THE
epicurious
COOKBOOK

THE
epicurious
COOKBOOK

**More Than 250 of Our Best-Loved Four-Fork Recipes
for Weeknights, Weekends & Special Occasions**

tanya steel and the editors of epicurious

photographs by ellen silverman

Clarkson Potter/Publishers
New York

Copyright © 2012 by Condé Nast

Published in the United States by Clarkson
Potter/Publishers, an imprint of the Crown
Publishing Group, a division of Random
House, Inc., New York.
www.crownpublishing.com
www.clarksonpotter.com

CLARKSON POTTER is a trademark and
POTTER with colophon is a registered
trademark of Random House, Inc.

Some recipes contained within this book
were originally published in Epicurious.com,
Bon Appétit, Gourmet, Self, and *Cookie*.

Library of Congress Cataloging-in-
Publication Data
The Epicurious Cookbook / Tanya Steel and
the editors of Epicurious. — 1st ed.
    p.   cm.
    Includes index.
1. Cooking.   2. International
cooking.   3. Cookbooks.   I. Steel, Tanya
Wenman.   II. Epicurious.com.
    TX714.E655   2012
    641.5—dc23
2011047821

ISBN 978-0-307-98485-2
eISBN 978-0-307-98486-9

Printed in China

Photographs by Ellen Silverman
Cover photograph by Ellen Silverman

10 9 8 7 6 5 4 3 2 1

First Edition

contents

acknowledgments

We'd like to dedicate this book to you, our family!

While there were just a handful of people who worked day in and day out on this book, the real number is in the multi-millions: our enormous global family of passionate cooks are the real authors of this cookbook. So if you are among them, we'd like to start off by thanking you for your incisive, smart, creative, and oftentimes touching or funny comments on Epicurious's recipes.

Besides the dozens of talented home cooks whose families' favorite recipes appear in this book, we would also like to thank the test kitchens of *Gourmet* and *Bon Appétit* magazines, as well as the renowned chefs and cookbook authors whose recipes we are lucky enough to share with you.

The brilliant photographer Ellen Silverman made an enormous contribution to this cookbook. With her talented team, she brought these recipes to life with a visual impact that reflects the essence of Epicurious.

The team at Clarkson Potter—Doris Cooper, Angelin Borsics, and Marysarah Quinn—was incredibly wonderful to work with. Supportive, intelligent, sane, and organized; we couldn't have asked for better partners.

Finally, I'd like to personally thank my *über*-talented and hard-working team of editors and recipe testers, all of whom spent long hours laboring over the selection of recipes and comments, testing recipes, writing headnotes, editing recipes, compiling contracts, and keeping me from having a daily panic attack. They include Siobhan Adcock, Sara Bonisteel, Joanne Camas, Patrick Decker, Dana Fraser, Sarah Kagan, Carolina Santos-Neves, Joanna Rothkopf, Paige Ross, Lauren Salkeld, Tracey Seaman, Esther Sung, and last but definitely not least, Kendra Vizcaino.

Tanya Steel

Tanya Wenman Steel
Editor in chief
Epicurious

introduction

Epicurious is many things to many people: an unparalleled recipe database; an up-to-the-minute resource on the food world; a global community millions strong that comes together to share, contribute ideas, and, yes, debate with one another about all things food; an authoritative source on everything from how to make a velvety genoise to where to slurp soba in Tokyo; a place to watch videos of Mario cooking, Lidia roasting, and Alice in the garden . . .

Epicurious is a trusted friend you can now find everywhere: from your smartphone and laptop to the tablet, printer, refrigerator, and Web-enabled television. But there's one place we weren't—the printed page—until now. Despite frequent requests, we had never ventured into books, preferring to expand our digital offerings. But as Mae West said, too much of a good thing is a good thing, and as passionate cookbook collectors ourselves, we set out to compile all of our favorite favorites into a gorgeous bound book, to have and to hold from this day forward.

Epicurious began in 1995 as a tiny database of recipes hand-coded by a small order of monks in upstate New York. This was a time when "getting online" required "dialing up." You could microwave popcorn faster than load a site in those days. And if someone was trying to reach you by phone, tough luck—all they would get is a busy signal. Epicurious was one of the first consumer outposts in this virtual Wild West, and we earned our spurs as innovators not just in the realm of food content but also in technology and social media, as early providers of rate-and-review tools, user profiles (à la Facebook), cooking videos, nutritional analysis, dynamic wine recommendations, a group blog, an interactive map denoting seasonal ingredients, mobile apps, shopping lists, a universal recipe box, and functionality to download entire cookbooks into your recipe box.

No matter how you connect with our content, we are all at core a very large family of food lovers, who come together at the virtual hearth to cook, eat, and inspire one another. So with inspiration as our goal, we decided it was high time to invert the paradigm and create a printed collection of our greatest hits. After much searching and arguing—and arguing and searching—we selected the best Epicurious recipes. These are some of the most highly rated gems in our database of more than 30,000 professionally created recipes, the ones that the largest percentage of users have indicated they would make again. The recipes in this book come from a wide range of sources, including Epicurious's siblings, *Bon Appétit, Gourmet,* and *Self,* as well as some of the world's most revered chefs and authors, such as Tom Colicchio, David Chang, Jean-Georges Vongerichten, Jonathan Waxman, Edna Lewis, and Dorie Greenspan. And we augmented these treasured recipes with spectacular new shots by the preeminent food photographer Ellen Silverman. We sought to bring these recipes to life in a delicious and approachable way, imagining how they would likely look in your kitchen.

We think a lot about what you make in your kitchen, and a significant portion of the recipes in the book come from you. There are upward of 200,000 recipes from home cooks also in the Epicurious database, and we selected some of our favorites for this book, tested them in our kitchens, adapted them when we needed to, and edited them so everyone can follow along easily. In short, we treated them as we do the recipes we receive from top chefs, testing and perfecting them to make sure they work for the home cook and are the best they can be.

We've categorized the recipes into the four seasons, beginning with spring and progressing through winter. And while we recognize that winter in Maine feels different than winter in Miami, and that there will be a lot less local produce up north, some items feel appropriate in both places. We advocate shopping locally and seasonally whenever possible, but sometimes your supermarket produce aisle is your best friend. We chose all types of recipes, from breakfast and starters to mains for a busy weeknight, plus ones that speak to your inner weekend warrior. And we selected not only recipes just for ratings but also for range: some are for more advanced, confident cooks, while others are so easy even kids can whip them up. And all are family favorites.

Alongside each recipe, we've provided expert advice from our team of food editors, ranging from substitutions to menu ideas—all in the collaborative, confidence-building spirit of Epicurious. And because 96 percent of the professionally created recipes on Epicurious are reviewed by our users (thousands of times, in some cases, as with our most-reviewed recipe of all time, Double Chocolate Layer Cake, pages 2 and 384), we thought it wouldn't be an Epicurious cookbook without contributions from you. We know our huge, passionate family of members is the ultimate test kitchen, so we're including some of the best tips from home cooks for each professionally created recipe. Keep in mind that reader tips provide useful variations and suggestions but aren't always specific in the amounts they use, so experiment with their substitutions once you've mastered the recipe. Also remember that because the recipes come from many sources, including our very own kitchens, we've taken care to leave the recipe styling pretty much as it was originally, which might lead to some recipes calling for softened butter while others call for room temperature butter. But we know that small differences in recipe styling won't confound you.

We believe that cooking is one of the greatest ways to show love for others—and for oneself—and this book is our way of giving you one big hug.

Tanya Steel and the Editors of Epicurious

S

pring

poached eggs and parmesan cheese over toasted brioche *with pistou*

These are no ordinary poached eggs. Rich, tender toasted brioche—or challah, if you can't find it—adds subtle crunch while shaved Parmesan lends just the right hint of saltiness. But the real star is the pistou. France's version of pesto, this basil-and-garlic–infused oil brings an herbal vibrance to the beloved egg, cheese, and bread combo. You might want to make extra pistou; pour leftovers over pasta for an effortless dinner.

YIELD: MAKES 2 SERVINGS

⅓ cup (packed) fresh basil leaves
½ small garlic clove
6 tablespoons extra-virgin olive oil
4 large eggs
2 (½-inch-thick) slices brioche or egg
    bread, toasted and kept warm
Parmesan cheese shavings, for serving

"I served this to my boyfriend and his friend with a spring mix salad on the side as a dinner. They both raved! Very beautiful and gourmet-seeming recipe, but so simple, healthy, easy, and fresh."

OHILLARYO,
Ft. Lauderdale, Florida

1. Puree the basil, garlic, and oil in a mini processor until very smooth. Season the pistou to taste with salt and pepper.

2. Add enough water to a medium skillet to measure 1¼ inches deep. Sprinkle salt generously into the water. Bring the water to a simmer over medium heat. Crack the eggs 1 at a time and gently slip into the water. Cook until the egg whites are just set and egg yolks are still runny, about 3 minutes.

3. Place the hot toasts on individual plates. Top each with some Parmesan. Using a slotted spoon, transfer 2 eggs, well drained, to each piece of brioche. Sprinkle the eggs with salt and pepper. Drizzle with some of the pistou and serve.

soft scrambled eggs *with ricotta and chives*

There's no such thing as a bad scrambled egg, but this concoction, made creamy with fresh ricotta, comes close to the *perfect* scrambled egg. The eggs are partially cooked and cheese is added off the heat to impart a soft texture. Chives and fleur de sel give this breakfast a rustic feel. Substitute four egg whites for the two eggs and serve it with whole-wheat lavash to lighten up the dish, or dress it up with slices of smoked salmon, avocado, or bacon.

1. Whisk the eggs, chopped chives, and ¼ teaspoon fleur de sel in a medium bowl until well blended. Melt the butter in a heavy medium nonstick skillet over medium heat. When the foam subsides, add the eggs and stir with a heatproof silicone spatula until the eggs are almost cooked but still runny in parts, tilting the skillet and stirring with the spatula to allow any uncooked portion to flow underneath, about 2 minutes. Remove from heat. Add the ricotta and stir just until incorporated but clumps of cheese are still visible.

2. Arrange 2 toasts or 4 baguette slices on each of 2 plates. Spoon the scrambled eggs atop the toasts. Sprinkle with more fleur de sel and freshly ground pepper. Garnish with whole chives, if desired.

YIELD: MAKES 2 SERVINGS

4 large eggs
1 tablespoon chopped fresh chives
¼ teaspoon fleur de sel or kosher salt, plus more for sprinkling
1 tablespoon unsalted butter
½ cup fresh ricotta cheese
4 (⅓- to ½-inch-thick) slices whole-grain bread, or 8 whole-grain baguette slices, lightly toasted and buttered
Whole chives, for garnish

"Be forewarned: The ricotta quickly brings the warm eggs to room temperature, so make sure you take out the ricotta from the refrigerator in advance. Also, homemade or locally made ricotta makes all the difference in the final dish."

A cook, Winnetka, Illinois

buttermilk biscuits *with green onions, black pepper, and sea salt*

These sweet–savory biscuits put a fresh spin on the classic buttermilk variety. Self-rising flour saves precious prep time. In fact, from start to finish, the whole recipe can be completed in about 30 minutes. To enjoy these fresh out of the oven, measure and combine the dry ingredients in advance, then bake the biscuits at the last minute.

YIELD: MAKES ABOUT 14 BISCUITS

¾ cup chilled buttermilk
½ cup finely chopped green onions
2 cups self-rising flour
½ cup yellow cornmeal
3 tablespoons sugar
½ teaspoon coarsely ground black pepper, plus additional for sprinkling
½ cup (1 stick) chilled unsalted butter, cut into ½-inch cubes, plus 1 tablespoon melted butter

"The green onions are awesome with the buttermilk. I made my own self-rising flour by adding 1½ teaspoons baking powder (and ½ teaspoon salt) for every 1 cup all-purpose flour. Worked very well."

Harshie11, Madison, Wisconsin

1. Position a rack in the center of the oven and preheat to 425°F. Line a baking sheet with parchment paper. Combine the buttermilk and green onions in a medium bowl. Whisk the flour, cornmeal, sugar, and ½ teaspoon pepper in a large bowl to blend. Add ½ cup chilled butter cubes and rub in with fingertips until mixture resembles coarse meal. Add the buttermilk mixture and stir until moist clumps form.

2. Gather the dough together. Turn the dough out onto a floured surface and knead gently just to combine, about 3 or 4 turns. Roll out to a ¾-inch thickness. Using a floured 2-inch cookie or biscuit cutter, cut out rounds. Reroll the scraps and cut out additional rounds. Place rounds 2 inches apart on the prepared baking sheet. Brush the tops of the biscuits with melted butter. Sprinkle each lightly with coarse sea salt and additional ground pepper.

3. Bake the biscuits until golden and a tester inserted into the center comes out clean, about 20 minutes. Cool slightly. Serve warm or at room temperature.

orange poppyseed cake

Thank goodness Epicurious member **Mary Jean Goodman** from Woodbridge, Connecticut, has been testing and retesting different iterations for this breakfast cake since she tried it as a little girl. The recipe has seen many incarnations and is now perfection, yielding a sweet, crumbly slice that is perfect for brunch or a special occasion. Try substituting different citrus fruits to flavor the cake to your preference.

MAKE CAKE

1. Position a rack in the middle of the oven and preheat to 350°F. Generously butter a 10-cup Bundt pan, then lightly coat the inside with flour, shaking out any excess.

2. In a medium bowl, whisk together the flour, poppy seeds, baking powder, and salt. In the bowl of a stand mixer fitted with the paddle attachment, combine the sugar and butter and beat on high until light and fluffy, about 5 minutes. Add the eggs 1 at a time, beating well after each addition. Add the vanilla and almond extracts and the orange zest and beat for 30 seconds. With the mixer on low, add half the flour mixture, followed by the milk and then the remaining flour, beating just until combined after each addition.

3. Pour the batter into the prepared pan and bake until a tester inserted in the center comes out clean, about 1 hour and 15 minutes. Transfer the pan to a rack to cool for 20 minutes, then turn the cake out onto the rack.

MAKE GLAZE

In a small bowl, whisk together the confectioners' sugar, orange juice, and vanilla until smooth. Brush the glaze all over the surface of the warm cake and serve.

YIELD: MAKES 12 SERVINGS

FOR THE CAKE
3 cups all-purpose flour
¼ cup poppy seeds
1½ teaspoons baking powder
½ teaspoon salt
2¼ cups granulated sugar
1¼ cups (2½ sticks) unsalted butter, at room temperature
3 large eggs
1½ teaspoons pure vanilla extract
½ teaspoon almond extract
1 teaspoon finely grated orange zest
1¼ cups whole milk

FOR THE GLAZE
1 cup confectioners' sugar, sifted
¼ cup orange juice
¼ teaspoon pure vanilla extract

Special equipment: 10-cup Bundt pan

This recipe comes from a family friend, Sarah Friedman. She taught me to make some traditional Jewish food, which came in handy when I converted to the Jewish faith.

Don't be thrown off by the consistency of the batter, and be sure to glaze the cake while it is warm so it absorbs the glaze.
—Mary Jean Goodman

ultimate sticky buns

With their irresistible cinnamon-sugar flavor and easy preparation, these classic sticky buns are definitely the "ultimate" of their kind. The night before, prep the recipe to midway through step 3; once the buns are in the pan, pop them in the refrigerator to rise overnight. In the morning, let the buns rise at room temperature for an hour or so—just until they're doubled in size—then bake them and get ready to wow your friends and family. One note: The sweet sugar glaze that makes these buns sticky can also stick to the pan; grease the pans generously, and you won't have any trouble.

YIELD: MAKES 24 BUNS

FOR DOUGH
1 cup warm water (105°-115°F)
4 teaspoons active dry yeast
⅔ cup granulated sugar
½ cup (1 stick) unsalted butter, at room temperature
½ cup dry nonfat milk powder
1¼ teaspoons salt
2 large eggs
4¼ cups all-purpose flour, or more as needed

FOR GLAZE AND FILLING
1¼ cups (packed) light brown sugar
¾ cup (1½ sticks) unsalted butter, at room temperature
¼ cup honey
¼ cup dark corn syrup
¼ cup water
2 cups pecan halves
4 teaspoons granulated sugar
4 teaspoons ground cinnamon

Special equipment: 2 (10-inch) round cake pans

MAKE DOUGH

1. Mix ¼ cup warm water, the yeast, and a pinch of sugar in a small bowl. Let stand until foamy, about 8 minutes. Using an electric mixer, beat the remaining sugar, butter, milk powder, and salt in a large bowl until well blended. Beat in eggs 1 at a time. Mix in remaining ¾ cup warm water and the yeast mixture, then add 3 cups flour, 1 cup at a time. Using a rubber spatula, mix in 1 cup flour, scraping down sides of the bowl frequently (dough will be soft and sticky). Sprinkle ¼ cup flour onto your work surface and knead until dough is smooth and elastic, adding more flour if sticky, about 8 minutes.

2. Butter another large bowl. Add dough; turn to coat. Cover the bowl with plastic wrap and let dough rise in a warm area until doubled, about 2½ hours.

MAKE GLAZE AND FILL AND BAKE ROLLS

1. Butter 2 (10-inch) round cake pans with 2-inch-high sides. Beat the brown sugar, ½ cup butter, honey, corn syrup, and ¼ cup water in a medium bowl to blend. Spread half of the glaze in the bottom of each prepared pan. Sprinkle 1 cup pecans in each pan.

2. Punch down the dough. Divide the dough in half. Roll each dough piece out on a floured work surface to a 12 by 9-inch rectangle. Brush any excess flour off the dough. Spread the remaining butter over the dough rectangles, dividing equally. Mix the 4 teaspoons sugar and cinnamon in a small bowl. Sprinkle the cinnamon sugar over the rectangles.

3. Starting at one long side, tightly roll up each rectangle into a log. Cut each log into 12 rounds. Place the 12 rounds, cut side down, in each prepared pan, spacing evenly. Cover with plastic wrap (can be made 1 day ahead; refrigerate). Let the rolls rise in a warm area until almost doubled, about 1 hour (or 1 hour 25 minutes if refrigerated).

4. Preheat the oven to 375°F. Bake the buns until deep golden brown, about 30 minutes. Run a small knife around the pan sides to loosen the sticky buns. Turn hot buns out onto a platter. Cool about 30 minutes and serve.

"I used maple syrup in place of the dark corn syrup called for. I also made one pan with raisins and one with the pecans. These are wonderful, and I had to give the recipe out to practically every cook at brunch. A sure winner!"
A cook, Philadelphia, Pennsylvania

banana macadamia pancakes
with orange butter

Fluffy buttermilk banana pancakes get a unique makeover with the help of salty macadamia nuts and zesty orange butter. As the orange butter melts into each pancake, the bright, refreshing citrus notes lighten up this rich morning meal. Add some chocolate chips or use different nuts to customize your breakfast.

YIELD: MAKES 15 (4-INCH) PANCAKES

FOR ORANGE BUTTER
½ stick (¼ cup) unsalted butter, softened
½ teaspoon finely grated fresh orange zest
1½ teaspoons fresh orange juice
⅛ teaspoon salt

FOR PANCAKES
1½ cups all-purpose flour
3 tablespoons sugar
1½ teaspoons baking powder
½ teaspoon baking soda
¼ teaspoon salt
1½ cups well-shaken buttermilk
3 tablespoons unsalted butter, melted
2 large eggs
1 teaspoon vanilla extract
1 ripe large banana
½ cup salted roasted macadamia nuts, chopped (2½ ounces)
Maple syrup, for serving

"I used two bananas and mashed them into the batter, added blueberries one time and strawberries the second time I made this recipe (as I prefer fruit to nuts), and doubled the orange zest in the butter for a bit more flavor. I also drizzled a bit of honey over the pancakes."
A cook, Beachwood, Ohio

MAKE ORANGE BUTTER
Stir together all the orange butter ingredients in a small bowl until combined well.

MAKE PANCAKES
1. Whisk together the flour, sugar, baking powder, baking soda, and salt in a medium bowl. Whisk together the buttermilk, 2 tablespoons melted butter, the eggs, and vanilla in a large bowl until smooth. Add the flour mixture and whisk until just combined. Cut the banana into bits and fold into batter along with nuts. (Batter will be very thick.)

2. Brush a 12-inch nonstick skillet with some of remaining tablespoon melted butter and heat over moderate heat until hot but not smoking. Working in batches of 3, pour ¼ cup batter per pancake into the hot skillet and cook until bubbles appear on the surface and undersides are golden brown, 1 to 2 minutes. Flip the pancakes with a spatula and cook until golden brown and cooked through, 1 to 2 minutes more. Transfer to a large plate and loosely cover with foil to keep warm, then make more pancakes, brushing skillet with butter for each batch. Serve with orange butter and maple syrup.

member recipe

cardamom iced tea

This recipe is a peek inside the magic hat of cookbook author and New York City caterer **Serena Bass.** There's nary a tea leaf in sight of this spicy and refreshing "tea"—rather, it's made from a fragrant combination of apples and cardamom spice. Be sure to use high-quality juice, not from concentrate, such as Adam and Eve apple juice or cloudy, fresh-pressed apple juice.

YIELD: MAKES 8 (8-OUNCE) SERVINGS

64 ounces clear apple juice
⅓ cup whole green cardamom pods
Thin apple slices, for garnish

I developed this when I needed a nonalcoholic cocktail for an Iranian wedding. With a slice of red-skinned apple and a sprig of mint, it looked fantastic. You can add a slug of Appletons-Estate golden rum to take it to a new level.

—Serena Bass

1. In a large saucepan over low heat, combine the apple juice and cardamom pods. Warm gently, without simmering, for 1 hour. Remove the tea from the heat and let it cool. Transfer to an airtight container or the original juice bottle, seal, and refrigerate overnight.

2. Pour the tea through a fine-mesh strainer into a glass pitcher, discarding the cardamom pods. Serve over ice and garnish with apple slices.

member recipe

cuppa cuppa cuppa dip

Of this luxurious and simple party dip recipe, Epicurious Connecticut member **Peg Dimmick** notes, "This is an old favorite of mine that my mother and my grandmother made, and was reintroduced to me by a cousin a couple of years ago at a family gathering." As the title suggests, the recipe ingredients couldn't be easier to remember, measure, and memorize.

YIELD: MAKES 4 TO 6 SERVINGS

1 cup mayonnaise
1 cup shredded imported Swiss cheese
   (4 ounces)
1 cup minced onion
Crackers or pita chips, for serving

1. Position a rack in the middle of the oven and preheat the oven to 350°F.

2. In a medium bowl, stir together the mayonnaise, cheese, and onion. Transfer to a shallow 1-quart baking dish and bake until golden brown and bubbly, about 25 minutes.

3. Serve with crackers or pita chips.

prosciutto-wrapped asparagus spears

This elegant, delicious appetizer has long been a favorite among Epicurious members. It's important to let the blanched asparagus cool completely before assembling these spears. They can be prepared up to a day in advance.

1. Trim the asparagus stalks so that the spears are 5 inches long. In a deep skillet, bring 1½ inches of salted water to a boil and cook the asparagus until they are crisp-tender, about 2 minutes. In a colander, drain the asparagus and rinse under cold water. Dry the asparagus well on paper towels.

2. In a small bowl, mash the Boursin with a fork until it is smooth. Cut 1 slice of prosciutto lengthwise into 1-inch strips and spread each strip with about ½ teaspoon Boursin. Spread about ¼ teaspoon mustard over the Boursin and wrap each strip in a spiral around an asparagus spear, trimming any excess. Make more hors d'oeuvres with the remaining prosciutto, Boursin, mustard, and asparagus spears in the same manner.

YIELD: MAKES 30 HORS D'OEUVRES— COUNT ON AT LEAST 3 PER PERSON!

30 medium-thin asparagus stalks
4 ounces peppered Boursin cheese, softened
¼ pound thinly sliced prosciutto
¼ cup honey mustard

"I cooked the asparagus in one can of chicken broth mixed with one cup of water . . . for 1½ minutes and then moved the asparagus to a bowl of ice water."
A cook, Dallas, Texas

salmon cakes *with lemon yogurt sauce*

Love crab cakes but want a change? These salmon cakes take fewer than 30 minutes to prepare. The recipe calls for pita pieces as a filler, but many Epicurious members subbed ¾ cup panko flakes for a lighter cake. The salmon cakes also make a clever fish taco when crumbled and served with jalapeños, corn, and the yogurt sauce.

1. Mix the salmon, pita, mayonnaise, egg, coriander, cayenne, 1 tablespoon chives, 1 teaspoon lemon zest, and ½ teaspoon salt. Season with black pepper and form into 4 cakes about 4 inches in diameter.

2. Heat the oil in a 12-inch heavy nonstick skillet over medium-high heat until it shimmers. Cook the salmon cakes, turning over once, until golden and just cooked through, 6 to 7 minutes total.

3. Stir together the yogurt, lemon juice, remaining ¼ teaspoon salt, 1 tablespoon chives, and ½ teaspoon lemon zest. Serve the salmon cakes with the sauce.

YIELD: MAKES 4 SERVINGS

1 pound skinless salmon fillet, cut into ½-inch pieces
2 (6-inch) pita rounds, or 3 slices firm white sandwich bread, torn into small pieces
¼ cup mayonnaise
1 large egg, lightly beaten
½ teaspoon ground coriander
¼ teaspoon cayenne
2 tablespoons chopped fresh chives
1½ teaspoons grated lemon zest
¾ teaspoon salt
2 tablespoons olive oil
¾ cup plain whole-milk yogurt
1 teaspoon fresh lemon juice
Lemon wedges, for serving

"I was worried about [the cakes] holding together, so I put half of the allotted salmon in the food processor, combined it with the chunked salmon, and formed the cakes. Also put them in the fridge for an hour beforehand. Would recommend adding spicy mustard, dill, and a little hot sauce to the yogurt for kicks."

Chaffism

sweet, tart, and spicy shrimp and cucumber salad

This healthy sprightly salad has a distinctly Asian kick to it. One of the best things about it is you can add just about any veggies you have—just be sure to cut them up into bite-size pieces. The dressing also makes a terrific marinade for fish or chicken.

YIELD: MAKES 6 TO 8 SERVINGS

FOR DRESSING

¼ cup fresh lime juice

3 tablespoons light brown sugar

2 tablespoons Asian fish sauce, such as nam pla or nuoc mam

2 tablespoons vegetable oil

1 tablespoon finely grated lime peel

1 teaspoon hot chile paste, such as sambal oelek

1 teaspoon grated peeled fresh ginger

FOR SALAD

2 pounds (about 8) Persian or Japanese cucumbers

1½ teaspoons salt

1 tablespoon vegetable oil

¾ cup lightly salted roasted peanuts

1 pound cooked deveined peeled medium shrimp

4 cups thinly sliced napa cabbage

1 large red bell pepper, seeded and cut into matchsticks

3 green onions, cut into matchsticks

½ cup fresh cilantro leaves

½ cup torn fresh Thai or regular basil leaves

2 teaspoons black sesame seeds, toasted

MAKE DRESSING

Whisk together all dressing ingredients in a small bowl; let the dressing stand while preparing the salad.

MAKE SALAD

1. Peel half of the cucumbers; cut in half lengthwise and scoop out seeds with a small spoon. Cut into ¼-inch cubes (about 2 cups) and place in a large strainer set over a bowl.

2. Cut off the ends from the remaining cucumbers and cut in half lengthwise. Scoop out the seeds. Cut the halves crosswise into ¼-inch-thick slices (about 2½ to 3 cups); add to the strainer. Sprinkle with the salt; let drain 30 minutes.

3. Heat the oil in a heavy medium skillet over medium-high heat. Add the peanuts; sauté until golden. Using a slotted spoon, transfer the peanuts to paper towels to drain.

4. Combine the shrimp, cabbage, bell pepper, green onions, cilantro, and basil in a large bowl.

5. Pat the cucumber pieces dry and add to the salad. Toss with the dressing; sprinkle with peanuts and black sesame seeds, and serve.

"I've made this twice and will be making it again for a dinner party. If you are going to skip the salting and draining the cucumbers step, keep in mind that you will want to serve it ASAP, otherwise you are going to have a very watered down, mushy salad."

Masshomechef, Portland, Maine

oysters *with champagne-vinegar mignonette*

This traditional take on broiled oysters is an elegant way to begin a dinner party—just multiply the servings by the number of guests. The French mignonette sauce offers an acidic complement to the briny shellfish, while Champagne grapes lend fruity sweetness. If Champagne grapes are unavailable, use seedless red table grapes instead. If you feel unsure about how to shuck an oyster, just purchase them on the half shell.

YIELD: MAKES 2 SERVINGS

FOR MIGNONETTE
2 teaspoons Champagne vinegar
1½ teaspoons finely chopped shallot
Pinch of coarsely ground black pepper
Pinch of sugar
1 teaspoon finely chopped fresh flat-leaf
  parsley leaves

FOR OYSTERS
1½ cups kosher or other coarse salt
½ dozen small oysters, such as Kumamoto
  or Prince Edward Island, shells
  scrubbed well, shucked, and oysters
  left on the half shell, their liquor
  reserved; oysters picked over for shell
  fragments
½ tablespoon unsalted butter, cut into
  6 pieces
1 small cluster Champagne grapes, or
  2 finely diced seedless red grapes

Special equipment: Shallow flameproof
  baking dish

do ahead:

The **MIGNONETTE,** without parsley, can be made 1 day ahead and chilled, covered.

MAKE MIGNONETTE
Stir together the vinegar, shallot, pepper, and sugar and let stand 30 minutes.

MAKE OYSTERS
1. Preheat the broiler. Spread ¾ cup kosher salt in an 8- to 10-inch shallow flameproof baking dish or pan. Arrange the oysters in their shells atop the salt, then top each with a piece of butter.

2. Broil 4 to 6 inches from the heat until the butter is melted and sizzling and the edges of the oysters are beginning to curl, 1 to 2 minutes.

3. Stir the parsley into the mignonette. Divide the remaining ¾ cup kosher salt between two plates and arrange 3 oysters on each. Spoon ¼ teaspoon mignonette over each oyster and sprinkle oysters with grapes. Serve warm.

"Although I usually like fresh oysters plain, this recipe really added a special something. I served the mignonette in a tiny bowl so my guests could spoon it on if they desired . . . they became addicted to it like I did!"

Dunnkit, Seattle, Washington

pea salad *with radishes and feta cheese*

Crunchy, zesty, and light: what else could one want in a warm-weather salad? Radishes are thinly sliced and mingle with shelled fresh peas, while feta cheese and honey provide a special salty sweetness. Pea sprouts can be found at natural-food stores and Asian markets.

1. Heat a small skillet over medium heat. Add the cumin seeds and toast until aromatic, about 2 minutes. Cool; grind finely in spice mill. Whisk together the lime juice, honey, and cumin in a small bowl. Gradually whisk in the olive oil; stir in the dill. Season with salt and pepper.

2. Cook the peas in a pot of boiling salted water until almost tender, about 5 minutes for fresh (or about 2 minutes for frozen). Drain; rinse under cold water, then drain well. Transfer to a large bowl. Add the radishes, feta, and dressing; toss. Season with salt and pepper. If using pea tendrils or sprouts, divide among bowls. Divide salad among bowls. Serve.

YIELD: MAKES 4 TO 6 SERVINGS

2 teaspoons cumin seeds
2 tablespoons fresh lime juice
2 teaspoons honey
¼ cup extra-virgin olive oil
3 tablespoons chopped fresh dill
4 cups shelled fresh peas (from about 4 pounds peas in pod), or 1 pound frozen petite peas
1 bunch radishes, trimmed, halved, and thinly sliced
1 cup crumbled feta cheese (about 4 ounces)
3 cups fresh pea tendrils, coarsely chopped, or pea sprouts (optional)

> **do ahead:**
>
> The **DRESSING** can be made 1 day ahead. Cover and chill. Bring to room temperature.

"I used edamame in place of the peas (had them in the freezer) and put them on a bed of Boston lettuce and baby spinach to get more greens in."

Ecf13, Cleveland, Ohio

thai cabbage salad

member recipe

A great recipe is like a strong friendship—it gets better with age. Epicurious member **Sooz Wolhuter** of Laguna Beach, California, crafted this cabbage salad years ago, riffing on a coleslaw recipe. The blend of ribboned cabbage, carrots, cucumbers, peppers, and green onions mixed with spicy soy and chile garlic is perfect for large gatherings. If peanuts aren't enough protein for you, add some seared Ahi tuna or grilled sliced chicken to bulk it up.

YIELD: MAKES 20 SERVINGS

FOR DRESSING

½ cup rice vinegar

¼ cup soy sauce

2 tablespoons sugar or honey

1 tablespoon chile garlic sauce

1 teaspoon sesame oil

4 garlic cloves, minced

1 to 2 fresh serrano chiles, seeds and ribs removed, minced

½ cup vegetable oil

FOR SALAD

1 head green cabbage, quartered, cored, and thinly sliced

3 medium carrots, grated

1 medium cucumber, peeled and finely diced

1 large red bell pepper, finely diced

5 to 6 green onions (white and light green parts only), thinly sliced on a diagonal

½ cup finely chopped fresh cilantro leaves

1 cup unsalted dry-roasted peanuts, coarsely chopped

do ahead:

The **DRESSING** can be made ahead and refrigerated, in the glass jar or another airtight container, up to 1 week. Whisk or shake before using.

MAKE DRESSING

In a small bowl or glass jar with a tight-fitting lid, whisk together the vinegar, soy sauce, sugar or honey, chile garlic sauce, sesame oil, garlic, and chiles. Slowly whisk in the vegetable oil or, if using a jar, add the vegetable oil, seal the jar, and shake vigorously.

MAKE SALAD

In a large salad bowl, toss together the cabbage, carrots, cucumber, and red bell pepper. Shake or whisk the dressing thoroughly, then pour it over the salad and toss to coat the vegetables. Add the onions and cilantro and toss again. Sprinkle the salad with peanuts and serve.

I threw this together for a potluck and it's been a mainstay ever since.

—Sooz Wolhuter

indian spiced carrot soup *with ginger*

If you're one of those folks with serious misgivings about cooked carrots (too soft, too bland, too . . . orange), this spicy South Asian starter will likely change your mind. Puréeing the carrot with broth and an aromatic mixture of spices produces an exceptionally rich, velvety texture. Like a little more heat? Kick it up a notch by increasing the amount of ginger, curry powder, or coriander while the pot is simmering. But be sure to remember the garnish: creamy yogurt will actually enhance the layers of flavor in the soup. This healthy option is great as a first course at a dinner party or makes a simple lunch for the kids.

1. Grind coriander and mustard seeds in a spice mill to a fine powder. Heat oil in a heavy large pot over medium-high heat. Add the ground seeds and curry powder; stir 1 minute. Add the ginger; stir 1 minute. Add the next 3 ingredients. Sprinkle with salt and pepper; sauté until the onions begin to soften, about 3 minutes. Add 5 cups broth; bring to boil. Reduce heat to medium-low; simmer uncovered until the carrots are tender, about 30 minutes. Cool slightly.

2. Working in batches, purée in a blender until smooth. Return the soup to the pot. Add more broth by ¼ cupfuls if too thick. Stir in the lime juice; season with salt and pepper.

3. Ladle soup into bowls. Garnish with yogurt and serve.

"Delicioso! I had way too many carrots, and this recipe was a fantastic solution to my problem. I used the coconut milk and doubled the spices. Then I garnished it with a dollop of sour cream and lime zest. Loved sooo much, I bought more carrots."

Princekuyper, California

YIELD: MAKES 6 TO 8 SERVINGS

1 teaspoon coriander seeds
½ teaspoon yellow mustard seeds
3 tablespoons peanut oil
½ teaspoon curry powder (preferably Madras)
1 tablespoon minced peeled fresh ginger
2 cups chopped onions
1½ pounds carrots, peeled, thinly sliced into rounds (about 4 cups)
1½ teaspoons finely grated lime peel
5 cups (or more) low-salt chicken broth or vegetable broth
2 teaspoons fresh lime juice
Plain yogurt, for garnish

do ahead:

The **SOUP** can be made 1 day ahead through step 2. Cool slightly. Chill uncovered until cold, then cover and keep chilled. Reheat before serving.

belgian leek tart *with aged goat cheese*

A savory tart with a flaky crust by Molly Wizenberg of Orangette.com fame is perfect for a party or potluck because it can be served (and devoured) at room temperature and also can be made a day ahead. The recipe calls for making a leek confit, whose recipe yields a bit more than you'll need for this tart. Serve any extra confit over a hearty fish like salmon.

YIELD: MAKES 6 TO 8 SERVINGS

FOR CRUST

About 4 tablespoons ice water
¾ teaspoon apple cider vinegar
1½ cups unbleached all-purpose flour
¾ teaspoon salt
½ cup (1 stick) plus 1 tablespoon chilled unsalted butter

FOR FILLING

½ cup whole milk
½ cup heavy whipping cream
1 large egg
1 large egg yolk
¼ teaspoon salt
½ cup crumbled aged goat cheese (such as Bûcheron), rind trimmed
1½ cups Leek Confit (recipe follows)

Special equipment: 1 (9-inch) round tart pan with removable bottom

> **do ahead:**
>
> The **DOUGH** can be made 3 days ahead. Keep refrigerated. Allow dough to soften slightly at room temperature before rolling out.

MAKE CRUST

1. Combine the ice water and vinegar in a small bowl. Blend the flour and salt in a food processor. Cut in the butter using on/off turns until the mixture resembles coarse meal. With the machine running, slowly add the water-vinegar mixture, processing until moist clumps form. If dough seems dry, add additional ice water by teaspoonfuls.

2. Gather the dough into a ball; flatten into a disk. Wrap in plastic and refrigerate at least 2 hours.

3. Position a rack in the center of the oven and preheat the oven to 375°F. Roll the dough out on a lightly floured work surface to a 12-inch round. Transfer to a 9-inch tart pan with a removable bottom. Press the dough onto the bottom and up the sides. Fold in the overhang and press to extend the dough ½ inch above the sides of the pan. Line the pan with foil and dried beans or pie weights. Bake until the dough looks dry and set, about 30 minutes. Remove the foil and beans and continue to bake until crust is pale golden, 20 to 25 minutes longer. Remove from the oven and cool while preparing the filling.

MAKE FILLING AND BAKE TART

Whisk the milk, cream, egg, egg yolk, and salt in a medium bowl to blend. Sprinkle ¼ cup of the cheese over the bottom of the crust; spread the leek confit over and sprinkle with the remaining cheese. Pour the milk mixture over. Bake until the filling has puffed, is golden in spots, and the center looks set, 35 to 40 minutes. Transfer to a rack; cool slightly. Remove the pan sides. Serve warm or at room temperature.

leek confit

Melt the butter in a large pot over medium-low heat. Add the leeks; stir to coat. Stir in the water and salt. Cover the pot; reduce heat to low. Cook until the leeks are tender, stirring often, about 25 minutes. Uncover and cook to evaporate excess water, 2 to 3 minutes. Serve warm.

"This has to be one of the most delicious and simple appetizers I've ever made! The leek confit is out of this world and is so versatile to serve with eggs and even on a slice of bread."
Laduque66, San Diego, California

YIELD: MAKES 2 CUPS CONFIT

¼ cup (½ stick) unsalted butter
4 large leeks (white and pale green parts only), halved lengthwise, cut crosswise into ¼-inch-thick slices (about 5 cups)
2 tablespoons water
½ teaspoon salt

do ahead:

The **LEEK CONFIT** can be made 1 week ahead. Keep chilled. Rewarm before using.

lemon gnocchi *with spinach and peas*

Lemon lovers adore this simple and satisfying pasta. Lemon zest and juice brighten the peas and spinach while lightening the creamy Parmesan sauce. You can also use penne, orecchiette, or another small pasta. To cut back on calories, use whole milk or half-and-half in place of some or all of the heavy cream.

YIELD: MAKES 4 SERVINGS

1 cup frozen baby peas (not thawed)
½ cup heavy cream
¼ teaspoon dried red pepper flakes
1 garlic clove, smashed
¼ teaspoon salt
3 cups (packed) baby spinach (3 ounces)
1 teaspoon grated lemon zest
1½ teaspoons fresh lemon juice
1 pound dried gnocchi
¼ cup grated Parmesan cheese

"This recipe is delicious; it has become one of my favorites. It's also one of my emergency meals, since I always have gnocchi around and peas and spinach in the freezer. Easy and versatile! You can throw in whatever you happen to have on hand . . . mushrooms, bacon, asparagus, chicken . . . just don't omit the lemon! The lemon is what makes this dish special."

Ma_licious, Berlin, Germany

1. Simmer the peas with the cream, red pepper flakes, garlic, and salt in a 12-inch heavy skillet, covered, until tender, about 5 minutes.

2. Add the spinach and cook over medium-low heat, uncovered, stirring, until wilted. Remove from the heat and stir in the lemon zest and juice.

3. Meanwhile, cook the gnocchi in a pasta pot of boiling salted water (3 tablespoons salt for 6 quarts water) until al dente. Reserve ½ cup pasta-cooking water, then drain the gnocchi.

4. Add the gnocchi to the sauce along with the cheese and some of the reserved cooking water and stir to coat. Thin with additional cooking water, if necessary.

lobster pasta *in a roasted corn and sweet bacon cream*

Here's a restaurant-quality sauce that is rich and luxurious but easy enough to make at home. Professional cook and Epicurious member **Thomas Campbell** of New London, Connecticut, invented it, and his favorite part of the recipe is the bacon-flavored liquid; it adds a slightly sweet but smoky flavor to the sauce, and tastes even better after the flavors have time to mingle.

YIELD: MAKES 6 SERVINGS

3 ears of corn, shucked
4 tablespoons olive oil
1 tablespoon brown sugar
½ teaspoon kosher salt
¼ teaspoon freshly ground black pepper
8 ounces thick-cut bacon, coarsely chopped
2 shallots, minced
2 garlic cloves, minced
¼ cup dry white wine
1 quart heavy cream
1 pound short-cut pasta, such as penne or rigatoni
1 pound cooked lobster meat, coarsely chopped
2 tablespoons minced fresh oregano leaves
¼ cup (loosely packed) fresh basil, cut into chiffonade

I like to serve this sauce with orecchiette, farfalle, or mini penne. This recipe makes a lot of sauce but it pays to make a big batch and freeze it for future use.

–Thomas Campbell

1. Position a rack in the middle of the oven and preheat the oven to 375°F. Cut the corn kernels off the cobs, reserving the cobs. Spread the kernels, in a single layer, on a large baking sheet. Add 2 tablespoons of the olive oil, the brown sugar, salt, and pepper and toss to coat. Roast until the kernels are tender and light golden brown, about 20 minutes.

2. In a large, straight-sided sauté pan over moderate heat, heat the remaining 2 tablespoons olive oil until hot but not smoking. Add the bacon and cook, stirring occasionally, until it turns golden brown and the fat has been rendered out, 8 to 10 minutes. Transfer the bacon to a paper-towel–lined plate and pour off all but 1 tablespoon of the bacon fat in the skillet.

3. Return the pan with the bacon fat to moderate heat. Add the shallots and garlic, and sauté, stirring occasionally, until tender, about 1 minute. Add the white wine and bring to a gentle boil. Continue boiling, scraping up any browned bits, until most of the wine has evaporated, 2 to 3 minutes. Add the cream and the reserved corncobs and return to a boil. Reduce the heat to moderately low and simmer, uncovered, until reduced by half, about 25 minutes.

4. Meanwhile, in a large pot of boiling salted water, cook the pasta until tender. Drain well and return it to the pot it was cooked in.

5. Once the cream is reduced, add the roasted corn, lobster meat, and herbs and continue simmering until the lobster is heated through, 5 to 6 minutes. Remove and discard the corncobs and season mixture with salt and pepper. Add the lobster cream sauce and the reserved bacon to the pot of cooked pasta and toss well to combine. Serve immediately.

linguine *with herb broth and clams*

The key to this classic pasta dish is using the best-quality white wine you have; contrary to popular belief, the quality of the wine is directly proportional to the quality of the broth. Make it a meal with a crusty warm Italian loaf and a glass of the leftover wine.

1. Melt the butter with the olive oil in a heavy large pot over medium heat. Add the onions and cook until soft, stirring often, about 5 minutes. Add the garlic and stir 1 minute. Add the tomatoes and cook until beginning to soften, stirring often, about 2 minutes. Add the white wine and 1 cup of water and bring to boil. Reduce the heat to low, cover, and simmer 20 minutes to blend flavors.

2. Add the clams, cover, and cook until clams open, 3 to 5 minutes (discard any clams that do not open). Transfer the clams to a large bowl; tent with foil to keep warm.

3. Stir the basil, parsley, oregano, and red pepper flakes into broth. Add the linguine. Boil until the pasta is almost tender but still very firm to the bite, stirring often and adding water by tablespoonfuls if too dry.

4. Return clams with any accumulated juices to the pot. Cover and simmer until clams are heated through and pasta is tender but still firm to the bite, about 3 minutes longer. Season to taste with salt and pepper.

5. Transfer the linguine and clam mixture to a large shallow platter and serve.

"The broth was so flavorful, and cooking the linguine in it infused the pasta with umami goodness. I used shrimp instead of clams. I boiled them in the broth for just a few minutes as the recipe instructs for clams, then removed them to a bowl and cooked the pasta. I added probably ¼ cup more water by the tablespoon. Delicious."
Hlehkw, Ormond Beach, Florida

YIELD: MAKES 4 SERVINGS

¼ cup (½ stick) butter
2 tablespoons olive oil
2 medium onions, chopped
6 garlic cloves, peeled and smashed
2 medium tomatoes, cored and chopped
3 cups dry white wine
3 pounds Manila clams or small littleneck clams, scrubbed
⅓ cup thinly sliced fresh basil leaves
¼ cup chopped fresh parsley
¼ cup chopped fresh oregano
2 pinches dried red pepper flakes
8 ounces linguine

do ahead:

The **BROTH** can be made 1 day ahead. Cool slightly, then cover and refrigerate. Bring to a boil before adding clams.

"*I made extra curry sauce, some jasmine rice, and steamed some fresh veggies real fast, and turned it into a full meal. I also used popcorn-size shrimp instead of jumbo, and although there were more to dip and fry, it worked really well with the rice and veggies.*"

A cook, Vermont

lime and coconut shrimp
with red curry sauce

Ice-cold ginger ale is just one of the secrets to chef Kevin Rathbun's Asian-inspired shrimp appetizer. The woody and fragrant kaffir lime leaf is another and can be found in the freezer section of Asian or Thai grocery stores. Rathbun's restaurant in Atlanta also serves this dish with chicken or tofu in place of the shrimp.

MAKE CURRY SAUCE

Combine all the ingredients for the sauce in a heavy medium saucepan. Bring to a boil over medium-high heat, whisking to blend. Reduce the heat to medium and simmer 1 minute. Remove from heat. Cover and let sauce stand at room temperature 10 minutes for flavors to blend. Strain. Season sauce to taste with salt and pepper.

MAKE KAFFIR LIME BATTER

Using on/off turns, mix the flour, cornstarch, lime leaves, curry paste, sugar, and salt in a food processor until blended. Transfer the mixture to a medium metal bowl. Gradually whisk in ¾ cup of ginger ale.

MAKE SHRIMP

1. Add enough oil to a heavy large saucepan to measure 1½ inches deep. Attach a deep-fry thermometer to the side of the pan (do not allow tip to touch bottom of pan). Heat the oil to 370°F to 380°F.

2. Place the cornstarch in a shallow bowl. Place the coconut in a medium bowl. Lightly dredge the shrimp in the cornstarch, shaking off excess. Working in batches, dip the shrimp in batter to coat lightly, allowing excess batter to drip off, then dredge shrimp in the coconut. Fry the shrimp until cooked through and coconut is golden, about 2 minutes. Transfer to paper towels to drain.

3. Divide the warm curry sauce among six plates. Stand 3 shrimp back-to-back on each plate. Garnish with cilantro sprigs and lime leaves and serve.

YIELD: MAKES 4 TO 6 SERVINGS

FOR CURRY SAUCE

1 (13.5- to 14.5-ounce) can unsweetened
   coconut milk
12 whole green cardamom pods, crushed
3 fresh kaffir lime leaves (3 double leaves)
2 garlic cloves, chopped
2 tablespoons (packed) light brown sugar
1 tablespoon grated lemon peel
1 tablespoon fresh lime juice
1 tablespoon Thai red curry paste
2 teaspoons Asian fish sauce, such as nam
   pla or nuoc mam

FOR KAFFIR LIME BATTER

¾ cup all-purpose flour
¼ cup cornstarch
2 teaspoons minced kaffir lime leaves
   (3 to 4 double leaves)
1½ teaspoons Thai red curry paste
1 teaspoon (packed) light brown sugar
½ teaspoon salt
¾ cup ice-cold ginger ale

FOR SHRIMP

About 6 cups peanut oil, for frying
½ cup cornstarch
2½ cups sweetened flaked coconut
18 uncooked large shrimp (about
   1 pound), peeled, deveined, and
   butterflied, tails left intact
Fresh cilantro sprigs and kaffir lime
   leaves, for garnish

seared scallops *with tomato beurre blanc*

Homemade tomato beurre blanc gives this dish a sophisticated French feel. But it's easy enough to make for a casual family meal; serve it with rice or a crusty bread to soak up the rich sauce.

YIELD: MAKES 6 SERVINGS

FOR TOMATO BEURRE BLANC
¼ cup (packed) soft dried tomatoes, not packed in oil (1¼ ounces)
1½ sticks (¾ cup) unsalted butter, softened
⅛ teaspoon salt
⅓ cup minced shallots
⅔ cup dry white wine
3 tablespoons water
1 teaspoon fresh lemon juice

FOR SCALLOPS
2 pounds large sea scallops (30), tough muscle removed from side of each if necessary
About 2 tablespoons vegetable oil

"Made this for a large group as part of a 'surf and turf' with smoked beef tenderloin. Big hit! I doubled the beurre blanc recipe, and we just had the leftovers spooned over a simple baked fish."

A cook, Michigan

MAKE TOMATO BEURRE BLANC

1. Soak the tomatoes in warm water until softened, 20 to 25 minutes. Drain and pat dry, then mince. Stir together the tomatoes, butter, and salt, then form into an 8-inch log on a sheet of plastic wrap and chill, wrapped in plastic wrap, until firm, about 1 hour. Cut tomato butter into 12 equal pieces.

2. Cook the shallots in 1 piece of tomato butter (keep remaining butter chilled) in a small heavy saucepan over moderately low heat, stirring, until softened, about 3 minutes. Add the wine and boil until liquid is reduced to about ⅓ cup, about 10 minutes.

3. Reduce the heat to low and whisk in the remaining cold tomato butter 1 piece at a time, adding each piece before previous one has completely melted and lifting pan from heat occasionally to cool mixture (sauce should not get hot enough to separate). Whisk in the water and lemon juice, then season with salt and pepper.

4. Transfer the tomato beurre blanc to a bowl and keep warm, covered, in a larger bowl of warm water.

MAKE SCALLOPS

1. Pat the scallops dry and season with salt and pepper. Heat 1 teaspoon oil in a 12-inch nonstick skillet over moderately high heat until hot but not smoking, then sear 6 to 8 scallops, turning once, until golden brown and just cooked through, 2 to 4 minutes total.

2. Transfer cooked scallops to a platter, and loosely cover with foil to keep warm. Sear remaining scallops in same manner, wiping out skillet and adding about 1 teaspoon oil between batches.

3. Spoon 3 tablespoons tomato beurre blanc onto each of six plates, then top with scallops.

bass satay *with asparagus*

Sam Hazen, the former executive chef of New York celebrity hangout Tao, created this broiled fish dish seasoned with the Japanese trifecta of sake, mirin, and miso. A great riff on beef satay, this appetizer can be marinated up to a day ahead for a quick weeknight snack or full meal when served with rice. Avoid unsustainable Chilean sea bass; look for white sea bass from California, black cod, Pacific or Alaskan halibut, or striped bass.

1. Combine the marinade ingredients. Reserve 2 tablespoons and marinate the bass in the rest (covered, in the refrigerator) for 24 hours.

2. Preheat broiler. Spear each piece of fish on a wooden skewer. Place in a foil-lined pan and broil until sauce caramelizes, 3 or 4 minutes.

3. Toss the asparagus with the oil, salt, and pepper. Heat a sauté pan (no oil) over high heat, 7 minutes. Add the asparagus; sauté all sides.

4. Arrange the asparagus on a plate. Top with the bass, drizzle with the reserved marinade, and garnish with chives. (Note: To evaporate alcohol, increase sake and mirin to 1¼ cups each. Simmer until mixture is reduced by half and is syrupy.)

YIELD: MAKES 2 SERVINGS

FOR MARINADE
1 cup sake
1 cup mirin
1 cup miso
1 cup sugar
½ cup chopped peeled fresh ginger
½ cup chopped garlic

FOR SATAY
2 pieces (2 ounces each) sea bass
4 thick spears peeled asparagus, trimmed
    to 4 inches long
1 tablespoon olive oil
1 tablespoon minced fresh chives

Special equipment: 2 wooden skewers

"The work is the day before, but the broiling part is fast. Served over sushi rice it makes for a good, filling meal. I made it for a dinner party for eight, which included a restaurant chef who was blown away."

Keough, Memphis, Tennessee

cioppino

Shrimp, scallops, crab, clams, and red snapper make up this 60-minute fish stew, a dish that sounds Old World Italian but most likely originated in the Italian-Portuguese neighborhood of San Francisco known as North Beach. Although the recipe may seem overwhelming at first, the ingredient list is in fact just made up of kitchen pantry staples and seafood. To cut costs, double up on the least expensive wild seafood and omit the priciest. Serve with a toasted baguette.

YIELD: MAKES 6 SERVINGS

4 large garlic cloves, minced
2 medium onions, finely chopped
1 Turkish bay leaf or ½ California bay leaf
1 teaspoon dried oregano, crumbled
1 teaspoon dried red pepper flakes
1½ teaspoons salt
½ teaspoon black pepper
¼ cup olive oil
1 green bell pepper, seeded and cut into
    ¼-inch dice
2 tablespoons tomato paste
1½ cups dry red wine
1 (28- to 32-ounce) can whole plum
    tomatoes, drained, reserving juice,
    chopped
1 cup bottled clam juice
1 cup chicken broth
1 (1-pound) king crab leg, thawed if frozen
18 small (2-inch) hard-shelled clams
    (1½ pounds), such as littlenecks,
    scrubbed
1 pound skinless red snapper or halibut
    fillets, cut into 1½-inch pieces
1 pound large shrimp (16 to 20), shelled
    (tails and bottom segment of shells left
    intact) and deveined
¾ pound sea scallops, tough muscle
    removed from side of each if necessary
¼ cup finely chopped fresh flat-leaf parsley
3 tablespoons finely chopped fresh basil
Shredded fresh basil leaves and small
    whole leaves, for garnish
Focaccia or sourdough bread, for serving

1. In an 8-quart heavy pot over moderate heat, cook the garlic, onions, bay leaf, oregano, and red pepper flakes with salt and pepper in the oil, stirring, until onions are softened, about 5 minutes. Stir in the bell pepper and tomato paste and cook, stirring, 1 minute more. Add the wine and boil until reduced by about half, 5 to 6 minutes. Then add the tomatoes with their juice, the clam juice, and chicken broth and simmer, covered, 30 minutes. Season with salt and pepper. (Can be made 1 day ahead; refrigerate.)

2. While stew is simmering, hack the crab leg through the shell into 2- to 3-inch pieces with a large heavy knife. Add the crab pieces and clams to the stew and simmer, covered, until clams just open, 5 to 10 minutes, checking every minute after 5 minutes and transferring opened clams to a bowl with tongs or a slotted spoon. (Discard any unopened clams after 10 minutes.)

3. Lightly season the fish fillets, shrimp, and scallops with salt and add to the stew, then simmer, covered, until just cooked through, about 5 minutes. Discard the bay leaf, then return the clams to the pot and gently stir in the parsley and basil.

4. Serve the cioppino immediately in large soup bowls, garnishing with basil.

"I used mussels, halibut, squid, scallops, and shrimp. My family loved it. I make a batch of the basic broth to portion and freeze. It will make a superfast and easy meal just by adding some fresh seafood."
A cook, Seattle, Washington

spicy sesame noodles
with chopped peanuts and thai basil

This Thai-inspired noodle dish dovetails four essential flavors: sweet, sour, salty, and bitter. Seek out Thai basil, which imparts clean, crisp notes of anise and mint.

YIELD: MAKES 4 TO 6 SERVINGS

1 tablespoon peanut oil
2 tablespoons minced peeled fresh
    ginger
2 garlic cloves, minced
3 tablespoons Asian sesame oil
2 tablespoons soy sauce
2 tablespoons balsamic vinegar
1½ tablespoons sugar
1 tablespoon hot chili oil, or to taste
1½ teaspoons salt
1 pound fresh Chinese egg noodles or
    fresh angel hair pasta
12 green onions (white and pale green
    parts only), thinly sliced
½ cup coarsely chopped roasted peanuts
¼ cup thinly sliced fresh Thai basil leaves

"Tasty dish, easy to take to other houses for BBQs, and it goes wonderfully with grilled salmon or chicken, or on its own for lunch the next day."

JoeyLGH, Amherst, Massachusetts

1. Heat the peanut oil in a small skillet over medium heat. Add the ginger and garlic; sauté 1 minute. Transfer to a large bowl. Add the sesame oil, soy sauce, vinegar, sugar, chili oil, and salt; whisk to blend.

2. Place the noodles in a sieve over the sink. Separate the noodles with your fingers and shake to remove excess starch. Cook in a large pot of boiling salted water until just tender, stirring occasionally. Drain and rinse under cold water until cool. Drain thoroughly. Transfer the noodles to the bowl with the sauce. Add the green onions and toss to coat noodles. Let stand at room temperature until noodles have absorbed dressing, tossing occasionally, about 1 hour.

3. Stir in the peanuts and Thai basil; toss again. Season noodles to taste with salt and pepper. Serve at room temperature.

indo-chinese lettuce wraps

Epicurious member **Neel N. Patel** of Chicago was inspired to make this when a friend asked for lettuce wraps for a party. The resulting marriage of cuisines incorporates Asian aromatics and Indian spices and a Mexican staple in a fragrant dish with garam masala, cumin, coriander, garlic, and ginger. If spicy is how you like to roll, include some of the jalapeño seeds. And while romaine lettuce leaves are sturdy and flavorful, butterhead varieties such as Boston or Bibb are more pliable and lend a more tender bite.

1. In a small bowl, whisk together the garam masala, cumin, coriander, and cayenne.

2. In a large sauté pan over moderate heat, heat the oil until hot but not smoking. Add the onion and sauté, stirring occasionally, until translucent, about 3 minutes. Add the jalapeño, garlic, and ginger and sauté, stirring occasionally, 2 minutes.

3. Add the chicken and sauté, breaking up any lumps with a wooden spoon, until no longer pink, about 3 minutes. Stir in the spice mixture, along with the salt and ketchup, and sauté 1 minute.

4. Stir in ¼ cup water and sauté, stirring occasionally, until the chicken is cooked through, about 6 minutes. Stir in 1 tablespoon cilantro, then transfer to a medium bowl.

5. Serve the chicken alongside the lettuce leaves and the remaining ½ cup chopped cilantro. To eat, pile chicken onto a lettuce leaf and top with cilantro.

YIELD: MAKES 4 SERVINGS

2 teaspoons garam masala
2 teaspoons ground cumin
2 teaspoons ground coriander
½ teaspoon cayenne
3 tablespoons vegetable oil
½ large yellow onion, cut into medium dice
1 large fresh jalapeño chile, seeded and minced
3 garlic cloves, minced
1 (1-inch) piece fresh ginger, peeled and coarsely grated
1 pound ground chicken
1 teaspoon salt
2 tablespoons ketchup
½ cup plus 1 tablespoon chopped fresh cilantro leaves
2 romaine hearts, leaves separated

I love making shareable, small dishes as it facilitates conversation. Besides, why have one tasty dish when you can have five?

I like to serve this family style, with the filling in a large bowl and lettuce cups and lime wedges piled next to it.
—Neel N. Patel

wild mushroom pizzas *with*
caramelized onions, fontina, and rosemary

You may want to offer silent thanks to the unnamed genius who invented personal-size pizzas, as you won't want to share even one bite of this luscious blend of flavors. Atlanta's Woodfire Grill came up with a mix of earthy wild mushrooms with sweet caramelized onions and rich fontina. Watching pennies? Choose common button mushrooms or rehydrate a dried-mushroom mix.

YIELD: MAKES 6 INDIVIDUAL PIZZAS

7 tablespoons butter
2 tablespoons plus 1 teaspoon grapeseed oil
3 medium onions, halved lengthwise, thinly sliced crosswise (about 6 cups)
2 pounds assorted wild mushrooms, such as cremini, oyster, chanterelle, stemmed shiitake, cut into bite-size pieces
6 garlic cloves, minced
2 tablespoons minced shallot
2 cups dry white wine
1 tablespoon minced fresh rosemary
Pizza Dough (recipe follows)
Cornmeal, for dusting
Garlic oil
3 cups grated fontina cheese (about 10 ounces)

"Spread oil on the pizza crust and tossed a little with uncooked shiitakes. Topped pizza with caramelized onions, roasted garlic cloves, more rosemary, the mushrooms, Parmesan, and some fresh-cracked-pepper goat cheese from the farmers' market. Delicious!"

A cook, Somerville, Massachusetts

1. Melt 3 tablespoons butter with 2 tablespoons grapeseed oil in a heavy large skillet over medium heat. Add the onions and sauté until golden, about 45 minutes. Season with salt and pepper.

2. Melt the remaining 4 tablespoons butter with 1 teaspoon grapeseed oil in another heavy large skillet over medium-high heat. Add the mushrooms, garlic, and shallot; sauté 4 minutes. Add the wine and simmer until almost all the liquid is absorbed, stirring frequently, about 13 minutes. Add the rosemary; season with salt and pepper.

3. Position the rack in the bottom third of the oven. Place heavy 17-by-11-inch baking sheet on the rack (invert if rimmed). Preheat the oven to 500°F at least 30 minutes before baking. Roll out 2 dough disks on a lightly floured surface to 8-inch rounds, allowing the dough to rest a few minutes if it springs back. Sprinkle another baking sheet (invert if rimmed) with cornmeal. Transfer one dough round to the second baking sheet. Lightly brush the dough with garlic oil. Sprinkle with ½ cup cheese. Scatter 2½ tablespoons of the onions over the cheese. Scatter ½ cup of the mushrooms over the onions. Sprinkle with salt.

4. Position the baking sheet with the pizza at the far edge of one side of the hot baking sheet. Tilt the sheet and pull it back slowly, allowing the pizza to slide onto the hot sheet. Repeat with the second dough disk, repeating the garlic oil, cheese, onions, mushrooms, and salt, and slide the second pizza onto the other half of the hot baking sheet. Bake pizzas 6 minutes. Rotate the pizzas half a turn, then bake until crust is deep brown, about 6 minutes

longer. Using a large spatula, carefully transfer the pizzas to the cutting board. Let rest 1 minute. Slice into wedges and serve.

5. Repeat with remaining ingredients to make 4 more pizzas.

pizza dough

1. Brush a large bowl with oil. Mix the warm water and sugar in a food processor. Sprinkle the yeast over; stir to dissolve. Let stand until the mixture bubbles, about 10 minutes. Add the flour, oil, and salt. Process 1 minute.

2. Transfer the dough to a floured surface; knead until smooth, about 5 minutes. Place in prepared bowl, turning to coat dough with oil. Cover the bowl with plastic wrap and let rise in a warm draft-free area until doubled in volume, about 1 hour.

3. Sprinkle cornmeal over rimmed baking sheet. Divide the dough into 6 equal portions; roll each into a ball. Lightly spray a large sheet of plastic wrap with nonstick spray; place over the dough balls, sprayed side down. Refrigerate 1 hour before rolling and baking.

YIELD: ENOUGH TO MAKE 6 INDIVIDUAL PIZZAS

1½ cups warm water (110°–115°F)
1½ tablespoons sugar
3 teaspoons active dry yeast (about 1½ envelopes)
4½ cups all-purpose flour
4½ tablespoons olive oil
2¼ teaspoons salt
Cornmeal, for dusting
Nonstick vegetable-oil spray

Asparagus, Fingerling Potato, and Goat Cheese Pizza (page 50)

Wild Mushroom Pizza with Caramelized Onions, Fontina, and Rosemary (page 46)

Caprese Pizza
(page 51)

asparagus, fingerling potato, and goat cheese pizza

Potato may not be your everyday kind of pizza topping, but its tender texture and buttery flavor just work, especially when paired with goat cheese. Replacing half the fingerlings with yams adds a touch of sweetness (not to mention beta-carotene). Make sure the pizza crust is rolled thick enough to stand up to the hearty toppings. Serve with a green salad for a delicious vegetarian dinner, or cut into small wedges to make it cocktail-party perfect.

YIELD: MAKES 4 SERVINGS

5 ounces fingerling potatoes
Cornmeal, for sprinkling
½ Pizza Dough (page 47)
2 tablespoons extra-virgin olive oil
1 garlic clove, pressed
4 green onions, thinly sliced
1⅓ cups grated whole-milk mozzarella cheese (about 6 ounces)
4 ounces soft fresh goat cheese, crumbled
8 ounces asparagus, trimmed, each spear cut in half lengthwise, then crosswise into 2- to 3-inch pieces
½ cup grated Parmesan cheese

"I used my own crust and added a bit of fresh rosemary before baking because I had some and it sounded good. I love potatoes on pizza, and the flavors in this one are complex without being heavy. I almost hate to say it because it's such a good veggie recipe, but some really good bacon could make this exceptional."

Cibomiele, Colorado

1. Place the potatoes in a small saucepan. Add enough water to cover by 1 inch. Sprinkle with salt. Bring to a boil and cook until potatoes are tender, about 10 minutes. Drain. Cool. Cut potatoes into thin slices.

2. Preheat the oven to 450°F. Sprinkle a rimless baking sheet with cornmeal. Roll and stretch the pizza dough to a 16 by 11-inch oval. Transfer to baking sheet. Mix 1 tablespoon olive oil and the garlic in a small bowl. Brush garlic oil over the dough. Sprinkle three-fourths of the green onions over, then the mozzarella, leaving a ½-inch plain border. Top with the potato slices and goat cheese. Toss the asparagus and remaining 1 tablespoon oil in a medium bowl. Scatter the asparagus over the pizza. Sprinkle with Parmesan, then lightly with salt and generously with pepper.

3. Bake the pizza until the crust is browned and the asparagus is tender, about 18 minutes. Transfer to a cutting board. Sprinkle with remaining green onions. Cut into pieces.

caprese pizza

The best Italian ingredients comingle in this delicious pizza from Epicurious member **Saatchiken**.

MAKE VEGETABLES

1. Position a rack in the middle of the oven and preheat the oven to 300°F.

2. Arrange the tomatoes (cut side up), onion, and garlic (cut side up) on a large baking sheet. Drizzle with the olive oil and sprinkle with the thyme, sugar, salt, and pepper. Roast the vegetables until the onion is tender and the garlic is golden brown, about 1 hour. Transfer the vegetables to a rack to cool.

3. Once the vegetables are cool enough to handle, squeeze the roasted garlic from its skins into a small bowl. Using a spoon, mash the garlic into a paste. Cut the root end off each onion wedge and separate the slices.

MAKE PIZZA

1. In a medium saucepan over moderate heat, bring the balsamic vinegar and sugar to a boil. Simmer, uncovered, until reduced by half, about 10 minutes. Cool to room temperature.

2. Position a rack in the middle of the oven and preheat the oven to 450°F.

3. Lightly dust a work surface with flour and roll out the pizza dough to a 12- to 14-inch diameter, ¼ inch thick. Sprinkle the cornmeal evenly over a pizza pan or baking sheet and lay the dough on top. Spread the mashed roasted garlic evenly over the dough and arrange the onion, tomatoes, and mozzarella evenly on top of that.

4. Bake the pizza until the crust is golden on the bottom and the cheese is melted, 12 to 15 minutes.

5. Garnish the pizza with the grated Parmesan, balsamic reduction, toasted pine nuts, and arugula. Serve immediately.

YIELD: MAKES 4 SERVINGS

FOR VEGETABLES

12 Roma (plum) tomatoes, halved
1 large red onion, cut into 8 wedges
2 heads of garlic with skin on, top ¼ inch cut off to expose each clove
¼ cup extra-virgin olive oil
1 tablespoon fresh thyme, chopped, or 1 teaspoon dried
1 tablespoon sugar
1 teaspoon kosher salt
½ teaspoon freshly ground black pepper

FOR PIZZA

1 cup balsamic vinegar
¼ cup sugar
¼ cup all-purpose flour
1 pound prepared pizza dough
¼ cup cornmeal
1 (8-ounce) ball fresh mozzarella, cut into ¼-inch-thick slices, or 6 ounces (1½ cups) coarsely shredded mozzarella
2 tablespoons freshly grated Parmesan cheese
2 tablespoons pine nuts, toasted
1 cup baby arugula

do ahead:

The **BALSAMIC REDUCTION** can be cooled and refrigerated, covered, for up to 2 weeks.

The **VEGETABLES** can be roasted and refrigerated, in separate covered containers, for up to 3 days.

braised chicken *with tomatoes and olives*

With only twenty-five minutes of active prep time, even a less-experienced cook can add this timeless chicken recipe to his or her repertoire. The simple dinner utilizes produce of southern France—olives, onions, and fennel—cooked in the same pan as the chicken and sauce. Substitute a combination of dried thyme, fennel, basil, and savory if you can't find herbes de Provence. Serve this in the backyard with a baguette and a bottle of Côtes de Provence, and have yourself a true *pique-nique français.*

YIELD: MAKES 4 SERVINGS

1 pound ripe tomatoes (3 to 4 medium), cut into wedges
1 large onion, cut into wedges, leaving root ends intact
½ cup drained brine-cured black olives, pitted if desired
4 large garlic cloves, sliced, plus 1 teaspoon minced
3 tablespoons olive oil
2 teaspoons herbes de Provence
½ teaspoon fennel seeds
1½ teaspoons salt
¾ teaspoon black pepper
1 whole (3½ pound) chicken
Chopped fresh flat-leaf parsley, for garnish
Crusty bread, for serving

Equipment: kitchen string

"I've been cooking for 30 some years, and this is one of the flat-out finest chicken dishes, period. Double the vegetables and serve it with basmati rice. Easy, elegant, and literally finger-lickin' good."

Raedwulf, the Okanagan, Canada

1. Preheat a convection oven to 400°F or a regular oven to 425°F, with the rack in the middle.

2. Toss together the tomatoes, onion, olives, sliced garlic, 2 tablespoons oil, 1 teaspoon herbes de Provence, the fennel seeds, ½ teaspoon salt, and ¼ teaspoon pepper in a 13 by 9-inch or other 3-quart shallow baking dish. Push the vegetables to the sides of the dish to make room for the chicken.

3. Stir together the minced garlic, remaining 1 teaspoon salt and ½ teaspoon pepper, remaining teaspoon herbes de Provence, and remaining tablespoon olive oil.

4. Remove excess fat from the chicken and pat dry, then rub inside and out with the seasoning mixture. Tie the legs together with string, then put the chicken in the baking dish.

5. Roast until an instant-read thermometer inserted into the thickest part of a thigh (do not touch bone) registers 170°F, about 1 hour in a convection oven, 1 to 1¼ hours in a regular oven.

6. Let the chicken stand 10 minutes before carving. Garnish with parsley. Serve with vegetables and pan juices.

green pozole *with chicken*

Chicken makes this ceremonial Aztec soup healthier than the pork-based original. While this does require some preparation, the extra time and effort pay off with an intense, flavorful entrée.

COOK CHICKEN:

1. Bring 8 cups of water, the bay leaf, half of the onion, half of the garlic, and 1 teaspoon salt to a boil, covered, in a heavy 6-quart pot, then reduce the heat and simmer 10 minutes. Add the chicken and poach at a bare simmer, uncovered, skimming off any foam, until just cooked through, about 20 minutes.

2. Transfer the chicken to a cutting board to cool. Pour the broth through a fine-mesh sieve into a large bowl, discarding solids, and reserve. When chicken is cool enough to handle, coarsely shred with your fingers.

MAKE SAUCE WHILE CHICKEN COOLS

1. Cook the pumpkin seeds in a dry small skillet over low heat, stirring occasionally, until puffed but not browned (seeds will pop as they puff), 6 to 7 minutes. Transfer to a bowl to cool completely, then finely grind in a grinder.

2. Simmer the tomatillos and remaining onion in the remaining cup water in a 3-quart saucepan, covered, until tender, about 10 minutes. Drain the vegetables and purée in a blender with the jalapeños, ¼ cup cilantro, the epazote, remaining garlic, and remaining 1½ teaspoons salt.

3. Heat the oil in a 4- to 5-quart heavy pot over moderately high heat until hot but not smoking, then add the purée (use caution as it will splatter and steam). Cook, uncovered, stirring frequently, until thickened, about 10 minutes. Stir in the pumpkin seeds and 1 cup of the reserved broth and simmer 5 minutes. Stir in the shredded chicken, the hominy, and 3 more cups of broth and simmer, partially covered, 20 minutes.

4. Stir in the remaining ½ cup cilantro and serve the pozole in deep bowls with accompaniments.

YIELD: MAKES 6 GENEROUS SERVINGS

FOR THE CHICKEN
9 cups water
1 Turkish or ½ California bay leaf
1 large white onion, halved lengthwise
   and thinly sliced
6 garlic cloves, chopped
2½ teaspoons salt
3 pounds skinless boneless chicken thighs

FOR THE SAUCE
½ cup hulled (green) pumpkin seeds, not
   roasted (2¼ ounces)
1 pound tomatillos, husked
2 fresh jalapeño chiles, quartered
   (including seeds)
¾ cup chopped fresh cilantro
1 teaspoon dried epazote or oregano
   (preferably Mexican), crumbled
2 tablespoons vegetable oil
2 (15-ounce) cans white hominy, rinsed
   and drained
Diced radish; cubed avocado tossed
   with lime juice; shredded romaine;
   chopped white onion; lime wedges;
   dried oregano

Special equipment: Electric coffee/spice
   grinder

> ### do ahead:
>
> The **CHICKEN** can be cooked and shredded 1 day ahead and chilled in 4 cups reserved broth. Measure out 1 cup broth before proceeding.

grilled jerk chicken *with papaya salsa*

This spicy standout nails the difficult balance of sweet and fiery that characterizes the best jerk, cutting the heat of the Scotch bonnet chiles with a mixture of allspice, cinnamon, nutmeg, and brown sugar. The soy sauce adds a sticky-salty-caramel note when the meat is grilled. Because jerk seasoning can burn easily, make sure to use indirect heat when grilling the meat. Serve with rice, beans, and plenty of ice-cold beer. (And be sure to use gloves when handling the peppers.)

YIELD: MAKES 8 SERVINGS

FOR JERK MARINADE
3 green onions, chopped
4 large garlic cloves, chopped
1 small onion, chopped
4 to 5 fresh Scotch bonnet or habanero
    chiles, stemmed and seeded
¼ cup fresh lime juice
2 tablespoons soy sauce
3 tablespoons olive oil
1½ tablespoons salt
1 tablespoon brown sugar
1 tablespoon fresh thyme leaves
2 teaspoons ground allspice
2 teaspoons black pepper
¾ teaspoon freshly grated nutmeg
½ teaspoon ground cinnamon

FOR CHICKEN
4 chicken breast halves with skin and
    bones (3 pounds), halved crosswise
2½ to 3 pounds chicken thighs and
    drumsticks
Papaya Salsa (recipe follows)

Special equipment: Gas or charcoal grill
    (optional)

MAKE MARINADE
Blend all marinade ingredients in a blender until smooth.

MARINATE AND GRILL CHICKEN
1. Divide the chicken pieces and marinade in 2 sealable plastic bags. Seal the bags, pressing out excess air, then turn bags over several times to distribute marinade. Put bags of chicken in a shallow pan and marinate, chilled, turning once or twice, for 1 day.

2. Let chicken stand at room temperature 1 hour before cooking.

COOK CHICKEN USING CHARCOAL GRILL
1. Open the vents on the bottom of the grill and on the lid. Light a large chimney of charcoal briquettes (about 100) and pour them evenly over one side of a bottom rack (you will have a double or triple layer of charcoal).

2. When the charcoal turns grayish white and you can hold your hand 5 inches above the rack for 3 to 4 seconds, sear the chicken in batches on a lightly oiled rack over the coals until well browned on all sides, about 3 minutes per batch. Move the chicken as seared to the side of the grill with no coals underneath, then cook, covered with the lid, until cooked through, 25 to 30 minutes more.

3. Serve the chicken with the papaya salsa.

COOK CHICKEN USING GAS GRILL
1. Preheat the burners on high, then adjust heat to moderate. Cook chicken until well browned on all sides, 15 to 20 minutes. Adjust the heat to low and cook chicken,

covered with lid, until cooked through, about 25 minutes more.

2. Serve the chicken with papaya salsa.

COOK CHICKEN USING AN OVEN

If you can't grill, you can roast the chicken in two large shallow (1-inch-deep) baking pans in the upper and lower thirds of a 400°F oven, switching the position of the pans halfway through the roasting, 40 to 45 minutes total.

"This is an excellent marinade—something magical happens when it hits the grill. In the future, I'm going to make this marinade in batches and keep it in the fridge for easy access—it turns boring old chicken breasts into something amazing."

A cook, Los Angeles, California

papaya salsa

In a large bowl, stir together all the ingredients; serve. This can be made up to 1 hour ahead, kept at room temperature, or kept, covered, in the refrigerator overnight.

YIELD: MAKES ABOUT 4½ CUPS

2 pounds papaya (2 preferably pink-fleshed strawberry variety), peeled, seeded, and cut into ¼-inch dice
1½ cups diced (¼-inch) fresh pineapple (from ½ small pineapple)
2 green onions, finely chopped
1 small garlic clove, minced
2 tablespoons fresh lime juice
½ teaspoon salt
¼ teaspoon black pepper

asian pork and mushroom burger wraps

Soy sauce, sriracha, hoisin, and Asian sesame oil assert an Eastern influence on the traditional burger. Since the burgers and sauce can both be made ahead of time, this is a versatile, no-fuss meal perfect for a dinner party or after-work bite. With the lettuce, bell pepper, carrot, and cilantro in separate bowls, guests can customize their burgers as they please.

YIELD: MAKES 6 SERVINGS

2 tablespoons canola or peanut oil
2 tablespoons minced lemongrass (from bottom 3 inches of about 4 stalks)
2 garlic cloves, minced
4 ounces fresh shiitake mushrooms, stemmed, caps chopped
1 teaspoon kosher or other coarse salt
1¾ pounds ground pork shoulder (from Boston butt)
2 tablespoons soy sauce
3 teaspoons Asian sesame oil
¾ teaspoon cracked black peppercorns
½ cup hoisin sauce
1 tablespoon minced peeled fresh ginger
1 tablespoon unseasoned rice vinegar
1 teaspoon hot chili sauce (such as sriracha)
Nonstick vegetable-oil spray
2 heads of Bibb lettuce, cored, leaves separated
1 cup matchstick strips of red bell pepper
1 cup matchstick strips of peeled carrot
⅓ cup fresh cilantro leaves

Special equipment: Gas or charcoal grill

1. Heat the oil in a large skillet over medium-high heat. Add the lemongrass and garlic; sauté 2 minutes. Add the mushrooms. Sprinkle with ½ teaspoon salt; sauté until mushrooms are tender, about 4 minutes. Remove from the heat; cool in skillet.

2. Place the pork in a large bowl. Mix in 1 tablespoon soy sauce, 1 teaspoon sesame oil, the cracked pepper, and remaining ½ teaspoon salt, then fold in the mushroom mixture. Using 2 generous tablespoonfuls for each, shape mixture into 18 patties, each about 2¼ inches in diameter; arrange on a plastic-lined baking sheet.

3. Whisk the hoisin sauce, ginger, vinegar, chili sauce, remaining 1 tablespoon soy sauce, and remaining 2 teaspoons sesame oil in small bowl. Set sauce aside.

4. Spray a grill rack with nonstick spray. Prepare grill to medium-high heat. Grill the burgers until cooked through, about 3 minutes per side.

5. Arrange burgers on a platter; set out sauce. Place the lettuce, bell pepper, carrot, and cilantro in separate bowls. Serve, suggesting guests wrap burgers in lettuce leaves and add sauce and vegetables as desired.

"Used a beef/pork/veal mixture and didn't bother making patties. Browned meat, added mushrooms and seasonings and mixed everything together in a big bowl and, WAL-LAH, lettuce wraps. Very delicious!"
Honoree77, Point Pleasant, New Jersey

old-fashioned ham
with brown sugar and mustard glaze

This sweet and savory ham, created by chef and Edna Lewis confidant Scott Peacock, gives us a whole new reason to look forward to Easter. Smothered in mustard and drizzled with honey, this is an old-fashioned Southern dish that's simple and impressive.

1. Preheat the oven to 325°F. Place the ham in a large roasting pan. Pour the apple juice over the ham. Cover the ham completely with parchment, then cover the ham and roasting pan completely with heavy-duty foil, sealing tightly at edges of pan. Bake the ham until an instant-read thermometer inserted into center of the ham registers 145°F, about 3 hours 45 minutes. Remove the ham from the oven. Increase the oven temperature to 375°F.

2. Remove the foil and parchment from the ham. Drain and discard the liquids from the roasting pan. Cut off rind and all but a ¼-inch-thick layer of fat from the ham and discard. Using a long sharp knife, score the fat in a 1-inch-wide, ¼-inch-deep diamond pattern. Spread the mustard evenly over the fat layer on the ham. Pat the brown sugar over the mustard coating, pressing firmly to adhere. Drizzle the honey evenly over.

3. Bake until the ham is well glazed, spooning any mustard and sugar glaze that slides into the roasting pan back over the ham, about 30 minutes. Transfer the ham to a serving platter; let cool at least 45 minutes. Slice the ham and serve slightly warm or at room temperature.

YIELD: MAKES 10 SERVINGS

1 (10-pound) smoked ham with rind, preferably shank end
1 cup unsweetened apple juice or apple cider
½ cup whole-grain Dijon mustard
⅔ cup (packed) light brown sugar
¼ cup honey

"For the mustard, we usually mix half whole-grain and creamy mustards—mostly because we never have enough of one or the other. We also baste the ham a couple of times after putting the glaze on, and it seems to get down into the ham a little better when we do that. Leftovers from this recipe are heavenly."

Krich231

pork tenderloin *with spiced rhubarb chutney*

Tender pork is roasted with rich, warmly spiced chutney so that the fruity condiment gets a chance to cook into the meat. The woody, sweet notes of the chutney are also great atop chicken, lamb, or duck—or just on a spoon, straight. Rhubarb is at its prime in spring so for a fall-friendly chutney, replace it with fresh apples and figs.

MAKE CHUTNEY

Combine the sugar, vinegar, ginger, garlic, cumin, cinnamon, cloves, and red pepper flakes in a heavy large Dutch oven. Bring to a simmer over low heat, stirring until the sugar dissolves. Add the rhubarb, onion, and dried cherries; increase the heat to medium-high and cook until rhubarb is tender and mixture thickens slightly, about 5 minutes. Cool completely.

MAKE PORK

Preheat the oven to 400°F. Sprinkle the pork with the cumin. Season with salt and pepper. Heat the oil in a heavy large skillet over high heat. Add the pork and brown on all sides, about 5 minutes. Transfer the meat to a roasting pan. Brush with 6 tablespoons chutney. Roast until an instant-read thermometer inserted into the center registers 155°F, brushing occasionally with 6 more tablespoons chutney, about 25 minutes. Slice the pork into medallions. Garnish with cilantro and serve with remaining chutney.

> *"The leftover chutney made amazing toasted sandwiches with ham and Camembert the next day."*
>
> **Nzjulz**

YIELD: MAKES 4 SERVINGS

FOR CHUTNEY

¾ cup sugar
⅓ cup cider vinegar
1 tablespoon minced peeled fresh ginger
1 tablespoon ground garlic powder
1 teaspoon ground cumin
½ teaspoon ground cinnamon
½ teaspoon ground cloves
¼ teaspoon dried red pepper flakes
4 cups (½-inch) cubed fresh rhubarb
    (about 1½ pounds)
½ cup (generous) chopped red onion
⅓ cup dried tart cherries or golden raisins
    (about 2 ounces)

FOR PORK

2 pork tenderloins (about 1½ pounds
    total), trimmed
2 teaspoons ground cumin
1 tablespoon olive oil
Fresh cilantro sprigs, for garnish

---

do ahead:

The **CHUTNEY** can be made 1 day ahead. Cover and chill. Bring to room temperature before using.

pan-seared rib-eye steaks
with porcini and rosemary rub

Master the art and science of meat preparation with this simple recipe from Aidells Sausage founder Bruce Aidells. He starts with grass-fed boneless rib eye and a simple soy-sauce marinade. But the secret to this meat's success is the porcini-focused spice rub. Dress it up with Wild Mushroom–Potato Gratin (page 272) or down with fries and beer on a Friday night in.

YIELD: MAKES 4 TO 6 SERVINGS

2 (2-inch-thick) grass-fed boneless rib-eye steaks (about 3 pounds total)
½ cup soy sauce
¼ ounce dried porcini mushrooms
1 tablespoon finely chopped fresh rosemary
2 teaspoons coarsely ground black pepper
1 tablespoon olive oil

"Great recipe, the crust was delicious. I added minced oregano. I seared it and then finished it in a 375 oven till medium rare. Served with sesame asparagus and baked sweet potato fries. YUMMY."
Chefmugs, Venice, Florida

1. Place the steaks and soy sauce in a large resealable plastic bag. Seal the bag, releasing excess air; turn to coat. Let the steaks marinate at room temperature 2 hours, turning occasionally.

2. Process the porcini mushrooms in a spice mill to a fine powder. Mix 1½ tablespoons mushroom powder, the rosemary, and pepper in a small bowl (reserve any remaining powder for another use).

3. Drain the steaks; pat dry. Sprinkle the mushroom-rosemary rub generously over both sides of the steaks, pressing to adhere.

4. Heat the oil in a heavy large skillet (preferably cast iron) over medium-high heat. Fry the steaks until browned and cooked to desired doneness, about 8 minutes per side for rare, adjusting heat to medium if browning too quickly.

5. Transfer the steaks to a plate; tent with foil to keep warm. Let rest 10 minutes. Cut into ½-inch-thick slices and serve.

steak *with parmesan butter, balsamic glaze, and arugula*

The bold pairing of sharp, salty Parmesan with a sweet vinegar and brown-sugar glaze transcends any steak lover's expectations. Both the butter and the glaze boost the juiciness of the meat, while peppery arugula sets a light and refreshing backdrop. Feel free to substitute your preferred cut of meat, and finish the plate with a baked sweet potato.

1. Mix the grated cheese and butter in a small bowl. Season generously with salt and pepper; set aside.

2. Sprinkle the steak generously with salt and pepper. Heat the oil in a medium skillet over medium-high heat. Add the steak; cook to desired doneness, about 4 minutes per side for medium-rare. Transfer to a plate.

3. Add the vinegar, shallots, and brown sugar to the skillet; boil until reduced to a glaze, stirring constantly, about 1 minute.

4. Divide the arugula and Parmesan shavings between 2 plates. Squeeze the lemon over. Slice the steak; place slices atop the arugula. Top the steak with Parmesan butter and drizzle lightly with the glaze.

YIELD: MAKES 2 SERVINGS

2 tablespoons grated Parmesan cheese, plus Parmesan cheese shavings
1½ tablespoons butter, at room temperature
1 (12-ounce) rib-eye steak
1 teaspoon olive oil
¼ cup balsamic vinegar
¼ cup finely chopped shallots
½ teaspoon (packed) dark brown sugar
4 cups (lightly packed) arugula
2 large lemon wedges

"Definitely need good ingredients— when there's so few. Bust out fresh Parmesan, and the bite of the arugula is the perfect balance. I used sirloin instead of rib eye for a less fatty cut."
A cook, Hampton, Connecticut

roasted lamb chops
with charmoula and skillet asparagus

Charmoula, an aromatic Middle Eastern herb and garlic sauce, combines mint, parsley, sweet smoked paprika, cilantro, and cumin. It comes together in minutes in the food processor, and the lamb can marinate all day.

YIELD: MAKES 4 SERVINGS

FOR CHARMOULA

1 tablespoon cumin seeds

1½ cups (lightly packed) fresh flat-leaf parsley leaves

½ cup (lightly packed) fresh mint leaves

½ cup (lightly packed) fresh cilantro leaves

2 large garlic cloves

1 tablespoon sweet smoked paprika (pimentón dulce) or Hungarian sweet paprika

1 teaspoon kosher or other coarse salt

¼ teaspoon cayenne

6 tablespoons extra-virgin olive oil

1 tablespoon fresh lemon juice

FOR LAMB

8 (1¼- to 1½-inch-thick) lamb loin chops (about 2⅔ pounds)

1 tablespoon butter

1 tablespoon extra-virgin olive oil

1½ pounds thin asparagus, trimmed, peeled, tops cut into 3-inch-long pieces, stalks cut into ½-inch pieces

3 tablespoons chopped shallots

1 teaspoon finely grated lemon peel

"This is a glamorous dish that is easy to prepare. I added extra lemon juice for some spunk and served it with roasted baby potatoes and French green beans with garlic."

Delspina, Purdys, New York

MAKE CHARMOULA

Heat a small skillet over medium heat. Add the cumin seeds and toast until aromatic and slightly darker, stirring occasionally, about 2 minutes. Transfer to a food processor. Add the parsley, mint, cilantro, garlic, paprika, salt, and cayenne to processor. Using on/off turns, process until a coarse paste forms. With the machine running, gradually add 4 tablespoons of olive oil. Transfer 2 tablespoons charmoula to a small bowl; whisk in the lemon juice and remaining 2 tablespoons oil. Cover and chill sauce to serve with lamb.

MAKE LAMB

1. Transfer the remaining charmoula to a large resealable plastic bag. Add the lamb chops; seal the bag and turn to coat well. Chill at least 4 hours and up to 24 hours.

2. Let the lamb and charmoula sauce stand in a bowl at room temperature for 1 hour.

3. Preheat the oven to 500°F. Line a rimmed baking sheet with foil and place a rack on the prepared baking sheet. Place the lamb on the rack and sprinkle with salt and pepper. Roast until a thermometer inserted into the center registers 130°F for medium-rare, about 13 minutes. Transfer the lamb to a platter. Tent with foil and let rest 5 minutes.

4. Melt the butter with oil in a heavy large skillet over high heat. Add the asparagus and sauté until tender, stirring often, about 3 minutes. Add the shallots and lemon peel; sauté 1 minute. Season to taste with salt and pepper.

5. Place 2 lamb chops on each of 4 plates. Divide the asparagus among the plates. Drizzle the lamb and asparagus with charmoula sauce, passing any remaining sauce alongside.

chili con carne
with chili cheddar shortcakes

Few comfort foods hit the spot like a good chili. Don't forget the Cheddar shortcakes; the light, fluffy consistency of the dough pairs perfectly with this Tex-Mex staple.

YIELD: MAKES 6 SERVINGS

FOR SHORTCAKE BISCUITS
1½ cups all-purpose flour
2 teaspoons baking powder
½ teaspoon baking soda
½ teaspoon salt
2 tablespoons cold unsalted butter, cut into bits
¼ pound sharp Cheddar cheese, coarsely grated (about 1½ cups)
4 (2-inch) pickled jalapeño chiles, seeded and minced (wear rubber gloves)
1 cup sour cream

FOR CHILI CON CARNE
2 large onions, chopped (about 3 cups)
¼ cup vegetable oil
1 tablespoon minced garlic
2 carrots, thinly sliced
3 pounds boneless beef chuck, coarsely ground in batches in a food processor or by butcher
¼ cup chili powder
1 tablespoon ground cumin
2 tablespoons paprika
1 tablespoon crumbled dried oregano
1 tablespoon dried red pepper flakes, or to taste
2 (8-ounce) cans tomato sauce
1¼ cups beef broth
3 tablespoons cider vinegar
1 (19-ounce) can kidney beans, rinsed and drained
2 green bell peppers, seeded and chopped

MAKE THE SHORTCAKE BISCUITS
Preheat the oven to 425°F. Into a large bowl, sift together the flour, baking powder, baking soda, and salt. Add the butter, and blend the mixture until it resembles coarse meal. Stir in the cheese and chiles, add the sour cream, and stir the mixture until it just forms a soft but not sticky dough. Knead the dough gently 6 times on a lightly floured surface, then roll or pat it out until ½ inch thick. With a 3½-inch cookie cutter, cut out 6 rounds. Lay the rounds on an ungreased baking sheet and bake for 15 to 17 minutes, or until they are golden.

MAKE THE CHILI CON CARNE
1. In a heavy large Dutch oven, cook the onions in the oil over moderately low heat, stirring occasionally, until they are softened. Add the garlic and carrots, and cook the mixture, stirring, for 1 minute. Add the chuck and cook it over moderate heat, stirring and breaking up any lumps, for 10 minutes, or until it is no longer pink.

2. Add the chili powder, cumin, paprika, oregano, and red pepper flakes and cook the mixture, stirring, for 1 minute. Add the tomato sauce, broth, and vinegar. Bring the mixture to a boil, and simmer it, covered, stirring occasionally, for 50 minutes to 1 hour, or until the meat is tender.

3. Add the kidney beans, bell peppers, and salt and black pepper to taste and simmer the mixture, uncovered, for 15 minutes, or until the bell peppers are tender.

4. Arrange a biscuit, reheated and split, on each of six dinner plates, spoon the chili con carne over the bottom half, and cover it with the top half of the biscuit.

roasted potato salad

This classic potato salad is from the grandmother of Epicurious member **Beatlebailey:** "The flavor of this potato salad always brings back the wonderful memories of all the times we spent together."

1. Position a rack in the middle of the oven and preheat the oven to 425°F.

2. On a large rimmed baking sheet, toss the potatoes and the olive oil. Season with salt and pepper and roast until just fork-tender, about 30 minutes. Set aside to cool completely.

3. In a large bowl, whisk together the mayonnaise, mustard, lemon juice, and parsley. Add the potatoes, eggs, bacon, and onion and toss to combine. Season with salt and pepper, cover, and refrigerate for at least 2 hours and up to 24 hours before serving.

YIELD: MAKES 8 SERVINGS

2 pounds (1½-inch diameter) red-skinned potatoes, quartered lengthwise
2 tablespoons olive oil
½ cup mayonnaise
1½ tablespoons Creole mustard
2 tablespoons lemon juice
2 to 3 tablespoons finely chopped fresh flat-leaf parsley
4 hard-cooked eggs, sliced crosswise
8 ounces bacon, cooked until crisp and crumbled or finely chopped
½ small red onion, thinly sliced

parmesan creamed corn

Add some Parmesan cheese to creamed corn and what you get is something worthy of your best special-occasion roast, courtesy of Epicurious member **Judym1us.**

YIELD: MAKES 6 TO 8 SERVINGS

2 tablespoons unsalted butter
1 tablespoon all-purpose flour
1 cup half-and-half
½ teaspoon salt
⅛ teaspoon cayenne
20 ounces frozen corn kernels, thawed
¾ cup finely grated Parmigiano-Reggiano cheese

1. Position a rack in the middle of the oven and preheat the oven to 425°F. Butter a shallow 1½- to 2-quart baking dish.

2. In a medium saucepan over moderate heat, melt the butter. Whisk in the flour and cook, whisking constantly, for 1 minute. Whisk in the half-and-half, salt, and cayenne, then reduce the heat and simmer, stirring occasionally, until thickened, about 3 minutes. Stir in the corn and ¼ cup of the cheese. Transfer to the prepared baking dish, top with the remaining ½ cup cheese, and bake until browned and bubbly, about 15 minutes.

mashed potatoes
with prosciutto and parmesan cheese

Methods of mashed potato preparation are constantly reimagined, and this incarnation of the beloved dish stands with the best of them. The recipe, a perfect side for pork chops, draws on traditional Italian ingredients: aged Parmesan for pungency, thinly sliced and chopped prosciutto for texture, and fresh rosemary as the finishing touch.

YIELD: MAKES 8 SERVINGS

3¼ pounds russet potatoes, peeled, cut into 1-inch pieces

4 large garlic cloves, peeled

½ cup (1 stick) butter

3½ ounces thinly sliced prosciutto, finely chopped

¾ teaspoon minced fresh rosemary, plus additional for garnish

¾ cup whole milk, or more as needed

1 cup freshly grated Parmesan cheese (about 3 ounces)

do ahead:

The **MASHED POTATOES** (through step 3) can be prepared 6 hours ahead. Cover and chill. Stir over low heat to rewarm, adding more milk by tablespoonfuls, if desired.

1. Cook potatoes and garlic in a large pot of boiling salted water until the potatoes are very tender, about 15 minutes. Drain; return the potatoes and garlic to the same pot.

2. Meanwhile, melt the butter in a heavy small saucepan over medium heat. Add the prosciutto and ¾ teaspoon minced rosemary and sauté until fragrant, about 2 minutes.

3. Add the prosciutto mixture and the milk to the potatoes and garlic. Mash well, adding more milk by tablespoonfuls if potatoes are dry. Mix in ¾ cup cheese. Season with salt and pepper.

4. Transfer the potatoes to a bowl. Sprinkle with the remaining ¼ cup cheese; garnish with fresh rosemary and serve.

"Awesome spuds! I made them in the morning, adding a little extra warm milk to keep them from drying out in the oven later, and then before dinner, I rewarmed them for about 40 minutes at 325° in a convection oven. Great do-ahead dish."

A cook, Walnut Creek, California

serrano ham and poblano corn pudding

Mexican chef Roberto Santibañez invented this dish. Fresh corn adds a bright note to the buttery pudding, which pairs well with ribs, chicken, or salmon. Not a meat eater? Omit the ham without missing out on the bold variety of flavors. The pudding calls for instant corn masa mix, sometimes called masa harina, which can be found in the international aisle of the grocery store. This recipe easily doubles or triples for larger gatherings.

1. Char the chiles over a gas flame or in a broiler until blackened on all sides. Enclose in a paper bag for 15 minutes. Peel and seed the chiles, then cut lengthwise into ¼-inch-wide strips.

2. Preheat the oven to 350°F. Generously butter a 13 by 9-inch glass baking dish. Combine 1½ cups of corn, the eggs, butter, salt, and baking powder in a blender. Blend until almost smooth. Transfer the mixture to a large bowl. Add the sour cream and masa; stir until blended. Stir in the ham, cheese, chiles, and remaining ½ cup corn. Transfer the mixture to the prepared baking dish. Bake until the corn pudding is puffed and golden brown in spots on top, about 40 minutes.

YIELD: MAKES 12 SERVINGS

2 large poblano chiles
2 cups fresh corn kernels (2 large ears), or 2 cups frozen, thawed kernels
2 large eggs
½ cup (1 stick) butter, melted, slightly cooled
1 teaspoon salt
Large pinch of baking powder
1 cup sour cream
½ cup instant corn masa mix
4 ounces ¼-inch-thick slices Serrano ham or prosciutto, cut into ¼-inch cubes (about 1 cup)
1 cup coarsely grated Manchego cheese (about 4½ ounces)

"I made a double batch, then froze it for a quick microwave meal."
A cook, Los Angeles, California

spring vegetables *with shallots and lemon*

Fava beans, asparagus, and sugar snap peas are the essence of the season in this vibrant spring dish with a citrus twist; the caramelized shallots are a sweet counterpoint to the zesty zing of the fresh lemon. While this makes a terrific side dish for roasted meats like ham, turkey, or chicken, you can also toss it with pasta or rice for a main-course meal.

YIELD: MAKES 6 SERVINGS

2 tablespoons olive oil
1 tablespoon unsalted butter
4 shallots, cut crosswise into thin slices
1 pound sugar snap peas, trimmed
1 pound asparagus, trimmed and cut
    diagonally into ½-inch slices
3 pounds fresh fava beans, shelled,
    blanched in boiling water 1 minute,
    and outer skins removed; or 1 pound
    frozen Fordhook lima beans, blanched
    and, if desired, skinned
2 (3-inch) strips lemon zest removed with
    a vegetable peeler and cut crosswise
    into julienne strips
2 teaspoons fresh lemon juice

"This is a great side dish to complement any spring menu. I served it with a lemon-thyme roasted chicken, and it got rave reviews. The fava beans were great, but a lot of effort. I used half edamame and half fava."
A cook, Los Angeles, California

1. In a large skillet, heat 1 tablespoon oil and ½ tablespoon butter over moderately high heat until foam subsides. Sauté the shallots, stirring, until tender, about 2 minutes. With a slotted spoon, transfer the shallots to a bowl.

2. In fat remaining in skillet, sauté the snap peas with salt to taste, stirring occasionally, until crisp-tender. Add to shallots in bowl.

3. In skillet, heat remaining tablespoon oil and ½ tablespoon butter over moderately high heat until foam subsides. Sauté the asparagus with salt to taste, stirring occasionally, until crisp-tender.

4. Add the fava or lima beans and sauté, stirring occasionally, 2 minutes. Add the zest, lemon juice, snap peas and shallots, and salt and pepper to taste and sauté, stirring, until just heated through.

beet and carrot pancakes

Made with shredded beets and carrots, these pancakes are substantial enough to be a vegetarian main course but mild enough to play second fiddle to roast chicken or pork. Pull out the food processor to shred the carrots and beets in minutes. Or pick up a bag of shredded carrots from your supermarket to save time. Luscious crème fraîche can take the place of the sour cream garnish, if desired, and both can be dressed up with chopped fresh chives or dill.

1. Preheat the oven to 300°F. Place a baking sheet in the oven. Combine the beets, carrots, and onion in a large bowl. Mix in the egg, salt, and pepper. Add the flour; stir to blend well.

2. Heat 1½ tablespoons of oil in a heavy large skillet over medium heat. Using ⅓ cup beet mixture for each pancake, drop 4 pancakes into the skillet. Flatten each into a 3-inch round. Cook until brown and cooked through, about 4 minutes per side. Transfer the pancakes to the baking sheet in the oven; keep warm. Repeat with remaining beet mixture, making 4 more pancakes.

3. Serve pancakes with sour cream.

YIELD: MAKES 8 SERVINGS

1⅓ cups (packed) coarsely shredded peeled beets (2 medium)
1 cup coarsely shredded peeled carrots (2 medium)
1 cup thinly sliced onion
1 large egg
½ teaspoon salt
¼ teaspoon pepper
¼ cup all-purpose flour
3 tablespoons olive oil
Low-fat sour cream, for serving

"I love it when a very simple dish is so flavorful! And inexpensive! I added a dash of rosemary to the 'batter' and improvised a yogurt sauce (with cilantro, lime, garlic powder, salt, and pepper) to use as a garnish. It turned out perfectly."
Mustardgreen, Portland, Oregon

black bean and tomato quinoa

High in protein, low in price, fast to make, and gluten-free, quinoa is the ultimate grain. With this much-beloved recipe, watch lime juice, black beans, and tomatoes transform a "health food" into a must-make side dish perfect for barbecues or school lunches. The flavors get more concentrated over time, so make it a day ahead for maximum impact. Use olive oil instead of butter to make it vegan.

YIELD: MAKES 4 SERVINGS

2 teaspoons grated lime zest
2 tablespoons fresh lime juice
2 tablespoons unsalted butter, melted and cooled
1 tablespoon vegetable oil
1 teaspoon sugar
1 cup quinoa
1 (14- to 15-ounce) can black beans, rinsed and drained
2 medium tomatoes, diced
4 green onions, chopped
¼ cup chopped fresh cilantro leaves

"I 'cheated' and followed the much simpler directions on the bag of quinoa, which was to simmer it for 15 minutes, and voilà! Done! Added fresh salsa with all the same ingredients, extra cilantro, a dash of rice vinegar, and followed a few other people's suggestions for avocado. Delicious!"

Sgmoise, Charleston, South Carolina

1. Whisk together the lime zest and juice, butter, oil, sugar, ½ teaspoon salt, and ¼ teaspoon pepper in a large bowl.

2. Wash the quinoa in 3 changes of cold water in a bowl, draining in a sieve each time.

3. Cook the quinoa in a medium pot of boiling salted water (1 tablespoon salt for 2 quarts water), uncovered, until almost tender, about 10 minutes. Drain in a sieve, then set the sieve in the same pot with 1 inch of simmering water (the water should not touch the bottom of the sieve).

4. Cover the quinoa with a folded kitchen towel, then cover the sieve with a lid (don't worry if the lid doesn't fit tightly) and steam over medium heat until tender, fluffy, and dry, about 10 minutes. Remove the pot from the heat and remove the lid. Let stand, still covered with the towel, 5 minutes.

5. Add the quinoa to the dressing and toss until the dressing is absorbed, then stir in remaining ingredients and salt and pepper to taste.

mediterranean couscous and lentil salad

The perfect compromise between a grain and a salad, this refreshing Mediterranean side makes a lovely accompaniment to grilled lamb for a backyard barbecue. Or, highlight its Middle Eastern influences by pairing it with baba ghanoush and a platter of stuffed grape leaves. Add personal touches by substituting your favorite herb for the mint, topping off the salad with a squeeze of lime and a bit of orange zest, or using spinach instead of arugula. However you decide to frame it, you'll be set up for a nice snack the next day.

1. In a small saucepan, simmer the lentils in water to cover by 2 inches until tender but not falling apart, 15 to 20 minutes. Drain well. Transfer the hot lentils to a bowl and stir in 1 tablespoon vinegar and salt and pepper to taste. Cool the lentils completely, stirring occasionally.

2. In a saucepan, bring 1¼ cups water to a boil and add the couscous and ½ teaspoon salt. Remove the pan from the heat and let couscous stand, covered, 5 minutes. Fluff the couscous with a fork and transfer to a large bowl. Stir in 1 tablespoon oil and cool completely, stirring occasionally.

3. In a small bowl, whisk together the garlic paste, remaining 2 tablespoons vinegar, remaining 3 tablespoons oil, and salt and pepper to taste. Stir the lentils and dressing into the couscous.

4. Just before serving, stir in the herbs, tomatoes, and feta, and season with salt and pepper.

"I replaced the couscous with quinoa to add even more protein and fiber (amazing taste and texture). The feta can also be replaced with goat cheese."

Vaccosni, California

YIELD: MAKES 6 SERVINGS

1 cup lentilles du Puy (French green lentils) or brown lentils
3 tablespoons white-wine vinegar
1¼ cups water
1 cup couscous
½ teaspoon salt
¼ cup olive oil, preferably extra-virgin
1 large garlic clove, minced and mashed to a paste with ¼ teaspoon salt
½ cup finely chopped fresh mint leaves
1 bunch arugula, stems discarded and leaves washed well, spun dry, and chopped
2 cups vine-ripened cherry tomatoes, halved
¼ pound feta, crumbled (about 1 cup)

do ahead:

Chill the **SALAD,** covered, at least 3 hours and up to 24 hours.

haricot vert and red onion salad
with pistou

Pistou, the simple combination of fresh basil, garlic, and olive oil, introduces the same savory spirit when tossed with tender, buttery green beans. One of the secrets to this salad is soaking the red onions: a quick water bath moderates their intensity without diminishing their crunch.

MAKE PISTOU

Purée all pistou ingredients in a food processor until basil is finely chopped.

MAKE SALAD

1. Soak the onion in cold water 15 minutes, then drain in a colander and pat dry.

2. Cook the beans in a 6- to 8-quart pot of boiling salted water, uncovered, stirring occasionally, until just tender, 3 to 6 minutes, then drain in a large colander. Transfer to a large bowl of ice and cold water to stop cooking, then drain again and pat dry.

3. Toss the beans and onion with the pistou. Season with salt and pepper.

"Great recipe. I made it for a family gathering, and it was the first dish to disappear. Garlic lovers will adore it. For a faster version, use prepared pesto. It is a great make-ahead recipe."
A cook, Lexington, Kentucky

YIELD: MAKES 6 SERVINGS

FOR PISTOU

2 cups loosely packed fresh basil leaves
6 garlic cloves, minced (1½ tablespoons)
¼ cup plus 2 tablespoons extra-virgin olive oil
½ teaspoon fine sea salt

FOR SALAD

1 medium red onion, halved lengthwise, then thinly sliced crosswise
1½ pounds haricots verts or other thin green beans, trimmed

do ahead:

The **PISTOU** can be made 6 hours ahead and transferred to a small bowl, then chilled, covered.

The **BEANS** can be cooked 1 day ahead and chilled in a sealed large plastic bag lined with paper towels.

three-bean salad

Good looking and versatile, this colorful salad features a winning trio of beans—edamame, black-eyed peas, and black beans—bathed in a citrus- and spice-infused dressing that's all kinds of satisfying. Vary the taste effect by adding crumbled feta or tossing in some garbanzo beans.

YIELD: MAKES 6 SERVINGS

1½ cups (8 ounces) frozen shelled
 edamame
¼ cup olive oil
1 teaspoon ground cumin
1 (15-ounce) can black beans, drained
 and rinsed
1 (15-ounce) can black-eyed peas,
 drained and rinsed
½ cup chopped red onion
2 cups thinly sliced celery
2 tablespoons fresh lime juice
½ cup chopped fresh cilantro leaves
1 teaspoon finely chopped garlic
1½ teaspoons salt
¼ teaspoon black pepper

"Have made this many times, both as written and with adjustments. Good both ways. Tonight had no black-eyed peas, but added corn, red pepper, more lime juice, and less oil. Very good!"

Mlfitzgerald

1. Cook the edamame in a 1½- to 2-quart saucepan of boiling salted water, uncovered, 4 minutes. Drain in a colander, then rinse under cold water to stop the cooking.

2. Heat the oil in a small heavy skillet over moderately low heat until hot but not smoking, then cook the cumin, stirring, until fragrant and a shade darker, about 30 seconds. Pour into a large heatproof bowl.

3. Add the edamame, black beans, peas, onion, celery, lime juice, cilantro, garlic, salt, and pepper to the cumin oil and toss to coat. Let stand 10 minutes for flavors to blend.

tarragon shallot egg salad sandwiches

With a few simple additions—chopped shallots and tarragon vinegar—basic egg salad is transformed. Because some of these ingredients pack quite a punch, try making this recipe a day in advance to allow the flavors to mellow and blend together.

MAKE EGG SALAD

1. Cover the eggs with cold water by 1 inch in a 2-quart heavy saucepan and bring to a rolling boil, partially covered. Reduce the heat to low and cook the eggs, covered completely, 30 seconds. Remove pan from heat and let the eggs stand in hot water, covered, 15 minutes.

2. Transfer the eggs with a slotted spoon to a bowl of ice and cold water and let stand 5 minutes (to cool). Peel eggs and finely chop.

3. Stir together the eggs and remaining salad ingredients in a bowl with a fork.

MAKE SANDWICHES

Spread some mayonnaise (if using) on the bread and make sandwiches with the egg salad and pea shoots.

"An open-faced sandwich topped with smoked salmon makes this, accompanied by a salad, an elegant lunch."

Mourmand, Miami Beach, Florida

YIELD: MAKES 6 SANDWICHES

FOR EGG SALAD

8 large eggs
½ cup mayonnaise
3 tablespoons finely chopped shallots
1½ tablespoons finely chopped fresh
    tarragon leaves, or to taste
2 teaspoons tarragon vinegar or
    white-wine vinegar
¼ teaspoon salt, or to taste
¼ teaspoon black pepper, or to taste

FOR SANDWICHES

Mayonnaise for spreading on bread
    (optional)
12 slices seedless rye bread or
    6 kaiser rolls
3 cups (3 ounces) tender pea shoots or
    shredded lettuce

do ahead:

The **EGG SALAD** can be made 1 day ahead and chilled, covered.

tuscan tuna-and-bean sandwiches

The classic tuna sandwich gets a healthy makeover with this Italian-style recipe that replaces mayo with a luscious cannellini bean spread. The garlicky mixture, when layered with watercress, gives the flaked tuna an unexpectedly delicious taste. Adjust the lemon juice and garlic that go into the beans to your taste and then spoon onto a crusty piece of rustic Italian bread or a panini roll.

YIELD: MAKES 4 SERVINGS

FOR BEANS

1 (14- to 15-ounce) can cannellini beans, rinsed and drained
2 garlic cloves, finely chopped
1 tablespoon fresh lemon juice
2 tablespoons olive oil
2 tablespoons chopped fresh flat-leaf parsley or basil
¼ teaspoon salt
¼ teaspoon black pepper

FOR TUNA SALAD

2 (6-ounce) cans Italian tuna in oil, drained
2 tablespoons finely chopped fresh basil or flat-leaf parsley
¼ cup pitted kalamata or other brine-cured black olives, finely chopped
1 celery rib, finely chopped
2 tablespoons finely chopped red onion
2 tablespoons olive oil
1 tablespoon fresh lemon juice
¼ teaspoon salt
⅛ teaspoon black pepper

FOR SANDWICHES

8 (⅓-inch-thick) slices rustic Italian bread (from a round crusty loaf); or 4 (4-inch-long) oval panini rolls
1 cup (loosely packed) trimmed watercress sprigs

MAKE BEANS

Coarsely mash the beans with a fork in a bowl, then stir in the garlic, lemon juice, oil, parsley, salt, and pepper.

MAKE TUNA

Flake the tuna in a bowl with a fork, then stir in the basil, olives, celery, onion, oil, lemon juice, salt, and pepper until combined.

ASSEMBLE SANDWICHES

Spoon one-fourth of the bean mixture on a slice of bread, then top with one-fourth of the tuna salad, some watercress, and a slice of bread. Make 3 more sandwiches in the same manner.

"I tossed the bean and tuna mixture together without mashing the beans. With a nice bread and the watercress on the side, it was a more salady but equally satisfying meal. Regular water-packed tuna works just fine."
A cook, San Francisco, California

chicken salad tea sandwiches
with smoked almonds

Chicken salad sandwiches aren't always exciting, but with the simple addition of shallot and tarragon, plus a bit of crunch from smoked almonds, this rises above the ordinary. It's great served over greens and sprinkled with the addictive nuts. For a healthier sandwich use whole-wheat bread and substitute low-fat Greek yogurt for some or all the mayonnaise; with such a flavor-packed base, you won't miss the fat.

1. In a deep 12-inch skillet, bring the broth or water to a boil and add the chicken breasts in one layer. Reduce the heat and poach the chicken at a bare simmer, turning once, 7 minutes. Remove the skillet from the heat and cool the chicken in the cooking liquid 20 minutes. Discard the skin and shred the chicken fine.

2. In a large bowl, stir together the chicken, ½ cup of the mayonnaise, the shallot, tarragon, and salt and pepper to taste.

3. Make 12 sandwiches with the chicken salad and bread, pressing together gently. With a 2-inch round cutter, cut 2 rounds from each sandwich.

4. Put the almonds on a small plate and spread the edges of the rounds with the remaining ½ cup mayonnaise to coat well. Roll the edges in the almonds.

YIELD: MAKES 24 TEA SANDWICHES

3 cups chicken broth or water
2 whole boneless chicken breasts with skin (about 1½ pounds), halved
1 cup mayonnaise
⅓ cup minced shallots
1 teaspoon minced fresh tarragon leaves
24 very thin slices homemade-type white bread
½ cup finely chopped smoked almonds (about 2 ounces)

do ahead:

The **SANDWICHES** may be made 2 hours ahead, wrapped in plastic wrap, and chilled.

"This is my favorite chicken salad recipe! I have made it with regular and smoked almonds (whatever I can find). I mix the almonds in the chicken salad to save time in preparation."
A cook, Asheville, North Carolina

muffaletta salad and sandwiches

When it comes to building a prime muffaletta, the bread may be more important than the olives, meats, and cheeses it's married to. In New Orleans, this hefty must-have "sando" is constructed on a round, soft Sicilian loaf. In this version, Epicurious member **Mike19711** uses focaccia. When serving large parties, use a soft Italian bread, a 9-inch round, or a long 14-inch loaf. Try and hold out until the olive salad has marinated for at least 24 hours; trust us, it will make the meal that much more authentic.

YIELD: MAKES 4 TO 6 SERVINGS

FOR OLIVE SALAD
1 cup kalamata olives, pitted and chopped
1 cup green olives, pitted and chopped
¼ cup finely diced roasted red bell pepper
1 tablespoon minced red onion
2 garlic cloves, minced
2 tablespoons minced fresh flat-leaf parsley leaves
¼ cup extra-virgin olive oil
2 teaspoons red-wine vinegar

FOR SANDWICHES
1 (9 by 11-inch) piece focaccia
Extra-virgin olive oil
6 ounces capicolla
4 ounces thinly sliced Genoa salami
4 ounces thinly sliced mortadella
4 ounces thinly sliced pepperoni
4 ounces sliced mozzarella
4 ounces thinly sliced provolone

1. In a medium bowl, toss together the olives, roasted peppers, onion, garlic, parsley, oil, and vinegar. Cover and refrigerate at least 1 hour and up to 2 days.

2. Split the focaccia horizontally and brush both cut sides with oil. Layer the capicolla, salami, mortadella, pepperoni, mozzarella, and provolone to completely cover the bottom half of the bread.

3. Spread the olive salad in an even layer on top and cover with the other piece of bread, leaving a small border along the edge. Press the sandwich together, carefully slice into portions, and serve.

pão de queijo

These crisp yet chewy cheese puffs are traditional staples in Brazil. Epicurious member **InewportTX,** from Pflugerville, Texas, recommends cooking the balls in mini-muffin cups, as the dough will be fairly runny. Find tapioca flour (also known as manioc starch and tapioca starch) at specialty markets like Whole Foods.

1. Position a rack in the lower third of the oven and preheat the oven to 400°F. Lightly butter 2 mini-muffin pans.

2. In a small saucepan over moderate heat, combine the milk, butter, and salt. Warm the mixture just until boiling, then remove from the heat and gradually whisk in 1 cup of the tapioca flour. Transfer to the bowl of a stand mixer fitted with the paddle attachment. With the mixer on low, gradually add another ½ cup tapioca flour, followed by the eggs, and then the remaining ½ cup of tapioca flour and beat until well blended. With the mixer still on low, add the cheese and beat to combine. The dough will be sticky.

3. Spoon 1½-inch scoops of dough into the prepared mini muffin cups and bake until puffed and golden brown, about 25 minutes. Serve warm.

YIELD: MAKES 2 DOZEN PUFFS

1 cup low-fat milk
½ cup (1 stick) unsalted butter
1 teaspoon salt
2 cups tapioca flour
2 large eggs, lightly beaten
1½ cups freshly grated Parmesan cheese

Special equipment: 2 mini-muffin pans with 12 (1-ounce) cups

irish soda bread *with raisins and caraway*

This recipe comes from the mother of a September 11 victim; it was a favorite of her son, a chef for Cantor Fitzgerald, and will no doubt be a favorite of yours. When originally submitting it to *Bon Appétit,* Patrice Bedrosian encouraged readers "to enjoy this delicious and comforting Irish bread, to smile, and to remember the love between a mother and son."

1. Preheat the oven to 350°F. Generously butter a heavy ovenproof 10- to 12-inch skillet with high sides. Whisk the flour, sugar, baking powder, salt, and baking soda in a large bowl to blend. Add the butter; using fingertips, rub in until coarse crumbs form. Stir in the raisins and caraway seeds. Whisk the buttermilk and egg in a medium bowl to blend. Add to dough; using wooden spoon, stir just until well incorporated (dough will be very sticky).

2. Transfer the dough to the prepared skillet; smooth the top, mounding slightly in center. Using a small sharp knife dipped into flour, cut a 1-inch-deep *X* in the top center of dough. Bake until the bread is cooked through and a tester inserted into the center comes out clean, about 1 hour 15 minutes. Cool the bread in the skillet 10 minutes. Turn out onto a rack and cool completely.

"This rivaled my mother's breads, and she made several types. Irish soda breads are generally easier to make anyway, but this one couldn't be simpler to put together. In case your breads dry too quickly a day later, place the bread in a plastic bag and zap it in a microwave oven for a few seconds. It will revive quite nicely. This version also toasts well."

Aleugene, USA

YIELD: MAKES 8 TO 10 SERVINGS

5 cups all-purpose flour
1 cup sugar
1 tablespoon baking powder
1½ teaspoons salt
1 teaspoon baking soda
½ cup (1 stick) unsalted butter, cut into cubes, at room temperature
2½ cups raisins
3 tablespoons caraway seeds
2½ cups buttermilk
1 large egg

do ahead:

The **BREAD** can be made 1 day ahead. Wrap tightly in foil; store at room temperature.

chocolate macaroon bars

The moist and toothsome coconut macaroon becomes a delicious (and infinitely more portable) bar cookie when built upon a dense shortbread base. The result is a surefire bake-sale winner, a kid-pleasing picnic finale, and an inviting edible gift for holidays or birthdays.

YIELD: MAKES 24 BARS

FOR SHORTBREAD BASE
¾ cup (1½ sticks) unsalted butter
2 cups all-purpose flour
½ cup (packed) light brown sugar
½ teaspoon salt

FOR TOPPING
4 large egg whites
1 cup granulated sugar
1 teaspoon pure vanilla extract
½ cup all-purpose flour
1 (7-ounce) bag sweetened flaked
    coconut (about 2⅔ cups)
1½ cups semisweet chocolate chips

do ahead:

The **BAR COOKIES** keep, covered, 5 days at room temperature.

"Delicious! I thought it might be fun to add ⅓ cup white chocolate chips and ⅓ cup chopped pecans to the coconut mixture. My guests loved them!"

A cook, Wenham, Massachusetts

MAKE SHORTBREAD BASE

1. Preheat the oven to 350°F. Place the rack in the middle of the oven.

2. Cut the butter into ½-inch pieces. In a food processor, process the butter, flour, sugar, and salt until mixture begins to form small lumps. Sprinkle the mixture into a 13 by 9-inch baking pan, and with a metal spatula, press evenly onto bottom. Bake the shortbread until golden, about 20 minutes.

MAKE TOPPING

1. In a bowl, whisk together the whites, sugar, and vanilla until combined well and stir in the flour and coconut.

2. Sprinkle the chocolate chips evenly over the hot shortbread. Let chips melt and spread evenly over shortbread base. Drop small spoonfuls of coconut mixture onto the chocolate and spread evenly with a fork. Bake until top is golden, about 30 minutes. Cool completely in pan and cut into 24 bars.

rugelach

Traditionally for Jewish holidays, these little pastries are perfect any time. While making rugelach may seem daunting, this recipe gives you helpful tips that cut the time and effort required.

1. Whisk together the flour and salt in a small bowl. Beat together the butter and cream cheese in a large bowl with an electric mixer until combined well. Add the flour mixture and stir with a wooden spoon until a soft dough forms. Gather the dough into a ball and wrap in plastic wrap, then flatten (in wrap) into a roughly 7 by 5-inch rectangle. Chill until firm, 8 to 24 hours.

2. Put the oven rack in the middle position and preheat the oven to 350°F. Line the bottom of 2 large shallow baking pans with parchment paper and have 3 additional sheets of parchment ready. Cut the dough into 4 pieces. Chill 3 pieces, wrapped in plastic wrap, and roll out the remaining piece into a 12 by 8-inch rectangle on a well-floured surface with a floured rolling pin. Transfer the dough to 1 of the parchment-lined pans and chill while rolling out the remaining dough in same manner, transferring each to another sheet of parchment and stacking on top of pan.

3. Whisk ½ cup sugar with the cinnamon. Arrange one dough rectangle on a work surface with a long side nearest you. Spread ¼ cup preserves evenly over the dough. Sprinkle ¼ cup raisins and a rounded ¼ cup walnuts over the jam, then sprinkle with 2 tablespoons cinnamon sugar.

4. Using the parchment, roll up the dough tightly into a log. Place seam side down in the second baking pan, then pinch the ends closed and tuck underneath. Make 3 more logs and arrange 1 inch apart. Brush the logs with milk and sprinkle each with 1 teaspoon of the remaining granulated sugar. With a sharp large knife, make ¾-inch-deep cuts crosswise in the dough (not all the way through) at 1-inch intervals. (If dough is too soft to cut, chill 20 to 30 minutes longer.) Bake until golden, 45 to 50 minutes. Cool to warm in the pan on a rack, about 30 minutes, then transfer the logs to a cutting board and slice the pastries.

YIELD: MAKES ABOUT 44 RUGELACH

2 cups all-purpose flour
½ teaspoon salt
1 cup (2 sticks) unsalted butter, softened
8 ounces cream cheese, softened
½ cup plus 4 teaspoons sugar
1 teaspoon ground cinnamon
1 cup apricot preserves or raspberry jam
1 cup loosely packed golden raisins, chopped
4 ounces shelled walnuts, finely chopped (1¼ cups)
Milk, for brushing cookies

"Perfect rugelach recipe, especially the dough. Key is to definitely keep the dough cold—chill overnight and work with only a fourth at a time, and it becomes a snap. I also used a food processor and just threw butter and cream cheese in first, then dry ingredients; pulsed just until it clumps. I used dried cranberries, as I didn't have raisins, and it was a great twist. I also added some chocolate chips just to take it over the top."
Juliedbell, Oakland, California

buttermilk panna cotta

This velvety pudding is the brainchild of chef and cookbook author Sara Foster; and like many of her recipes, it's a masterpiece of simple goodness that needs no extra bells or whistles. But it's amenable to a variety of sauces and toppings. Try soaking the fresh berries in port to make a memorable dessert.

YIELD: MAKES 6 SERVINGS

2 tablespoons water
1½ teaspoons unflavored gelatin
Nonstick vegetable-oil spray
1 cup heavy whipping cream
1 teaspoon finely grated lemon peel
½ cup sugar
2 cups buttermilk
2 teaspoons pure vanilla extract
Assorted frozen berries (such as
    blackberries, blueberries, and
    raspberries), thawed

Special equipment: 6 (¾-cup) ramekins
    or custard cups

do ahead:

The **PANNA COTTA** (through step 2) can be made 2 days ahead. Cover and keep chilled.

1. Pour the 2 tablespoons water into a small bowl; sprinkle the gelatin over. Let stand until the gelatin softens, about 10 minutes. Lightly spray 6 (¾-cup) ramekins or custard cups with nonstick spray.

2. Heat the cream, lemon peel, and sugar in a medium saucepan over medium-high heat, stirring constantly until the sugar dissolves. Increase the heat and bring just to a low boil, stirring occasionally. Add the gelatin mixture; remove from the heat. Stir until gelatin dissolves. Cool mixture to lukewarm, stirring often. Stir in the buttermilk and vanilla; divide the mixture among prepared ramekins. Refrigerate the panna cotta until set, about 4 hours.

3. Using a small sharp knife, cut around the panna cotta in each ramekin. Place a plate atop each ramekin and invert, allowing the panna cotta to settle onto the plate. Top with berries and serve chilled.

"The texture and flavor are perfect. I don't bother unmolding, and just served with fresh berries on top. Sometimes I substitute the cream with an equal part of milk. The result tastes just as good but the texture is slightly less silky. It's also easy to overheat the milk, so more care must be taken."

A cook, Boston, Massachusetts

carrot cake ice cream

Here's a gluten-free ice cream from Epicurious member **Lorelei Lee** of Philadelphia, complete with the taste of carrot cake. A cooling treat, this dish is perfect for a sunny day. Cream cheese, sugar, and milk provide the backbone for the simple dish, while cinnamon, ginger, nutmeg, and shredded carrot give it that carrot cake feel. Like most homemade ice creams, this dessert should be eaten within a few days.

1. In a medium pot over moderate heat, combine ½ cup milk with the sugar, cinnamon, ginger, and nutmeg and simmer until the sugar dissolves.

2. In a medium bowl, whisk the cream cheese until smooth. Add the warm milk mixture and whisk until the cream cheese melts and the mixture is smooth. Whisk in the vanilla, lemon juice, carrots, and salt. Cover and chill the ice cream base until cold, at least 6 hours or overnight.

3. Process the base in an ice cream machine according to the manufacturer's instructions, then transfer to an airtight container and freeze until hard, about 3 hours.

YIELD: MAKES ABOUT 1 QUART

1¾ cups whole milk
¾ cup sugar
½ teaspoon ground cinnamon
½ teaspoon ground ginger
⅛ teaspoon ground nutmeg
1 (8-ounce) package cream cheese, at room temperature
¼ teaspoon pure vanilla extract
1½ teaspoons lemon juice
1 medium carrot, coarsely grated (about ½ cup)
⅛ teaspoon kosher salt

Special equipment: 1-quart ice-cream maker

salted caramel ice cream

Inspired by Brittany's traditional salted caramel candies, this is a knockout ice cream. If you've never made caramel before, be prepared for what will seem like violent splattering when the cream is added to the hot, melted sugar. Relax—this is normal and subsides quickly. The other crucial moment comes when you slowly add the steamy milk mixture to the eggs. If curdling does occur, simply strain the mixture to ensure the smoothest possible custard.

1. Heat 1 cup sugar in a dry 10-inch heavy skillet over medium heat, stirring with a fork to heat sugar evenly, until it starts to melt, then stop stirring and cook, swirling the skillet occasionally so sugar melts evenly, until it is dark amber.

2. Add 1¼ cups cream (mixture will spatter) and cook, stirring, until all of caramel has dissolved. Transfer to a bowl and stir in the sea salt and vanilla. Cool to room temperature.

3. Meanwhile, bring the milk, remaining 1 cup cream, and remaining ¼ cup sugar just to a boil in a small heavy saucepan, stirring occasionally.

4. Lightly whisk the eggs in a medium bowl, then add half of the hot milk mixture in a slow stream, whisking constantly. Pour mixture back into the saucepan and cook over medium heat, stirring constantly with a wooden spoon, until the custard coats the back of a spoon and registers 170°F on an instant-read thermometer (do not let boil). Pour the custard through a fine-mesh sieve into a large bowl, then stir in the cooled caramel.

5. Chill the custard, stirring occasionally, until very cold, 3 to 6 hours. Freeze the custard in an ice cream maker according to manufacturer's directions (it will still be quite soft). Transfer the ice cream to an airtight container and put in the freezer to firm up.

YIELD: MAKES ABOUT 1 QUART

1¼ cups sugar
2¼ cups heavy cream
½ teaspoon flaky sea salt, such as Maldon
½ teaspoon pure vanilla extract
1 cup whole milk
3 large eggs

Special equipment: 1-quart ice-cream maker

"I liked how it tasted when I added more salt, but remember that the more salt you add, the longer the ice cream takes to set in the freezer. It helps to chill the custard in the fridge overnight before freezing it in the machine and develops the flavors nicely, too! It is divine topped with candied bacon."

**Gramercygirl305,
New York, New York**

lemon ice cream sandwiches
with blueberry swirl

Ice cream sandwiches are hard to hate, especially this one. What can be wrong with a dessert that combines sweet blueberries, tart lemon ice cream, and buttery blondie-like cookies? Store-bought vanilla ice cream gets a flavor lift with the addition of lemon juice and zest, plus an easy (as in three minutes' prep time) blueberry compote.

YIELD: MAKES 8 SERVINGS

FOR LEMON ICE CREAM
2 pints premium vanilla ice cream
1 tablespoon grated lemon zest
2 tablespoons fresh lemon juice

FOR BLUEBERRY COMPOTE
2 cups blueberries (10 ounces)
¼ cup granulated sugar
2 (3 by 2½-inch) strips lemon zest
1 tablespoon fresh lemon juice
2 teaspoons cornstarch

FOR SANDWICH LAYERS
1 cup all-purpose flour
½ teaspoon baking powder
¼ teaspoon baking soda
¼ teaspoon salt
½ cup (1 stick) unsalted butter, softened
¾ cup (packed) light brown sugar
1 large egg
½ teaspoon pure vanilla extract

Special equipment: 2 (8-inch) square baking pans 2 inches deep; small offset spatula

do ahead:

The **ICE CREAM SANDWICHES** can be made 1 week ahead and frozen in pan, wrapped in plastic wrap and then in foil. Cut before serving.

MAKE LEMON ICE CREAM
1. Transfer the ice cream to a microwave-safe bowl and microwave at 30 percent power in 10-second intervals, stirring, until softened, about 50 seconds total. Or allow the ice cream to soften at room temperature.

2. Stir in the lemon zest and juice. Spread the ice cream thinly in a 13 by 9-inch baking dish and freeze while making the compote and sandwich layers.

MAKE BLUEBERRY COMPOTE
1. Cook the blueberries, sugar, and zest in a 12-inch heavy skillet over medium-high heat, thoroughly crushing the blueberries with a potato masher, until juices are released and sugar has dissolved, about 2 minutes.

2. Stir together the lemon juice and cornstarch, then stir into the blueberry mixture. Boil, stirring, 1 minute; mixture will thicken.

3. Transfer the blueberry compote to a bowl and chill until cold, about 1 hour. Discard the lemon zest.

MAKE SANDWICH LAYERS
1. Preheat the oven to 375°F, with rack in the middle. Butter 2 (8-inch) square baking pans and line with foil, leaving a 1-inch overhang on each side, then butter the foil.

2. Whisk together the flour, baking powder, baking soda, and salt in a small bowl. Beat together the butter and brown sugar in a large bowl with an electric mixer at medium-high speed until pale and fluffy, about 3 minutes. Beat in the egg and vanilla. At low speed, add the flour mixture in 2 batches, mixing until just combined.

3. Divide the batter between the baking pans and spread in a thin, even layer with an offset spatula. Bake until golden brown but still tender, 10 to 12 minutes. Cool completely in pans, about 30 minutes.

ASSEMBLE SANDWICHES

1. Let ice cream soften for 5 minutes, then dollop tablespoons of blueberry compote on it and swirl it gently through the softened ice cream with a spoon. Spoon all of the ice cream over one sandwich layer (in pan) and spread evenly using a clean offset spatula. Invert the second sandwich layer over the ice cream, pressing gently to form an even sandwich. Wrap the baking pan in plastic wrap and freeze until firm, at least 2 hours.

2. Transfer the frozen sandwich to a cutting board using the overhang. Trim the edges if desired, then cut into 8 pieces.

"I turned the blondies into brownies with a few tablespoons of cocoa, used vanilla ice cream, and tossed a bunch of frozen raspberries into the middle as well. Make the brownies in a cookie sheet with parchment—it's relatively simple. They get rave reviews."

A cook, Canada

frozen lemon ginger snap pie

This mix of refreshing lemon and spicy ginger snaps in the form of a frosty, zesty pie is perfect for spring parties. The ginger snap crust is ridiculously easy. Consider topping the pie's creamy citrus with a sweet dash of raspberry sauce.

YIELD: MAKES 8 TO 10 SERVINGS

FOR CRUST

1½ cups finely crushed ginger snaps
    (6 ounces)
5 tablespoons unsalted butter, melted
2 tablespoons sugar

FOR ICE CREAM

1½ cups heavy cream
1 cup whole milk
¾ cup plus 2 tablespoons sugar
4 teaspoons finely grated fresh lemon zest
⅛ teaspoon salt
6 large egg yolks
⅔ cup fresh lemon juice
Lemon slices, for garnish

Special equipment: 10-inch ceramic pie
    plate; ice-cream maker

---

do ahead:

The **ICE CREAM** can be made 2 days ahead of assembling pie. Soften in refrigerator about 30 minutes before spreading in crust. Assembled pie can be frozen up to 3 days.

"The ginger snap crust was a huge hit, and the lemon was just lemony enough. I would suggest making some extra crust and scattering that over the top of the pie."

Jsaturley, Concord, New Hampshire

MAKE CRUST

1. Preheat the oven to 350°F.

2. Toss together the cookie crumbs, butter, and sugar with a fork until crumbs are moistened. Press evenly onto bottom and up the side of a 10-inch glass or ceramic pie plate. Bake the crust in the middle of the oven 7 minutes, then cool on a rack.

MAKE ICE CREAM

1. Bring the cream, milk, sugar, zest, and salt to a boil in a 2-quart heavy saucepan, stirring until sugar is dissolved. Whisk the yolks in a bowl until blended, then add the hot cream mixture in a slow stream, whisking. Transfer the custard back to the saucepan and cook over moderately low heat, stirring constantly with a wooden spoon, until thick enough to coat back of a spoon and mixture registers 175° to 180°F on an instant-read thermometer, 3 to 5 minutes (do not let boil). Immediately pour the custard through a fine-mesh sieve into a clean bowl, then stir in the lemon juice.

2. Cool the custard to room temperature, stirring occasionally, then chill, its surface covered with a round of wax paper, until cold, about 3 hours. Freeze the custard in an ice cream maker, following manufacturer's directions.

3. Spread the ice cream evenly in the crust and wrap the pie plate in wax or parchment paper, then in plastic wrap. Freeze until firm, at least 2 hours.

4. About 20 minutes before serving, put the pie in the refrigerator to soften.

lemon curd tart *with olive oil*

Even if you consider yourself a cook and not a baker, you can manage this recipe from Les Petits Farcis in Nice, France. The shortbread-like almond crust is a pleasingly rich base for the delicate custard. Try using Meyer lemons or adding minced rosemary to the crust.

MAKE TART SHELL

1. Pulse the almonds with the flour, sugar, and salt to a fine powder in a food processor. Add the butter and pulse until the mixture resembles coarse meal with some small (roughly pea-size) butter lumps.

2. Add the yolk and oil and pulse until just incorporated and a very soft dough has formed. Spread the dough evenly over the bottom and up the side of a 9-inch round tart pan with an offset spatula. Chill until firm, about 30 minutes.

3. Preheat the oven to 425°F, with the rack in the middle.

4. Line shell with foil or parchment and weight it with dried beans or pie weights. Bake the shell until golden brown all over, about 13 minutes. Transfer to a rack to cool completely, about 30 minutes.

MAKE LEMON CURD

1. Grate enough zest from the lemons to measure 1 table-spoon, then squeeze ¾ cup juice from the lemons.

2. Whisk together the lemon zest and juice, sugar, cornstarch, and whole eggs and yolks in a medium saucepan. Bring to a boil over medium heat, whisking constantly, and boil, still whisking, for 2 minutes. Remove from the heat and whisk in the butter and oil until smooth.

ASSEMBLE TART

Pour the lemon curd into the cooled shell and chill until set, at least 2 hours.

YIELD: **MAKES 6 SERVINGS**

FOR TART SHELL

2 tablespoons almonds with skins, toasted and cooled
¾ cup all-purpose flour
¼ cup confectioners' sugar
Pinch of fine sea salt
½ stick (4 tablespoons) cold unsalted butter, cut into ½-inch cubes
1 large egg yolk
3½ tablespoons fruity olive oil, preferably French

FOR LEMON CURD

3 large lemons
¾ cup granulated sugar
2 teaspoons cornstarch
2 large eggs plus 2 large yolks
½ stick (4 tablespoons) unsalted butter, cut into ½-inch cubes
2 tablespoons fruity olive oil, preferably French

Special equipment: 9-inch round tart pan with removable bottom; small offset spatula

do ahead:

The **TART SHELL** can be made 1 day ahead and kept, loosely covered, at room temperature.

The **ASSEMBLED TART** can be chilled up to 4 hours.

lattice-topped strawberry-rhubarb pie

When strawberries and rhubarb are at the peak of freshness, buy some, if only to make this pie. Be mindful of adding water slowly to the dough to achieve flaky perfection. Depending on the room temperature and humidity, the dough may need less or more water than the recipe calls for.

YIELD: MAKES 8 SERVINGS

FOR CRUST

3 cups all-purpose flour

2½ teaspoons granulated sugar

¾ teaspoon salt

⅔ cup chilled vegetable shortening, cut into pieces

½ cup plus 2 tablespoons (1¼ sticks) chilled unsalted butter, cut into pieces

About 10 tablespoons ice water

FOR FILLING

3½ cups (½-inch-thick) sliced trimmed rhubarb (1½ pounds untrimmed)

1 (16-ounce) container strawberries, hulled, halved (about 3½ cups)

½ cup (packed) light brown sugar

½ cup granulated sugar

¼ cup cornstarch

1 teaspoon ground cinnamon

¼ teaspoon salt

1 large egg yolk, beaten to blend with 1 teaspoon water, for glaze

do ahead:

The **CRUST** can be made 1 day ahead. Keep chilled. Let dough soften slightly at room temperature before rolling.

MAKE CRUST

Combine the flour, sugar, and salt in a food processor. Using on/off pulses, cut in the shortening and butter until coarse meal forms. Blend in enough ice water 2 table-spoons at a time to form moist clumps. Gather the dough into a ball; cut in half. Flatten each half into a disk. Wrap separately in plastic; refrigerate until firm, about 1 hour.

MAKE FILLING

1. Preheat the oven to 400°F. Combine the fruit, sugars, cornstarch, cinnamon, and salt in a large bowl. Toss gently to blend.

2. Roll out one dough disk on a floured work surface to a 13-inch round. Transfer to a glass pie dish. Trim the excess dough, leaving a ¾-inch overhang.

3. Roll out the second dough disk on a lightly floured surface to a 13-inch round. Cut into 14 (½-inch-wide) strips. Spoon the filling into the crust. Arrange 7 dough strips atop the filling, spacing evenly. Form a lattice by placing the remaining dough strips in opposite directions atop the filling. Trim the ends of the dough strips even with the overhang of the bottom crust. Fold the strip ends and overhang under, pressing to seal. Crimp edges decoratively.

4. Brush the glaze over the crust; transfer the pie to a baking sheet. Bake 20 minutes. Reduce the oven tempera-ture to 350°F. Bake the pie until golden and the filling thickens, about 1 hour 25 minutes. Transfer the pie to a rack and cool completely.

"I baked this pie for my husband's
birthday and used leftover rhubarb,
strawberries, and (1½ cups) apricots.
It was absolutely delicious."
Gunzen, Gunzenhausen, Germany

key lime pie *with almond crumb crust*

Squeezing a half-cup of fresh Key lime juice is quite the upper-arm workout, but the hard labor is worth it. In this recipe the traditional graham cracker crust gets a dose of lightly toasted ground almonds. If you don't have a food processor, purchased almond flour works just as well. Go with the meringue topping, or replace it with whipped cream for a silky bite.

YIELD: MAKES 6 TO 8 SERVINGS

FOR CRUST

1 cup zwieback crumbs or graham cracker crumbs

⅔ cup blanched almonds, toasted lightly, cooled completely, and ground fine in a food processor

½ stick (¼ cup) unsalted butter, melted and cooled

¼ cup sugar

FOR FILLING

3 large eggs, separated, the whites at room temperature

1 (14-ounce) can sweetened condensed milk

½ cup Key lime juice (available bottled at specialty food shops) or fresh lime juice (about 3 limes)

⅓ cup sugar

Special equipment: 10-inch pie plate

"Instead of grinding the almonds finely, I coarsely chopped them and mixed with the graham cracker crumbs. The larger pieces of almond gave the crust a nutty and crunchy consistency that contrasted well with the smooth filling."

A cook, Washington, D.C.

1. Preheat the oven to 350°F, with the rack in the middle.

2. In a medium bowl, combine well the crumbs, almonds, butter, and sugar. Press the mixture onto the bottom and up the side of a 10-inch pie plate. Bake the shell for 10 minutes, or until it is browned lightly. Let the shell cool on a rack.

3. In a large bowl, beat the yolks with the condensed milk and stir in the lime juice, a little at a time, stirring to combine the filling well. Spoon the filling into the cooled shell and chill the pie for 1 hour.

4. Preheat the oven to 350°F. In a bowl, beat the egg whites with a pinch of salt until they hold soft peaks. Add the sugar, beating, 1 tablespoon at a time, and beat the meringue until it holds stiff peaks. Spread the meringue over the filling and bake for 15 minutes, or until the meringue is just golden. Chill the pie for 2 hours.

triple-layer carrot cake
with cream cheese frosting

This carrot cake from Becky Guyton, a home cook in Ohio, is one of our most beloved recipes, perhaps because it achieves the perfect balance of tangy and sweet, spongy and creamy, dense and light. Originally appearing in a 1994 *Bon Appétit* column, it's almost as moist as bread pudding. To cut back on the sweetness, just reduce the amount of sugar in the icing to three cups.

MAKE CAKE

1. Preheat the oven to 325°F. Lightly grease 3 (9-inch) round cake pans. Line the bottom of the pans with wax paper. Lightly grease the wax paper.

2. Using an electric mixer, beat the sugar and oil in a large bowl until combined. Add the eggs 1 at a time, beating well after each addition. Sift the flour, baking powder, baking soda, salt, cinnamon, and nutmeg into the sugar and oil mixture. Stir in the carrots, chopped pecans, and raisins.

3. Pour the batter into the prepared pans, dividing equally. Bake until a toothpick inserted into the center of each comes out clean and cakes begin to pull away from sides of pans, about 45 minutes. Cool in pans on racks 15 minutes. Turn out the cakes onto the racks and cool completely.

MAKE FROSTING AND ICE CAKE

1. Using an electric mixer, beat all the ingredients in a medium bowl until smooth and creamy.

2. Place one cake layer on a platter. Spread with ¾ cup frosting. Top with another cake layer. Spread with ¾ cup frosting. Top with remaining cake layer.

3. Using an icing spatula, spread the remaining frosting in decorative swirls over the sides and top of cake. Serve cake cold or at room temperature.

"Wonderfully light, moist and tasty. I divided the batter into 2 pans instead of 3 and baked it for about 45 minutes. Since this was just a two-layer cake, I halved the frosting and added some grated lemon zest, which improved the taste."
A cook, Hudson Valley, New York

YIELD: MAKES 10 SERVINGS

FOR CAKE

2 cups granulated sugar
1½ cups vegetable oil
4 large eggs
2 cups all-purpose flour
2 teaspoons baking powder
2 teaspoons baking soda
1 teaspoon salt
1 teaspoon ground cinnamon
¾ teaspoon ground nutmeg
3 cups finely grated peeled carrots (about 1 pound)
½ cup chopped pecans (about 1½ ounces)
½ cup raisins

FOR FROSTING

4 cups confectioners' sugar
2 (8-ounce) packages cream cheese, at room temperature
½ cup (1 stick) unsalted butter, at room temperature
4 teaspoons pure vanilla extract

Special equipment: 3 (9-inch) round cake pans with 1½-inch sides

do ahead:

The **CAKE LAYERS** can be baked 1 day ahead. Wrap tightly in plastic and store at room temperature.

The **CAKE** can be completely assembled and frosted 2 days ahead. Cover with cake dome and refrigerate.

"I made this cake for Thanksgiving because my daughter has a gluten allergy, and it was fantastic, receiving rave reviews! I topped the cake with fresh fruit: raspberries, blueberries, strawberries, kiwi, and mango. It was beautiful as well as flavorful."

Glutenfreemom, Walnut Creek, California

gluten-free lemon layer cake

This lemon layer cake is the ultimate dessert for anyone with a gluten-free diet. You may need to hit up a specialty shop or go online for some of the ingredients, but it's well worth the effort. A brown-rice flour mix combined with the xanthan gum creates light, moist cake layers, while guar gum thickens the rich, silky curd. Generous amounts of lemon zest, juice, and extract infuse the layers, filling, and frosting, adding up to a full-on citrus celebration. Make this cake—or turn it into cupcakes—for birthdays, barbecues, or holidays.

MAKE CAKE LAYERS

1. Put the oven rack in the middle position and preheat the oven to 350°F. Brush 2 (9-inch) round cake pans with canola oil. Line the bottom of each pan with a round of parchment or wax paper, then oil the paper.

2. Whisk together the flour mix, salt, baking powder, and xanthan gum until combined well. Stir together the milk, canola oil, vanilla, and zest in another bowl.

3. Beat together the sugar and eggs in a large bowl with an electric mixer at medium speed just until combined, about 1 minute. Reduce the speed to low and add the flour and milk mixtures alternately in batches, beginning and ending with the flour mixture and mixing until just combined.

4. Divide the batter evenly between the cake pans, smoothing the tops, and bake until a wooden pick or skewer inserted in the center of each cake layer comes out clean, 35 to 40 minutes.

5. Cool the cake layers in pans on racks 10 minutes. Run a thin knife around edge of one cake layer and invert rack over cake pan, then invert cake onto rack. Repeat with the second layer.

6. Peel off the paper and cool layers completely.

YIELD: MAKES 8 SERVINGS

FOR CAKE LAYERS

2½ cups Brown-Rice Flour Mix (recipe follows)

½ teaspoon salt

1 tablespoon baking powder

1 teaspoon xanthan gum

1 cup milk

1 cup canola oil, plus more for greasing pans

1 teaspoon pure vanilla extract

1 tablespoon finely grated fresh lemon zest

2 cups granulated sugar

4 large eggs

do ahead:

The **CAKE LAYERS** can be made (but not halved) 1 day ahead and cooled completely, then kept, wrapped well in plastic wrap, at room temperature.

The **CAKE** can be completely assembled and frosted 4 hours ahead and kept at room temperature, or 1 day ahead and chilled, loosely covered. Bring to room temperature before serving.

recipe continues

FOR LEMON CURD

2 teaspoons finely grated fresh lemon
    zest
¼ cup fresh lemon juice
¼ cup plus 2 tablespoons granulated
    sugar
3 large egg yolks
¼ teaspoon guar gum
½ stick unsalted butter, cut into
    tablespoon pieces
¼ teaspoon lemon extract

FOR LEMON FROSTING

1 cup (2 sticks) unsalted butter, softened
3 ½ cups confectioners' sugar
¼ cup fresh lemon juice
½ teaspoon lemon extract
2 teaspoons finely grated fresh lemon
    zest

Special equipment: 2 (9-inch) round cake
    pans

---

do ahead:

The **LEMON CURD** can be made and
chilled up to 3 days.

MAKE CURD

1. Whisk together the zest, lemon juice, sugar, yolks, a pinch of salt, and the guar gum in a 1-quart heavy saucepan. Add the butter and cook over moderately low heat, whisking constantly, until the curd is thick enough to hold the marks of a whisk and the first bubbles appear on the surface, about 5 minutes. Whisk in the extract.

2. Immediately pour the hot curd into a bowl, then cover the surface with wax paper and chill until cold, about 30 minutes.

MAKE FROSTING

Beat the butter with an electric mixer at high speed until light and fluffy, about 1 minute. Reduce the speed to low and add the confectioners' sugar, lemon juice, extract, and zest, then mix until creamy and smooth, about 2 minutes.

FROST CAKE

1. Halve each cake layer horizontally using a long serrated knife. Spread the bottom half of each cake layer with half of the lemon curd, then top with remaining cake layers to form two sandwiched cakes.

2. Put one sandwiched cake on a cake stand or platter and spread a heaping ½ cup frosting over top, then cover with remaining sandwiched cake. Frost the top and sides of cake with remaining frosting.

---

brown-rice flour mix

YIELD: MAKES 3 CUPS

2 cups brown-rice flour (extra finely
    ground)
⅔ cup potato starch
⅓ cup tapioca flour

Put all ingredients into a sealable airtight container and shake until combined well.

mascarpone cheesecake
with balsamic strawberries

This cheesecake from California's Wente Vineyards is ethereal and easy. An Italian grandmother might scold you for not using ricotta, but good-quality mascarpone will yield a smoother, richer, and denser cheesecake. Feel free to experiment with different kinds of biscotti such as chocolate, but really, what makes this cheesecake are the balsamic strawberries, which are sweet and tart—the perfect counterpart to the cheesecake's richness.

1. Tightly wrap the outside of the springform pan with 2 layers of heavy-duty foil. Mix the biscotti crumbs and butter in a bowl. Press the mixture evenly onto the bottom (not sides) of the prepared pan. Chill 30 minutes.

2. Preheat the oven to 350°F. Using an electric mixer, beat the cream cheese, mascarpone, and 1¼ cups sugar in a large bowl until smooth. Add the eggs 1 at a time; beat just until blended.

3. Spread the cheese mixture evenly over the crust in the pan. Place the pan in a large roasting pan. Pour enough hot water into the roasting pan to come halfway up the sides of the springform pan. Bake until the cheesecake is golden and the center of the cake moves only slightly when the pan is shaken, about 1 hour 10 minutes.

4. Transfer the cake to a rack; cool 1 hour. Chill overnight.

5. Mix the strawberries, remaining ½ cup plus 2 tablespoons sugar, and the vinegar in a large bowl. Let stand at room temperature until juices form, about 30 minutes.

6. Cut the cake into wedges. Spoon the strawberries alongside and serve.

YIELD: MAKES 8 TO 10 SERVINGS

1½ cups ground crumbs from purchased almond biscotti (about 6 ounces)
6 tablespoons (¾ stick) unsalted butter, melted
2 pounds cream cheese, at room temperature
8 ounces mascarpone cheese
1¾ cups plus 2 tablespoons sugar
2 large eggs
3 cups quartered hulled strawberries (about 1½ [12-ounce] baskets)
¼ cup balsamic vinegar

Special equipment: 9-inch springform pan with 2¾-inch sides

do ahead:

The **CAKE** can be made 2 days ahead. Cover and keep chilled. Remove from refrigerator 30 minutes before serving.

"Take an additional cup of strawberries and purée them. Add the purée while you beat up the cream cheese and eggs. Cheesecake came out just perfect and with a hint of strawberry flavor."

A cook, Burlingame, California

strawberry shortcake
with buttermilk biscuits

In this classic take on strawberry shortcake, tender buttermilk biscuits are piled high with fresh berries and lush, vanilla-scented whipped cream. We like the biscuits fresh out of the oven, but they can be baked a few hours in advance; return them to the oven for five minutes, and they'll be as good as new.

YIELD: MAKES 4 SERVINGS

2 (1-pound) baskets strawberries, hulled and halved (or quartered if very large; about 7 cups)
½ cup plus 3 tablespoons granulated sugar
2 tablespoons raspberry preserves
1 cup chilled heavy whipping cream
1 teaspoon pure vanilla extract
Buttermilk Biscuits (recipe follows)
Confectioners' sugar

1. Combine the strawberries, ½ cup sugar, and the raspberry preserves in a large bowl; toss to coat. Let stand until syrup forms, tossing occasionally, about 1 hour.

2. Beat the chilled whipping cream, vanilla, and remaining 3 tablespoons sugar in another large bowl until stiff peaks form.

3. Cut the Buttermilk Biscuits in half. Place each biscuit bottom in a shallow bowl. Top each generously with strawberries and whipped cream. Cover the fruit and cream with the biscuit tops. Dust the biscuits with confectioners' sugar and serve.

buttermilk biscuits

YIELD: MAKES 4 BISCUITS

2 cups all-purpose flour
1 tablespoon sugar
2 teaspoons baking powder
½ teaspoon salt
10 tablespoons (1¼ sticks) chilled unsalted butter, cut into pieces
⅔ cup plus 1 tablespoon chilled buttermilk

1. Preheat the oven to 375°F. Sift the flour, sugar, baking powder, and salt into a large bowl. Add the butter and rub in with your fingertips until mixture resembles coarse meal. Gradually add the buttermilk, tossing with a fork until large moist clumps form. Gather the dough into a ball.

2. Divide the dough into 4 pieces. Shape each piece into a 3-inch round. Transfer to a baking sheet, spacing evenly.

3. Bake the biscuits until a tester inserted into the center comes out dry, about 20 minutes (biscuits will be pale). Transfer the biscuits to a rack and cool to lukewarm.

"This recipe is a keeper. I made six biscuits instead of four and used a combo of blueberries and strawberries."

A cook, New Jersey

sum

mango lassi

This frothy Southeast Asian favorite is easy to make and even easier to slurp down. Customize your drink with mint or cumin for a summer barbecue, baby shower, or birthday; you can even spice it up your drink with ground chiles or fresh ginger.

YIELD: MAKES 2 SERVINGS

¾ cup peeled and chopped mango
¾ cup low-fat yogurt
3 tablespoons sugar
¼ cup milk
½ teaspoon lemon juice
¼ cup mango sorbet
⅓ cup cold water
9 to 10 ice cubes

1. Purée the mango with the yogurt and sugar in a blender. Add the milk, lemon juice, and sorbet, and blend until smooth. Add the cold water and ice, and blend to the desired consistency.

2. Pour into a tall glass or 2 small glasses. Serve with a straw.

fruit salad *with ginger syrup*

The combination of stone fruits, berries, and melon, dressed in a simple but zingy ginger syrup, makes for a seasonal dish that's elegant enough for a party and easy enough for a creative topping to your morning bowl of quinoa or oatmeal.

YIELD: MAKES 4 SERVINGS

FOR GINGER SYRUP
3 cups water
2 cups sugar
2 cups thinly sliced fresh ginger (about a 10-inch piece), unpeeled

FOR FRUIT SALAD
4 cups (1-inch pieces) summer fruit, such as mixed berries, melons, peaches, and/or nectarines
3 tablespoons small fresh mint leaves

MAKE SYRUP
1. Bring the water, sugar, and ginger to a boil in a 2-quart saucepan, then stir until the sugar is dissolved.

2. Simmer the syrup 10 minutes, stirring occasionally, then remove from the heat and let steep 15 minutes. Pour the ginger syrup through a sieve into a bowl, discarding ginger. Chill, covered, at least 2 hours.

MAKE FRUIT SALAD
Toss the fruit and mint with ¼ cup of the syrup, or to taste.

meyer lemon and dried blueberry scones

These slightly sweet and perfectly tart scones are quick and easy for breakfast, brunch, or an afternoon snack. Meyer lemons, a cross between a lemon and an orange, are sweeter and less acidic than regular lemons. They're gaining in popularity and more widely available, but if you can't find any, just use a standard lemon. Likewise, dried blueberries can often be found at specialty food stores and good supermarkets, but dried cranberries are easier to find and make an excellent substitute.

1. Position a rack in the top third of the oven and preheat the oven to 425°F. Line a large baking sheet with parchment.

2. Whisk the flour and ½ cup sugar in a large bowl. Using your fingertips, rub in the chilled butter until pieces are the size of small peas. Add the dried wild blueberries and toss to coat.

3. Mix 1 cup buttermilk and the finely grated lemon peel in a glass measuring cup. Pour the buttermilk mixture into the dry ingredients and stir until a dough begins to form (some of the flour will not be incorporated).

4. Transfer the dough to a lightly floured work surface and gather together. Knead the dough briefly, about 5 turns. Divide the dough in half. Form each dough half into a ball and flatten into a 1-inch-thick disk. Cut each disk into 6 wedges.

5. Transfer the scones to the prepared baking sheet, spacing 1 inch apart. Brush the tops with the remaining 1 tablespoon buttermilk and sprinkle with the remaining 1½ tablespoons sugar. Bake until the scones are golden brown on top and a toothpick inserted into the center comes out clean, about 25 minutes.

YIELD: MAKES 12 SERVINGS

3 cups self-rising flour
½ cup plus 1½ tablespoons sugar
¾ cup (1½ sticks) chilled unsalted butter, cut into ½-inch cubes
1½ cups dried wild blueberries (about 10 ounces)
1 cup plus 1 tablespoon buttermilk
1½ tablespoons finely grated Meyer lemon peel or regular lemon peel

"I make them pretty often. I will regularly substitute orange zest for the lemon if I don't have one in the house. Great with lemon curd!"

Koontzie, California

zucchini raisin bran muffins

This recipe is a great way to use the extra zucchini from the garden or farmers' market and is chockfull of healthy ingredients. For an even more nutritious version, substitute the same amount of applesauce for the butter, and brown sugar instead of white.

YIELD: MAKES 12 MUFFINS

⅔ cup all-purpose flour
⅔ cup whole-wheat flour
⅔ cup Miller's Bran (see Note*)
2 teaspoons baking powder
¾ teaspoon salt
1 teaspoon ground cinnamon
¼ teaspoon ground cloves
½ cup (1 stick) unsalted butter, softened
⅔ cup sugar
2 large eggs
1 teaspoon pure vanilla extract
¼ cup milk
½ cup raisins
½ cup chopped walnuts
2 cups coarsely grated zucchini

Special equipment: 12-cup muffin tin

* Note: Available at natural foods stores, specialty
  foods shops, and some supermarkets

"My zucchini was rather large and had a soft center, so although it wasn't specified, I scooped it out, grating only the firm flesh. This recipe produced a sturdy-looking muffin with a nice, light texture. The kids loved them!"

Ckarrowsmith, Calgary, Canada

1. Preheat the oven to 375°F.

2. In a medium bowl, whisk together the flours, bran, baking powder, salt, cinnamon, and cloves. In a large bowl with an electric mixer, cream the butter with the sugar until the mixture is light and fluffy. Add the eggs 1 at a time, beating well after each addition, and beat in the vanilla. Beat the flour mixture into the butter mixture, beat in the milk, and stir in the raisins, walnuts, and zucchini.

3. Divide the batter among 12 well-buttered or paper-lined ½-cup muffin tins and bake the muffins in the middle of the oven for 25 to 30 minutes, or until a tester comes out clean. Turn the muffins out onto a rack and let them cool.

basil lime spritzer

Serve this spritzer as a rejuvenating treat in the summer heat, or try the basil lime syrup drizzled over your favorite melon. If you decide to add alcohol to a few glasses, garnish with either a fresh sprig of basil or a lime wheel to differentiate them from the virgin drinks.

YIELD: MAKES 1 SERVING

2 tablespoons Basil Lime Syrup (recipe
    follows)
Sparkling water
Basil sprig, for garnish

Pour the syrup into an ice-filled tall glass and top off with sparkling water. Stir, then garnish with a basil sprig.

basil lime syrup

YIELD: MAKES ABOUT 1 CUP

¾ cup sugar
Zest of 1 lime, removed in strips with a
    vegetable peeler
½ cup fresh lime juice
¼ cup water
1 cup loosely packed fresh basil leaves

*"I served as an opening drink for
my dinner party and it was a
great hit. It is also quite good with
some tequila."*
A reviewer, Toronto, Canada

1. Bring the sugar, zest, juice, and water to a boil, stirring until sugar is dissolved. Remove from the heat and let syrup stand, uncovered, 15 minutes.

2. Discard the zest and transfer the syrup to a blender. Add the basil and blend 20 seconds. Pour through a fine-mesh sieve lined with a rinsed and squeezed paper towel into a bowl or glass measuring cup, then cool.

vegetable summer rolls

Attention, parents: If you're looking for a veggie-packed, kid-pleasing recipe—one that children as young as two can help you prepare—this is it. Set up a workstation with the ingredients, parchment paper for easy cleanup, and a pastry brush, and let the kids "paint" the lettuce leaves with peanut sauce.

MAKE SAUCE

Cook the onion, garlic, and red pepper flakes in the oil in a small heavy saucepan over moderate heat, stirring, until pale golden, about 4 minutes. Whisk in the remaining sauce ingredients. Simmer, whisking, 1 minute, then cool.

MAKE SUMMER ROLLS

1. Cover the noodles with boiling water and soak 15 minutes, then drain well in a sieve. Pat dry between paper towels and toss with vinegar and salt to taste.

2. Put a double thickness of paper towel on a work surface and fill a shallow baking pan with warm water. Soak a rice-paper round (make sure there are no holes) in warm water until pliable, 30 seconds to 1 minute, then transfer to paper towels.

3. Arrange a piece of lettuce on the bottom half of the soaked rice paper, folding or tearing to fit and leaving a 1-inch border along edge. Spread one-fourth of the peanut sauce over the lettuce and top with one-fourth each of mint, basil, cabbage, and noodles. Roll up the rice paper tightly around the filling and, after rolling halfway, arrange one-fourth of the cilantro and carrot along the crease. Then fold in the sides and continue rolling. Transfer the summer roll to a plate and cover with dampened paper towels.

4. Make 3 more rolls in same manner. Serve rolls halved on the diagonal.

"Love the rolls and the sauce (minus the tomato paste). I use the sauce for lots of other things— over a cold veggie-noodle-almond salad is great."
A cook, Carbondale, Colorado

YIELD: MAKES 4 SERVINGS

FOR PEANUT SAUCE

3 tablespoons finely chopped onion
1 small garlic clove, minced
¾ teaspoon dried red pepper flakes
1 teaspoon vegetable oil
3 tablespoons water
1 tablespoon creamy peanut butter
1 tablespoon hoisin sauce
1 teaspoon tomato paste
¾ teaspoon sugar

FOR SUMMER ROLLS

1 ounce bean thread noodles (cellophane noodles)
1 tablespoon seasoned rice vinegar
4 (8-inch) rice-paper rounds, plus additional in case some tear
2 red-leaf lettuce leaves, ribs cut out and discarded and leaves halved
¼ cup fresh mint leaves
¼ cup fresh basil leaves, preferably Thai
½ cup thinly sliced napa cabbage
¼ cup fresh cilantro leaves
⅓ cup coarsely shredded carrot (1 medium)

do ahead:

The **SUMMER ROLLS** may be made 6 hours ahead and chilled, wrapped in dampened paper towels and kept in a sealed plastic bag. Bring the rolls to room temperature before halving and serving.

zucchini patties *with feta*

After tasting this Mediterranean and Middle Eastern delight, even avowed zucchini haters will sing the vegetable's praises. If you don't have—or you dislike—dill, use other herbs such as basil, chives, and mint, and try French or Bulgarian feta for a milder and less salty alternative to the Greek cheese. Serve these zucchini patties with traditional meze dishes such as tzatziki, labaneh, tabbouleh, fattoush, olives, dolma, hummus, and kibbeh, for an array of appetizers.

YIELD: MAKES ABOUT 18 PATTIES

2½ cups coarsely grated zucchini (from about 3 medium)
1 teaspoon salt
1 large egg and 1 large egg yolk
½ cup all-purpose flour, or more as needed
½ cup crumbled feta cheese
1 cup chopped fresh flat-leaf parsley leaves
½ cup chopped green onions
1½ tablespoons chopped fresh dill
½ cup olive oil, or as needed
½ cup corn oil, or as needed
Plain Greek yogurt, for serving

do ahead:

The **ZUCCHINI PATTIES** can be made 1 day ahead. Place on a baking sheet, cover, and chill. Rewarm, uncovered, in a 350°F oven 12 minutes.

1. Toss the zucchini and ½ teaspoon salt in a large bowl. Let stand 5 minutes, then transfer to a sieve. Press out the excess liquid.

2. Place the zucchini in a dry bowl. Mix in the egg, yolk, ½ cup flour, the cheese, and remaining ½ teaspoon salt. Mix in the parsley, onions, and dill. If the batter is very wet, add more flour by spoonfuls until it is stiffer.

3. Heat 2 tablespoons olive oil and 2 tablespoons corn oil in a large skillet over medium heat. Working in batches, drop the batter by rounded tablespoonfuls into the skillet. Fry the patties until golden, 5 minutes per side, adding more olive oil and corn oil as needed. Transfer to paper towels to drain. Serve with yogurt.

"These are so good! I served them with tzatziki, and they were out of this world!"
Antigone66, Virginia

spicy adobo shrimp cocktail

Fiery adobo sauce is the secret ingredient in this classic first course. Chopped cucumber, crunchy celery, and silky avocado help round out the spicy sauce, making it hearty enough for a quick and easy light lunch and perfect for a hot summer afternoon.

1. Cook the shrimp in lightly salted boiling water until just cooked through, 2 to 3 minutes, then drain. Chill until cold, about 10 minutes.

2. Gently stir together the remaining ingredients, then stir in the shrimp. Serve in bowls or festive glasses.

"We had a dinner party for eight, and everyone loved this. I put the celery in, and the crunch was what made it so unusual with the creaminess of the avocado (which I doubled). I used halved grape tomatoes."
Mnikolaisen, St. Louis, Missouri

YIELD: MAKES 4 SERVINGS

¾ pound peeled and deveined medium shrimp

1 celery rib, sliced

1 firm ripe 6- to 8-ounces avocado, chopped

1 Kirby cucumber, peeled and chopped

1 plum tomato, seeded and chopped

3 tablespoons finely chopped white onion

1 small garlic clove, minced

2 tablespoons chopped fresh cilantro

¼ cup ketchup

3 tablespoons fresh lime juice

1 teaspoon adobo sauce from canned chipotles in adobo

2 tablespoons water

½ teaspoon salt

savory summer tarts

These versatile small tartlets can take top billing for a light lunch or play appetizer to a lazy weekend brunch. A creamy custard forms the backdrop for three fillings: goat cheese and tomato; crab and tarragon; and pea, onion, and pancetta. The empty pastry shells can be baked up to a day in advance, then filled and finished when you're ready to eat. Pack them for a picnic—they'll easily travel!

MAKE PASTRY DOUGH

1. Blend together the flour, butter, and salt in a bowl with your fingertips or a pastry blender (or pulse in a food processor) just until mixture resembles coarse meal with some roughly pea-size butter lumps. Drizzle 5 tablespoons ice water evenly over the mixture and gently stir with a fork (or pulse) until incorporated. Squeeze a small handful of dough: if dough doesn't hold together, add more ice water, ½ tablespoon at a time, stirring until incorporated. Do not overwork dough, or pastry will be tough.

2. Turn out the dough onto a work surface and divide into 4 portions. With the heel of your hand, smear each portion once or twice in a forward motion to help distribute fat. Gather all of dough together, with a pastry scraper if you have one, and form into 2 (5-inch) squares. Chill, wrapped in plastic wrap, until firm, at least 1 hour.

MAKE TART SHELLS

1. Arrange 12 (4-inch) flan rings, tart rings, or ramekins on 2 parchment-lined baking sheets. Roll out one portion of dough on a lightly floured surface with a lightly floured rolling pin into a 16 by 10-inch rectangle. Cut into 6 rough squares.

2. Gently fit each square into a ring (do not stretch dough). Trim the excess dough flush with the rim. Lightly prick each shell several times with a fork and chill until firm, about 30 minutes. Repeat with remaining dough and rings.

3. Preheat the oven to 375°F with racks in upper and lower thirds.

recipe continues

YIELD: MAKES 12 (4-INCH) TARTS

FOR PASTRY DOUGH

2½ cups all-purpose flour
1 cup (2 sticks) cold unsalted butter, cut into ½-inch pieces
½ teaspoon salt
5 to 8 tablespoons ice water

FOR GOAT CHEESE AND TOMATO FILLING

8 haricots verts, trimmed and cut into 1½-inch pieces
8 grape or cherry tomatoes, halved
4 (¼-inch-thick) rounds soft mild goat cheese (from a small log)
2 teaspoons finely chopped fresh chives

do ahead:

The **TART SHELLS** can be baked 1 day ahead and kept on trays at room temperature, wrapped tightly in plastic wrap. Filled baked tarts can be kept at cool room temperature 2 hours.

"I also made one giant tart, which impressed my guests to no end."
[see Cook's Note, following page]
A cook, New York City

y

w

FOR CRAB AND TARRAGON FILLING

2 tablespoons finely chopped shallot
1½ tablespoons extra-virgin olive oil
½ cup (½-inch) bread cubes
½ cup jumbo lump crab meat, picked
    over (2 ounces)
1½ teaspoons finely chopped fresh
    tarragon leaves
¼ teaspoon grated lemon zest
2 pinches cayenne

FOR PEA, ONION, AND
PANCETTA FILLING

2 green onions, thinly sliced
½ tablespoon extra-virgin olive oil
¼ cup thawed frozen baby peas
4 thin slices pancetta

FOR CUSTARD

¾ cup whole milk
¾ cup heavy cream
3 large eggs and 1 large egg yolk
¾ teaspoon salt
½ teaspoon black pepper

Special equipment: 12 (4-inch) flan rings

cook's note:

To make 1 large (11-inch) **TART**,
prepare a half recipe of dough, and
when fitting it into the tart pan,
cut off the excess dough, leaving a
½-inch overhang, and fold overhang
inward. Press the dough against the
side of the pan, pushing dough
¼ inch above rim. Choose a filling
and triple the ingredients (for a large
pea tart, you'll need only 5 slices
pancetta); use the entire custard
recipe. Bake the shell as above, then
bake the filled tart 30 to 35 minutes.

4. Line the shells with foil (not heavy-duty) and fill with pie weights. Bake until the sides are set, about 20 minutes. Carefully remove the weights and foil and bake the shells until golden brown all over, 5 to 8 minutes. Cool completely on baking sheets on racks, then remove the flan rings.

5. Reduce the oven temperature to 350°F.

ASSEMBLE GOAT CHEESE AND TOMATO TARTS

Cook the haricots verts in salted boiling water until crisp-tender, about 3 minutes. Drain and divide among 4 tart shells along with the tomatoes, then top with a round of cheese. Reserve chives.

ASSEMBLE CRAB AND TARRAGON TARTS

Cook the shallot in ½ tablespoon oil in a small skillet over medium heat until softened, about 1 minute. Transfer to a small bowl. Heat the remaining tablespoon oil in a skillet over medium heat, then cook the bread, stirring, until golden. Toss the croutons with the shallot and divide among 4 tart shells. Toss the crab with the tarragon, zest, and cayenne and add to the same shells.

ASSEMBLE PEA, ONION, AND PANCETTA TARTS

Cook the onions in the oil in a clean small skillet over medium heat until softened, about 1 minute. Stir in the peas and warm through, then divide mixture among remaining 4 tart shells. Add the pancetta to the skillet and cook, turning once, until just crisp. Reserve pancetta.

MAKE CUSTARD AND BAKE TARTS

1. Whisk together the custard ingredients and divide among the shells. Sprinkle the chives over the goat cheese tarts and top the pea tarts with the pancetta.

2. Bake the tarts on baking sheets until the custard is just set, about 20 minutes. Cool slightly.

mango salad *with grilled shrimp*

This tropical dish, adapted from the Mnemba Island Lodge off the coast of Zanzibar, pairs chile-spiced mangos with freshly grilled shrimp. Complex in flavor and easy in execution, this sweet, spicy, and creamy entrée makes a balanced and beautiful meal that Epicurious members make again and again.

MAKE MANGO SALAD

Whisk together the brown sugar and lime juice in a large bowl until sugar is dissolved. Whisk in chile, shallot, cilantro, and mint. Add the mangos, tossing gently.

MAKE SHRIMP AND FINISH SALAD

1. Beginning at thick end, insert a skewer lengthwise through each shrimp to straighten. Transfer to a tray.

2. Prepare the grill.

3. Whisk together the oil, jalapeño, cumin, and salt, then brush on the skewered shrimp until well coated. Grill the shrimp, turning occasionally, until lightly charred and just cooked through, about 4 minutes.

4. Toss the mango salad again and divide among 4 plates. Arrange 4 shrimp on top of each serving.

"I made the mango salad and skewered shrimp (with marinade poured on top) in advance and refrigerated while I went to a graduation ceremony. When we returned, I simply grilled some rustic bread with olive oil, layered each plate with greens, grilled shrimp, and served—beautiful, delicious, a real (healthy) winner."
A cook, Los Altos, California

YIELD: MAKES 4 SERVINGS

FOR MANGO SALAD

2 tablespoons dark brown sugar
2 tablespoons fresh lime juice
1 (4-inch-long) fresh hot red chile, thinly sliced, including seeds
1 medium shallot, thinly sliced
¼ cup chopped fresh cilantro leaves
2 tablespoons chopped fresh mint leaves
2 firm-ripe mangos, peeled, pitted, and thinly sliced

FOR SHRIMP

16 jumbo shrimp (1¼ pounds), shelled, leaving tail and adjoining first segment attached, and deveined
2 tablespoons vegetable oil
1 fresh jalapeño chile, minced, including seeds
2 teaspoons ground cumin
½ teaspoon salt
Lime wedges

Special equipment: 16 (8-inch) wooden skewers (optional); gas or charcoal grill

shrimp bisque

When developing this recipe, Epicurious member **Joan Higgins** of Pearl River, New York, decided to use extra shrimp to make sure that her diners had a piece of shrimp with each spoonful. The bisque's base is indulgent, too—half-and-half infused with earthy nutmeg and enlivened with paprika. Even with its deep flavor and silky texture, Higgins says the best thing about this recipe is that it's foolproof.

YIELD: MAKES 4 SERVINGS

5 tablespoons unsalted butter
¾ pound large shrimp, peeled and
    deveined, shells reserved
1 bay leaf
4 cups water
½ medium onion, finely diced
1 celery rib, finely diced
⅛ teaspoon dried thyme, crumbled
½ cup dry Sherry
2 tablespoons all-purpose flour
1½ cups half-and-half, heated until hot
3 tablespoons tomato paste
2 teaspoons sweet paprika
⅛ teaspoon freshly ground nutmeg

do ahead:

The **SHRIMP STOCK** can be made ahead and refrigerated, covered, up to 3 days.

Be sure to use fresh, high-quality ingredients; never use frozen shrimp; and make sure you cook your roux long enough so you don't get a floury taste.
—Joan Higgins

1. In a large, heavy saucepan over moderately high heat, melt 1 tablespoon of butter. Add the shrimp shells and sauté, stirring frequently, until golden, about 5 minutes. Add the bay leaf and water, and bring to a boil. Reduce the heat to moderately low and simmer, uncovered, 25 minutes. Strain the stock through a fine-mesh sieve into a medium bowl. Set aside.

2. In a large sauté pan over moderately high heat, melt 1 tablespoon of the butter. Add the shrimp and sauté, stirring frequently, until pink, 2 to 3 minutes. Transfer to a medium bowl and let cool. Reserve 4 shrimp for garnish and coarsely chop the rest.

3. In the same pan over moderately high heat, melt 2 table-spoons of butter. Add the onion and celery and sauté, stirring occasionally, until soft, about 8 minutes. Add the thyme and Sherry, and bring to a simmer. Continue simmering, scraping up any browned bits on the bottom of the pan, until liquid is absorbed, about 2 minutes. Transfer to a blender, add the reserved shrimp stock, and purée until smooth. Set aside.

4. In a medium saucepan over low heat, melt the remaining tablespoon butter. Whisk in the flour and cook, whisking constantly, until the mixture bubbles, about 3 minutes. Whisk in the hot half-and-half in a steady stream. Add the puréed shrimp stock mixture, tomato paste, paprika, and nutmeg, and chopped shrimp. Season with salt and pepper and stir to combine. Cook over moderate heat until heated through, about 2 minutes.

5. Divide the soup among 4 bowls and garnish each with the reserved shrimp. Serve immediately.

tomato and watermelon salad
with feta and toasted almonds

Watermelon and heirloom tomatoes work together to create a juicy and flavorful arrangement that is sweet and tangy. Use different-colored watermelon with tomatoes for a stunning presentation. Heaping the salad over a crunchy base of fresh arugula keeps the various flavors in check.

1. Combine the melon and tomatoes in a large bowl. Sprinkle with 1 teaspoon fleur de sel and toss to blend; let stand 15 minutes. Add 4 tablespoons oil, the vinegar, and herbs to the melon mixture. Season to taste with pepper and more salt, if desired.

2. Toss the arugula in a medium bowl with the remaining 1 tablespoon oil. Divide the arugula among plates. Top with the melon salad; sprinkle with feta cheese and toasted almonds, and serve.

"This salad is surprising and amazing. Definitely drain the watermelon and tomatoes before tossing; they will sweat a lot and the salad can quickly turn into soup. Also be sparing with the almonds . . . they are a nice surprise when you don't let them overtake the combination of flavors."

Vintagesoul, Los Angeles, California

YIELD: MAKES 6 TO 8 SERVINGS

8 cups (1¼-inch) chunked seedless watermelon (from about 6-pound melon)

3 pounds ripe tomatoes (preferably heirloom) in assorted colors, cored, cut into 1¼-inch chunks (about 6 cups)

1 teaspoon fleur de sel or kosher salt, or more as needed

5 tablespoons extra-virgin olive oil

1½ tablespoons red-wine vinegar

3 tablespoons chopped assorted fresh herbs (such as dill, basil, and mint)

6 cups fresh arugula leaves or small watercress sprigs

1 cup crumbled feta cheese (about 5 ounces)

½ cup sliced almonds, lightly toasted

grilled caesar salad

With just 2 minutes on the grill, crisp romaine develops a smoky, charred flavor without wilting. Add a garlicky anchovy dressing, freshly grated Parmigiano-Reggiano, and grill-toasted croutons, and you have a whole new way to enjoy classic Caesar salad. The salad pairs with all your barbecue favorites, but a hearty steak is its perfect match. Prep the dressing in advance—store it in the refrigerator and give it a good shake before using—and grill the romaine while your meat rests.

1. Purée the anchovies, garlic, oil, salt, and pepper in a blender until smooth.

2. Prepare a grill for direct-heat cooking over medium-hot charcoal (moderate heat for gas).

3. Brush both sides of the baguette slices with some of the anchovy dressing, then grill the bread, turning over occasionally, until toasted, 1 to 2 minutes. Add the egg and lemon juice to the dressing in the blender and blend until emulsified, 1 to 2 minutes. Season with salt.

4. Cut the romaine hearts in half lengthwise, then grill, cut sides down, covered only if using a gas grill, until grill marks just appear, about 2 minutes. Cut the romaine crosswise into 2-inch-wide strips and transfer to a bowl.

5. Halve or quarter the toasts and add to the romaine along with the cheese.

6. Toss the salad with just enough dressing to coat and serve immediately.

YIELD: MAKES 6 SERVINGS

2 flat anchovy fillets, drained and chopped
1 small garlic clove, chopped
½ cup extra-virgin olive oil
¼ teaspoon salt
¼ teaspoon black pepper
12 (½-inch-thick) slices baguette
1 large egg
2 tablespoons fresh lemon juice, or to taste
3 hearts of romaine (18 ounces)
½ cup finely grated Parmigiano-Reggiano cheese (about 1 ounce)

Special equipment: Gas or charcoal grill

"This is a fantastic summer salad, and incredibly quick and easy. I used 1 teaspoon anchovy paste (total) for the two fillets. We will be having this often with grilled chicken or steak."
TacomaFoodie, Washington

faux arrabbiata *with penne*

Arrabbiata (Italian for "angry") sauce is a heated-up version of your classic marinara, made from garlic, tomatoes, red chiles, and olive oil. What makes this a "faux" arrabbiata is the ever-so-slightly unorthodox addition of basil, lemon, and balsamic vinegar, which add sweetness to the sauce. Cookbook author and Epicurious member **Serena Bass** notes, "Mince the lemon with a sharp knife rather than grate, as it is nice to get little pieces of zest to bite on. And don't be tempted to cook this for longer than 10 minutes, as it will lose its fresh TKO punch. I like this sauce with penne or spaghettini."

YIELD: MAKES 4 SERVINGS

2 tablespoons olive oil
1 tablespoon unsalted butter
5 large garlic cloves, minced
1 teaspoon dried red pepper flakes
1 (28-ounce) can crushed tomatoes
Zest of 1 lemon, minced
½ teaspoon salt
½ teaspoon freshly ground black pepper
1 pound penne, spaghettini, or other
    pasta
1 tablespoon balsamic vinegar
¼ cup chopped fresh basil leaves

1. In a medium saucepan over moderate heat, heat the oil and butter. Add the garlic and red pepper flakes and cook, stirring occasionally, until the garlic is fragrant and lightly golden, 1 to 2 minutes. Add the tomatoes, lemon zest, salt, and pepper and bring to a boil. Reduce the heat to low and simmer, partially covered, until slightly reduced, about 15 minutes.

2. Meanwhile, in a large pot of boiling salted water, cook the pasta until tender. Drain well and return it to the pot it was cooked in. Add the sauce, vinegar, and basil, and toss to combine. Serve immediately.

ORZO *with grilled shrimp, summer vegetables, and pesto vinaigrette*

Served cold or at room temperature, this colorful orzo is picnic and party ready. Save yourself some time—and effort—by buying peeled and deveined shrimp, and look for bocconcini, which are tiny mozzarella balls, usually sold in water. With precut veggies, this salad is a snap.

1. Cook the orzo in a large pot of boiling salted water until tender but still firm to bite, stirring occasionally. Drain. Rinse with cold water; drain well. Transfer to a large bowl and toss with 1 tablespoon oil.

2. Prepare the grill to medium-high heat. Whisk 2 tablespoons oil and 2 tablespoons vinegar in a small bowl. Brush the zucchini and bell pepper with the oil mixture, then sprinkle with salt and pepper. Whisk the pesto, lime juice, remaining 3½ tablespoons oil, and remaining 2 tablespoons vinegar in a small bowl for the pesto vinaigrette. Place the shrimp in a medium bowl. Add 2 tablespoons pesto vinaigrette; toss to coat.

3. Grill the zucchini and bell pepper until crisp-tender, about 3 minutes per side for zucchini and 4 minutes per side for bell pepper. Transfer to work surface.

4. Sprinkle the shrimp with salt and pepper; then grill until charred and cooked through, 2 to 3 minutes per side. Place the shrimp in the bowl with the orzo. Chop the zucchini and bell pepper; add to the bowl with the orzo. Add the remaining vinaigrette, the tomatoes, sliced basil, and mozzarella; toss to combine. Season to taste with salt and pepper.

5. Garnish shrimp with basil sprigs and serve cold or at room temperature.

"Made my own pesto, and used asparagus and summer squash (didn't have zucchini)—also had to roast the veggies thanks to a grill malfunction. Grown-ups and kids alike had seconds."
Emiyeric, San Antonio, Texas

YIELD: MAKES 6 SERVINGS

8 ounces orzo (about 1⅓ cups)
6½ tablespoons extra-virgin olive oil
4 tablespoons red-wine vinegar
2 medium zucchini or summer squash, cut lengthwise into ¼-inch-thick slices (about 9 ounces total)
1 red or yellow bell pepper, quartered
3 tablespoons favorite pesto
2 tablespoons fresh lime juice
1 pound large shrimp, peeled and deveined
2 large heirloom tomatoes, cored, cut into ½-inch cubes (about 2 cups)
½ cup thinly sliced fresh basil leaves, plus sprigs for garnish
1 (8-ounce) ball fresh mozzarella cheese, cut into ½-inch cubes

Special equipment: Gas or charcoal grill

do ahead:

The **ORZO** can be made 2 hours ahead. Cover; chill.

chilled soba *with tofu and sugar snap peas*

When the heat is on, there's no better way to cool down than with a bowl of chilled noodles. To make this truly vegetarian and vegan friendly, seek out a ponzu sauce without dashi, an ingredient made with dried fish. Two brands worth considering are Marukan and Wan Ja Shan. For die-hard meat eaters, add some thin slices of cold beef.

YIELD: MAKES 6 SERVINGS

FOR SAUCE

1 large dried shiitake mushroom
2½ cups water
8 (1-inch) pieces kombu (dried kelp)
½ cup soy sauce, preferably Japanese
¼ cup mirin (Japanese sweet rice wine)
3 tablespoons ponzu sauce (not containing dashi)
1 tablespoon sugar
1 tablespoon Asian sesame oil

FOR SOBA

1 pound sugar snap peas, thinly sliced
10 ounces baby spinach (16 cups)
1 pound dried soba noodles
1 (14- to 18-ounce) package silken tofu
1 cup thinly sliced green onions
2 tablespoons thin matchsticks of peeled fresh ginger

do ahead:

The **SAUCE** can be made 3 days ahead and chilled.

MAKE SAUCE

1. Simmer the mushroom in the water in a small saucepan, covered, for 15 minutes. Add the kombu and barely simmer, covered, 5 minutes more. Remove from heat and let stand, covered, 5 minutes. Strain liquid through a fine-mesh sieve into a large glass measure, pressing on and discarding solids.

2. Return 2 cups liquid (add water, if necessary) to the saucepan. Add the soy sauce, mirin, ponzu, sugar, and ¼ teaspoon salt and bring to a boil, stirring until sugar has dissolved. Remove from heat. Stir in the sesame oil, then cool in the pan set into a large ice bath.

COOK NOODLES AND VEGETABLES

1. Blanch the snaps peas in a large pot of unsalted boiling water until crisp-tender, about 2 minutes. Transfer with a slotted spoon to a large colander set into an ice bath to stop the cooking. Lift the colander to drain, then transfer peas to a bowl.

2. Meanwhile, return the cooking water to a boil. Blanch the spinach until just wilted, about 30 seconds, then cool and drain in same manner. Squeeze out excess water. Add to the peas.

3. Return the cooking water to a boil. Add the noodles and cook according to package directions, stirring occasionally, until tender. Drain in a colander and rinse with cold water. Cool in an ice bath until very cold (add more ice to water as necessary). Drain well.

4. Carefully drain the tofu and pat dry. Cut into ¾-inch cubes.

5. Whisk the sauce, then pour 1½ cups sauce into a large bowl. Add the noodles, sugar snaps, spinach, and half of the onions and toss.

6. Serve in shallow bowls, topped with tofu, remaining scallions, and ginger. Drizzle with some of the remaining sauce and serve remainder on the side.

"I was taken aback by the amount of sauce, but it was great. So that the noodles and tofu don't soak up all the sauce, it is a good idea to add the remaining sauce just before serving."

Blinknoodle, Canada

quick paella

Bring the vibrant colors and fresh flavors of this Spanish dish to your table in under an hour. Spicy chorizo, fresh shrimp, roasted peppers, and tangy artichoke hearts melt together on a bed of saffron-infused rice in an easy dish, ideal for summer sharing. Personalize your paella by adding a favorite shellfish or throwing in some cooked onions.

YIELD: MAKES 4 SERVINGS

¾ pound cooked chorizo or linguiça
    sausage, cut into chunks
4 tablespoons olive oil
1 (1-pound) bag saffron rice, such as Vigo
1 (9-ounce) package frozen artichoke
    hearts, thawed and drained
1 (8-ounce) jar roasted red peppers,
    drained and sliced
2 cups chicken or fish broth, or wine
2 cups water
1 pound large shrimp, peeled
1 cup frozen peas, defrosted

"It was fast and easy, a good break from grilling during a hot Texas summer. I made it almost exactly as written, except I used fresh red peppers, andouille sausage, and frozen artichoke hearts."

Pamthecook, Dallas, Texas

1. In a large skillet with a lid, brown the sausage in the oil until crisp, about 5 minutes.

2. Add the rice, artichoke hearts, peppers, broth or wine, and water. Bring to a boil. Reduce the heat, cover, and simmer until most of the liquid is absorbed, about 20 minutes.

3. Stir in the shrimp and peas. Cover and continue cooking until the shrimp are opaque, 5 to 7 minutes.

mussels and fries *with mustard mayonnaise*

Although there's no substitute for enjoying a pot of freshly steamed mussels on the coast of France, this 30-minute supper is a pretty good substitute. The briny flavor and deep garlic aroma of stewed mussels are surprisingly simple to recreate. Crunchy french fries (whether frozen or homemade) and a mellow mustard mayonnaise round out this classic meal. Served with crusty bread, these mussels can create an intimate weekend dinner or an easy weekday escape.

1. Cook the fries according to package instructions and keep warm in the oven if necessary.

2. Meanwhile, cut the onion into very thin slices with the slicer, then cook with garlic and a pinch of salt in the butter in a wide heavy medium pot over medium-high heat, covered, stirring occasionally, until pale golden.

3. While the onion cooks, whisk together the mustard and water until smooth, then whisk in the mayonnaise and about ¼ teaspoon pepper.

4. Add the wine to the onion and briskly simmer, covered, stirring occasionally, until the onion is almost tender, about 5 minutes. Add the mussels and cook, covered, stirring occasionally, until mussels are just open wide, 4 to 6 minutes, checking frequently after 4 minutes and transferring as cooked to a bowl. (Discard any mussels that remain unopened.)

5. Stir the parsley into the cooking liquid and season with salt. Pour liquid over mussels, then serve with fries and mustard mayonnaise.

YIELD: MAKES 2 SERVINGS

1 (15- to 16-ounce) package frozen french fries
1 small onion
2 garlic cloves, forced through a press
3 tablespoons unsalted butter
2 teaspoons dry mustard
2 teaspoons water
½ cup mayonnaise
1 cup dry white wine
2 pounds cultivated mussels, rinsed
2 tablespoons chopped fresh flat-leaf parsley
Crusty bread, preferably a baguette

Special equipment: Mandoline

cook's note:

This **RECIPE** can be doubled in an 8-quart heavy pot.

"Delicious, quick, and cheap. This recipe required exactly 30 minutes and less than $15, including the baguette. (Okay, I used cheap leftover wine.)"
A cook, Berkeley, California

grilled tuna salade niçoise

The crisp beans and potatoes can be cooked an hour ahead and kept at room temperature, but toss the potatoes with the dressing while they are still warm. To soak up any extra herbed garlicky goodness, serve with the Garlic Bruschetta.

YIELD: MAKES 6 SERVINGS

FOR DRESSING

¼ cup red-wine vinegar
2½ tablespoons minced shallot
2 teaspoons Dijon mustard
1 large garlic clove, minced and mashed
    to a paste with ½ teaspoon salt
Rounded ½ teaspoon anchovy paste
1 cup extra-virgin olive oil
1½ teaspoons minced fresh thyme
1½ tablespoons finely chopped fresh
    basil

FOR SALAD

12 ounces green beans (preferably
    haricots verts), trimmed
1½ pounds small (1- to 2-inch) potatoes,
    preferably Yukon Gold
1½ pounds (1-inch-thick) tuna steaks
Vegetable oil, for brushing
¼ cup drained bottled capers (1½ ounces)
12 ounces Boston lettuce (2 heads), leaves
    separated and large ones torn into
    pieces
1 pint cherry or grape tomatoes
⅔ cup Niçoise or other small brine-cured
    black olives
4 hard-cooked large eggs, quartered
3 tablespoons finely chopped fresh
    parsley and/or basil

Special equipment: Gas or charcoal grill
    (see Note)

MAKE DRESSING

Whisk together the vinegar, shallot, mustard, garlic paste, and anchovy paste in a small bowl until combined well, then add the oil in a slow stream, whisking until emulsified. Whisk in the thyme, basil, and salt and pepper to taste.

MAKE SALAD

1. Cook the beans in a 4- to 6-quart pot of boiling salted water, uncovered, until crisp-tender, 3 to 4 minutes, then immediately transfer with a slotted spoon to a bowl of ice and cold water to stop the cooking. Add the potatoes to the boiling water and simmer, uncovered, until tender, 15 to 20 minutes, then drain in a colander. Halve the potatoes while still warm (peel, if desired) and toss with 2 tablespoons dressing in a bowl, then cool.

2. Prepare grill for cooking. If using a charcoal grill, open the vents on the bottom of the grill, then light the charcoal. The charcoal fire is medium-hot when you can hold your hand 5 inches above rack for 3 to 4 seconds. If using a gas grill, preheat to high, covered, 10 minutes, then reduce the heat to moderately high.

3. Brush the tuna with oil and season with salt and pepper, then grill on lightly oiled rack, uncovered, turning over once, until browned on outside but still pink in center, 6 to 8 minutes total. Let the tuna stand 3 minutes, then break into large (3-inch) pieces. Transfer the tuna to a large platter and drizzle with 2 to 3 tablespoons dressing and top with capers.

4. Transfer the potatoes to the platter with the tuna, reserving the bowl. Drain the beans and pat dry. Toss the beans in the bowl with 1 tablespoon dressing and salt and pepper to taste, then transfer to the platter. Toss the lettuce in the bowl with 2 tablespoons dressing and salt and pepper to taste, then transfer to the platter. Toss the tomatoes in the bowl with 1 tablespoon dressing and salt and pepper to taste, then transfer to the platter.

5. Arrange the olives and eggs on the platter and sprinkle the salad with parsley and/or basil. Serve the salad with the remaining dressing on the side.

cook's note:

The **TUNA** can also be cooked in a hot, lightly oiled ridged grill pan over moderately high heat.

"I used salmon instead of tuna, since my local grocery store didn't have tuna. The dressing and capers still went very well. I also added a fresh sliced radish for crunch."

Tara305

garlic bruschetta

On a baking sheet, toast the bread slices in batches under a preheated broiler about 3 inches from the heat for about 1 minute on each side, or until they are golden, transferring them as they are toasted to a work surface. Rub one side of each toast slice with the cut side of a garlic clove, brush it with some of the oil, and season it with salt.

YIELD: MAKES 8 SERVINGS

8 (¾-inch-thick) slices crusty peasant bread, preferably from a large round loaf
3 garlic cloves, halved crosswise
6 tablespoons olive oil, preferably extra-virgin

"We love this salad. I often serve it
with mixed greens or arugula. I've
done it with peaches when I
couldn't get nectarines and with
shrimp and chicken when I
couldn't get scallops."
Mgoeh, New Mexico

grilled scallops and nectarines
with corn and tomato salad

Grilled nectarines add an unexpected sweetness to this summer dish. The smoky, buttery scallops and caramelized fruit give farmers' market corn and tomatoes a new way to shine. And it gets a kick from *piment d'Espelette,* a French hot red chile ground into a powder, and available at specialty foods stores; but chili powder is a fine alternative.

MAKE DRESSING

Whisk the lime juice, lime peel, and piment d'Espelette in a small bowl. Gradually whisk in the oil. Season with fleur de sel and pepper.

MAKE BASIL PURÉE

Blanch the basil in a small pot of boiling salted water 30 seconds; drain. Squeeze to remove as much water as possible, then coarsely chop. Purée the basil and oil in a blender until smooth. Transfer to a small bowl. Season to taste with fleur de sel.

MAKE SALAD

1. Prepare a grill to medium-high heat. Brush the scallops and nectarines with oil; sprinkle with salt and pepper. Grill the scallops until slightly charred and cooked through, about 2 minutes per side. Grill the nectarines until slightly charred, about 1½ minutes per side. Transfer the scallops and nectarines to a plate.

2. Arrange 4 scallops on each of 6 plates. Toss the corn and 2 tablespoons dressing in a medium bowl. Toss the tomatoes with 1 tablespoon dressing in another bowl; season to taste with salt and pepper.

3. Spoon corn around scallops. Scatter tomatoes over corn. Arrange nectarine wedges decoratively on plates. Drizzle some dressing over scallops, then spoon some basil purée over. Sprinkle the sliced basil and fleur de sel over the corn and tomatoes and serve.

YIELD: MAKES 6 SERVINGS

FOR DRESSING
3 tablespoons fresh lime juice
1½ teaspoons finely grated lime peel
⅛ teaspoon (generous) piment d'Espelette or chili powder
3 tablespoons extra-virgin olive oil
Fleur de sel

FOR BASIL PURÉE
¾ cup (loosely packed) fresh basil leaves
¼ cup extra-virgin olive oil
Fleur de sel

FOR SALAD
24 large sea scallops, side muscles removed, patted dry
3 firm but ripe nectarines (white or yellow), each cut into 6 wedges
Olive oil, for brushing
1½ cups fresh corn kernels, cut from 2 large ears of corn
24 grape or cherry tomatoes, halved
⅓ cup thinly sliced fresh basil leaves
Fleur de sel

Special equipment: Gas or charcoal grill

do ahead:

The **DRESSING** and **BASIL PURÉE** can be made 1 day ahead. Cover and chill separately. Bring both to room temperature before using.

tuna kebabs *with ginger-chile marinade*

The combination of plump fresh fish, juicy red bell peppers, sweet onion squares, and pungent cilantro makes for an eye-catching presentation. For additional color, thread yellow, orange, and green bell peppers onto the skewers, or you can tame the heat with thick peach slices. And feel free to swap wooden skewers for the metal variety; just be sure to give them the requisite pregrilling soak of about 30 minutes. Serve these lively kebabs with a simple green salad.

YIELD: MAKES 4 SERVINGS

3 tablespoons unseasoned rice vinegar
2 tablespoons finely grated peeled fresh
  ginger
2 tablespoons peanut oil
2 tablespoons Asian sesame oil
2 tablespoons soy sauce
2 tablespoons honey
1 tablespoon chopped fresh cilantro,
  plus additional to taste
1 serrano chile, seeded and minced
Freshly ground white pepper
1½ pounds (1¼-inch thick) ahi tuna, cut
  into 1¼-inch cubes
Nonstick vegetable-oil spray
1 large red bell pepper, cut into 1-inch
  squares
1 large sweet onion (such as Maui or
  Vidalia), cut into 1-inch squares

Special equipment: 6 (12-inch) metal
  skewers; gas or charcoal grill

1. Whisk the vinegar, ginger, oils, soy sauce, honey, cilantro, and chile in a medium bowl to blend; season to taste with white pepper. Transfer 3 tablespoons of the marinade to a small bowl and reserve. Add the tuna to the remaining marinade in a medium bowl and toss to coat. Refrigerate at least 30 minutes and up to 45 minutes.

2. Spray a grill rack with nonstick spray. Prepare a grill to medium-high heat. Alternate the tuna cubes, bell pepper squares, and onion squares on each of 6 metal skewers. Grill to desired doneness, turning frequently, about 4 minutes total for medium-rare. Transfer to a platter. Drizzle the reserved marinade over and sprinkle skewers with cilantro, to taste.

"This was superb! Definitely double the sauce. I served it over rice with grilled baby bok choy."
Phylora, Mill Valley, California

grilled salmon and baby bok choy *with ginger and garlic*

Salmon, bok choy, ginger, and garlic are packed in foil and cooked on the grill for an easy dinner from Epicurious member **Maggieingl.** Sake and soy sauce create steam within the foil pack so be cautious when opening them—the steam can be extremely hot right off the grill. Add fluffy jasmine rice for an inventive midweek feast.

1. Prepare a gas or charcoal grill to moderately high heat.

2. Trim ⅛ inch from the bottom of each bok choy, then cut into quarters. Wash the bok choy in several changes of cold water and dry in a colander or salad spinner.

3. In a small bowl, whisk together the sesame oil, sake, soy sauce, garlic, and ginger.

4. On a large baking sheet, arrange 2 (12 by 24-inch) pieces of heavy-duty foil, overlapping them in the center to form a cross. Brush the entire surface of the salmon with the sesame oil mixture, then sprinkle with salt and pepper and place skin side down in the center of the foil. Arrange the bok choy on top of the salmon, then fold the foil into a packet, sealing in the salmon and bok choy.

5. Transfer the foil packet to the grill and cook until the salmon is just opaque in center, about 15 minutes. Transfer to a cutting board, open the foil slightly, and let stand 10 minutes.

6. Remove the salmon and bok choy from the foil and cut the salmon into 8 servings. Divide the bok choy among 8 plates and top each with a piece of salmon. Garnish plates with lime wedges and serve immediately.

YIELD: MAKES 8 SERVINGS

8 baby bok choy (about ¾ pound), bruised outer leaves removed
1 tablespoon Asian sesame oil
2 tablespoons sake or rice wine vinegar
2 tablespoons soy sauce
2 garlic cloves, minced
1 (1-inch) piece fresh ginger, peeled and minced
1 (2-pound) salmon fillet with skin
2 limes, cut into quarters

Special equipment: Gas or charcoal grill

grilled shrimp satay
with peaches and bok choy

Consider this colorful dish a step in the direction of rescuing the true Southeast Asian satay from its overdone-chicken-on-a-stick reputation. Tender shrimp, bright bok choy, and sweet stone fruit, all grilled together, make for a nontraditional but nonetheless scrumptious complement to a sauce that strikes the perfect sweet, spicy balance.

YIELD: MAKES 4 SERVINGS

6 tablespoons smooth natural peanut butter, stirred to combine
⅓ cup (packed) dark brown sugar
3 tablespoons seasoned rice vinegar
2 tablespoons soy sauce
2 to 3 teaspoons hot chile paste, such as sambal oelek
9 tablespoons peach nectar
3 peaches or nectarines, each cut into 6 wedges
16 large shrimp, peeled and deveined
6 heads of baby bok choy, halved lengthwise

Special equipment: Gas or charcoal grill

"Nice, really quick dinner. We didn't do the bok choy but instead served with some sautéed snow peas and jasmine rice, and it was a great combination."
A cook, Apex, North Carolina

1. Prepare a grill to medium-high heat.

2. Whisk the peanut butter, sugar, vinegar, soy sauce, chile paste, and 5 tablespoons of the nectar until smooth; season sauce with pepper.

3. Arrange the peaches, shrimp, and bok choy on the grill. Brush with the remaining 4 tablespoons nectar; brush lightly with ¼ cup sauce. Sprinkle with salt and pepper. Grill until the peaches are slightly charred, the shrimp are just opaque in the center, and the bok choy halves are just tender, about 2 minutes per side for peaches and 3 minutes per side for shrimp and bok choy.

4. Mound the shrimp, bok choy, and peaches on a platter. Drizzle with some sauce. Serve with the remaining sauce.

shrimp tikka *with fresh mango chutney*

Tossed in a dynamic spice paste, these little shrimp aren't shy: assertive heat from ginger, jalapeño, and garlic is balanced by the pungency of garam masala. Try sautéing or steaming the shrimp if you don't own a grill. To make a heartier meal, place the shrimp on a bed of basmati rice and boil the marinade for 5 minutes to pour over the top.

MARINATE SHRIMP

Purée the oil, lime juice, jalapeño, ginger, garlic, and spices in a blender until smooth. Pour into a sealable bag, then add the shrimp and marinate at cool room temperature, turning bag occasionally, 30 minutes. Soak the wooden skewers in water for 30 minutes.

MAKE CHUTNEY

Toast the cumin in a dry small skillet over medium heat, stirring occasionally, until fragrant, about 1 minute. Stir together the remaining chutney ingredients, then sprinkle with the toasted cumin.

MAKE KEBABS

1. Prepare the grill for direct-heat cooking over hot charcoal or preheat to medium-high heat for gas.

2. Thread 4 shrimp onto each skewer, leaving small spaces between them. Put on a tray.

3. Oil the grill rack, then grill the skewers, covered only if using a gas grill, turning once, until just cooked through, 4 to 6 minutes total. Serve with the chutney and lime wedges.

"My family inhaled them! I doubled the marinade to use again with chicken later in the week."
Kmacbeth1, Los Gatos, California

YIELD: MAKES 6 SERVINGS

FOR SHRIMP

¼ cup vegetable oil
2 tablespoons fresh lime juice
1 (1-inch) piece fresh jalapeño chile, chopped (about 2 teaspoons)
1 (1-inch) piece peeled fresh ginger, chopped
1 large garlic clove, smashed
2 teaspoons garam masala
¾ teaspoon ground turmeric
⅛ teaspoon grated nutmeg
½ teaspoon salt
2 pounds large shrimp in shell, peeled, leaving tail fan attached

FOR CHUTNEY

1 teaspoon ground cumin
¼ teaspoon salt
1 large (¾-pound) unripe mango, peeled and chopped
⅓ seedless cucumber, peeled and chopped (¾ cup)
½ cup chopped red onion
1 to 2 teaspoons minced fresh jalapeño chile with seeds
3 tablespoons fresh lime juice
3 tablespoons thinly sliced mint leaves
3 tablespoons chopped fresh cilantro

Lime wedges, for serving

Special equipment: 10 (12-inch) wooden skewers; gas or charcoal grill

fish taco platter

Crispy, crunchy, spicy, and best of all, easy, from chefs Bruce Aidells and Nancy Oakes. Fill a few bowls with lime cream, tangy tomatillo salsa, and quick-pickled toppings (all of which can be made in advance) for a make-your-own taco buffet. Baja purists, feel free to insist on mahimahi for the fish, but sea bass, tilapia, cod, and catfish all stand up equally well to the buttermilk batter.

MAKE PICKLED RED ONION AND JALAPEÑOS

Place the onion and jalapeños in a heatproof medium bowl. Mix the vinegar, lime juice, and salt in a small saucepan. Bring just to boil, stirring until salt dissolves. Pour over the onion and jalapeños. Let stand at room temperature at least 1 hour and up to 8 hours.

MAKE BAJA CREAM

Whisk all ingredients in a small bowl.

MAKE TOMATILLO SALSA VERDE

1. Preheat the oven to 375°F. Lightly oil a medium roasting pan. Char half of the tomatillos, white parts of the green onions, and the jalapeño directly over a gas flame or in the broiler. Transfer the charred vegetables to the roasting pan. Add the remaining tomatillos and the garlic cloves to the pan. Roast until all the vegetables are soft, about 12 minutes. Cool.

2. Stem and seed the jalapeño. Place all the roasted vegetables, green onion tops, the cilantro, and 1 tablespoon lime juice in a blender. Purée until smooth, stopping to push vegetables down into blades several times. Transfer to a medium bowl. Season with salt and more lime juice, if desired.

MAKE TACOS

1. Mix the buttermilk, cilantro, hot pepper sauce, 1 teaspoon salt, and the lime juice in a large bowl. Add the fish; toss. Cover; chill at least 1 hour and up to 3 hours.

2. Preheat the oven to 300°F. Wrap the tortillas in foil; place in the oven to warm. Whisk the flour and remaining

recipe continues

YIELD: MAKES 6 TO 8 SERVINGS

FOR PICKLED RED ONION AND JALAPEÑOS

1 red onion (about 12 ounces), halved lengthwise, cut thinly crosswise
5 small jalapeño chiles
2 cups seasoned rice vinegar
3 tablespoons fresh lime juice
1 tablespoon coarse kosher salt

FOR BAJA CREAM

½ cup mayonnaise
½ cup sour cream
2 tablespoons fresh lime juice
1 teaspoon finely grated lime peel
Pinch of salt

FOR TOMATILLO SALSA VERDE

12 ounces tomatillos, husked and stemmed
4 green onions, white and green parts separated
1 jalapeño chile
2 garlic cloves, unpeeled
1¼ cups (packed) fresh cilantro leaves
1 tablespoon fresh lime juice, or more as needed

"I suggest making all of the toppings the day before—and make extra so you can use them on everything you eat that week. I especially love the pickled onions, which just get better with time."
Sthomp, Boston, Massachusetts

FOR TACOS

2 cups buttermilk

½ cup chopped fresh cilantro leaves

3 tablespoons hot pepper sauce

3 teaspoons kosher or other coarse salt

1 tablespoon fresh lime juice

2 pounds skinless halibut, sea bass, or
    striped bass fillets, cut into ½-inch
    strips

16 (6-inch) corn tortillas

2 cups self-rising flour

Vegetable oil, for frying

Fresh salsa and guacamole, for serving

do ahead:

The **PICKLED RED ONION AND
JALAPEÑOS** can be made 1 week
ahead. Cover and refrigerate.

The **BAJA CREAM** can be made
3 days ahead. Cover and refrigerate.

2 teaspoons salt in a medium bowl. Add enough oil to a large skillet to reach a depth of 1 inch. Heat the oil until a thermometer registers 350°F.

3. Working in batches, remove the fish from the marinade and dredge in the flour. Carefully add the fish to the skillet, cover partially, and fry until golden brown, turning occasionally, about 4 minutes. Transfer fish to a paper-towel–lined baking sheet to drain, then place in the oven to keep warm.

4. Set up a buffet with all the taco fixings, along with fresh salsa and guacamole.

peruvian grilled chicken

The classic recipe easily serves four, but the Peruvian tradition is to serve each person a half chicken, so feel free to offer more generous portions. Pair this enticing dish with Peru's beloved Pisco Sour cocktail for an authentic South American experience.

MARINATE CHICKEN

Blend the soy sauce, lime juice, garlic, cumin, paprika, oregano, pepper, and oil in a blender. Put the chicken in a large sealable bag and add the marinade. Seal the bag and marinate, chilled, 8 to 24 hours.

GRILL CHICKEN

1. If using a charcoal grill, open the vents on the bottom and in lid of grill. Light a large chimney starter full of charcoal, preferably hardwood. When the coals are lit, dump them out along opposite sides of bottom rack, leaving a space free of coals (the size of the quartered chicken) in middle. When you can hold your hand 5 inches above the grill rack directly over coals for 3 to 4 seconds, coals will be medium-hot. If using a gas grill, preheat all burners on high, then reduce the heat to medium-high.

2. Drain the chicken. Discard the marinade, then pat the chicken dry. Oil the grill rack, then grill the chicken over the area with no coals, skin side down first, covered, then turning over once, until cooked through, 30 to 35 minutes (add charcoal to maintain heat). Serve with lime wedges.

"A lot of flavor for a little effort . . . My eleven-year-old son, who usually barely notices his food, made a special point of asking me to add it to the regular rotation. Makes very tasty quesadillas later."

Laurena, San Francisco Bay Area, California

YIELD: MAKES 2 TO 4 SERVINGS

⅓ cup soy sauce
2 tablespoons fresh lime juice
5 garlic cloves
2 teaspoons ground cumin
1 teaspoon paprika
½ teaspoon dried oregano
½ teaspoon black pepper
1 tablespoon vegetable oil
1 whole chicken (about 3½ pounds), quartered
Lime wedges, for serving

Special equipment: Gas or charcoal grill (optional; see Note)

cook's note:

If you aren't able to grill outdoors, the quartered **CHICKEN** can be roasted in the middle of a 500°F oven in a 13 by 9-inch roasting pan with 1 cup water for 30 minutes; then tented with foil and roasted until browned and cooked through, about 15 minutes more.

grilled citrus chicken under a brick

Cooking with a brick might sound strange, but it is the key step in this Tuscan chicken dish. The brick flattens the butterflied chicken so it cooks faster and more evenly, keeping the bird moist and tender. Orange slices placed under the chicken's skin and a zesty herb marinade give this dish a smoky citrus flavor. Serve with a light salad for lunch, or pair it with a hearty potato dish and crunchy green vegetables for dinner.

YIELD: MAKES 4 SERVINGS

1 cup fresh orange juice
⅓ cup fresh lime juice
¼ cup fresh lemon juice
2 tablespoons olive oil
1 tablespoon finely chopped fresh
    oregano
3 teaspoons salt
2 teaspoons finely chopped fresh
    rosemary
1 garlic clove, chopped
1 chicken (about 3¾ pounds), neck and
    giblets removed, butterflied
1 teaspoon Hungarian sweet paprika
1 teaspoon black pepper
Nonstick vegetable-oil spray
1½ oranges

Special equipment: 2 foil-wrapped bricks
    (or cast-iron skillet); gas or charcoal
    grill

do ahead:

The **MARINADE** can be made 1 day ahead. Keep chilled.

"This is a really nice recipe for grilled chicken, and very easy to prepare in advance for a weekday dinner."
Happybaker1, Milwaukee, Wisconsin

1. Whisk the juices, oil, oregano, 1 teaspoon salt, the rosemary, and garlic in a glass baking dish. Add the chicken to marinade, turning to coat. Chill 2 hours, turning occasionally.

2. Mix the remaining 2 teaspoons salt, the paprika, and pepper in small bowl.

3. Spray a grill rack with nonstick spray. Prepare a grill to medium heat. Cut ½ orange into ¼- to ⅛-inch-thick slices.

4. Remove the chicken from the marinade; pat dry. Loosen the skin from the chicken breast and slide 1 to 2 orange slices between the skin and breast. Loosen the skin from the thighs and slide 1 to 2 orange slices between skin and thighs. Rub the paprika mixture over both sides of the chicken.

5. Place the chicken skin side down on the grill. Place the foil-wrapped bricks or a cast-iron skillet atop the chicken (if using bricks, position 1 brick over the top half of the chicken and 1 brick over the bottom half). Cover and grill until skin is crisp and brown, about 15 minutes. Remove bricks or skillet. Using tongs or 2 large spatulas, turn the chicken. Replace the bricks or skillet and cook, covered, until the chicken is cooked through, about 20 minutes longer. Let chicken rest 10 minutes.

6. Meanwhile, place a whole orange on the grill and cook until slightly charred, turning often, about 1 minute. Cut into wedges and serve alongside for squeezing over chicken.

southwestern lime chicken
with ancho chile sauce

Tender chicken shot through with a simple marinade and livened with a spicy-sweet Tex-Mex sauce works well for a casual dinner party or a regular old Wednesday night. This dish, originally from Golden Annie's in Frisco, Colorado, can be prepared in advance, although don't worry if you only have time to let the chicken marinate a few hours.

1. Combine the lime juice, soy sauce, oil, sugar, herbs, garlic, chili powder, and cayenne in a medium bowl; whisk to blend. Place the chicken in a 13 by 9-inch glass baking dish 2 inches deep. Pour the marinade over. Cover and refrigerate overnight, turning occasionally.

2. Prepare a grill to medium-high heat. Remove the chicken from the marinade and grill until just cooked through, turning occasionally, about 10 minutes. Place 1 cheese slice atop each chicken piece; cover the grill and cook until the cheese melts, about 2 minutes. Transfer the chicken to plates. Serve with Ancho Chile Sauce.

YIELD: MAKES 8 SERVINGS

½ cup fresh lime juice
6 tablespoons soy sauce
¼ cup vegetable oil
2 tablespoons sugar
2 tablespoons chopped fresh oregano
1 tablespoon chopped fresh rosemary
1 tablespoon minced garlic
1½ teaspoons chili powder
½ teaspoon cayenne
8 skinless boneless chicken breast halves
8 slices Monterey Jack cheese
Ancho Chile Sauce (recipe follows)

Special equipment: Gas or charcoal grill

ancho chile sauce

1. Place the chiles in a medium metal bowl. Pour enough boiling water over the chiles to cover. Let stand until soft, about 30 minutes. Drain, reserving ½ cup of the soaking liquid.

2. Purée the chiles, 3 tablespoons soaking liquid, and the lime juice in a blender until smooth. Transfer to a small bowl. Whisk in the mayonnaise, brown sugar, oregano, rosemary, and cumin. Season to taste with salt and pepper.

YIELD: MAKES ABOUT 1¼ CUPS

3 ancho chiles, stemmed, seeded, and
    torn into pieces
2 tablespoons fresh lime juice
½ cup mayonnaise
2 tablespoons (packed) brown sugar
1 tablespoon chopped fresh oregano
1 teaspoon chopped fresh rosemary
½ teaspoon ground cumin

"I don't use the melted cheese on top, as I typically serve with halved bell peppers that I grill and melt pepper Jack cheese in them."
A cook, San Diego, California

deviled fried chicken

"Deviled" is just a Southerner's way of saying "don't forget the spice." If you like deviled eggs, you'll probably love deviled chicken, marinated in a blend of buttermilk, cayenne, and dry mustard, then coated and fried. Like most good things that come out of the South, this recipe demands a leisurely pace. You'll want to marinate the chicken for at least a day, and then allow the chicken to rest in the seasoning for about an hour prior to frying. This is a supremely portable and packable recipe, since the chicken is delicious either hot or cold.

YIELD: MAKES 4 SERVINGS

2 cups buttermilk
¼ cup Dijon mustard
2 tablespoons onion powder (with green onion and parsley)
5 teaspoons salt
4 teaspoons dry mustard
4 teaspoons cayenne pepper
2½ teaspoons ground black pepper
1 (3- to 3¼-pound) chicken, backbone removed, chicken cut into 8 pieces, skinned (except wings)
3 cups all-purpose flour
1 tablespoon baking powder
1 tablespoon garlic powder
About 5 cups peanut oil, for frying

Special equipment: Deep-fry thermometer

"Be sure to remove any fried bits of coating that may be left in the oil before adding the next batch of pieces. Otherwise the excess batter bits will burn and/or stick to the chicken pieces as they fry. Serve with coleslaw, potato salad, and homemade cherry pie for a Southern feast."

Aldodson, Franklin, Kentucky

1. In a 1-gallon resealable plastic bag, mix the buttermilk, mustard, 1 tablespoon onion powder, 1 teaspoon salt, 1 teaspoon dry mustard, 1 teaspoon cayenne, and 1 teaspoon pepper. Add the chicken pieces. Seal the bag, eliminating air. Turn the bag to coat the chicken evenly. Refrigerate at least 1 day and up to 2 days, turning bag occasionally.

2. Whisk the flour, baking powder, garlic powder, remaining 1 tablespoon onion powder, 4 teaspoons salt, 3 teaspoons dry mustard, 3 teaspoons cayenne, and 1½ teaspoons pepper in a 13 by 9-inch glass dish. With marinade still clinging to the chicken pieces (do not shake off excess), add the chicken to the flour mixture, turning to coat thickly. Let the chicken stand in the flour mixture for 1 hour, turning chicken occasionally to recoat with flour mixture.

3. Pour the oil to a depth of 1¼ inches into a 10- to 11-inch pot. Attach a deep-fry thermometer. Heat the oil over medium-high heat to 350°F. Add 4 pieces of chicken, skin side down. Reduce the heat to medium-low and fry 5 minutes, adjusting heat to maintain oil temperature between 280° and 300°F (oil should bubble constantly around chicken). Using wooden spoons, turn the chicken over. Fry 7 minutes. Turn the chicken over again. Fry until deep golden brown and cooked through, about 3 minutes longer. Using the same spoons, transfer the chicken to a large rack set on a baking sheet.

4. Reheat the oil to 350°F. Repeat frying with the remaining 4 pieces of chicken. Serve the chicken warm or at room temperature within 2 hours, or chill up to 1 day and serve cold.

coffee-rubbed cheeseburgers
with texas barbecue sauce

Coffee and burgers are not your everyday combination, but you'll be surprised at the depth and complexity that freshly ground beans deliver when combined with brown sugar, pepper, coriander, and oregano. Bacon, along with the smoked cheese, is added to the patties while they finish up on the grill. Spoon on the Texas Barbecue Sauce, and crack open a brew.

YIELD: MAKES 8 SERVINGS

FOR COFFEE RUB
1 tablespoon freshly ground coffee powder
2 teaspoons (packed) light brown sugar
2 teaspoons freshly ground black pepper
½ teaspoon ground coriander
½ teaspoon dried oregano
½ teaspoon fine sea salt

FOR BURGERS
8 slices applewood-smoked bacon
1 pound ground chuck, preferably grass-fed
1 pound ground sirloin, preferably grass-fed
8 slices smoked provolone, smoked caciocavallo, or smoked Gouda cheese (about 8 ounces)
8 potato-bread hamburger buns
8 slices red onion
8 slices ripe tomato
Texas Barbecue Sauce (recipe follows)

Special equipment: Gas or charcoal grill

---

do ahead:

The **COFFEE RUB** can be made 1 week ahead. Store airtight at room temperature.

The **BACON** can be cooked and the **BURGERS** can be formed 8 hours ahead. Cover separately and chill.

MAKE COFFEE RUB
Mix all the ingredients in a small bowl.

MAKE BURGERS
1. Cook the bacon in a large skillet until crisp. Transfer to paper towels to drain. Break in half. Gently mix the chuck and sirloin in a large bowl. Form the meat into 8 patties, each 3 ½ to 4 inches in diameter and ⅓ to ½ inch thick. Using your thumb, make a slight indentation in the center of each burger.

2. Prepare the grill to medium-high heat. Sprinkle 1 teaspoon coffee rub on the top side of each burger. Place the burgers rub side down on the grill rack. Grill until slightly charred, about 4 minutes; turn.

3. Place 2 bacon halves atop each burger. Cook 3 minutes.

4. Top each burger with 1 cheese slice. Cover grill and cook until the cheese melts, about 1 minute longer.

5. Place the burgers atop the bottom halves of the buns. Top with the onion and tomato slices. Spoon a dollop of barbecue sauce over and cover with bun tops. Serve, passing additional sauce alongside.

"I used organic, grass-fed beef and smoked Gouda. Family devoured them. For the sauce, I used just a bit of chipotle hot sauce, as we like flavor, not heat. Then I let the sauce sit on superlow heat for an hour or two. Fantastic."

Wdm

texas barbecue sauce

Melt the butter in a medium saucepan over medium heat. Add the garlic; stir 30 seconds. Stir in ketchup and all remaining ingredients. Bring to a boil. Reduce the heat to medium-low; simmer until reduced to 1⅓ cups, stirring occasionally, about 15 minutes. Season with salt and pepper.

YIELD: MAKES ABOUT 1⅓ CUPS

1 tablespoon butter
1 garlic clove, minced
1 cup ketchup
⅓ cup (packed) light brown sugar
⅓ cup Worcestershire sauce
¼ cup fresh lemon juice
1 chipotle chile from canned chipotle chiles in adobo, minced with seeds
¼ teaspoon cayenne

do ahead:

The **SAUCE** can be made 1 week ahead. Cool slightly, cover, and chill.

coleslaw

No summer barbecue would be complete without a big bowl of creamy, tangy coleslaw. Use the Texas Barbecue Sauce above for a touch of Southwestern flavor.

Mix the mayonnaise, vinegar, barbecue sauce, and sugar in a large bowl. Mix in the cabbage. Season with salt and pepper. Chill at least 1 hour.

YIELD: MAKES 12 CUPS

1 cup mayonnaise
6 tablespoons cider vinegar
6 tablespoons barbecue sauce
3 tablespoons sugar
12 cups (lightly packed) shredded green cabbage (about 2 small heads)

Coffee-Rubbed Cheeseburgers with
Texas Barbecue Sauce (page 148)

Dominican Chimichurri
Burgers (page 152)

dominican chimichurri burgers

These multispiced patties are a step up from basic backyard burgers, infused with a laundry list of herbs and chopped veggies. Grab a handful of napkins and prepare for a messy masterpiece.

YIELD: MAKES 4 SERVINGS

1¼ pounds ground beef chuck
1 medium onion, finely chopped
½ large red bell pepper, diced
2 garlic cloves, minced
⅓ cup chopped fresh cilantro
1 teaspoon dried oregano
2 teaspoons soy sauce
1 tablespoon Worcestershire sauce
½ teaspoon salt
½ teaspoon pepper
4 hamburger buns, split
2 cups thinly sliced green cabbage
1 medium carrot, coarsely grated
1 small red onion, cut into rings
1 medium tomato, sliced ¼ inch thick
2 tablespoons ketchup
2 tablespoons mayonnaise
1 tablespoon yellow mustard

"Very nice and tasty. It reminded me of the burgers from the street stands in many different countries. Make sure to pack the burgers tightly . . . they can fall apart pretty easily."
Alshash, Minneapolis, Minnesota

1. Mix the beef, onion, bell pepper, garlic, cilantro, oregano, soy sauce, Worcestershire sauce, salt, and pepper. Form into 4 (4½-inch-wide) patties.

2. Heat a large griddle or 12-inch heavy skillet over medium heat until hot, then lightly toast the buns.

3. Oil the griddle, then cook the patties, turning once, about 8 minutes total for medium-rare. Transfer to the buns.

4. Mix the cabbage, carrot, and salt to taste, then cook, turning occasionally, until slightly wilted, about 2 minutes. Divide among burgers.

5. Oil the griddle again, then sear the onion and tomato, turning once, until slightly charred, about 2 minutes total. Divide among burgers.

6. Stir together the ketchup, mayonnaise, and mustard, then top burgers with sauce.

mushroom kasha burgers
with chipotle mayonnaise

This grain-based veggie burger is an excellent change from traditional bean or tofu varieties. Cooked kasha's firmness balances the soft sautéed vegetables for a robust texture.

1. Bring water to a boil in a 1½-quart heavy saucepan, then stir in the kasha. Cover and reduce the heat to low, then cook until the kasha is tender and the water is absorbed, about 10 minutes. Transfer to a bowl and cool. Break one-third of the mushrooms into a food processor and pulse until finely chopped, then transfer to a bowl. Repeat with the remaining 2 batches of mushrooms, transferring to the bowl.

2. Cook the onion and bell pepper in the butter in a 12-inch heavy skillet over medium heat, stirring occasionally, until softened, about 5 minutes. Add the chopped mushrooms, the garlic, ¾ teaspoon salt, and ½ teaspoon pepper and cook over medium-high heat, stirring occasionally, until any liquid the mushrooms give off is evaporated and the mushrooms begin to brown, 8 to 10 minutes. Transfer the mixture to a large bowl, then stir in the kasha, parsley, soy sauce, and ½ cup bread crumbs until combined well. Cool 10 minutes, then stir in the egg until combined well.

3. Line a platter with foil. Spread the remaining 1 cup bread crumbs in a shallow baking dish. Form one-fourth of the mushroom mixture (about ¾ cup) into a ¾-inch-thick patty (3½ inches in diameter), then dredge in bread crumbs, knocking off excess, and transfer to the platter. Form and dredge 3 more patties, transferring each to platter. Chill the patties, loosely covered with plastic wrap, 1 hour.

4. Heat the oil in a clean 12-inch heavy skillet over medium-high heat until it shimmers, then fry the patties, turning over once, until deep golden, about 4 minutes total. Transfer the patties to paper towels to drain (patties will be soft).

5. Meanwhile, whisk together the mayonnaise and chipotle sauce. Spread the bread with chipotle mayonnaise and sandwich each mushroom patty between 2 slices.

YIELD: MAKES 4 SERVINGS

⅔ cup water
⅓ cup coarse kasha (whole roasted buckwheat groats)*
1 pound portobello mushrooms, stems discarded
1 cup finely chopped onion
1 cup finely chopped red bell pepper
3 tablespoons unsalted butter
2 garlic cloves, finely chopped
3 tablespoons finely chopped fresh flat-leaf parsley
1 teaspoon soy sauce
1½ cups fine dry bread crumbs
1 large egg, lightly beaten
¼ cup olive oil
½ cup mayonnaise
1 tablespoon Tabasco chipotle sauce, or to taste
8 large oval slices rye bread, cut into 4½-inch rounds if desired, lightly toasted

* Sold at health food stores

do ahead:

The **PATTIES** can be formed, without bread-crumb coating, 12 hours ahead and chilled, covered.

"I used a 2-tablespoon cookie scoop and I got a total of 22 slider-size patties out of this recipe."
Akalish, New York City

bourbon-glazed baby back ribs

These ribs spend about an hour bathing in pineapple juice while they cook. A glaze combining Asian ingredients—hoisin and plum sauces plus hot chile paste—with bourbon, honey, and molasses is brushed on the meat while it's finished on the grill. The slightly spicy ribs will be on everyone's favorite food list.

YIELD: MAKES 6 SERVINGS

5 tablespoons honey
¼ cup bourbon
1½ tablespoons hoisin sauce
1 tablespoon Dijon mustard
1 tablespoon plum sauce
1½ teaspoons unsulfured (light) molasses
1½ teaspoons soy sauce
1½ teaspoons Worcestershire sauce
¾ teaspoon hot chile paste, such as
    sambal oelek
¼ teaspoon salt
¼ teaspoon ground black pepper
2 (2¼ to 2½-pound) racks of baby back
    pork ribs
1 cup unsweetened pineapple juice

Special equipment: Gas or charcoal grill

do ahead:

The **GLAZE** can be made 1 day ahead. Cover and refrigerate.

The **RIBS** can be made 1 day ahead (through step 3). Cover with plastic wrap; refrigerate.

1. Whisk the honey, bourbon, hoisin, mustard, plum sauce, molasses, soy sauce, Worcestershire, chile paste, salt, and pepper in a small bowl.

2. Preheat the oven to 350°F. Place a long sheet of heavy-duty foil on each of 2 large rimmed baking sheets. Sprinkle the rib racks on all sides with salt and pepper. Place one rib rack on each foil sheet. Fold up the sides of each foil sheet around the rib rack to form a boat-like shape.

3. Pour ½ cup pineapple juice over each rib rack. Fold up foil to seal packets. Bake until ribs are tender, about 1 hour. Remove the ribs from the foil packets. Transfer to a roasting pan; pour any juices from the foil over and cool.

4. Prepare a grill to medium heat. Cut each rib rack in half. Grill until browned, brushing frequently with glaze and turning often, about 10 minutes. Cut racks between bones into ribs.

"Didn't have plum sauce so used fig preserves and didn't have chile paste so used chili and garlic sauce. Yummy!! Baked for 2½ hours at 275°F then broiled with glaze for a few minutes on each side. Served with corn cakes and salad and full-bodied Spanish wine."

Maywall

pork barbecue sandwiches *with coleslaw*

Serious about pulled pork? Do it right with this hard-core recipe, which seasons the meat in three stages, so that each bite is flavorful and tender. Serve on a toasted bun with the coleslaw.

MAKE BARBECUE SAUCE

Melt the butter in a heavy large saucepan over medium heat. Add the onion and sauté 3 minutes. Add the remaining sauce ingredients and bring to a boil, stirring frequently. Reduce the heat and simmer until the sauce is reduced to 2⅔ cups, stirring occasionally, about 30 minutes. Season to taste with salt and pepper.

MAKE DRY SEASONING RUB

Mix all ingredients in a small bowl.

MAKE BARBECUE MOP

Mix all ingredients in bowl. Set aside until ready to use.

MAKE PORK

1. Place the pork, fat side up, on the work surface. Cut each pork piece lengthwise in half, forming total of 4 long strips. Place the pork on a baking sheet. Sprinkle the rub all over the pork, rubbing it in and covering completely. Cover and chill at least 2 hours and up to 6 hours.

2. Place the wood chips in a large bowl. Cover with cold water and let stand 30 minutes. Place a handful of torn newspaper into the bottom of a charcoal chimney. Top with 25 charcoal briquettes. Remove the upper rack from a charcoal grill. Place the chimney on the lower grill rack. Light the newspaper and let the charcoal burn until gray ash color, about 30 minutes.

3. Open 1 bottom grill vent. Turn out the hot charcoal onto one side of the lower rack. Using a metal spatula, spread the charcoal to cover approximately one-third of the rack. Remove 1 cup of wood chips from the water and drain (keep remaining chips in water). Scatter over the coals (avoid using too many wet chips, which may douse the fire). Fill a foil loaf pan halfway with water and place on the lower grill rack on the opposite side of the coals.

YIELD: MAKES 12 SANDWICHES

FOR BARBECUE SAUCE
¼ cup (½ stick) unsalted butter
6 tablespoons minced onion
1⅓ cups cider vinegar
1⅓ cups ketchup
1 cup (packed) dark brown sugar
1 teaspoon Worcestershire sauce
¼ teaspoon cayenne

FOR DRY SEASONING RUB
3 tablespoons coarsely ground black
    pepper
3 tablespoons dark brown sugar
3 tablespoons paprika
2 tablespoons salt
1 teaspoon cayenne

FOR BARBECUE MOP
1 cup cider vinegar
½ cup water
1 tablespoon Worcestershire sauce
1 tablespoon coarsely ground black
    pepper
1 tablespoon salt
2 teaspoons vegetable oil
½ teaspoon cayenne

> ## do ahead:
>
> The **SAUCE** can be prepared 1 week ahead. Cover and refrigerate.
>
> The **RUB** can be made 1 week ahead. Store airtight.

recipe continues

FOR PORK

2 untrimmed boneless halves of pork shoulder (Boston butt; about 6 pounds total weight)

12 soft hamburger buns with sesame seeds, warmed

12 cups coleslaw, homemade or store-bought

Coleslaw (page 149)

Special equipment: Charcoal grill with lid; chimney lighter; candy thermometer; 4 cups hickory wood (smoke) chips; 20-pound sack charcoal briquettes

"Used this for a big party. Rave reviews, many asked for the recipe. The hardest part was shredding the pork—that took time. This is definitely a plan-ahead dish, with all the smoking and shredding. I did use the bagged slaw, which saved cabbage chopping time."

A cook, Portland, Oregon

4. Place the upper grill rack on the grill. Arrange the pork fat side up on the upper grill rack above the loaf pan. Cover the grill with the lid, positioning the top vent directly over the pork. Place the stem of a candy thermometer through the top vent, with the gauge on the outside and the tip near the pork (thermometer should not touch meat or grill rack); leave in place during cooking. Check temperature after 5 minutes. Use the top and bottom vents to maintain a temperature range between 225° and 250°F, opening the vents wider to increase heat and closing to decrease heat. Leave any other vents closed.

5. After 30 minutes, light an additional 15 charcoal briquettes in the same charcoal chimney set atop bricks, cement, or other nonflammable surface. When the cooking temperature falls below 225°F, use oven mitts to lift off the upper grill rack with the pork and place on a heatproof surface. Using tongs, add half of the hot gray charcoal to the bottom rack. Sprinkle about 1 cup drained wood chips over the charcoal as well. Reposition the upper rack on the grill with the pork above the loaf pan. Brush the pork lightly with the mop. Cover with lid.

6. About once an hour, light more charcoal in the chimney and replenish the charcoal and wood chips as necessary to maintain a temperature between 225° and 250°F, brushing the pork lightly with the mop each time the grill is opened. Open the grill only when necessary and cover as quickly as possible to minimize loss of heat and smoke. Cook the pork until an instant-read thermometer inserted into the center of the meat registers between 165° and 170°F, turning occasionally, about 3 hours total. Transfer the pork to a baking sheet. Let stand 10 minutes.

7. When cool enough to handle, shred the pork into bite-size pieces, discarding any fat. Mix any meat juices accumulated on the baking sheet into the pork. Spoon the pork onto bottom halves of buns. Drizzle with sauce. Top with coleslaw and bun tops.

grilled butterflied leg of lamb
with lemon, herbs, and garlic

Looking for a spectacular dish to wow friends and family? Give them some leg. Have your butcher butterfly the leg of lamb, and use metal skewers to secure any loose meat as it cooks. If you find yourself with leftovers, pair them with toasted pita and hummus.

MAKE HERB RUB

Finely chop the garlic and in a small bowl stir together with the remaining rub ingredients.

MAKE LAMB

1. Put the lamb in a large dish and, with tip of a sharp small knife held at a 45-degree angle, cut ½-inch-deep slits all over lamb, rubbing the herb mixture into the slits and all over the lamb. Marinate the lamb at room temperature 1 hour.

2. Prepare a grill.

3. Lightly pat the lamb dry. On a lightly oiled rack set 5 to 6 inches over glowing coals (or in a medium-hot gas grill), grill the lamb about 10 minutes on each side, or until an instant-read thermometer horizontally inserted into the thickest part of the meat registers 125°F for medium-rare. (Alternatively, roast the lamb in a roasting pan in the middle of a 425°F oven about 25 minutes.)

4. Transfer the lamb to a cutting board. Halve and seed the lemon. Squeeze the juice over the lamb and let stand, loosely covered with foil, 15 minutes.

5. Cut the lamb into slices and serve with any juices that have accumulated on the cutting board.

YIELD: MAKES 8 SERVINGS

FOR HERB RUB

8 garlic cloves
3 tablespoons chopped fresh thyme leaves
2 tablespoons chopped fresh rosemary leaves
2 tablespoons chopped fresh parsley leaves
½ teaspoon freshly ground black pepper
1 tablespoon kosher or other coarse salt
3 tablespoons olive oil

FOR LAMB

1 (7- to 8-pound) leg of lamb, trimmed of all fat, boned, and butterflied by butcher (4 to 4 ¾ pounds boneless)
1 lemon

Special equipment: Gas or charcoal grill (optional)

"This is the best recipe for lamb I've ever tried. I serve it regularly at dinner parties and have adapted it for other cuts of lamb. The fresh herb rub is great on rack of lamb, served with a wild mushroom risotto and steamed green beans, then drizzled with the lemon-flavored jus."
A cook, British Columbia, Canada

grilled asian flank steak *with sweet slaw*

With just a few ingredients, many of which are probably already in your pantry, you get a satisfying and flavor-packed meal with this steak and slaw combo. Red jalapeños are simply the ripe form of the green ones, and either version works in this slaw. If you're nervous about the heat, remove the seeds and veins from the peppers or use one instead of two. Serranos make a spicier substitute.

1. Prepare a grill to medium heat. Mix the soy sauce, oil, 3 teaspoons ginger, and the garlic in a resealable plastic bag. Add the flank steak and seal the bag; turn to coat. Let stand at room temperature 30 minutes, turning occasionally.

2. Stir the sugar and vinegar in a small saucepan over medium heat until the sugar dissolves; remove from the heat. Add the jalapeños and remaining 2 teaspoons ginger.

3. Place the cabbage and ½ cup green onions in a medium bowl. Pour the vinegar mixture over and toss to coat. Season with salt and pepper. Let stand while grilling steak, tossing occasionally.

4. Grill the steak until cooked to desired doneness, about 6 minutes per side for medium-rare. Transfer to a work surface. Let rest 10 minutes. Slice the steak thinly against grain. Sprinkle the remaining ¼ cup green onions over the slaw.

YIELD: MAKES 4 SERVINGS

¼ cup soy sauce
5 tablespoons vegetable oil
5 teaspoons minced peeled fresh ginger
1 garlic clove, pressed
1 (1½-pound) flank steak
3 tablespoons sugar
3 tablespoons seasoned rice vinegar
2 red jalapeño chiles, thinly sliced into rounds
5 cups thinly sliced napa cabbage (about 9 ounces)
¾ cup chopped green onions

Special equipment: Gas or charcoal grill

"Made this following the directions (except that I broiled the flank steak because of the weather) and it was a big hit with the family. The marinade is not too overpowering for the children. The slaw was especially good. I will definitely use the dressing again and might add a few more veggies to the slaw, like carrots and peppers."
A cook, Bellevue, Washington

chili beef skewers

Chef Jean-Georges Vongerichten shares his secret beef skewer recipe from his famed restaurant Spice Market in New York City. Alternate the beef and peppers on each skewer to achieve a balance between charred and crunchy, juicy and tender. And don't forget the creamy citrus-basil dipping sauce.

YIELD: MAKES 4 SERVINGS

FOR MARINADE AND BEEF
½ cup fresh cilantro leaves
4 garlic cloves, thinly sliced
3 tablespoons low-sodium soy sauce
1 teaspoon grated orange zest
1 teaspoon sriracha sauce
2 teaspoons Asian fish sauce, such as nam pla or nuoc mam
1 teaspoon brown sugar
1 pound lean beef sirloin, cut into ⅛-inch strips

FOR DIPPING SAUCE
½ cup low-fat mayonnaise
2 tablespoons chopped fresh basil leaves
1 tablespoon fresh lime juice

1 each red, green, and yellow bell pepper, cored, seeded, and cut into 2½-inch pieces (optional)
Nonstick vegetable-oil spray

Special equipment: 8 wooden skewers; gas or charcoal grill

1. Soak the skewers for 30 minutes.

2. Purée the cilantro, garlic, soy sauce, orange zest, sriracha, 1 teaspoon fish sauce, and the sugar in a food processor. Transfer the marinade to a resealable plastic bag; add the beef. Seal the bag, toss, and set aside 30 minutes.

3. Combine the mayonnaise, basil, lime juice, and remaining 1 teaspoon fish sauce in a small bowl.

4. Thread 4 pieces of bell pepper and 2 beef strips on each skewer, alternating the beef and peppers. Coat the grill rack with vegetable-oil spray; heat the grill to high, then cook until meat is no longer pink, about 3 minutes.

"I have vegetarians in the family, so I substitute extra-firm organic tofu for the beef. A great vegetarian meal with baked yams."
A cook, Vancouver, Canada

porterhouse steak
with pan-seared cherry tomatoes

When an amazing necklace meets a little black dress, or when a red silk tie meets a gray flannel suit, something basic is magically transformed into something stylish and memorable. Just so with the seared tomatoes that top off this delicious steak dinner. The bright summery topping makes a chunky, natural sauce for the steak and creates a meal that's more than the sum of its parts.

1. Preheat the oven to 375°F, with a rack in the middle.

2. Heat 1 tablespoon oil in a 12-inch heavy skillet (preferably cast-iron) over medium-high heat until it shimmers.

3. Meanwhile, pat the steaks dry and sprinkle with salt and pepper. Sear the steaks 1 at a time, turning once, until well browned, about 10 minutes total per steak.

4. Transfer the steaks to a shallow baking pan (do not clean skillet) and cook in the oven until an instant-read thermometer inserted in the center registers 120°F for medium-rare, about 6 minutes. Transfer to a platter and let stand 15 minutes.

5. While steaks stand, pour off the oil from the skillet. Add the remaining 2 tablespoons oil and heat over medium-high heat until it shimmers, then sauté the garlic until golden, about 2 minutes. Transfer with a slotted spoon to a plate.

6. Add the tomatoes and thyme to the hot oil (be careful; oil will spatter), then lightly season with salt and pepper and cook, covered, stirring occasionally, just until tomatoes begin to wilt, about 2 minutes. Stir in any meat juices from the platter, then scatter the basil over the tomatoes and spoon over the steaks.

YIELD: MAKES 4 SERVINGS

3 tablespoons olive oil
2 (1½-inch-thick) porterhouse steaks
    (about 1¾ pounds each)
4 teaspoons kosher salt
1½ teaspoons pepper
6 large garlic cloves, thinly sliced
    lengthwise
4 (½-pint) containers mixed cherry
    tomatoes
6 large sprigs fresh thyme
1½ cups coarsely torn fresh basil leaves

"I served this with polenta and a salad of shaved fennel that I tossed with some lemon, olive oil, Parmesan, and basil."
A cook, Ann Arbor, Michigan

dilled potato and pickled cucumber salad

Jazz up a traditional summer staple with this extra-fresh side dish. Usually potato salads are dense dishes drenched in mayonnaise, but this version provides a boost in flavor and texture with cucumbers, onions, radishes, and dill. Be sure to leave ample time for preparation, as the recipe requires you to pickle the cucumbers overnight. Prepare an extra batch; the pickled cucumbers make a great snack on their own and add a satisfying crunch to other salads and sandwiches and will last in the refrigerator for several days.

YIELD: MAKES 8 SERVINGS

6 tablespoons white vinegar
4 teaspoons kosher salt, plus more as needed
2 (1-pound) English hothouse cucumbers, very thinly sliced
½ cup plus 3 tablespoons chopped fresh dill
3¼ pounds Yukon Gold potatoes (about 10 medium), unpeeled
1 cup very thinly sliced white onion
8 radishes, trimmed, thinly sliced
¾ cup mayonnaise
Small radishes with green tops, for garnish

do ahead:

The **SALAD** can be made 1 day ahead. Cover and refrigerate.

"Well worth the pickling work the night before. The cucumbers were ultra salty—I remedied this by rinsing them in water, then in vinegar, followed by the drying time."
Whiterabbbit, Orange County, California

1. Stir the vinegar and 4 teaspoons coarse salt in a small bowl until the salt dissolves. Place the cucumbers and ½ cup dill in a heavy 1-gallon resealable plastic bag. Add the vinegar mixture; seal the bag. Turn several times to coat. Refrigerate overnight, turning bag occasionally.

2. Pour the cucumber mixture into a large sieve set over a bowl. Drain at least 1 hour and up to 3 hours. Discard brine.

3. Cook the potatoes in a large pot of boiling salted water until tender, about 30 minutes. Drain. Cool the potatoes completely. Peel the potatoes; quarter lengthwise. Cut crosswise into ½-inch-thick slices. Place the potatoes in a large bowl; sprinkle generously with coarse salt and pepper.

4. Add the drained cucumbers, onion, sliced radishes, and remaining 3 tablespoons dill; toss to blend. Let stand 1 hour. Stir the mayonnaise into the salad. Season generously with salt and pepper, if desired.

5. Mound the salad in a bowl; garnish with whole radishes. Serve cold or at room temperature.

sweet potato salad
with spicy peanut dressing

This summery way to serve yams is great with hoisin-glazed ribs or pork chops. Experiment by swapping the spuds for rice to create another filling vegetarian meal, or serve the creamy dressing as a dip for chicken satay.

1. Whisk the vinegar, soy sauce, mayonnaise, ginger, sesame oil, garlic, peanut butter, chili-garlic sauce, and sugar in a medium bowl to blend.

2. Add enough water to a large saucepan to reach a depth of ½ inch. Bring to a boil; add the sweet potatoes and cook until just tender, about 5 minutes. Drain; cool.

3. Mix the sweet potatoes, dressing, peas, and green onions in a large bowl. Season the salad with salt and pepper.

4. Sprinkle the salad with peanuts and serve.

"I made it as called for, except that I used light mayo and threw the dressing into the blender. I doubled it, and didn't think I'd have enough of it the way people were eating it."

A cook, Chicago, Illinois

YIELD: MAKES 6 TO 8 SERVINGS

¼ cup rice vinegar
¼ cup soy sauce
3 tablespoons mayonnaise
4 teaspoons minced peeled fresh ginger
4 teaspoons Asian sesame oil
4 garlic cloves, minced
1 tablespoon peanut butter
2 teaspoons chili-garlic sauce
1½ teaspoons light brown sugar
2 pounds red-skinned sweet potatoes, peeled and cut into ½-inch cubes
1½ cups sugar snap peas, cut crosswise into ½ inch pieces
1 cup thinly sliced green onions
⅓ cup coarsely chopped dry-roasted peanuts

do ahead:

The **DRESSING** can be made 4 hours ahead. Cover and refrigerate.

baked zucchini fries
with tomato coulis dipping sauce

Zucchini replaces the traditional starchy potato, making this a great way to get your kids to love their veggies. Plus, the dipping sauce is ketchup on steroids.

1. Combine the coulis ingredients in a blender and pureé. Transfer to a sauté pan and cook over medium heat until fragrant and warmed through, 3 to 5 minutes. Transfer to the refrigerator to cool.

2. Preheat the oven to 350°F.

3. In a medium bowl, combine the bread crumbs, salt, and pepper. Place the flour in another medium bowl and the eggs in a smaller bowl. Dip the zucchini sticks first in the flour until lightly coated, then in the beaten eggs. Roll them in the bread-crumb mixture until well covered.

4. Transfer the zucchini pieces to a nonstick baking sheet and bake until the zucchini is tender but the coating is crisp, about 20 minutes. Let the fries cool slightly before eating. Serve with the coulis as a dipping sauce.

YIELD: MAKES 6 TO 8 SERVINGS

FOR TOMATO COULIS
1 pound ripe tomatoes, peeled, cored, and diced
2 tablespoons white-wine vinegar
1 tablespoon honey
1 tablespoon minced shallot or onion
2 teaspoons chopped fresh basil
Kosher salt and freshly ground black pepper

FOR FRIES
1 cup unseasoned bread crumbs
½ teaspoon kosher salt
¼ teaspoon freshly ground black pepper
1 cup all-purpose flour
2 large eggs, lightly beaten
3 medium zucchini, cut lengthwise into 2-inch-long pieces ¼ inch thick

"I served the fries with ranch dressing instead, and that was really yummy!"
Jennchsm01, Austin, Texas

corn on the cob *with cheese and lime*

Like Mexico's better-known culinary exports—guacamole, tacos, and tequila—Mexican-style corn (*elote*) is finding its place in restaurants, street carts, and home kitchens across North America. Given how available the ingredients are and how quickly it can be prepared, it's no wonder that it's a new favorite. Grilling lends an earthiness to the corn, but if grilling is not an option, boil it instead. It's worth seeking out cotija, a Mexican cow's-milk cheese, but in a pinch, Parmesan or feta will do.

YIELD: MAKES 2 SERVINGS

4 ears of corn in the husk
¼ cup mayonnaise
⅛ teaspoon cayenne, or to taste
¾ cup shredded cotija or feta cheese
Lime wedges, for serving

Special equipment: Gas or charcoal grill

"I recommend mixing the lime juice into the mayonnaise. We tried it both ways and prefer that to drizzling on top of the cheese."
Thomaskurt, Seattle, Washington

1. Prepare the grill.

2. Soak the corn in the husk in cold water 10 minutes. Drain and grill on a rack set 5 to 6 inches over glowing coals until husks are charred, about 10 minutes. Shuck the corn and grill until kernels are browned in spots, about 10 minutes.

3. While corn is grilling, in a small bowl, whisk together the mayonnaise and cayenne. Using the small teardrop-shaped holes on a four-sided grater, grate the cheese.

4. Brush the mayonnaise mixture onto the hot corn and sprinkle with cheese.

5. Serve corn on the cob with lime wedges.

stewed corn and tomatoes *with okra*

Maque choux, a traditional Cajun dish of fresh corn, stewed tomatoes, and tender okra, is guaranteed to bring a burst of juicy heat to herb-roasted chicken or a meaty white fish. Mop up the savory side with a corn muffin or pair it with freshly grated Parmesan cheese. Requiring nothing more than chopping and sautéing, this side is an easy go-to dish for summertime fare.

YIELD: MAKES 6 SERVINGS

6 green onions, chopped
1 fresh jalapeño chile, finely chopped, with seeds
1 large green bell pepper, coarsely chopped
½ teaspoon salt
3 tablespoons unsalted butter
1 pound ripe tomatoes, coarsely chopped
3 cups corn kernels (5 to 6 ears)
½ pound small fresh okra, trimmed, keeping stem end intact

"I added fresh basil at the end to really perk up the flavors. Best served at room temperature, this dish travels well to potluck gatherings."

A cook, Washington, D.C.

1. Cook the onions, jalapeño, bell pepper, and salt in the butter in a 12-inch heavy skillet over medium heat, stirring occasionally, until onions begin to brown, 7 to 9 minutes. Stir in the tomatoes and cook, stirring occasionally, until broken down into a sauce, about 15 minutes.

2. Add the corn and okra and cook, stirring occasionally, until just tender, about 15 minutes.

roasted tomatillo salsa

Freshly husked and oven-broiled, roasted tomatillos provide a smoky warmth you just won't find in jarred salsa. To reduce the sodium here, use half the suggested amount of salt; the flavor will pick right back up with tortilla chips. While fresh tomatillos are an end-of-summer through fall item, you can use the canned variety to whip this up; and play around with the pepper selection to personalize your dip and control the heat.

1. Preheat the broiler.

2. If using fresh tomatillos, remove the husks and rinse the tomatillos under warm water to remove stickiness. If using canned tomatillos, drain and measure out 2 cups.

3. Broil the chiles, garlic, and fresh tomatillos (do not broil canned) on the rack of a broiler pan 1 to 2 inches from heat, turning once, until tomatillos are softened and slightly charred, about 7 minutes.

4. Peel the garlic and pull off the tops of the chiles. Purée all the ingredients in a blender.

"Not for the faint of tongue! The smell of roasted tomatillos, serranos, and garlic will transport you to Mexico when you purée. Mixes lusciously with mashed avocado and added to scrambled eggs or as a topping for grilled fish."
Domessmith, Irvine, California

YIELD: MAKES ABOUT 3 CUPS

1½ pounds fresh tomatillos, or
   3 (11-ounce) cans tomatillos
5 serrano chiles
3 garlic cloves, unpeeled
½ cup fresh cilantro leaves
1 large onion, coarsely chopped
2 teaspoons coarse salt

do ahead:

The **SALSA** can be made 1 day ahead and covered and chilled.

avocado-mango salsa

For your next Tex-Mex dinner, opt for this colorful summer salsa that features seasonal ingredients such as avocado, green onions, and mango. Serve it with black beans and rice, or heap it on jerk chicken or grilled fish for a fresh and healthy lunch or dinner any night of the week.

YIELD: MAKES ABOUT 3 CUPS

1 ripe mango, peeled, seeded, and diced
1 medium tomato, seeded and diced
2 green onions, finely sliced
¼ cup fresh lime juice
1 jalapeño chile, minced
1 avocado, peeled, seeded, and diced

1. Combine the mango, tomato, onions, lime juice, and jalapeño in a bowl.

2. Stir in the diced avocado and season to taste with salt and pepper.

"This recipe is amazing. I have used it with tilapia, grilled salmon, as a filling for veggie spring rolls, and as an appetizer with chips. Each time it has been a hit!"

Thorpc, Chicago, Illinois

guacamole *with fresh corn and chipotle*

Add a chipotle chile for a subtle kick to this chunky guacamole, then serve it with multicolored corn tortilla chips for a stunning platter. Double the recipe if you plan to serve a crowd.

YIELD: MAKES ABOUT 2 CUPS

2 large ripe avocados (about 1½ pounds), halved, pitted, and peeled
1 tablespoon fresh lime juice
1 ear of corn (raw or cooked)
1 plum tomato, seeded and diced
2 green onions, chopped
1 chipotle chile from a can, finely chopped
¼ cup sour cream

1. Mash the avocados with the lime juice in a medium bowl. Using sharp knife, remove the kernels from the corn cob and add to avocado mixture. Stir in the tomato and green onions.

2. Combine the chipotle and sour cream in a small bowl; whisk to blend. Stir the cream mixture into the avocado mixture. Season with salt.

"I grill the corn directly on a grate over charcoal before cutting it off the cob and adding it to the recipe."

A cook, Atlanta, Georgia

do ahead:

The **GUACAMOLE** can be made 4 hours ahead. Place plastic wrap directly onto surface of guacamole and refrigerate.

greek salad *with orzo and black-eyed peas*

This salad is low in calories and high in fiber, so why not double the recipe? The ingredients can be assembled in jars and stored in your fridge, making it easy to pack and carry to work or the beach. Simply mix it up and serve at room temperature with a side of toasted pita chips so you can scoop up every bit of the oregano and vinegar dressing.

1. Cook the orzo according to package instructions. Drain in a sieve and rinse under cold water until cool. Drain well.

2. Toss the black-eyed peas, tomato, and parsley with the vinegar, 1 tablespoon oil, ½ teaspoon salt, and ¼ teaspoon pepper. Marinate, stirring occasionally, 15 minutes.

3. Meanwhile, toss together the orzo, remaining 1 tablespoon oil, the cucumber, olives, onion, lemon zest and juice, oregano, remaining ½ teaspoon salt, and remaining ¼ teaspoon pepper in a large bowl.

4. Divide the black-eyed-pea mixture (with juices) among the jars and layer the orzo salad, romaine, and feta on top. Add 1 or 2 peperoncini to each jar.

"I've also put this inside a pita, inside a tortilla, and on top of baby spinach."

Hollie26, Kitchener, Canada

YIELD: MAKES 4 SERVINGS

¾ cup orzo
1 (15-ounce) can black-eyed peas, drained and rinsed
1 large tomato, diced (1 cup)
2 tablespoons chopped fresh flat-leaf parsley
2 tablespoons red-wine vinegar
2 tablespoons extra-virgin olive oil
1 teaspoon salt
½ teaspoon black pepper
½ seedless cucumber, halved lengthwise, cored, and diced (1 cup)
½ cup pitted kalamata olives, slivered
⅓ cup thinly sliced red onion
1 teaspoon grated lemon zest
2 tablespoons fresh lemon juice
1 tablespoon finely chopped fresh oregano leaves
2 to 3 cups coarsely chopped romaine
½ pound feta, crumbled (1 cup)
4 to 8 peperoncini

Pita chips, for serving

Special equipment: 4 (16-ounce) wide-mouth jars or containers with lids

do ahead:

ASSEMBLED JARS can be chilled up to 6 hours. Serve at room temperature.

spanish rice plus

This dish from Epicurious member **Christopher Curtis** of Halifax, Canada, pairs well with Mexican, barbecue, or various fish dishes. Easy to make, the rice is infused with natural smoke from the grilled corn and peppers. Add chipotles to enhance that smokiness, or throw in some sausage, such as chorizo, for a meaty main course.

YIELD: MAKES 6 TO 8 (SIDE DISH) SERVINGS

1 ear of corn, shucked
1 red bell pepper
1 green bell pepper
1 fresh jalapeño chile
1 tablespoon olive oil
1 small sweet onion, diced
2 shallots, minced
4 garlic cloves, minced
1 cup long-grain white rice
1 (28-ounce) can diced tomatoes,
    or 3 cups diced fresh
1 (15-ounce) can black beans, rinsed and
    drained
2 tablespoons coarsely chopped pitted
    green olives
½ teaspoon cayenne
1 teaspoon kosher salt
1 teaspoon freshly ground black pepper
½ cup water
¼ cup (loosely packed) coarsely chopped
    fresh cilantro leaves

Special equipment: Gas or charcoal grill

1. Preheat the grill to moderately high heat. Grill the corn, red and green peppers, and jalapeño until charred, about 4 minutes for the jalapeño and 8 minutes for the corn and bell peppers. Transfer the corn to a plate to cool.

2. Place the peppers in a bowl, cover with plastic wrap, and let cool. When cool enough to handle, gently remove the skin from each pepper, then chop the flesh and remove and discard the seeds. Once the corn is cool enough to handle, cut the kernels off the cob.

3. In a large, straight-sided skillet over moderate heat, heat the oil until hot but not smoking. Cook the onion, shallots, and garlic, stirring occasionally, until aromatic and just beginning to soften, about 5 minutes. Add the rice and continue cooking, stirring occasionally, until pale golden brown, about 5 minutes. Add the tomatoes and their juices, black beans, olives, cayenne, salt, and pepper. Stir in the corn, bell peppers, and jalapeño, and add water.

4. Cook, stirring occasionally, until the rice is tender, about 20 minutes. Transfer to a serving bowl, garnish with the cilantro, and serve immediately.

My family loves to have fajitas, enchiladas, or ribs when we get together for big family meals. When I served Spanish Rice, they loved it, so then the trick was to adjust the recipe to better complement the flavors of whatever was being served. This version is their favorite.

—Christopher Curtis

gingered bulgur salad *with grapes*

This bulgur salad makes a delicious and healthy side. It travels well, too.

1. In a bowl, stir together the bulgur and salt. Stir in the hot water and let stand, covered, 30 minutes.

2. Slice the grapes and chop the cilantro. Mince the garlic. In a small bowl, combine the grapes, cilantro, garlic, ginger, lemon juice, and oil. Fluff the bulgur with a fork and stir in the grape mixture.

YIELD: MAKES 2 SERVINGS

½ cup bulgur
¾ teaspoon salt
⅔ cup boiling water
½ cup seedless green grapes
⅓ cup (packed) fresh cilantro leaves
1 garlic clove
1 teaspoon grated peeled fresh ginger
2 tablespoons fresh lemon juice
2 tablespoons olive oil

bevy of beans and basil

This salad is a beautiful chorus of peas and pods. Cook all the beans in the same pot so you boil the water only once.

1. Blanch the fava beans in a pot of boiling well-salted water 1 minute, then transfer with a slotted spoon to an ice bath to stop the cooking. Transfer again to a small bowl.

2. Cook the Romano beans in the same pot of boiling water, stirring occasionally, until just tender, about 5 minutes, then transfer with a slotted spoon to an ice bath to stop the cooking. Drain well and transfer to a bowl. Cook the green beans in the same pot until just tender, 6 to 7 minutes, then transfer to ice bath. Add to the Romano beans. Gently peel the skins from the fava beans, then add to other beans.

3. Cut the basil into very thin shreds. Cook the garlic in the oil with a rounded ¼ teaspoon each of salt and pepper in a 12-inch heavy skillet over medium heat, stirring occasionally, 1 minute. Add the beans, the water, and lemon zest and cook, stirring occasionally, until heated through. Stir in the basil and the lemon juice and remove from heat. Season with salt and additional lemon juice, if desired. Serve beans warm or at room temperature.

YIELD: MAKES 4 TO 6 SERVINGS

1 pound fresh fava beans, shelled, or
   1 cup shelled fresh or frozen edamame
¾ pound young fresh Romano beans
   (Italian flat beans), stemmed and cut
   diagonally into 1½- to 2-inch pieces
½ pound green or wax beans, trimmed
   and halved crosswise
¼ cup (packed) basil leaves
2 garlic cloves, finely chopped
3 tablespoons extra-virgin olive oil
3 tablespoons water
1½ teaspoons grated lemon zest
2½ teaspoons fresh lemon juice, or to
   taste

vietnamese chicken sandwich (*banh mi*)

A symbol of France's influence on Vietnam, the *banh mi* sandwich showcases the tangy pickled vegetables of Southeast Asia in a French baguette piled with meat and pâté. This recipe calls for liverwurst instead of the traditional pork pâté, and roast chicken, though roast pork can be substituted for a richer flavor. Spice lovers should add a few dashes of sriracha, the sandwich's customary condiment.

YIELD: MAKES 4 SERVINGS

½ pound daikon, peeled
1 carrot, peeled
½ cup rice vinegar (not seasoned)
1 tablespoon sugar
½ teaspoon salt
1 (24-inch) soft baguette
2 tablespoons vegetable oil
1 tablespoon Asian fish sauce, such as nam pla or nuoc mam
½ teaspoon soy sauce
¼ pound liverwurst
2 fresh jalapeño chiles, thinly sliced
½ sweet onion, cut into ¼-inch rings
¾ cup (packed) cilantro sprigs
2 cooked chicken breasts from a rotisserie chicken, thinly sliced
Lettuce leaves
2 tablespoons mayonnaise

"The only modification I made was to decrease the fish sauce to 1½ teaspoons. Also drained the slaw by squeezing it thoroughly with my hands till almost dry. Great sandwich with and without mayo."

A cook, Riverside, California

1. Preheat the oven to 350°F, with the rack in the middle.

2. Shred the daikon and carrot in a food processor fitted with the medium shredding disk. Stir together the vinegar, sugar, and salt and toss with the shredded vegetables. Let the slaw stand, stirring occasionally, 15 minutes.

3. Meanwhile, heat the baguette on the rack in the oven until crusty, about 5 minutes. Cut off and discard the round ends, then split the baguette lengthwise.

4. Mix the oil, fish sauce, and soy sauce and brush on the cut sides of the bread. Spread the liverwurst on the bottom layer of bread and top with the chiles, onion, and cilantro.

5. Drain the slaw in a colander.

6. Arrange the chicken, slaw, and lettuce on the cilantro. Spread the top layer of bread with mayonnaise and cut the sandwich crosswise into fourths.

crispy pancetta, burrata, and tomato sandwiches

Think the BLT couldn't get any better? This recipe pumps up the flavors of the classic sandwich with gourmet Italian ingredients like pancetta and arugula. Burrata, which means "butter" in Italian, has an exterior similar to mozzarella but with a soft center that gives it a creamy, spreadable quality. Plain mozzarella will do, but try to find this extra-special cheese, sold at specialty foods stores, Italian markets, and cheese shops. It's worth the effort.

YIELD: MAKES 6 SERVINGS

4 (3-ounce) packages thinly sliced pancetta
6 (¾-inch-thick) slices ripe Costoluto Genovese tomatoes or other red heirloom tomatoes
½ cup (packed) coarsely torn fresh basil leaves
6 tablespoons extra-virgin olive oil
2 teaspoons dried oregano
½ teaspoon fleur de sel or kosher salt
Freshly ground black pepper
12 (½-inch) slices egg bread or brioche, lightly toasted
18 ounces burrata cheese
About 4 cups baby arugula or mixed microgreens

do ahead:

The **PANCETTA** can be cooked 2 hours ahead. Let stand at room temperature.

1. Working in batches, cook the pancetta in a heavy large skillet over medium heat until brown and crisp, about 6 minutes per batch. Transfer to paper towels to drain.

2. Place the tomato slices in a shallow baking dish. Add the basil, oil, oregano, and fleur de sel. Sprinkle with pepper and turn to coat. Let stand at least 30 minutes and up to 1 hour.

3. Place 6 toasted bread slices on a work surface. Divide the burrata among the bread slices and spread to edges. Top each with 1 tomato slice, then the pancetta slices, dividing equally. Top with arugula. Cover with the remaining 6 toasted bread slices, and press each slightly to adhere. Cut each sandwich in half and serve.

"Buffalo mozzarella was an easy substitution and was delicious! I used homemade bread, which kicked it up a notch, but even without that, it would have been fabulous."

Dag556, Washington, D.C.

featherlight yeast rolls

These yeast rolls are the creation of legendary chef and cookbook author Edna Lewis. The mashed potato is traditional in yeast dough and tenderizes both the rolls and contributes to their airy rise. Serve piping hot from the oven, or bake them in advance and warm before serving.

1. Cover the potato with cold water in a medium saucepan. Bring to a boil, then simmer, covered, until very tender, about 10 minutes. Reserving 1 cup cooking liquid, drain potato. Meanwhile, melt 2½ tablespoons butter. Mash the hot potato in a large bowl with a fork. Stir in the milk, salt, 2 tablespoons sugar, and 2 tablespoons melted butter (mixture will be lumpy).

2. Cool ½ cup cooking liquid to warm (105 to 115°F). Stir in the yeast and let stand until foamy, about 5 minutes. (If mixture doesn't foam, start over with new yeast and remaining cooking liquid.) Stir the yeast mixture into the potato mixture, then stir in the flour with a wooden spoon until a soft dough forms.

3. Turn out the dough onto a floured surface and knead, dusting the surface and your hands with just enough flour to keep the dough from sticking, until smooth and elastic, about 10 minutes (dough will be slightly sticky). Brush a large bowl with some of remaining melted butter, then turn dough in bowl to coat. Cover tightly with plastic wrap and let rise in the refrigerator, 8 to 12 hours.

4. Punch down the dough (do not knead), then halve. Roll each half into a 12-inch-long log on a lightly floured surface with lightly floured hands. Cut each log into 12 pieces and roll each into a ball. Arrange ½ inch apart in a buttered 13 by 9-inch baking pan. Cover the pan with a kitchen towel (not terry cloth). Let the rolls rise at warm room temperature until doubled (they will fill pan), 1 to 1½ hours.

5. Preheat the oven to 375°F, with a rack in the middle. Melt the remaining 1½ tablespoons butter. Brush the top of the rolls with melted butter and bake until golden brown, 25 to 30 minutes. Loosen the edges with a sharp knife, then transfer the rolls to a rack and cool slightly.

YIELD: MAKES 2 DOZEN ROLLS

1 russet (baking) potato (½ pound), peeled and cut into 1-inch pieces
½ stick (4 tablespoons) unsalted butter
½ cup whole milk
1 teaspoon salt
2 tablespoons sugar
1 (¼-ounce) package active dry yeast
2⅔ cups all-purpose flour

cook's note:

The **ROLLS** are best the day they're baked but can be frozen, wrapped well, up to 1 month. Thaw, then reheat, uncovered, on a baking sheet in a 350°F oven, 5 to 10 minutes.

"Put the potato through a ricer—it was a snap and produced a light, fluffy mashed potato that mixed easily with the rest of the ingredients."
Airportannie, Elizabethtown, Kentucky

summer fruit *with praline fondue*

This deconstructed praline version of fondue wows time and again thanks to its simplicity and unexpected flavor. While it's great any time of year, it's especially suited to the summertime, when you want to keep cooking to a minimum and you have an abundance of berries, melons, peaches, and grapes at peak flavor. This setup is ideal for parties, as it encourages interaction; there'll be no wallflowers when you set this out.

YIELD: MAKES 4 SERVINGS

½ cup crème fraîche
1 cup plus ½ tablespoon (packed) dark
    brown sugar
½ cup chopped toasted pecans
Assorted fresh fruit (cherries, grapes,
    berries, sliced peaches, and plums,
    etc.)
6 tablespoons unsalted butter
2 tablespoons water
2½ tablespoons dark rum
1 teaspoon pure vanilla extract

"This was so easy, and with peaches, cherries, plums, grapes, and mango, it was hard to say which fruit tasted the best with the sauce, nuts, and double-thickened cream."

A cook, Sydney, Australia

1. Beat together in a medium bowl the crème fraîche and ½ tablespoon brown sugar. Transfer to a small serving bowl.

2. Place the pecans in another small serving bowl. Place the crème fraîche and nuts on a platter and surround with the fruit.

3. Melt the butter in a medium nonstick skillet over medium heat. Increase the heat to medium high and add the remaining 1 cup sugar and the water. Stir 1 minute (mixture will bubble vigorously), then stir in the rum and vanilla.

4. Transfer the butterscotch to a bowl. Serve with the crème fraîche, nuts, and fruit.

pistachio semifreddo

An airy dessert, this creamy semifreddo can stand alone on the dessert platter or top a cake as a dreamy icing. Using whipped raw egg whites (be sure they are from very fresh eggs) adds lift to this easy dessert, and slowly folding the meringue into the cream gives it a light texture. Save time by freezing it the day before, and sprinkle some cracked pistachios on top for a crunch.

1. Pulse 1 cup of pistachios with ½ cup plus 2 tablespoons sugar in a food processor until very finely ground. Add the remaining ½ cup pistachios and pulse until just coarsely ground.

2. Beat the egg whites in a bowl with an electric mixer at medium speed until they just hold soft peaks. Beat in the remaining ¼ cup plus 2 tablespoons sugar, a little at a time, then increase the speed to high and beat until the meringue just holds stiff, glossy peaks. Beat the cream with the almond extract in a wide bowl with mixer at high speed until it just holds soft peaks.

3. Fold the meringue into the cream gently but thoroughly, then fold in the nut mixture in the same manner. Spoon into a 2-quart dish and freeze, covered, until firm enough to scoop, about 4 hours. Let soften slightly before serving.

YIELD: MAKES 2 QUARTS

1½ cups shelled salted pistachios
   (6½ ounces)
1 cup sugar
6 large egg whites
2 cups chilled heavy cream
¼ teaspoon almond extract

"I lined a loaf pan and put a layer of chopped nuts in the bottom before putting the custard in. Makes for a beautiful presentation when unmolded. Served with butter cookies and a drizzle of dark chocolate sauce."
A cook, Crystal Coast, North Carolina

peach sorbet

This refreshing dessert from Epicurious member **Danita Sam Lai** of Los Angeles is a crisp, delicious treat. Limoncello and Grand Marnier are optional but recommended, as the alcohol imparts a pleasing softness to the finished sorbet. Keep in mind that alcohol slows the freezing process, so freeze overnight before serving—unless you're one of the many folks who likes a slightly slushier sorbet, in which case a few hours in the freezer will do nicely.

YIELD: MAKES ABOUT 1 QUART

4 large peaches, peeled, pitted, and
    roughly chopped (about 4 cups total)
Juice of 1 orange
Juice of 1 lemon
1⅓ cups sugar
2 tablespoons limoncello (optional)
3 tablespoons orange-flavored liqueur,
    such as Grand Marnier (optional)

Special equipment: ice-cream maker

1. In a blender, combine the peaches, orange and lemon juice, sugar, limoncello, and liqueur. Process the mixture until very well blended and smooth, about 45 seconds.

2. Transfer to a medium bowl, cover, and refrigerate until cold, at least 6 hours or overnight.

3. Process the sorbet in an ice-cream maker according to the manufacturer's instructions, then transfer to an airtight container and freeze overnight.

peaches and cream yogurt pops

Amaretto makes this a grown-up treat. If you want the kids to enjoy these as well but don't want to forgo the almond flavor, use a nonalcoholic Amaretto syrup such as Monin. Or omit the syrup. Just be sure to stick with thick Greek-style yogurt for an unbeatably luscious, creamy pop.

Purée all the ingredients in a blender until smooth. Pour into the molds. Freeze 30 minutes. Insert the sticks, then freeze until firm, about 24 hours.

"This recipe is also an excellent foundation for other yogurt/fruit pops. I just made strawberry ones using this recipe as a guideline."

A cook, Nashville, Tennessee

YIELD: MAKES 8 ICE POPS

3 ripe peaches (about 1 pound), peeled, pitted, and chopped
¾ cup Greek-style yogurt (5 ounces)
½ cup superfine sugar
1 teaspoon fresh lemon juice
⅓ cup water
⅛ teaspoon salt
2 tablespoons Amaretto liqueur

Special equipment: 8 (⅓-cup) ice pop molds and 8 wooden sticks

frozen mango, blackberry cassis, and vanilla mosaic

This dessert is so stunning your guests will wonder if it's art or food. Orange-hued mango sorbet, deep purple blackberries, and cloudlike vanilla ice cream fit together in a mosaic of luscious, vibrant flavors. Indulge your creative side and layer the ingredients decoratively, filling any cracks with blackberry purée. When everything is assembled, freeze the sweet terrine anywhere from three hours to five days.

1. Put the sorbet and ice cream in the refrigerator until evenly softened, 45 minutes to 1 hour. Meanwhile, purée the blackberries, sugar, and cassis in a blender until smooth, then strain through a fine-mesh sieve set over a bowl, pressing on and then discarding solids. Freeze to thicken slightly until ice cream is ready, 20 to 40 minutes, then stir until smooth.

2. Lightly oil a 9 by 5-inch loaf pan, then cut a piece of parchment to fit the bottom and long sides of pan, leaving at least 3 inches of overhang on each side.

3. Fill the pan decoratively with spoonfuls of sorbet and ice cream, pressing down and filling the empty spaces with blackberry purée as you go. Smooth the top, pressing down with the back of a spoon to eliminate air spaces, then fold the parchment flaps over the top and freeze until solid, at least 3 hours.

4. To unmold, run a thin knife along the short sides of the pan to loosen, then open the parchment and invert onto a flat serving dish, discarding the parchment.

5. Cut the mosaic into ½-inch-thick slices.

YIELD: MAKES 10 TO 12 SERVINGS

2 pints mango sorbet
1 pint vanilla ice cream
6 ounces fresh blackberries (1½ cups)
¼ cup sugar
2 tablespoons crème de cassis (black currant liqueur)

Special Equipment: a 9 by 5 by 3-inch loaf pan or other 7- to 8-cup-capacity mold

do ahead:

The **MOSAIC** can be made 5 days ahead and frozen, covered with plastic wrap.

"I made twice the amount of blackberry sauce and used the extra to decorate the slices. I also served with a whipped cream flavored with cassis and sprinkled toasted almond slices over the top."

Goodman1, New Jersey

classic sour cherry pie *with lattice crust*

This soul-satisfying, butter-crusted, fruit-filled dessert is a straight-up American classic. The flaky, beautifully woven topping offers a tempting peek of whole cherries in all their fresh, tart glory, with none of the gelatinous, sticky-sweet filling you find in most cherry pies. It's so easy and popular you might want to double the recipe and make two.

YIELD: MAKES 8 SERVINGS

FOR CRUST
2½ cups unbleached all-purpose flour
1 tablespoon sugar
¾ teaspoon salt
1 cup (2 sticks) chilled unsalted butter, cut into ½-inch cubes
5 tablespoons ice water, or more as needed

FOR FILLING
1 cup plus 1 tablespoon sugar
3 tablespoons cornstarch
¼ teaspoon salt
5 cups whole pitted sour cherries or dark sweet cherries (about 2 pounds unpitted)
1 teaspoon fresh lemon juice (if using sour cherries), or 3 tablespoons fresh lemon juice (if using sweet cherries)
½ teaspoon vanilla extract
2 tablespoons (¼ stick) unsalted butter, cut into ½-inch cubes
About 1 tablespoon milk

Vanilla ice cream, for serving

> ### do ahead:
> The **DOUGH** can be made 2 days ahead. Keep chilled. Let dough soften slightly before rolling out.

MAKE CRUST

1. Whisk the flour, sugar, and salt in a large bowl to blend. Add the butter and rub in with your fingertips until small pea-size clumps form.

2. Add 5 tablespoons ice water; mix lightly with a fork until the dough holds together when small pieces are pressed between fingertips, adding more water by teaspoonfuls if dough is dry.

3. Gather the dough together; divide into 2 pieces. Form each piece into ball, then flatten into disks and wrap in plastic. Refrigerate at least 30 minutes.

MAKE FILLING

1. Position a rack in the lower third of the oven and preheat the oven to 425°F. Whisk 1 cup sugar, the cornstarch, and salt in a medium bowl to blend. Stir in the cherries, lemon juice, and vanilla; set aside.

2. Roll out one dough disk on a floured surface to a 12-inch round. Transfer to a 9-inch glass pie dish. Trim the dough overhang to ½ inch. Roll out the second dough disk on the floured surface to a 12-inch round. Using a large knife or a pastry wheel with a fluted edge, cut 10 (¾-inch) strips from the dough round.

3. Transfer the filling to the dough-lined dish, mounding slightly in center. Dot with butter. Arrange the dough strips atop the filling, forming a lattice; trim the dough strip overhang to ½ inch. Fold the bottom crust up over the ends of the strips and crimp the edges to seal. Brush the lattice crust (not edges) with milk. Sprinkle the lattice with remaining 1 tablespoon sugar.

4. Place the pie on a rimmed baking sheet and bake 15 minutes. Reduce the oven temperature to 375°F. Bake the pie until the filling is bubbling and the crust is golden brown, covering the edges with a foil collar if browning too quickly, about 1 hour longer. Transfer the pie to a rack and cool completely.

5. Cut the pie into wedges and serve with vanilla ice cream.

"I really enjoy cherry pie, and this is hands down the best one I have ever had. I used 1 pound of sweet and 1 pound of sour cherries, and it turned out great."

Llyr, St. Louis, Missouri

fresh strawberry granita

This amazingly easy recipe is a perfect, slightly sweet ending to a decadent meal or an afternoon treat on a lazy Sunday. After blending the ingredients, all you need to do is let the mixture sit in the freezer.

1. Stir the hot water, sugar, and lemon juice in a small bowl until the sugar dissolves. Blend 3 cups of strawberries in a food processor until smooth. Add the sugar syrup and blend until combined.

2. Pour the mixture into a 13 by 9-inch nonstick metal baking pan. Freeze until icy around edges, about 25 minutes. Using a fork, stir the icy portions into the middle of the pan. Freeze until mixture is frozen, stirring the edges into the center every 20 to 30 minutes, about 1½ hours. Using a fork, scrape the granita into flaky crystals. Cover tightly and freeze.

3. Scrape the granita into bowls. Garnish with berries and serve.

"I used a mix of berries (strawberries, blackberries, and blueberries) and added the zest and flesh of one orange and a tablespoon of good balsamic vinegar. Delicious."

Briannawolf, San Francisco, California

YIELD: MAKES ABOUT 6 CUPS

1 cup hot water
¾ cup sugar
2 tablespoons fresh lemon juice
3 cups sliced hulled strawberries
    (1 pound whole berries), plus
    additional for garnish

Special equipment: 13 by 9-inch nonstick
    baking pan

do ahead:

The **GRANITA** can be made 1 day ahead. Keep frozen.

three-berry pie *with vanilla cream*

Take full advantage of summer's bounty with this luscious pie that needs only 40 minutes of active prep time. Choose the ripest seasonal berries from the farmers' market to create the gooey filling—the tartness of blackberries will perfectly mix with the sweetness of sugar and tapioca.

YIELD: MAKES 8 SERVINGS

1 cup granulated sugar
3 tablespoons cornstarch
2 tablespoons quick-cooking tapioca
¼ teaspoon salt
3 cups fresh blackberries (¾ to 1 pound)
2 cups fresh raspberries (½ to ¾ pound)
2 cups fresh blueberries (½ to ¾ pound)
Pastry Dough (recipe follows)
1 large egg, lightly beaten
1 tablespoon sanding or granulated sugar
Vanilla Cream (recipe follows)

"If the berries are frozen, I drain them well and up the tapioca and cornstarch. I also add a little cinnamon to both the crust and the pie. Work fast and keep your ingredients cold!"

A cook, Anchorage, Alaska

1. Put a large baking sheet in the middle of the oven and preheat the oven to 450°F.

2. Whisk together the sugar, cornstarch, tapioca, and salt, then toss with the berries.

3. Roll out one piece of dough (keep remaining piece chilled) on a lightly floured surface with a lightly floured rolling pin into a 13-inch round and fit into a 9-inch pie plate. Trim the edge, leaving a ½-inch overhang. Chill the shell.

4. Roll out the remaining piece of dough on a lightly floured surface with floured rolling pin into an 11-inch round.

5. Spoon the filling into the shell, then cover the pie with the pastry round and trim edge with kitchen shears, leaving a ½-inch overhang. Press the edges together, then crimp the edge decoratively. Brush the top of the pie with egg and sprinkle all over with sanding sugar. Cut 3 steam vents in top crust with a small sharp knife.

6. Bake the pie on the hot baking sheet in middle of oven 15 minutes, then reduce oven temperature to 375°F and continue to bake until crust is golden brown and filling is bubbling, about 45 minutes more.

7. Cool the pie on a rack at least 3 hours before serving to allow juices to thicken slightly (filling will still be juicy). Top with a dollop of Vanilla Cream.

pastry dough

1. Blend together the flour, butter, shortening, and salt in a large bowl with your fingertips or a pastry blender (or pulse in a food processor) until most of the mixture resembles coarse meal with some small (roughly pea-size) butter lumps. Drizzle evenly with 4 tablespoons ice water and gently stir with a fork (or pulse in food processor) until incorporated.

2. Squeeze a small handful of dough; if it doesn't hold together, add more ice water, 1 tablespoon at a time, stirring (or pulsing) until incorporated, then test again. (Do not overwork mixture, or pastry will be tough.)

3. Turn out the mixture onto a lightly floured surface and divide into 8 portions. With the heel of your hand, smear each portion once or twice in a forward motion to help distribute fat. Gather the dough together with a pastry scraper, if you have one, and press into 2 balls, then flatten each into a 5-inch disk. Wrap the disks separately in plastic wrap and chill until firm, at least 1 hour.

YIELD: MAKES ENOUGH FOR A DOUBLE-CRUST 9-INCH PIE

2½ cups all-purpose flour
¾ cup (1½ sticks) cold unsalted butter, cut into ½-inch cubes
¼ cup cold vegetable shortening
½ teaspoon salt
4 to 6 tablespoons ice water

do ahead:

The **DOUGH** can be chilled up to 1 day.

vanilla cream

Scrape the seeds from the vanilla bean with the tip of a knife into a bowl. Add the cream and sugar and beat with an electric mixer until cream just holds soft peaks.

YIELD: MAKES ABOUT 2 CUPS

½ vanilla bean, halved lengthwise, or 1 teaspoon vanilla extract
1 cup chilled heavy cream
2 tablespoons sugar

fruit crumble

With a recipe as simple as this, there's no reason not to make dessert. The fruit comes out soft and tender, while the crumble is crisp and light golden brown. Experiment with other seasonal fruit combinations: raspberries, blackberries, and blueberries are other summer options, while apples, pears, and quince are perfect for fall. All are delicious with a scoop of vanilla ice cream.

1. Preheat the oven to 425°F.

2. Pulse the flour, sugar, almonds, and salt in a food processor until nuts are chopped. Add the butter and pulse until the mixture begins to clump.

3. Spread the fruit in a 9½-inch deep-dish glass pie plate and sprinkle the topping over it.

4. Bake the crumble in the middle of the oven until fruit is tender and topping is golden brown, 25 to 30 minutes.

YIELD: MAKES 6 SERVINGS

¾ cup all-purpose flour
¾ cup sugar
½ cup sliced almonds
¼ teaspoon salt
½ cup (1 stick) cold unsalted butter, cut into ½-inch cubes
2 pounds plums, peaches, or nectarines (or a combination), pitted and cut lengthwise into ½-inch wedges
Vanilla ice cream, for serving

"I used oat flour and ¼ cup less sugar. I ate it while warm, by itself. I also sprinkled some fresh ground nutmeg (just a touch!) on the crumble before baking."
Dottz817, Boston, Massachusetts

mascarpone-filled cake
with sherried berries

Just before serving this light and simple buttermilk cake, drizzle the warm, syrupy berries on top. Serve for casual get-togethers or a birthday party, paired with a dessert wine.

YIELD: MAKES 8 TO 12 SERVINGS

FOR CAKE
2 cups sifted cake flour (not self-rising)
1 teaspoon baking powder
1 teaspoon baking soda
½ teaspoon salt
½ cup (1 stick) unsalted butter, softened
1 cup sugar
1 teaspoon pure vanilla extract
2 large eggs
1 cup well-shaken buttermilk

FOR BERRIES
½ cup fino (dry) Sherry
½ cup sugar
4 cups mixed berries, cut if large

FOR CREAM
8 ounces mascarpone (1 cup)
1 cup chilled heavy cream
¼ cup granulated sugar
Confectioners' sugar, for dusting

Special equipment: 9-inch round cake
    pan 2 inches deep

do ahead:

The **CAKE,** without cream, can be baked 1 day ahead. Wrap in plastic wrap once cool and keep at room temperature. The **BERRIES** can macerate at room temperature up to 2 hours.

MAKE CAKE

1. Preheat the oven to 350°F, with the rack in the middle. Butter the cake pan and line the bottom with a round of parchment, then butter the parchment.

2. Sift together the flour, baking powder, baking soda, and salt.

3. Beat together the butter and sugar in a large bowl with an electric mixer until pale and fluffy. Beat in the vanilla. Add the eggs 1 at a time, beating well after each addition. With mixer at low speed, beat in the buttermilk until just combined. Add the flour mixture in 3 batches, mixing after each addition until just combined.

4. Spread the batter in the cake pan, smoothing the top. Rap the pan on the counter to eliminate air bubbles.

5. Bake until golden and a wooden pick inserted in the center comes out clean, 35 to 40 minutes. Cool in the pan on a rack 10 minutes. Run a knife around the edge of the cake to loosen, then invert onto a plate. Discard the parchment and reinvert cake onto a rack to cool completely.

MACERATE BERRIES

Bring the Sherry and sugar to a boil in a small heavy saucepan, stirring until sugar has dissolved. Put the berries in a bowl and pour the hot syrup over them, gently tossing to coat. Let stand 15 minutes.

MAKE CREAM AND ASSEMBLE CAKE

1. Beat the mascarpone and cream with the granulated sugar in a large bowl until mixture just holds stiff peaks.

2. Halve the cake horizontally with a long serrated knife. Reserve top half. Put the bottom half on a plate, then spread evenly with all of the cream and replace top half. Dust with confectioners' sugar. Serve with berries.

"I did not have a long knife, so I cut very carefully around the cake (shallow cuts) and then used dental floss. Pass it through (start from back) one of the cuts carefully with a back-and-forth motion, bring the thread to the front, cutting the cake in two."

A cook, Washington, D.C.

pound cake
with blueberries and lavender syrup

Forget the boring "welcome to the neighborhood" pound cake of yesteryear! This dessert gets an aromatic lift from lavender syrup and fresh blueberries. The syrup can be made with either dried or fresh lavender flowers: dried will tint the syrup a pale purple, and fresh will infuse it with a more powerful floral taste.

YIELD: MAKES 6 TO 8 SERVINGS

FOR CAKE
2 cups all-purpose flour
½ teaspoon baking powder
¼ teaspoon salt
1 cup (2 sticks) unsalted butter, softened
1½ cups sugar
3 large eggs, at room temperature
1 teaspoon finely grated fresh lemon zest
1 teaspoon pure vanilla extract
½ cup whole milk, at room temperature

FOR BLUEBERRIES
¾ cup water
½ cup sugar
4 teaspoons dried edible lavender
   flowers, or 2 tablespoons fresh
2 teaspoons fresh lemon juice
10 ounces fresh blueberries (1 pint)

Special equipment: a 9 by 5 by 3-inch
   metal loaf pan

do ahead:

The **LAVENDER SYRUP** (without berries) can be made 2 hours ahead and kept, covered, at room temperature. The **CAKE** can be made 1 day ahead and cooled completely, then wrapped tightly in plastic wrap or kept in an airtight container at room temperature. Add berries to syrup just before serving.

MAKE CAKE

1. Put the oven rack in middle position and preheat the oven to 350°F. Generously butter and flour a 9 by 5-inch loaf pan, knocking out excess flour.

2. Whisk together the flour, baking powder, and salt. Beat together the butter and sugar in a large bowl with an electric mixer at medium-high speed until light and fluffy, about 3 minutes in a stand mixer or 5 minutes with a handheld. Add the eggs 1 at a time, beating well after each addition, then beat in the zest and vanilla. Reduce mixer speed to low and add the flour mixture and milk alternately in batches, beginning and ending with the flour and mixing until just incorporated.

3. Spoon the batter into the loaf pan and bake until golden and a wooden pick or skewer inserted in the center comes out with crumbs adhering, 1 to 1¼ hours. Cool the cake in the pan on a rack 30 minutes, then invert onto a rack and cool completely.

MAKE BLUEBERRIES

1. Bring the water and sugar to a boil in a small saucepan, stirring until sugar is dissolved. Remove from heat and stir in the lavender, then steep 30 minutes for dried lavender or 40 minutes for fresh.

2. Pour the syrup through a fine-mesh sieve into a bowl, discarding the lavender. Stir in the lemon juice and blueberries.

3. Spoon the berries and syrup over slices of cake just before serving.

raspberry buttermilk cake

This buttermilk cake begins with a fluffy, vanilla-infused batter that's topped with tart, sweet berries and covered in sugar, and then baked until golden brown.

YIELD: MAKES 6 SERVINGS

1. Preheat the oven to 400°F with the rack in the middle. Butter and flour a 9-inch round cake pan.

2. Whisk together the flour, baking powder, baking soda, and salt.

3. Beat the butter and ⅔ cup sugar with an electric mixer at medium-high speed until pale and fluffy, about 2 minutes, then beat in the vanilla. Add the egg and beat well.

4. At low speed, mix in the flour mixture in 3 batches, alternating with the buttermilk, beginning and ending with the flour, and mixing until just combined.

5. Spoon the batter into the cake pan, smoothing the top. Scatter the raspberries evenly over the top and sprinkle with the remaining 1½ tablespoons sugar.

6. Bake until cake is golden and a wooden pick inserted into the center comes out clean, 25 to 30 minutes. Cool in the pan 10 minutes, then turn out onto a rack and cool to warm, 10 to 15 minutes more. Invert onto a plate.

1 cup all-purpose flour
½ teaspoon baking powder
½ teaspoon baking soda
¼ teaspoon salt
4 tablespoons unsalted butter, softened
⅔ cup plus 1½ tablespoons sugar
½ teaspoon pure vanilla extract
1 large egg
½ cup well-shaken buttermilk
1 cup fresh raspberries (about 5 ounces)

"I substituted sour cherries for raspberries and almond extract for vanilla, and it was lovely! The sugar sprinkled over the top of the cake creates a crispy, golden, sparkly crust—no need to dress it up with frosting. I lined the pan with parchment."
Foodhappy, Edmonton, Canada

chocolate chip zucchini cake

More than one Epicurious editor considers this cake flawless: buttery and firm, sweet but not too sugary, moist but still cakey. If you're leery of the dense, oily texture of most zucchini bread, this zucchini cake will be a pleasant revelation. And if you're buried in a bounty of late-summer zucchini, this is a great go-to recipe to help burn through it using a short list of pantry staple ingredients. (Oh, and don't be afraid to eat it for breakfast!)

1. Preheat the oven to 350°F. Butter a 12-cup Bundt pan well and dust with some flour, knocking out excess.

2. Sift together the flour, baking soda, baking powder, and salt into a bowl. Beat together the butter and brown sugar in a large bowl with an electric mixer at high speed until pale and fluffy, about 3 minutes, then beat in the vanilla.

3. Reduce the mixer speed to medium and add the eggs 1 at a time, beating well after each addition and scraping down side of bowl occasionally, then beat until very smooth and fluffy, about 2 minutes more. Reduce the speed to low and add all but ½ cup of the flour mixture, mixing until just combined.

4. Toss the zucchini, chocolate chips, and walnuts with the remaining ½ cup flour mixture and add to the batter, then mix the batter with a rubber spatula (batter will be thick).

5. Spoon the batter into the prepared pan, smoothing the top. Bake in the middle of the oven, rotating the pan halfway through baking, until the side begins to pull away from the pan and a tester comes out clean, 45 to 50 minutes total.

6. Cool the cake in the pan on a rack 30 minutes, then run a thin knife around the outer and inner edges. Invert a rack over the pan, then invert the cake onto the rack. Cool completely.

YIELD: MAKES 8 TO 10 SERVINGS

2½ cups all-purpose flour
1 teaspoon baking soda
½ teaspoon baking powder
½ teaspoon salt
1 cup (2 sticks) unsalted butter, softened
1 cup (packed) light brown sugar
1 teaspoon pure vanilla extract
3 large eggs, at room temperature
2 cups coarsely grated zucchini
1 cup semisweet chocolate chips
½ cup walnuts, toasted and chopped

Special equipment: 12-cup Bundt or fleur-de-lis pan

"Made this in mini Bundts (muffin size) and served with brunch. My husband even ate one knowing there was a vegetable hiding inside. I did not peel the zucchini, but I think doing so might make it easier to sneak the veggie in."
A cook, Des Moines, Iowa

brownies
with caramel, fig, and cherry jam

member recipe

Greece is more synonymous with flaky, honeyed pastries than gooey brownies, but amid the hills of Crete, Epicurious member **Lisa Lindy** swirls a figgy-cherry caramel into a chocolaty batter before baking it into a moist-in-the-middle brownie. These fruity delights will provide sticky fingers and happy faces on kids and adults like.

YIELD: MAKES 16 TO 20 SQUARES

FOR JAM
¾ cup sugar
2 tablespoons water
⅓ cup heavy whipping cream
4 ounces dried black Mission figs
4 ounces dried tart cherries
1½ teaspoons balsamic vinegar

FOR BROWNIES
8 ounces bittersweet chocolate
½ cup (1 stick) unsalted butter
1¼ cups sugar
3 large eggs
1 tablespoon pure vanilla extract
1¼ cups all-purpose flour
¼ teaspoon baking powder
¼ teaspoon kosher salt
6 ounces chocolate chips

Special equipment: 13 by 9 by 2-inch pan

do ahead:

The **BROWNIES** can be baked ahead and kept, in an airtight container at room temperature, up to 3 days.

MAKE JAM

1. In a small pot over moderately high heat, bring the sugar and water to a boil. Cook the sugar until light golden brown, 3 to 5 minutes. Remove from the heat and carefully stir in the cream.

2. Add the figs, cherries, and balsamic vinegar, stirring to combine. Let the mixture rest until the fruit is softened, about 10 minutes.

3. Transfer the mixture to a food processor and process until smooth.

MAKE BROWNIES

1. Arrange a rack in the middle of the oven and preheat the oven to 350°F. Butter and flour a 13 by 9-inch pan.

2. In a small pot over moderately low heat, stir the bitter-sweet chocolate and butter until melted. Remove from the heat and cool for about 15 minutes.

3. In a medium bowl, whisk together the sugar, eggs, and vanilla. Add the cooled chocolate mixture and whisk to combine. Sift the flour, baking powder, and salt into the mixing bowl and gently stir to combine. Fold in the chocolate chips.

4. Transfer the batter to the prepared pan. Dollop the jam on top of the batter and, using a knife, swirl it into the batter. Bake the brownies until a toothpick inserted into the center is barely clean, 20 to 25 minutes. Cool the brownies completely in the pan before cutting and serving.

dark chocolate cherry oatmeal cookies

These chocolate delights manage to be both light and decadent at the same time. Dark chocolate mingles with earthy rolled oats as juicy bits of dried cherry add extra dimension to the already satisfying chewiness. "These cookies are best served light and fluffy, just baked through," notes Epicurious member **alyb2002,** the author of this recipe, and they are easy enough to be a cookie jar mainstay all-year round.

1. Position a rack in the middle of the oven and preheat the oven to 350°F. Butter 2 large baking sheets.

2. Into a medium bowl, sift together the flour, baking powder, baking soda, and salt. In the bowl of a stand mixer fitted with the paddle attachment, combine the butter and sugars and beat on medium speed, scraping the bowl occasionally, until light and fluffy, about 2 minutes. Add the eggs1 at a time, scraping down the bowl after each addition. Add the vanilla and beat until the mixture is thoroughly combined. With the mixer on low, add the flour mixture and stir, scraping down the bowl occasionally, until just combined. Add the oats, chocolate chips, and cherries to the dough and mix on low speed until just incorporated.

3. Drop the dough by heaping tablespoons onto the prepared cookie sheets, leaving about 2 inches between each cookie. Bake the cookies in batches, rotating the sheets halfway through baking, until pale golden brown, 12 to 14 minutes. Cool the cookies on the baking sheet for 5 minutes before transferring to a wire rack to cool completely. Continue baking cookies on cooled baking sheets.

YIELD: MAKES ABOUT 3 DOZEN COOKIES

3 cups all-purpose flour
1 teaspoon baking powder
1 teaspoon baking soda
1 teaspoon kosher salt
1 cup (2 sticks) unsalted butter, at room temperature
1 cup (packed) light brown sugar
1 cup granulated sugar
2 large eggs
2 teaspoons pure vanilla extract
1½ cups old-fashioned rolled oats
6 ounces dark chocolate chips
8 ounces dried cherries

Special equipment: 2 large baking sheets

fall

vanilla date breakfast smoothie

For a quick and easy glass of tranquillity, indulge in the mellow sweetness of vanilla and dates. This low-fat, creamy smoothie makes the perfect breakfast when you're on the go or an energizing shake after a workout. Toss in a banana and ½ cup almonds for a filling drink or substitute soy milk for dairy. To create a silkier consistency, soak the dates for about an hour and then blend until smooth.

YIELD: MAKES 2 SMOOTHIES

1 cup nonfat yogurt
1 cup nonfat milk
1 cup (packed) pitted Medjool dates
   (about 9 ounces)
½ teaspoon pure vanilla extract
2 cups ice cubes

"I puréed the dates in the food processor and froze the yogurt before adding to the blender."
A cook, San Diego, California

Purée the yogurt, milk, dates, and vanilla in a blender until smooth. Add the ice cubes; purée until the mixture is thick and smooth. Divide between 2 glasses and serve.

kitchen sink frittata

What makes this frittata so easy, according to Epicurious member **Carla Joy Zambelli** of Haverford, Pennsylvania, is that there's practically no shopping required. The frittata can be made with whatever produce you have on hand. Some easy add-ins include caramelized onions, mushrooms, diced kale, or collards. "It's an Italian version of a quiche—just without the fuss and crust," she says. Served with a lightly dressed arugula salad, it makes for a perfect start—or finish—to the day.

1. Preheat the oven to 400°F.

2. In a medium bowl, whisk together the eggs, cheese, cream, salt, and pepper.

3. In a 9- or 10-inch cast-iron pan over moderate heat, heat the butter until hot but not smoking. Add the sliced vegetables and sauté, stirring occasionally, until crisp-tender, about 3 minutes. Add the bacon and potato, and sauté, stirring occasionally, for 1 minute. Add the egg mixture and scramble for 3 to 4 minutes. Stir in the basil and then spread the egg mixture evenly in the pan.

4. Sprinkle the mozzarella and tomato on top, season with salt and pepper, and transfer the pan to the oven. Bake until the eggs are set and the cheese is melted, about 8 minutes. Cut into wedges to serve.

Look at the origins of pizza: It was created by Italian cooks to use what was at hand to create a meal. I view frittatas similarly. I love eggs, and when you want to jazz it up once in a while and not waste ingredients already in your kitchen, frittatas do that!

—Carla Joy Zambelli

YIELD: MAKES 4 SERVINGS

8 large eggs

2 tablespoons freshly grated Parmigiano-Reggiano cheese

1 tablespoon heavy cream or half-and-half

¼ teaspoon salt

¼ teaspoon freshly ground black pepper

2 tablespoons unsalted butter or extra-virgin olive oil

1½ cups thinly sliced raw vegetables, such as cremini mushrooms, bell peppers, and onions

1 cup cooked crumbled bacon, diced ham, or chopped sausage

½ cup diced cooked potato

2 tablespoons finely chopped fresh basil or flat-leaf parsley

4 ounces whole-milk mozzarella cheese, freshly grated

1 large plum tomato, diced

open-faced bacon and egg sandwiches
with arugula

Leave it to bad-boy bacon to show no-nonsense arugula a good time. This savory treat towers with layers of flavor and texture, from the deliciously runny yolks melding with the cool tomato and tangy vinaigrette, to the chewy bacon and crisp Italian bread. Add breakfast potatoes for a nice Sunday morning brunch.

1. Cook the bacon in a heavy large skillet over medium-high heat until brown and crisp; transfer to paper towels to drain.

2. Wipe out skillet. Brush the cut sides of the bread with 1 tablespoon oil. Place the bread cut side down in the skillet. Cook over medium heat until golden, about 3 minutes. Place 1 bread square, golden side up, on each of 2 plates. Top each with half of the bacon, then 2 tomato slices.

3. Whisk 1 tablespoon of oil, the shallot, and vinegar in a medium bowl to blend. Season the dressing with salt and pepper. Add the arugula and toss to coat.

4. Heat the remaining 1 tablespoon oil in the same skillet over medium heat. Crack the eggs into the skillet. Sprinkle with salt and pepper. Cook until the whites are set and the yolks are cooked as desired. Top each bread stack with arugula, egg, and cheese.

YIELD: MAKES 2 SERVINGS

5 bacon slices, halved crosswise
1 (4-inch) square ciabatta bread or focaccia, halved horizontally
3 tablespoons olive oil
4 large thin tomato slices
1 small shallot, chopped
½ tablespoon white-wine vinegar
1 cup (packed) arugula
2 large eggs
Parmesan cheese shavings, for serving

"Used leftover challah, and added a bit of fresh mozzarella on top of the warm bread. The best breakfast ever."
Obecca, Albuquerque, New Mexico

mushroom and fontina quiche

Quiche is a culinary workhorse—a great dish to have in your repertoire. Enjoy it on its own for breakfast or brunch, or pair it with a simple green salad, and you've got yourself a satisfying supper. And since it can be baked in advance and served warm or at room temperature, quiche is ideal for gatherings. This vegetarian rendition is packed with earthy mushrooms. Not a fan of fontina? Gruyère, Emmental, Provolone, and Gouda make excellent substitutes. And if you prefer a lighter quiche, skip the half-and-half and use whole milk instead.

YIELD: MAKES 8 SERVINGS

1 refrigerated pie crust (half of a 15-ounce package)
2 tablespoons (¼ stick) unsalted butter
⅔ cup chopped shallots (about 3 medium)
5 cups (12 to 14 ounces) sliced assorted fresh mushrooms (such as chanterelle, stemmed shiitake, oyster, cremini, and button), large mushrooms halved
4 large eggs
⅔ cup half-and-half
⅓ cup whole milk
½ teaspoon salt
½ teaspoon freshly ground black pepper
½ teaspoon freshly grated or ground nutmeg
1½ cups (packed) coarsely grated fontina cheese (about 7 ounces)

Special equipment: 9-inch deep-dish glass pie dish

"I just use baby portobello mushrooms and follow the recipe exactly. You can sauté your mushrooms the night before if you are making it for breakfast."
hannarose

1. Preheat the oven to 450°F. Unroll the crust completely and press firmly onto the bottom and up the sides of the pie dish. Bake until light golden brown, pressing on the sides of the crust with the back of a spoon if the crust begins to slide down the sides of dish, about 17 minutes. Reduce the oven temperature to 325°F.

2. Melt the butter in a heavy large skillet over medium-high heat. Add the shallots and sauté until beginning to soften, about 2 minutes. Add the mushrooms, sprinkle with salt and pepper, and sauté until tender and beginning to brown, about 8 minutes. Transfer to a plate; spread out to cool slightly.

3. Whisk the eggs, half-and-half, milk, salt, pepper, and nutmeg in a large bowl to blend. Stir in 1 cup fontina cheese and sautéed mushrooms. Pour the filling into the crust. Sprinkle the remaining ½ cup cheese over the quiche.

4. Bake the quiche until puffed, golden brown, and just set in the center, about 45 minutes. Cool 30 minutes. Cut into wedges to serve.

banana bread
with chocolate chips and walnuts

member recipe

Epicurious member **Marsha Klein** of Barrington, Rhode Island, shared her everything-but-the-kitchen-sink banana bread with our community, and it quickly became popular. Toasted walnuts and chocolate chips add texture, but this flexible recipe can easily be adapted to a baker's whim. The chocolate-averse can substitute dried fruit—golden raisins or blueberries—for the chips; the nut-allergic, shredded coconut; the health-conscious, white whole-wheat flour.

1. Preheat the oven to 350°F. Butter and flour a 9 by 5-inch metal loaf pan. Whisk the flour, baking soda, baking powder, and salt in a medium bowl to blend. Combine the chocolate chips and walnuts in a small bowl; add 1 table-spoon of the flour mixture and toss to coat.

2. In a stand mixer, beat the butter in a large bowl until fluffy. Gradually add the sugar, beating until well blended. Beat in the eggs 1 at a time. Beat in the mashed bananas, lemon juice, and vanilla. Beat in flour mixture.

3. Spoon one-third of the batter into the prepared pan. Sprinkle with half of the chocolate-chip and nut mixture. Spoon another one-third of batter into the pan. Sprinkle with the remaining nut mixture. Cover with the remaining one-third batter. Run a knife through the batter in a zigzag pattern.

4. Bake the bread until a tester inserted into the center comes out clean, about 1 hour and 5 minutes. Turn out onto a rack and cool.

YIELD: MAKES 1 (9-INCH) LOAF

1½ cups all-purpose flour
1 teaspoon baking soda
1 teaspoon baking powder
¼ teaspoon salt
¾ cup semisweet chocolate chips
¾ cup walnuts, toasted and chopped
½ cup (1 stick) unsalted butter, at room temperature
1 cup sugar
2 large eggs
1 cup mashed ripe bananas
2 tablespoons fresh lemon juice
1½ teaspoons vanilla extract

"I've gotten great reviews for this recipe every time I've served it. You can adjust the sugar depending on how ripe the bananas are. (The riper fruits require less sugar.) I also like to use the huge chunks of chocolate chips instead of the morsels. It's a very rich treat!"
A cook, Chicago, Illinois

crème brûlée french toast

Admittedly, the notion of crème brûlée might seem a bit much in the morning, but when coupled with French toast, it creates a whole new dish that is nothing short of brunch brilliance. Originally from the Inn at Sunrise Point in Camden, Maine, it makes for the ideal breakfast treat or a potluck pleaser of a dessert (one that can be assembled the night before). To make it kid-friendly, replace the Grand Marnier with the same amount of orange juice. And for a slightly healthier take, substitute whole-wheat challah and use 2% milk. Even then, you'll have a hard time sharing it with others.

YIELD: MAKES 6 SERVINGS

½ cup (1 stick) unsalted butter
1 cup (packed) light brown sugar
2 tablespoons corn syrup
1 (8- to 9-inch) round loaf country-style
  bread
5 large eggs
1½ cups half-and-half
1 teaspoon pure vanilla extract
1 teaspoon orange-flavored liqueur, such
  as Grand Marnier
¼ teaspoon salt

"Sometimes, I substitute the country bread for a French baguette so that there is more texture. I also like to sprinkle the top with fresh raspberries."
Kittysf, Oslo, Norway

1. In a small heavy saucepan, melt the butter with the brown sugar and corn syrup over moderate heat, stirring, until smooth. Pour into a 13 by 9-inch baking dish. Cut 6 (1-inch-thick) slices from the center portion of the bread, reserving the ends for another use, and trim the crusts. Arrange the bread slices in one layer in the baking dish, squeezing them slightly to fit.

2. In a bowl, whisk together the eggs, half-and-half, vanilla, liqueur, and salt until combined well and pour evenly over bread. Chill the bread mixture, covered, at least 8 hours and up to 1 day.

3. Preheat the oven to 350°F and bring the bread mixture to room temperature.

4. Bake the bread mixture, uncovered, in the middle of the oven until puffed and edges are pale golden, 35 to 40 minutes. Serve hot French toast immediately.

buttermilk pancakes
with maple syrup apples

This crêpelike pancake recipe might make you want to eat breakfast for dinner. The yellow cornmeal gives the cake a hearty flavor and a crisp crust, leading one reviewer to compare it to a hybrid Swedish-buttermilk pancake. Yogurt and scant mixing keep these cakes fluffy and airy. Make extra compote to use on oatmeal or ice cream.

MAKE MAPLE SYRUP APPLES

Melt the butter in a large nonstick skillet over medium-high heat. Add the apples and 1 tablespoon maple syrup; sauté until apples are tender, about 5 minutes. Mix in remaining ½ cup maple syrup and cinnamon.

MAKE PANCAKES

1. Combine the flour, cornmeal, sugar, baking powder and soda, and salt in a large bowl; whisk to blend. Whisk the buttermilk, yogurt, and egg in a medium bowl to blend; add to the dry ingredients and stir until just blended but still lumpy. Gently mix in the melted butter.

2. Heat a griddle or large nonstick skillet over medium heat. Spread a thin coating of butter over the griddle and let melt. Working in batches, drop the batter by ⅓ cupfuls onto the griddle, spacing apart. Cook the pancakes until brown on the bottom and bubbles form on top, about 3 minutes. Turn the pancakes over and cook until the bottoms are brown and pancakes are barely firm to touch. Transfer to plates. Repeat with the remaining batter, adding more butter to griddle as needed.

3. Spoon the apples over the pancakes. Serve, passing additional maple syrup.

YIELD: MAKES 4 SERVINGS

FOR MAPLE SYRUP APPLES

2 tablespoons (¼ stick) unsalted butter
3 large Golden Delicious apples, peeled, cored, and cut into ½-inch slices (about 1½ pounds)
1 tablespoon plus ½ cup pure maple syrup
½ teaspoon ground cinnamon

FOR PANCAKES

1 cup all-purpose flour
2 tablespoons yellow cornmeal
2 tablespoons light brown sugar
1 teaspoon baking powder
1 teaspoon baking soda
½ teaspoon salt
1 cup buttermilk
1 cup plain whole-milk yogurt
1 large egg
1½ tablespoons unsalted butter, melted
Unsalted butter, for griddle
Maple syrup, for serving

"This recipe has replaced all other Saturday morning pancake recipes. We're always in a rush to get to soccer, so we skip the apples and throw chocolate chips and bananas in the batter instead. The kids swear the chocolate chips help them play better."
A cook, New York, New York

bourbon chicken liver pâté

Bourbon puts a distinctively American spin on this classic French hors d'oeuvre. The booze also helps balance the rich and unctuous chicken livers, which are sautéed in a heady mix of onion, garlic, and herbs. While it needs to be chilled only for two hours before you can dig in, wait a day or two and you'll give the flavors a chance to really develop. For holiday celebrations, serve this pâté in a terrine. Alternatively, divide it among ramekins to create unique and indulgent hostess gifts.

YIELD: MAKES 8 TO 10 SERVINGS

¾ cup (1½ sticks) unsalted butter
1 cup finely chopped onion
1 large garlic clove, minced
1 teaspoon minced fresh thyme,
    or ¼ teaspoon dried
1 teaspoon minced fresh marjoram,
    or ¼ teaspoon dried
1 teaspoon minced fresh sage,
    or ¼ teaspoon dried
¾ teaspoon salt
¼ teaspoon black pepper
⅛ teaspoon ground allspice
1 pound chicken livers, trimmed
2 tablespoons bourbon
Fresh thyme, marjoram, or sage sprig,
    for garnish
Crackers or toasted baguette slices,
    for serving

Special equipment: 2½-cup crock or
    terrine or several small ramekins

do ahead:

The **PÂTÉ** can be chilled up to 2 weeks. Once butter seal has been broken, pâté keeps for up to 1 week chilled, its surface covered with plastic wrap.

1. Melt 1 stick butter in a large nonstick skillet over moderately low heat, then cook the onion and garlic, stirring, until softened, about 5 minutes. Add the herbs, salt, pepper, allspice, and livers and cook, stirring, until livers are cooked on the outside but still pink when cut open, about 8 minutes.

2. Stir in the bourbon and remove from the heat. Purée the mixture in a food processor until smooth, then transfer the pâté to a 2½-cup crock and smooth the top.

3. Melt the remaining 4 tablespoons butter in a very small heavy saucepan over low heat, then remove the pan from the heat and let the butter stand 3 minutes. If using an herb garnish, put a sprig on top of the pâté. Skim the froth from the butter, then spoon enough clarified butter over the pâté to cover its surface, leaving the milky solids in bottom of pan.

4. Chill the pâté until the butter is firm, about 30 minutes, then cover with plastic wrap and chill at least 2 hours more.

"Tweaked according to what I had at hand . . . used a nice rum instead of bourbon, skipped marjoram as I didn't have any, added some browned sage on top."

A cook, Dover, New Hampshire

crab hush puppies
with curried honey-mustard sauce

If you believe that frying makes everything taste better, get the oil ready, because after popping one of these hush puppies into your mouth, you'll quickly need countless more. Creole mustard, a Louisiana specialty, may not be readily available at your local market, but you can substitute whole-grain Dijon mustard. Having a deep-fry thermometer will make the frying process easier, as oil that's not hot enough will lead to greasy and soggy fritters. And to keep the oil temperature from dropping too much, cook the hush puppies in small batches as directed.

1. Stir the mustard, honey, and 1¼ teaspoons curry powder in a small bowl for dipping sauce.

2. Stir the cornbread mix, clam juice, and remaining ½ teaspoon curry powder in a medium bowl. Mix in the crab and ¾ cup of the onions.

3. Pour enough oil into a medium saucepan to reach a depth of 1½ inches. Attach a deep-fry thermometer to the side of the pan and heat the oil over medium heat to 320°F to 330°F. Working in batches, drop the batter into the oil by heaping teaspoonfuls. Fry until golden and cooked through, 1 to 1½ minutes. Transfer to paper towels to drain.

4. Sprinkle the hush puppies with the remaining onions. Serve with dipping sauce.

YIELD: MAKES ABOUT 30

¼ cup Creole mustard
¼ cup honey
1¾ teaspoons curry powder
1 cup just-add-water cornbread mix
¼ cup bottled clam juice
12 ounces fresh lump crab meat, diced
1 cup finely chopped green onions
Vegetable oil, for frying

Special equipment: Deep-fry
   thermometer

"I made these for a party, and they were much appreciated. I found that I could form the hush puppies ahead of time, chill them on a baking sheet, and then just fry them before serving. So simple."
Ihateblueberrles

potato samosa phyllo triangles

Potato samosas are one of the most popular Indian dishes, and one of the easiest to make. Traditionally, they're a little larger than the ones this recipe yields, but regardless of size, the mix of warming spices, potatoes, and peas makes for a delicious appetizer or snack. And because these are baked instead of fried, they're healthier. An easier alternative to using phyllo dough is to use wonton wrappers, but they will change the exterior texture from buttery and flaky to crispy and crunchy.

YIELD: MAKES 2 DOZEN SAMOSAS

1½ pounds Yukon Gold or other yellow boiling potatoes
1¾ teaspoons salt
1 large onion, chopped
1 teaspoon garam masala (Indian spice blend)
1 teaspoon cumin seeds
1 teaspoon coriander seeds
¼ cup vegetable oil
½ cup frozen peas, thawed
12 (17 by 12-inch) phyllo sheets, thawed if frozen
¾ stick unsalted butter, melted and cooled
Indian chutney, for serving

"Love this take on the traditional samosas, and the phyllo dough was a nice twist. I would probably add a little garlic next time and serve with apricot chutney."
ElsbethUK, Glastonbury, England

1. Peel the potatoes and cut into ½-inch cubes. Put in a medium saucepan with 1 teaspoon salt and enough water to cover by 1 inch. Simmer until tender, about 15 minutes, then drain in a colander.

2. Cook the onion, spices, and remaining ¾ teaspoon salt in the oil in a 12-inch nonstick skillet over medium-high heat, stirring occasionally, until golden brown, 8 to 10 minutes. Add the potatoes and peas and cook, stirring, 3 minutes, then remove from heat and cool slightly.

3. Preheat the oven to 375°F, with racks in upper and lower thirds.

4. Cover the stack of phyllo sheets with plastic wrap and a damp kitchen towel. Keeping the remaining phyllo covered and working quickly, place 1 sheet on a work surface. Gently brush with some melted butter, then lay a second sheet on top and brush with butter. Cut crosswise into 4 strips. Put 2 tablespoons filling near one corner of 1 strip and fold corner of phyllo over to enclose filling and form a triangle. Continue folding strip, maintaining triangle shape. Put samosa, seam side down, on a baking sheet. Make 3 more triangles in same manner. Repeat with remaining phyllo and filling.

5. Generously brush both sides of each samosa with butter and bake, turning the samosas over halfway through and switching position of sheets, until golden and crisp all over, about 25 minutes total. Cool slightly. Serve warm or at room temperature.

my mother-in-law's deviled eggs

Some family recipes are fiercely guarded secrets, hoarded for generations and never allowed to leave the lockbox, much less the house. **Rick Noonan**, an Epicurious member from Crofton, Maryland, got lucky with this one. He said, "My mother-in-law finally shared her recipe with me after nearly twelve years with her daughter. I guess I must be doing OK." Now, he's sharing it with the rest of us.

1. Gently remove the yolks from the egg halves and transfer to a small bowl. Using a fork, finely mash the egg yolks. Add the mayonnaise and mustard, season with salt and pepper, and stir until well blended. Add the celery and onions and stir to combine.

2. Spoon the yolk mixture into the egg halves. Arrange on a platter and garnish each egg with the chopped olives, if desired.

YIELD: MAKES 12 HORS D'OEUVRES

6 hard-cooked large eggs, halved
    lengthwise
¼ cup mayonnaise
2 teaspoons mustard
1 tablespoon finely chopped celery
1 tablespoon finely chopped green
    onions (white and light green parts
    only)
1 tablespoon finely chopped green olives
    (optional)

Be sure to incorporate all the ingredients very well. You can make minor adjustments to the quantity of mayo, mustard, salt, or pepper to suit individual tastes, but note that the egg yolk does a good job of hiding the seasonings, so unless you blend well you could end up with one egg that is too salty.

—Rick Noonan

roasted butternut squash and caramelized onion tart

Whether you serve this versatile vegetable and cheese tart for a savory lunch or as a rich first course, Epicurious users agree: Make sure to cook the onions until they're a caramelized brown. It takes time, but the sweet, tangy flavor is worth the effort. That said, if you're looking for shortcuts, it's easy to swap in puff pastry dough to save time making and baking the pie shell. Most of the recipe can be made in advance, and assembled and baked before serving.

YIELD: MAKES 6 TO 8 SERVINGS

Pastry Dough (recipe follows)
1 small butternut squash (about 1 pound)
1½ teaspoons olive oil, plus about
    2 teaspoons for brushing squash
1 small onion
1½ tablespoons unsalted butter
1 large egg and ½ large egg yolk
    (½ tablespoon)
⅓ cup heavy cream
¾ cup grated Italian fontina cheese (about
    2½ ounces)
⅓ cup freshly grated Parmesan cheese
    (about 1 ounce)
¼ cup crumbled mild soft goat cheese
    (about 1 ounce)
1½ teaspoons minced fresh herbs, such as
    rosemary, thyme, and marjoram leaves
½ teaspoon salt
Freshly ground black pepper
⅓ cup fine fresh bread crumbs

Special equipment: 11-inch round fluted
    tart pan with removable bottom

"Buy a slightly larger squash and a large onion. Then use the leftover purée, caramelized onions, and goat cheese the next day to make gourmet grilled cheese sandwiches."

A cook, Charlottesville, Virginia

1. On a lightly floured surface, roll out the dough into a 12-inch round about ⅛ inch thick. Fit the dough into an 11-inch tart pan with a removable fluted rim. Freeze the shell 15 minutes.

2. Preheat the oven to 375°F. Line shell with foil and fill with pie weights or raw rice. Bake the shell in the middle of the oven until the edge is pale golden, about 20 minutes. Carefully remove the foil and weights and bake 10 minutes more, or until the bottom is golden. Leave oven on. Cool shell in pan on a rack.

3. Halve the squash and scoop out the seeds. Lightly brush each cut side with about 1 teaspoon oil and roast the squash on a baking sheet, cut sides down, in the middle of the oven 40 minutes or until soft.

4. While squash is roasting, thinly slice the onion and cook in a heavy skillet in ½ tablespoon butter and the remaining 1½ teaspoons oil over moderate heat, stirring occasionally, until soft and golden brown, about 20 minutes.

5. Cool the squash and scoop out the flesh. In a food processor, purée the squash. Add the whole egg, egg yolk, and cream and blend well. Transfer the mixture to a large bowl and stir in the onion, cheeses, herbs, salt, and pepper to taste. Pour the filling into the shell, smoothing the top.

6. In a small skillet, melt the remaining tablespoon butter and stir in the bread crumbs until combined well. Sprinkle the bread crumb mixture evenly over the filling. Bake the tart in the middle of the oven 40 minutes, or until filling is set. Cool the tart in the pan on a rack 10 minutes and then carefully remove rim. Serve.

pastry dough

YIELD: MAKES ENOUGH DOUGH FOR 11-INCH TART

1¼ cups all-purpose flour
1 teaspoon sugar
½ teaspoon salt
½ cup (1 stick) cold unsalted butter,
   cut in pieces
¼ cup ice water

In a food processor, blend the flour, sugar, and salt until combined. Add the butter and pulse until most of the mixture resembles coarse meal, with remainder in small (roughly pea-size) lumps. Add 2 tablespoons of ice water and pulse just until incorporated. Test the mixture by gently squeezing a small handful: if it does not hold together, add enough remaining water, 1 tablespoon at a time, pulsing and testing, until mixture just forms a dough. Form dough into a disk. Chill the dough, wrapped in plastic wrap, 30 minutes before using.

roasted squash, red pepper, and jack cheese quesadillas
with chipotle lime sour cream dip

A creamy, savory-sweet purée of roasted vegetables replaces half the cheese in this colorful, vegetarian-friendly quesadilla. (Try serving the dip with raw veggies or even grilled corn.) Although dicing and then roasting the squash amps up the intensity of the roasted flavor, you can save some time by simply halving the squash before putting it into the oven and scooping out the flesh once it's soft.

YIELD: MAKES 4 SERVINGS

FOR DIP

1 canned chipotle chile in adobo, minced
2 teaspoons fresh lime juice
1 cup sour cream

FOR QUESADILLAS

1 ¾-pound seedless piece butternut squash, peeled and cut into ¾-inch dice (about 5 cups)
1 medium onion, unpeeled, cut into eighths
1 large garlic clove, unpeeled
1 tablespoon vegetable oil
8 (6-inch) flour tortillas
1 cup chopped red bell pepper (about 1 large)
1 cup coarsely grated Monterey Jack cheese
½ stick (¼ cup) unsalted butter, softened

do ahead:

The **DIP** may be made 2 days ahead and chilled, covered.

The **SQUASH PURÉE** may be made 2 days ahead and chilled, covered.

MAKE DIP

In a small bowl, stir the chile and lime juice into the sour cream until combined well.

MAKE QUESADILLAS

1. Preheat the oven to 400°F. In a shallow baking pan, arrange the squash, onion, and garlic in a single layer and drizzle with the oil, tossing to coat. Roast in the middle of the oven 15 minutes, or until the garlic is tender, and transfer garlic to a work surface. Roast squash and onion until tender, about 15 minutes more. Discard peels from onion and garlic.

2. In a food processor purée the squash, onion, and garlic with salt and pepper to taste until smooth.

3. Spread about one-fourth of the squash purée on each of 4 tortillas and sprinkle each with about one-fourth bell pepper and about one-fourth cheese. Top each quesadilla with a plain tortilla, pressing gently together. Spread each side of the quesadillas with ½ tablespoon butter.

4. Heat a griddle or 7-inch nonstick skillet over moderately high heat until hot and cook the quesadillas, 1 at a time, until golden, about 3 minutes on each side, transferring to a cutting board as they finish cooking.

5. Cut each quesadilla into 6 to 8 wedges and serve warm with the chipotle dip.

"Brown the quesadilla cheese side down first. Upon melting, it will act like glue and will make the thing easier to flip. I topped each finished wedge with a slice of avocado and a sprinkle of chopped cilantro."

Peppermill, Chicago, Illinois

black bean soup *with cumin and jalapeño*

This flavorful, filling stew was developed by home cook Jennifer Smith of Tyler, Texas, who hit on the perfect balance of jalapeño heat, aromatic cumin, and stick-to-your-ribs black beans. Best of all, it's a budget-friendly weeknight dish made of ingredients you probably have in your pantry. Jennifer's secret weapon: "A can of flavored diced tomatoes. They're great in chili and my black bean soup. I keep plenty of pantry staples, garlic, and herbs on hand to spice up whatever I'm making." Serve this soup over rice and some crusty bread for a simple meal, and you'll have healthy leftovers for lunch.

YIELD: MAKES 4 SERVINGS

2 tablespoons olive oil
1 medium onion, chopped
1 medium carrot, chopped
4 garlic cloves, chopped
2 teaspoons ground cumin
1 to 2 teaspoons chopped jalapeño chile
    with seeds
2 (15- to 16-ounce) cans black beans,
    with juice
1 (15-ounce) can diced tomatoes with
    juice
1½ cups low-sodium chicken broth
Chopped fresh cilantro, chopped green
    onions, and crumbled feta cheese, for
    serving

"I used dried black beans, which I cooked the night before. The soup turned out wonderfully. I served it with a dollop of plain yogurt, and plain nacho chips on the side. Next time I might add some fresh corn as well."

Ldubravcic, Vancouver, Canada

1. Heat the oil in a heavy large pot over medium-high heat. Add the onion, carrot, and garlic; sauté until vegetables begin to soften, about 6 minutes.

2. Mix in the cumin and 1 teaspoon jalapeño. Add the beans, tomatoes with juice, and broth; bring soup to boil. Reduce heat to medium, cover, and cook until carrot is tender, about 15 minutes.

3. Transfer 3 cups of the soup to a blender and purée until smooth. Return purée to pot. Simmer the soup until slightly thickened, about 15 minutes. Season to taste with salt, pepper, and remaining 1 teaspoon jalapeño, if desired.

4. Ladle the soup into bowls. Pass the cilantro, green onions, and feta cheese separately.

cheese fondue

Fondue may have been trendy in the 1960s and 1970s, but cheesy goodness has never really gone out of style. This recipe is straight from the Alps, and calls for the classic combination of Gruyère and Emmental. Melt them in a cast-iron fondue pot with the simmering wine before transferring the mix to your fondue stand. Of course, you can serve this with cut-up veggies and fruit, but bread is the true classic partner. Just know that if you lose your bread in the cheese, you'll need to kiss your neighbor. That's Swiss tradition.

YIELD: MAKES 6 SERVINGS

1 garlic clove, halved crosswise
1½ cups dry white wine
1 tablespoon cornstarch
2 teaspoons kirsch (optional)
½ pound Emmental cheese, coarsely
     grated (2 cups)
½ pound Gruyère cheese, coarsely grated
     (2 cups)
French bread cubes
Apples and pears, cored and cubed
Roasted potatoes, julienned
Pieces of bell pepper
Blanched broccoli florets

"We serve it with lots of pickled veggies on the side and dip things like broccoli, apples, bread, of course, pears, and whatever else we have in the house that sounds good with cheese!"
Mllejess, Boulder, Colorado

1. Rub the inside of a 4-quart heavy pot with the cut sides of the garlic, then discard the garlic. Add the wine to the pot and bring just to a simmer over moderate heat.

2. Stir together the cornstarch and kirsch (if using; otherwise, use water or wine) in a cup.

3. Gradually add the cheese to the pot and cook, stirring constantly in a zigzag pattern (not a circular motion) to prevent the cheese from balling up, until the cheese is just melted and creamy (do not let boil). Stir the cornstarch mixture again and stir into the fondue. Bring fondue to a simmer and cook, stirring, until thickened, 5 to 8 minutes.

4. Transfer the mixture to a fondue pot set over a flame. Dip pieces of bread, apple and pear, potatoes, bell pepper, and broccoli.

golden and crimson beet salad
with oranges, fennel, and feta

Oranges, fennel, and toasted hazelnuts perk up red and yellow beets in this versatile salad from Chef Alfred Portale of the long-beloved Gotham Bar and Grill in New York City. Equal parts rustic and refined, with an eye-catching mix of colors and sophisticated blend of ingredients, this salad is perfect as a dinner-party starter or main-course accompaniment. Try grilling the beets, instead of roasting, to add yet another layer of flavor.

YIELD: MAKES 6 SERVINGS

2 large (3-inch) red beets, all but 1 inch of tops trimmed
2 large (3-inch) golden beets, all but 1 inch of tops trimmed
5 tablespoons extra-virgin olive oil
4 oranges
1 small fresh fennel bulb, trimmed, quartered, cored, and cut into paper-thin strips
¼ cup finely chopped fresh mint leaves
¼ cup finely chopped fresh flat-leaf parsley
¼ cup hazelnuts, toasted, husked, and halved
1 small shallot, finely chopped
1 tablespoon balsamic vinegar
Kosher or other coarse salt
Freshly ground white pepper
1½ cups coarsely crumbled feta cheese

do ahead:

The **BEETS** can be roasted 1 day ahead. Cover and chill. Bring to room temperature before using.

1. Preheat the oven to 400°F. Place all the beets in a 9-inch square metal pan. Drizzle 3 tablespoons of oil over, sprinkle with salt and pepper, and toss to coat. Cover the pan with foil and roast the beets until tender, about 1½ hours. Uncover and cool completely.

2. Peel the beets, cut into ½-inch cubes, and place in a large bowl, each color on opposite side; sprinkle with salt and pepper.

3. Cut all peel and pith off the oranges. Working over a medium bowl to catch the juice, cut between the membranes, releasing the segments. Add 1 cup of orange segments and the fennel, mint, parsley, hazelnuts, and shallot to the bowl with the beets.

4. Transfer 2 teaspoons of orange juice to a small bowl; whisk in the vinegar and remaining 2 tablespoons olive oil. Season the dressing to taste with salt and white pepper. Stir into the beet mixture.

5. Mound the salad on a large platter. Drain the remaining orange segments; arrange on salad. Sprinkle with cheese.

"I serve it with a piece of grilled chicken for a nice light summer meal. I used pear-infused white balsamic vinegar and fresh basil (instead of mint). Substituted pine nuts for the hazelnuts. Fresh juicy oranges are a must for this to be right."
Hkohl, Coral Springs, Florida

lacinato kale and ricotta salata salad

These dark leafy greens never tasted better. Be sure to seek out lacinato kale (also sold as Tuscan kale, black kale, dinosaur kale, or cavolo nero), a variety that is noticeably more tender and mild than the common curly kale, also known as Scotch kale. Take the time to massage the leaves in oil with your hands; the result will be kale that seems to melt in your mouth. If ricotta salata isn't readily available at your market, try pecorino romano, another Italian cheese that's easy to grate and has a similar salty flavor.

1. Working in batches, cut the kale crosswise into very thin slices.

2. Whisk together the shallot, lemon juice, salt, and pepper in a small bowl, then add the oil in a slow stream, whisking until combined well.

3. Toss the kale and cheese in a large bowl with enough dressing to coat well, then season with salt and pepper.

YIELD: MAKES 6 SERVINGS

¾ to 1 pound lacinato kale or tender regular kale, stems and center ribs discarded
2 tablespoons finely chopped shallot
1½ tablespoons fresh lemon juice
¼ teaspoon salt
¼ teaspoon black pepper
4½ tablespoons extra-virgin olive oil
1 cup coarsely grated ricotta salata (2 ounces)

"I only used a couple tablespoons of olive oil—it didn't seem like it needed as much as the recipe indicated. And I didn't add any salt since my ricotta salata was already quite salty. This is the dish for anyone who doesn't like kale!"

A cook, Wisconsin

clementine jícama salad

In this unique and lively salad, juicy clementines combine with crunchy jícama, salty pumpkin seeds, and creamy queso fresco to create a vibrant yet harmonious medley of textures and flavor notes. The garlicky vinaigrette is versatile enough to use on almost any salad. For a healthy, quick dinner, top the salad with a piece of grilled mahimahi, or pair it with a piece of avocado toast and call it lunch.

YIELD: MAKES 8 SERVINGS

½ teaspoon chopped garlic
½ teaspoon salt
¼ cup fresh lime juice
6 tablespoons olive oil
½ teaspoon sugar
½ teaspoon black pepper
8 clementines, peeled and cut crosswise
    into ¼-inch-thick slices (1¾ pounds)
1 pound jícama, peeled and cut into
    ¼-inch-thick matchsticks (3 cups)
1 small red onion, thinly sliced
¾ cup (packed) cilantro sprigs
½ cup crumbled queso fresco or mild feta
⅓ cup raw green (hulled) pumpkin seeds
    (pepitas), toasted

do ahead:

The **VINAIGRETTE** can be made 4 hours ahead and kept at room temperature.

The **CLEMENTINES, JÍCAMA, AND ONION** can be cut 4 hours ahead and chilled.

1. Mince and mash the garlic to a paste with the salt, then whisk together with the lime juice, oil, sugar, and pepper in a large bowl.

2. Just before serving, add the clementines, jícama, onion, and cilantro and gently toss. Season with salt. Sprinkle with the cheese and pumpkin seeds.

"I used unsalted pistachio nuts instead of the pumpkin seeds, and it turned out delish. I think that adding avocado would also be an excellent decision."

A cook, Oslo, Norway

perfect pear salad

Created by Epicurious member **Kathe Miller** from Chelan, Washington, this beautiful salad has a wonderful presentation as well as a rich taste. Try it as a starter, or as a satisfying lunch. Miller recommends pears that are tender but crisp, giving the salad a divine texture and bite that is at once crunchy and juicy.

1. In a large skillet over moderately high heat, sauté the bacon, stirring occasionally, until crisp, 10 to 12 minutes. Using a slotted spoon, transfer to a paper-towel–lined plate to drain. Set aside.

2. In a medium bowl, whisk together the oil, vinegar, salt, and pepper. In a large bowl, toss the spinach with half the dressing.

3. Divide the spinach among 4 plates. Top with the pear slices. Sprinkle the bacon, cheese, red pepper, and shallot over each plate. Drizzle with the remaining dressing and serve immediately.

YIELD: MAKES 4 SERVINGS

10 slices thick-cut bacon, cut into large dice
6 tablespoons extra-virgin olive oil
¼ cup balsamic vinegar
¼ teaspoon coarse sea salt
⅛ teaspoon freshly ground black pepper
4 cups (loosely packed) baby spinach leaves
1 Anjou pear, peeled, cored, and cut lengthwise into ¼-inch-thick slices
¾ cup coarsely grated Asiago cheese (about 5 ounces)
½ cup red bell pepper, cut into fine dice
2 tablespoons shallot, minced

Don't put too much balsamic on the salads—it's easy to drown them. I like to serve these on pretty salad plates so that each one can be composed in the kitchen!
—Kathe Miller

roasted eggplant salad
with pita chips and yogurt sauce

Chef Joe Bonaparte, academic director of culinary arts at the Art Institute of Charlotte, North Carolina, must have had garden parties or afternoon snacks in mind when creating this enticing combination of eggplant, peppers, and tomatoes topped with parsley, basil, and chives.

YIELD: MAKES 8 SERVINGS

FOR SALAD
3 large eggplants (3 pounds total)
6 tablespoons fresh lemon juice
2 green bell peppers, cored, seeded, and finely diced
2 roasted red peppers, peeled, seeded, and diced
2 tomatoes, seeded and diced
15 yellow or red cherry tomatoes, quartered
4 garlic cloves, chopped
½ cup finely chopped flat-leaf parsley
¼ cup finely chopped fresh chives
2 tablespoons finely julienned fresh basil
1 tablespoon extra-virgin olive oil
½ teaspoon salt
⅛ teaspoon freshly ground black pepper

FOR YOGURT SAUCE
2 cups nonfat plain yogurt
½ cup peeled and diced cucumber
1 jalapeño chile, seeded and diced
1 tablespoon chopped fresh mint
2 tablespoons fresh lemon juice
2 teaspoons olive oil
½ teaspoon salt

FOR PITA CHIPS
4 whole-wheat pitas, each cut into 12 wedges
Vegetable oil cooking spray
2 tablespoons grated reduced-fat Parmesan cheese
2 tablespoons poppy seeds
1 tablespoon sesame seeds
¼ teaspoon freshly ground black pepper

MAKE EGGPLANT
Preheat the oven to 450°F. Line a baking sheet with foil. Poke holes in the eggplants with a fork. Roast until they collapse, 35 to 40 minutes. Cool slightly. Cut the eggplants open, scoop out flesh into a bowl, and discard skins. Mix the flesh with 4 tablespoons of the lemon juice. Let sit 10 minutes. Place the flesh in a fine-mesh strainer and press gently with a large spoon, squeezing out moisture. Chop the eggplant. Mix in the peppers, tomatoes, garlic, parsley, chives, basil, oil, and remaining 2 tablespoons lemon juice. Add salt and pepper.

MAKE YOGURT SAUCE
Mix ingredients in a bowl.

MAKE PITA CHIPS AND SERVE
Preheat the oven to 350°F. Coat one side of each pita wedge with cooking spray. Sprinkle each sprayed side with the Parmesan, seeds, and black pepper. Bake on foil until crisp, 6 to 7 minutes. Serve the eggplant salad with pita chips and yogurt sauce on the side.

"We make it often with mixed greens as a salad main dish (with hummus and tapenade on the side in addition to the yogurt). We add feta and olives to sort of 'meat it up' and it's tasty, hearty, and perfect for when vegetarian friends come to visit."

A cook, Madison, Wisconsin

roasted yellow pepper soup and roasted tomato soup *with serrano cream*

This roasted vegetable duo represents an unconventional combination of vibrant colors, rich aromatics, and sensual tastes. The soups are served as equal partners in one bowl—try each one separately, but be sure to stir them together to get the full experience.

MAKE PEPPER SOUP

1. In a heavy saucepan, cook the shallots, thyme, and salt and pepper to taste in the butter over moderately low heat, stirring, until the shallots are soft. Add the bell peppers and 1½ cups of the broth, and simmer the mixture, covered, for 12 to 15 minutes, or until the peppers are very soft.

2. In a blender, purée the soup in batches until it is very smooth, forcing it as it is puréed through a fine sieve set over the pan, cleaned, and whisk in the cream and enough additional broth to reach the desired consistency. Add the lemon juice and salt and pepper to taste.

MAKE TOMATO SOUP

1. Preheat the oven to 350°F. Spread the tomatoes, skin side down, in one layer in 2 foil-lined jelly-roll pans. Add the garlic to one of the pans, and bake the tomatoes and garlic for 45 minutes to 1 hour, or until the tomatoes are very soft and their skin is dark brown. Let the tomatoes and garlic cool in the pans on racks.

2. In a heavy saucepan, cook the shallots, oregano, and salt and pepper to taste in the butter over moderately low heat, stirring, until the shallots are soft. Add the tomatoes, garlic (skins discarded), and 1½ cups of the broth, and simmer the mixture, covered, for 15 minutes.

3. In a blender, purée the soup in batches until it is very smooth, forcing it as it is puréed through a fine sieve set over the pan, cleaned, and whisk in the cream and additional broth if necessary (both soups should have the same consistency). Add the lemon juice and salt and pepper to taste.

recipe continues

YIELD: MAKES 6 SERVINGS

FOR PEPPER SOUP

3 tablespoons finely chopped shallots
½ teaspoon dried thyme, crumbled
1 tablespoon unsalted butter
6 yellow bell peppers, roasted (see Note) and coarsely chopped (about 6 cups)
1½ cups low-sodium chicken broth, plus more as needed
¼ cup heavy cream
Fresh lemon juice

FOR TOMATO SOUP

3 pounds plum tomatoes, quartered lengthwise
3 large garlic cloves, unpeeled
3 tablespoons finely chopped shallots
½ teaspoon dried oregano, crumbled
1 tablespoon unsalted butter
1½ cups low-sodium chicken broth, plus more as needed
¼ cup heavy cream
Fresh lemon juice

FOR SERRANO CREAM

3 serrano chiles or jalapeños, seeded and finely chopped (wear rubber gloves)
1 large garlic clove, minced and mashed to a paste with ½ teaspoon salt
½ cup crème fraîche or sour cream

do ahead:

The **SOUP** may be made 1 day in advance, kept covered and chilled, and reheated.

cook's note:

Use a long-handled fork to char the **PEPPERS** over an open flame, turning them, for 2 to 3 minutes, or until the skins are blackened. (Or broil the peppers on the rack of a broiler pan under a preheated broiler about 2 inches from the heat. Turn them every 5 minutes, for 15 to 25 minutes, or until the skins are blistered and charred.) Transfer the peppers to a bowl and let them steam, covered, until they are cool enough to handle. Keeping the peppers whole, peel them starting at the blossom end; cut off the tops and discard the seeds and ribs.

do ahead:

The **SERRANO CREAM** may be made 1 day in advance, kept covered and chilled, and brought to room temperature before serving.

MAKE SERRANO CREAM

In a blender, blend the chiles, garlic paste, and crème fraîche until the mixture is combined well. (Be careful not to overblend the mixture or the cream may curdle.) Force the mixture through a fine sieve set over a small bowl.

SERVE SOUP

For each serving, ladle ½ cup of each soup into 2 glass measuring cups, then pour the soups simultaneously into a shallow soup bowl from opposite sides of the bowl. Drizzle some of the serrano cream over each serving.

"I make the pepper and tomato soups, freeze them without the cream, thaw them the day I plan to serve them, add the cream, and heat 'em."

A cook, Toronto, Canada

shrimp and penne rigate alfredo

member recipe

After many rounds of tweaking and perfecting, Epicurious member **Robert Belden** landed on a quick and easy formula for creamy and comforting Alfredo sauce. Although bathing fresh shrimp in a velvety blanket of cream and butter is a pairing that Belden says "is tough to beat," he admits to occasionally substituting seared scallops or grilled chicken for the shrimp. Alongside crisp homemade garlic bread, this pasta dish makes a satisfying dinner to share with a friend or keep all to yourself.

YIELD: MAKES 2 SERVINGS

1 cup penne rigate
1 tablespoon unsalted butter
1 small garlic clove, minced
1 cup heavy cream
½ pound (8 ounces) medium shrimp, peeled and deveined
½ cup small broccoli florets
1 cup freshly grated Asiago cheese

1. In a large pot of boiling salted water, cook the pasta until tender. Drain well and set aside.

2. In a 12-inch skillet over moderate heat, melt the butter. Add the garlic and sauté, stirring occasionally, until translucent, about 1 minute. Add the cream, shrimp, and broccoli and bring to a simmer. Continue cooking, stirring occasionally, until the shrimp is firm and the broccoli is crisp-tender, about 3 minutes. Add the pasta and stir to coat in the sauce. Sprinkle the cheese over the pasta, toss again, and season to taste with salt and pepper. Serve in warm, shallow bowls.

After having several somewhat disappointing versions of pasta Alfredo over the years, I wanted to create my own, with a rich and silky sauce. You can vary by using pecorino romano cheese, or crumbled Gorgonzola dolce for a little more sharp flavor to the sauce.

—Robert Belden

spicy mac and cheese *with pancetta*

Epicurious member **Tess Ellis** of Washington, D.C, drew inspiration from the ingredients she had on hand to create this eclectic take on a classic comfort food. The savory ingredients add dimension to the creamy dish, while the red pepper flakes add a touch of heat. To achieve a delicious crusty top, she suggests that you "put it under the broiler for a few minutes to give it a nice brown coating."

1. In a large, deep skillet over moderate heat, heat the oil. Add the pancetta and cook, stirring occasionally, for 3 minutes. Add the onion and sauté, stirring occasionally, until softened, about 5 minutes. Add the garlic, red pepper flakes, and mushrooms and sauté, stirring occasionally, until the mushrooms are tender, about 5 minutes. Add the tomatoes and their juices and bring to a boil. Reduce the heat to low, partially cover, and simmer, stirring occasionally, until thickened, about 15 minutes.

2. Position a rack in the middle of the oven and preheat the oven to 400°F. Butter the bottom and sides of a 2½-quart baking dish.

3. Meanwhile, in a large pot of boiling salted water, cook the pasta until tender. Drain well and return it to the pot it was cooked in. Add the mushroom-pancetta sauce, cream, and mozzarella and toss to combine. Transfer the pasta to the prepared baking dish, cover with foil, and bake until bubbling and beginning to brown, 20 to 25 minutes.

4. While the pasta is baking, in a small bowl, combine the butter with the bread crumbs and cheeses and stir to combine.

5. After the 20 to 25 minutes baking time, sprinkle the bread-crumb mixture on top of the pasta, making sure to cover the entire surface. Return the pasta to the oven and bake, uncovered, an additional 5 to 10 minutes. Let the mac and cheese stand 15 minutes before serving.

YIELD: MAKES 6 SERVINGS

1½ tablespoons extra-virgin olive oil
½ pound sliced pancetta, finely chopped
1 small onion, finely chopped
2 garlic cloves, minced
1 teaspoon dried red pepper flakes
4 ounces assorted mushrooms, quartered if large
1 (14-ounce) can diced fire-roasted tomatoes
½ pound elbow macaroni
1 cup heavy cream
5 ounces fresh mozzarella cheese, cut into ¼-inch dice
1 tablespoon unsalted butter, room temperature
6 tablespoons plain dry bread crumbs
2 tablespoons freshly grated Parmigiano-Reggiano cheese
2 tablespoons freshly grated Asiago cheese

Special equipment: 2½-quart oval or rectangular baking dish

I love bringing the dish to the table and watching everyone's eyes pop. It just looks fabulous right out of the oven. I try to serve it with something healthy (salad or roasted veggies), but more often than not those sit cold on the plate while everyone loads up for second helpings of the mac and cheese!

—Tess Ellis

farfalle *with sausage, tomatoes, and cream*

Here's a perfect pasta dish, a one-pan dream that pairs tomatoes with savory Italian sausage. Even picky eaters will love this simple dish, featuring a sweet, creamy sauce that can be spiced to taste with red pepper flakes. The whole thing comes together in under 15 minutes, making it an easy weeknight meal that's impressive enough for date night, too. This dish makes delicious leftovers, and cleanup is a breeze.

YIELD: MAKES 6 SERVINGS

2 tablespoons olive oil
1 pound sweet Italian sausages, casings removed
½ teaspoon dried red pepper flakes
1 cup chopped onion
3 garlic cloves, minced
1 (28-ounce) can crushed tomatoes with purée
½ cup heavy whipping cream
1 pound farfalle (bow-tie pasta)
½ cup (packed) chopped fresh basil
Freshly grated pecorino romano cheese, for serving

"I made it just a little healthier by using chicken sausage and light cream instead of regular sausage and whipping cream, and it still was really delicious."
Katiegrace31

1. Heat the oil in a heavy large skillet over medium-high heat. Add the sausage and red pepper flakes. Sauté until the sausage is no longer pink, breaking it up with the back of a fork, about 5 minutes. Add the onion and garlic; sauté until the onion is tender and the sausage is browned, about 3 minutes longer. Add the tomatoes and cream. Reduce the heat to low and simmer until the sausage mixture thickens, about 3 minutes. Season to taste with salt and pepper.

2. Meanwhile, cook the pasta in a large pot of boiling salted water until tender but still firm to the bite. Drain, reserving 1 cup cooking liquid. Return the pasta to same pot. Add the sausage mixture and toss over medium-low heat until the sauce coats the pasta, adding reserved cooking liquid by ¼ cupfuls if mixture is dry. Transfer the pasta to serving dish. Sprinkle with basil. Serve, passing cheese separately.

eggplant lasagne *with parsley pesto*

Meat lovers may smile politely and insist otherwise, but it's the rare vegetarian lasagne that truly pleases the committed carnivore. In the case of this exceptional recipe, the meaty texture of the eggplant makes a luscious stand-in for Bolognese sauce. Choose your eggplant wisely: a younger, smaller one will yield the tastiest results. Try white or Asian eggplant for a more mellow flavor.

MAKE BÉCHAMEL

Cook the garlic in the butter in a 3-quart heavy saucepan over moderately low heat, stirring, 1 minute. Add the flour and cook the roux, whisking, 3 minutes. Add the milk in a stream, whisking. Add bay leaf and bring to a boil over moderately high heat, whisking constantly, then reduce heat and simmer, whisking occasionally, until liquid is reduced to about 4 cups, about 10 minutes. Whisk in the salt and white pepper, then remove from heat and discard bay leaf. Cover the surface of the sauce with wax paper until ready to use.

MAKE PESTO AND RICOTTA MIXTURE

1. Coarsely chop ⅓ cup hazelnuts and reserve for sprinkling over the lasagne.

2. Purée the parsley, cheese, ⅔ cup oil, the garlic, 1 teaspoon salt, 1 teaspoon pepper, and the remaining 1 cup hazelnuts in a food processor until the pesto is smooth, about 1 minute.

3. Whisk the egg in a bowl, then stir in the ricotta, 1 cup parsley pesto, remaining teaspoon salt, and remaining ¼ teaspoon pepper until combined well.

4. Stir together the remaining ¼ cup pesto and remaining ¼ cup oil in a small bowl for drizzling over the lasagne.

ROAST EGGPLANT FOR LASAGNE

1. Put the oven racks in the upper and lower thirds of the oven and preheat the oven to 450°F. Oil 2 large baking sheets.

recipe continues

YIELD: MAKES 8 SERVINGS

FOR BÉCHAMEL

1 garlic clove, minced
3 tablespoons unsalted butter
5 tablespoons all-purpose flour
5 cups whole milk
1 Turkish or ½ California bay leaf
1 teaspoon salt
⅛ teaspoon white pepper

FOR PESTO AND RICOTTA MIXTURE

1⅓ cups hazelnuts (5½ ounces), toasted and loose skins rubbed off in a kitchen towel
4 cups loosely packed fresh flat-leaf parsley leaves
3 ounces Parmigiano-Reggiano, finely grated (1½ cups)
⅔ cup plus ¼ cup olive oil
2 garlic cloves, finely chopped
2 teaspoons salt
1¼ teaspoons black pepper
1 large egg
1 (15-ounce) container whole-milk ricotta

FOR LASAGNE

4 pounds medium eggplants, cut crosswise into ⅓-inch-thick slices
6 tablespoons olive oil
1 teaspoon salt
¾ teaspoon black pepper
9 (7 by 3½-inch) oven-ready lasagna noodles (sometimes called "no-boil"; 6 ounces)
1½ ounces Parmigiano-Reggiano, finely grated (¾ cup)

*"Doubled the recipe, froze one
without baking. Defrosted to room
temp and baked later with
success."*

A cook, Vancouver, Canada

2. Brush the eggplant with oil on both sides, then arrange
in a single layer on the baking sheets and sprinkle with
salt and pepper. Bake, switching position of sheets halfway through and turning slices over once, until tender,
20 to 25 minutes total.

ASSEMBLE LASAGNE

1. Move the oven rack to the middle position and reduce
the oven temperature to 425°F. Lightly oil a 13 by 9-inch
glass or ceramic baking dish and line a larger shallow
baking pan with foil.

2. Spread 1 cup béchamel in the baking dish and cover
with 3 pasta sheets, leaving spaces between sheets. Drop
1 cup ricotta mixture by spoonfuls over the pasta, spreading evenly (layer will be thin), then top with 1 layer of
eggplant, cutting the rounds to fit if necessary. Make
1 more layer each of béchamel, pasta, ricotta, and eggplant.
Spread with 1 cup béchamel and cover with remaining
3 pasta sheets. Spread remaining 1 cup ricotta mixture
over the pasta, then spread the ricotta with the remaining
béchamel and top with remaining eggplant in 1 layer (you
may have a few slices left over). Sprinkle the Parmigiano-
Reggiano over the eggplant and scatter with reserved
chopped hazelnuts.

3. Tightly cover the baking dish with oiled foil (oiled side
down), then set the dish in the foil-lined pan (to catch
drips). Bake the lasagne 30 minutes. Remove the foil, and
bake until golden and bubbling, 10 to 15 minutes more. Let
the lasagne stand 15 to 20 minutes before serving.

4. Serve drizzled with pesto.

wild mushroom lasagne

Mountains of porcini and white mushrooms lend deep woodsy notes to this hearty vegetarian entrée, while a béchamel sauce offers all the richness of a meat-filled version. Use a food processor to finely chop the fresh mushrooms; they'll cook more quickly. Members return to this recipe time and time again because its flavor far outweighs the fuss of assembling it. If you're short on time, make just the filling or the whole dish a day ahead of time.

YIELD: MAKES 6 SERVINGS

FOR MUSHROOM FILLING

3 cups water
2 ounces dried porcini mushrooms (about 1 cup)
2 pounds fresh white mushrooms
2 large zucchini (about 1 pound)
1 large onion
3 garlic cloves
5 tablespoons unsalted butter
6 tablespoons Sherry
2 teaspoons chopped fresh thyme leaves
2½ teaspoons salt
¼ teaspoon freshly ground black pepper

do ahead:

The **MUSHROOM FILLING** may be made 1 day ahead and chilled, covered.

The **SAUCE** may be made 1 day ahead and chilled, covered. Bring sauce to room temperature before proceeding.

The **LASAGNE** may be baked 1 day ahead and chilled, covered. Bring lasagne to room temperature and reheat before serving.

MAKE MUSHROOM FILLING

1. In a small saucepan, bring water to a boil and remove the pan from the heat. Stir in the porcini and soak 20 minutes. Lift out the porcini, squeezing out excess liquid, and reserve the soaking liquid. In a sieve, rinse the porcini to remove any grit and pat dry; chop and transfer to a large bowl. Simmer the soaking liquid until reduced to about ¼ cup. Pour the liquid through a sieve lined with a dampened paper towel into the bowl with the porcini.

2. Quarter the white mushrooms, and in a food processor, pulse in 3 batches until finely chopped. Cut the zucchini into ¼-inch dice. Chop the onion and mince the garlic.

3. In a 12-inch heavy skillet, heat 1 tablespoon butter over moderate heat until the foam subsides and cook one-third of the white mushrooms with 2 tablespoons Sherry, stirring, until the liquid the mushrooms give off is evaporated and they begin to brown. Add the mushroom mixture to the porcini. Cook the remaining mushrooms in 2 batches in the butter with the remaining Sherry in same manner and add to the porcini mixture.

4. In the skillet, cook the zucchini in 1 tablespoon butter until tender and stir into the porcini mixture. Cook the onion in the remaining tablespoon butter, stirring, until softened. Stir in the garlic, thyme, salt, and pepper and cook, stirring, until fragrant, about 30 seconds. Stir the onion into the mushroom mixture until combined.

MAKE SAUCE

In a 3-quart heavy saucepan, melt the butter over moderately low heat and whisk in the flour. Cook the roux, whisking, 3 minutes and then whisk in the milk. Bring the sauce to a boil, whisking constantly, and simmer, whisking occasionally, 3 minutes. Stir in the 1½ cups of Parmesan, the mustard, and salt. Remove the pan from the heat and cover surface with wax paper.

ASSEMBLE AND BAKE LASAGNE

1. Preheat the oven to 375°F and butter a 13 by 9-inch baking dish.

2. Spread 1¼ cups sauce in the baking dish and cover with 3 pasta sheets, making sure they don't touch each other. Spread one-third of the filling over the pasta sheets and top with 3 more pasta sheets, gently pressing down layers to remove air pockets. Top the pasta sheets with one-third mozzarella. Continue layering in same manner with sauce, pasta sheets, filling, and mozzarella, ending with mozzarella (dish will be filled to rim). Spread remaining sauce over top and sprinkle with remaining ½ cup Parmesan. On a foil-lined large baking sheet, bake the lasagne in middle of oven until bubbling and golden, about 45 minutes. Let lasagne stand 20 minutes.

FOR SAUCE

- 1 stick (½ cup) unsalted butter
- ½ cup all-purpose flour
- 5 cups whole milk
- 4½ ounces freshly grated Parmesan cheese (about 1½ cups)
- 2 teaspoons Dijon mustard
- 1½ teaspoons salt
- 18 (7 by 3½-inch) sheets no-boil lasagna noodles (about 1 pound)
- ½ pound freshly grated mozzarella (about 2 cups)
- 1½ ounces freshly grated Parmesan (about ½ cup)

"I cooked all the mushrooms at once, and then cooked the onion, garlic, and zucchini together and then combined them. Makes for fewer steps, and it came out fine. I also made the filling the night before and then assembled the day of, and it worked great."

A cook, Brookline, Massachusetts

vietnamese chicken

This unbelievable stir-fry is a cut way above your average one-wok wonder. Epicurious member **Thomas Spears** of Worcester, Massachusetts, puts his own spin on a classic combination of Southeast Asian flavors—lemongrass, turmeric, and fish sauce—with the richness of caramelized sugar. Feel free to temper the heat by using fewer Thai chiles. The quality of the fish sauce makes all the difference here. Spears notes, "I prefer the brand Thanh Ha Chanh Hieu Phu Quoc nuoc mam, based on its lower salt content and what I believe to have great flavor." Another tip: when slicing the lemongrass, flatten it with the back of your knife to release some extra flavor.

YIELD: MAKES 4 SERVINGS

2 (4- to 6-ounce) boneless skinless chicken breasts, cut into 1-inch cubes
5 tablespoons Asian fish sauce, such as nam pla or nuoc mam
3 tablespoons freshly ground black pepper
2 tablespoons sugar
2 tablespoons vegetable or sunflower oil
1 medium red onion, diced
2 stalks lemongrass, tough outer skin removed, minced
3 Thai chiles, seeds and ribs removed, minced
1 tablespoon turmeric
Steamed white rice or couscous, for serving
1 green onion (white and light green parts only), thinly sliced on a diagonal (optional)

1. In a large bowl, combine the chicken, fish sauce, pepper, and 1 tablespoon sugar. Toss to combine and set aside.

2. In small pot over moderately low heat, combine the oil and the remaining 1 tablespoon sugar. Cook until the sugar turns a deep golden caramel, about 90 seconds—the sugar cooks quickly so be careful not to burn it. Add the red onion and cook, stirring, until starting to soften, about 20 seconds. Remove from the heat.

3. Heat a wok or large shallow-sided skillet over high heat. Add both the onion mixture and chicken, and stir-fry until the chicken begins to turn golden brown, about 4 minutes. Add the lemongrass, chiles, and turmeric, and continue stir-frying until the chicken is cooked through, 2 to 4 minutes more. Serve the chicken over rice or couscous, garnishing with green onion, if desired.

I was having a few friends over for dinner and cocktails one winter night and I was going to make a big pot of tom kha gai (chicken galangal soup), but then wanted to do something else with the same ingredients. I was trying to think of holiday flavors, and for some reason caramel came to mind. I figured that the caramel would add a darker, earthier sweetness to a stir-fry. The sauce also kept the meat super-tender; I've made this so many times since then, and it's always been a winner!
—Thomas Spears

pasta fagiola

This hearty meal-in-a-bowl was recreated by Epicurious member **Alisa Guralnick**, from Encinitas, California, after trying a version of the divine soup at a restaurant in New York City. This recipe features sausage, white beans, spinach, pasta, and other veggies, making this a customizable recipe perfect for extra produce from community gardens, co-ops, or your own garden.

1. In a heavy large pot or Dutch oven over moderate heat, heat the olive oil until hot but not smoking. Add the sausage and cook, breaking up the meat with a spoon, until lightly browned. Add the onions and garlic and cook, stirring frequently, until tender, about 10 minutes.

2. Add the chicken broth, tomatoes, beans and their liquid, and water and bring to a simmer. Continue simmering, stirring occasionally, for 15 minutes. Add the pasta and cook at a gentle boil, raising the heat if necessary and stirring frequently, until tender, about 10 minutes. Add the spinach and cook, stirring occasionally, 3 more minutes. Season with salt and pepper. Divide the soup among bowls, garnish with the basil or parsley, and serve with freshly grated cheese.

You can make this from things you have on hand in the pantry and the freezer, or make it for a crowd by adding some extra vegetables, pasta, sausages. It is really easy and is better the second day, so maybe make it the day before and let it sit in the refrigerator. Then, serve it in big soup bowls with good, warm, crusty Italian bread and olive oil for dipping.
—Alisa Guralnick

YIELD: MAKES 6 TO 8 SERVINGS

1 tablespoon extra-virgin olive oil

1 pound mild Italian pork or turkey sausage, casings removed

2 large onions, chopped

4 garlic cloves, minced

2 (15-ounce) cans low-sodium chicken broth

1 (28-ounce) can diced tomatoes, drained

2 (15-ounce) cans cannellini beans, with their liquid

2 cups water

1½ cups small dried pasta, such as shells or elbow macaroni

10 ounces frozen spinach, thawed, squeezed to remove liquid, and chopped

2 tablespoons chopped fresh basil or flat-leaf parsley

Freshly grated Parmigiano-Reggiano cheese, for serving

risotto *with leeks, shiitake mushrooms, and truffles*

This dish is as good as the time and ingredients you put into it, so use quality ingredients and patience to get the flavors to harmonize. A teaspoon of white truffle oil can substitute for the black truffles.

MAKE LEEKS

Bring the leeks and cream to a boil in a heavy medium saucepan. Reduce the heat to medium and simmer until leeks are tender and cream is thick, stirring often, about 15 minutes. Season with salt and pepper.

MAKE MUSHROOMS

Preheat the oven to 400°F. Toss all the ingredients on a rimmed baking sheet. Sprinkle with salt and pepper. Roast until mushrooms are tender and light brown around edges, stirring occasionally, about 45 minutes.

MAKE RISOTTO

1. Melt 2 tablespoons butter in a heavy large saucepan over medium heat. Add the onion and cook until beginning to soften, about 5 minutes. Add the rice; stir 1 minute. Add the wine and stir until almost all the liquid is absorbed, about 1 minute.

2. Add 1 cup of hot broth. Simmer until the broth is almost absorbed, stirring often, about 4 minutes. Add more broth, 1 cup at a time, allowing each addition to be absorbed before adding next and stirring often, until the rice is tender and mixture is creamy, about 20 minutes longer.

3. Stir in the leek mixture, mushroom mixture, remaining 2 tablespoons butter, the cheese, and truffle. Transfer to a large bowl, sprinkle with parsley, and serve.

"It's really worth every second spent preparing it; the lavish flavors—creamy leeks, truffles, and shiitakes—work together magically."

Bounces

YIELD: MAKES 4 TO 6 SERVINGS

FOR LEEKS

2 large leeks (white and pale green parts only), halved and thinly sliced crosswise (about 2 cups)
¾ cup heavy whipping cream

FOR MUSHROOMS

1 pound shiitake mushrooms, stemmed and cut into ¼- to ⅓-inch-thick slices
1 large onion, halved and thinly sliced lengthwise
¼ cup (½ stick) butter, melted
1 tablespoon white truffle oil
1 teaspoon minced fresh thyme leaves

FOR RISOTTO

4 tablespoons (½ stick) butter
1 large onion, chopped
1½ cups arborio rice or medium-grain white rice
½ cup dry white wine
5 cups hot vegetable broth, or more as needed
½ cup grated Parmesan cheese
2 teaspoons shaved or chopped black truffle (optional)
Chopped fresh parsley leaves

do ahead:

The **LEEKS** can be made 1 day ahead. Cover and chill. Rewarm before continuing. The **MUSHROOMS** can be made 2 hours ahead.

seared scallops *with tarragon-butter sauce*

At the end of a long day, this quick seafood dish and a glass of Chardonnay will get you on your merry way toward a relaxing evening. A quick sear is all that meaty sea scallops require, and cooking them in butter creates a nutty, slightly toasted crust. Beurre blanc may be classically French, but it's also undeniably easy. This tarragon-infused version makes a luscious, slightly anise-flavored blanket for the scallops, which would be cozy atop a bed of sautéed baby spinach.

YIELD: MAKES 4 SERVINGS

1¼ pounds large sea scallops, tough ligament from side of each discarded
¼ teaspoon salt
½ teaspoon pepper
7 tablespoons unsalted butter, cut into tablespoons
2 tablespoons finely chopped shallot
¼ cup dry white wine
¼ cup white-wine vinegar
1 tablespoon finely chopped fresh tarragon

"Allow the liquid to reduce slowly, as it will deepen the flavor. I also used a tarragon white wine vinegar, which brought out the flavor even more. I poured about half the sauce over the scallops and saved the remaining to top our homemade popovers."
DKteachr7, Mapleville, Rhode Island

1. Pat the scallops dry and sprinkle with salt and pepper.

2. Heat 1 tablespoon butter in a 12-inch nonstick skillet over medium-high heat until the foam subsides, then sear the scallops, turning once, until golden brown and just cooked through, about 5 minutes total. Transfer to a platter.

3. Add the shallot, wine, and vinegar to the skillet and boil, scraping up any brown bits, until reduced to 2 tablespoons. Add the juices from the platter and if necessary boil until the liquid is reduced to about ¼ cup. Reduce the heat to low and add 3 tablespoons butter, stirring until almost melted, then add the remaining 3 tablespoons butter and swirl until incorporated and sauce has a creamy consistency. Stir in the tarragon and salt to taste; pour sauce over scallops.

spicy shrimp *with andouille sausage on grits*

No trip to South Carolina's Low-Country is complete without a nibble of the region's famed shrimp and grits. This recipe, from the Boathouse in Charleston, South Carolina, uses smoked andouille sausage and green hot pepper sauce to provide the essential kick, while a generous cup of whipping cream mellows the heat and smoothes the grits. Serve this for a casual dinner party, or use it to liven up a midweek meal. Epicurious members also serve this with pasta or polenta.

1. Combine the hot sauce, wine, shallot, lemon juice, and vinegar in a heavy medium saucepan. Boil over medium heat until reduced to ½ cup, about 15 minutes. Stir in ½ cup of the cream.

2. Bring the remaining ½ cup cream, the water, milk, and butter to a simmer in a heavy medium saucepan. Gradually whisk in the grits. Simmer until the grits are very soft and thickened, stirring frequently, about 1 hour.

3. Meanwhile, heat the olive oil in a heavy medium skillet over medium heat. Add the sausage, bell peppers, onion, and garlic; sauté until the vegetables are tender, about 8 minutes. Add the shrimp, tomatoes, and Cajun and Old Bay seasonings, and sauté until the shrimp are opaque in the center, about 6 minutes. Season to taste with salt and pepper.

4. Bring the hot pepper–cream sauce to a simmer. Spoon the grits onto 6 plates, dividing equally. Spoon the shrimp mixture over the grits. Drizzle the hot pepper–cream sauce over and serve.

"Made two small adjustments: One, I couldn't find andouille sausage, so I substituted chorizo, and it was delicious; two, I used fontina cheese with the grits."

Lwalsh, South Carolina

YIELD: MAKES 6 SERVINGS

⅓ cup green hot pepper sauce
¼ cup dry white wine
1 shallot, chopped
1 tablespoon fresh lemon juice
1 tablespoon rice vinegar
1 cup heavy whipping cream
5 cups water
3 cups whole milk
¼ cup (½ stick) unsalted butter
2 cups hominy grits
¼ cup olive oil
8 ounces andouille or other smoked
    sausage, sliced
1 red bell pepper, chopped
1 yellow bell pepper, chopped
½ cup minced onion
4 garlic cloves, chopped
30 uncooked large shrimp, peeled and
    deveined
4 plum tomatoes, chopped
1 teaspoon Cajun seasoning
1 teaspoon Old Bay seasoning

cedar-planked salmon *with maple glaze and mustard mashed potatoes*

The smoky flavor of the fish combined with a sweet maple sauce and mustardy potatoes adds up to a rustic fall meal that will win raves. Inspired by the open-fire plank-cooking techniques of northwest Native American cultures, this nontraditional version uses the oven instead of the grill. Be sure to presoak the plank overnight to prevent flare-ups, and if you don't have a plank, fear not: many Epi members report great success simply roasting the salmon in a pan with the glaze.

YIELD: MAKES 6 SERVINGS

1 cup pure maple syrup
2 tablespoons finely grated peeled fresh ginger
4 tablespoons fresh lemon juice
3 tablespoons soy sauce
1½ teaspoons minced garlic
1 (2½-pound) center-cut salmon fillet with skin
1 bunch green onions (green parts only)
Mustard Mashed Potatoes (recipe follows)

Special equipment: Untreated presoaked cedar plank about 17 by 10½ inches (optional)

do ahead:

The **MAPLE GLAZE** may be made 2 days ahead and chilled, covered. Bring to room temperature before proceeding.

The **POTATOES** may be made 1 day ahead. Chill in a buttered ovenproof dish, covered. Bring to room temperature before reheating, covered.

1. In a small heavy saucepan, simmer the maple syrup, ginger, 3 tablespoons lemon juice, soy sauce, garlic, and salt and pepper to taste until reduced to about 1 cup, about 30 minutes, and let cool.

2. Preheat the oven to 350° F. If using a cedar plank, lightly oil and heat the plank in the middle of the oven 15 minutes; or lightly oil a shallow baking pan large enough to hold the salmon.

3. Arrange the onion greens in one layer on the plank or in the baking pan to form a bed for the fish.

4. In another small saucepan, heat half of glaze over low heat until heated through to use as a sauce. Stir in the remaining tablespoon lemon juice. Remove the pan from the heat and keep sauce warm, covered.

5. Put the salmon, skin side down, atop the onion green and brush with the remaining glaze. Season the salmon with salt and pepper and roast in the middle of the oven until just cooked through, about 20 minutes if using a baking pan or about 35 minutes if using a plank.

6. Cut the salmon crosswise into 6 pieces. On each plate, arrange the salmon and onion greens on a bed of mashed potatoes. Drizzle the salmon with warm sauce.

"This salmon is great cooked and flaked on a salad lightly dressed with balsamic vinaigrette and garnished with a touch of freshly squeezed lemon."
Librarian4kids, Inverness, Scotland

mustard mashed potatoes

1. In a 5-quart kettle or pot, cover the potatoes with cold salted water by 2 inches and simmer until tender, 35 to 45 minutes. While potatoes are simmering, in a small saucepan, heat the milk with the butter over moderate heat until the butter is melted. Remove from the heat and keep the milk mixture warm, covered.

2. In a colander, drain the potatoes and cool just until they can be handled. Peel the potatoes, transferring to a large bowl. Add the mustard, salt and pepper to taste, and three-fourths of the hot milk mixture. With a potato masher, mash until smooth, adding more milk mixture if necessary to make the potatoes creamy.

YIELD: MAKES 6 SERVINGS

3 pounds Yukon Gold potatoes
1½ cups milk
6 tablespoons unsalted butter
3 tablespoons whole-grain or
    coarse-grain mustard

tilapia *with artichoke, caper, and cherry tomato sauce and israeli couscous*

member recipe

While some recipes require elaborate introductions justifying particular flavor combinations, the creation from Epicurious member **Sarah Perl** of Brooklyn, New York, needs little justification as it eventually won her a husband. Perl also praises the dish for its versatility: "It's simple enough for a weeknight dinner and special enough for a dinner party." So, choose a fresh fish fillet and serve up this dish in the name of romance.

YIELD: MAKES 2 SERVINGS

1 cup dry Italian-flavored bread crumbs
¼ cup freshly grated Parmigiano-
    Reggiano cheese (about 1 ounce)
¾ teaspoon coarse sea salt
⅛ teaspoon freshly ground black pepper
2 (8-ounce) tilapia fillets
3 tablespoons olive oil
1 cup chicken stock or low-sodium
    chicken broth
1 cup Israeli couscous
1 bunch green onions (white and light
    green parts only), thinly sliced
1 small red onion, finely diced
4 garlic cloves, minced
1 (6-ounce) jar marinated artichokes,
    drained and liquid reserved
½ cup cherry tomatoes, quartered
2 tablespoons bottled capers, drained
½ cup vegetable stock
1½ teaspoons unsalted butter
3 tablespoons lemon juice

Soon after I had successfully created this recipe, I was out with friends and my new creation came into the conversation. A few minutes later, a friend introduced me to a man and the recipe continued to be discussed among us all. A year and a half later, I am happily with this handsome food-loving gentleman, and we often joke about how it was my new tilapia recipe that connected us.

–Sarah Perl

1. On a large plate, stir together the bread crumbs, cheese, ½ teaspoon salt, and the black pepper. Rinse the tilapia fillets and pat dry, then coat on both sides with the bread-crumb mixture.

2. In a large nonstick skillet over moderately high heat, heat 2 tablespoons of the olive oil until hot but not smoking. Add the tilapia fillets and sauté, turning once, until golden and just cooked through, 4 to 5 minutes total. Transfer the tilapia to a plate and keep warm.

3. In a medium saucepan over moderately high heat, bring the stock to a boil. Remove from the heat and stir in the couscous and the remaining ¼ teaspoon salt. Let stand, covered, for 10 minutes, then stir in the green onions. Cover and keep warm.

4. While the couscous is standing, prepare the sauce: In the skillet that was used to cook the fish, heat the remaining 1 tablespoon olive oil over moderately low heat. Add the red onion and sauté, stirring frequently, about 1 minute. Add the garlic and sauté, stirring frequently, until the onion is soft, about 2 more minutes. Add the artichokes and sauté, stirring occasionally, about 2 more minutes. Add the tomatoes and capers and sauté, stirring occasionally, until the tomatoes start to soften, about 3 more minutes. Stir in the reserved artichoke liquid, the vegetable stock, butter, and lemon juice and simmer, stirring occasionally, until the sauce thickens slightly, about 3 more minutes.

5. Divide the couscous between 2 plates and top each with a tilapia fillet. Spoon the sauce over the fish and couscous and serve immediately.

oven-roasted sea bass
with ginger and lime sauce

Forget going out for dinner, this sea bass is dressed to impress in less than 20 minutes. The sauce begs to be scooped up, so be sure to serve this dish with fluffy basmati rice. Sauté snow peas or green beans in sesame oil and serve them alongside. And by all means, invite friends, as this dish can easily be doubled. (Most halibut, trout, salmon, cod, or tuna can take the place of the sea bass, so buy whatever is freshest and avoid the endangered Chilean sea bass.)

1. Preheat the oven to 500°F. Mix the lime juice, soy sauce, cilantro, ginger, and shallot with 3 teaspoons of oil in a small bowl. Season the sauce with salt and pepper.

2. Brush a 9-inch-diameter glass pie dish with the remaining 2 teaspoons oil. Arrange the fish in the prepared dish; turn to coat. Sprinkle with salt and pepper; spoon ½ tablespoon sauce over each fillet.

3. Roast the fish until just opaque in center, about 12 minutes. Top the fish with the remaining sauce and serve.

YIELD: MAKES 2 SERVINGS

2 tablespoons fresh lime juice
1½ tablespoons soy sauce
1 tablespoon chopped fresh cilantro
1 tablespoon chopped peeled fresh
  ginger
1 tablespoon minced shallot
5 teaspoons light or regular olive oil
2 (6-ounce) sea bass fillets, each about
  ¾ inch thick

"We make this once a week. There is usually too much for one night, so we make fish tacos with the leftovers. My friend loves the sauce so much she makes quarts of it for big parties to put on salmon and other fish."
Tribe, Laguna Beach, California

chicken and fall vegetable pot pie

Transform plain chicken breasts into a new feast with this succulent take on the pot pie. Make the filling the night before, then get to work on the aromatic herb crust, stuffed with thyme and butter. The pie demands a fair amount of preparation, but efforts will be rewarded with high praise. Halve the measurements for a weeknight dinner for the kids, or make the whole recipe to serve a crowd of eager guests. And feel free to throw in whatever produce you have on hand.

1. Butter a 4-quart oval baking dish. Place the chicken breasts in a heavy large pot. Add just enough broth to cover the chicken. Bring the broth to a boil, reduce heat to low, cover the pot and simmer until the chicken is just cooked through, skimming surface occasionally, about 20 minutes. Using tongs, transfer the chicken to a plate and cool.

2. Add the carrots and turnips to the broth in the pot. Simmer uncovered until the vegetables are just tender, about 10 minutes. Using a slotted spoon, transfer the vegetables to the prepared baking dish. Add the turnip greens to the broth and cook just until wilted, about 1 minute. Using a slotted spoon, transfer the greens to a colander; drain well. Add to the vegetables in the baking dish.

3. Strain the broth; reserve 4 cups. Remove the skin and bones from the chicken. Cut the meat into ½- to ¾-inch pieces. Add the chicken to the vegetables in the baking dish.

4. Melt the butter in the same pot over medium heat. Add the leeks, shallots, and thyme. Sauté until tender, about 8 minutes. Add the flour and stir 2 minutes. Stir in 4 cups broth and the wine. Increase the heat to high and bring to a boil, stirring constantly. Add the cream and boil until the sauce thickens enough to coat a spoon, whisking frequently, about 6 minutes. Season with salt and pepper. Pour the sauce over the mixture in the baking dish. Stir to blend. Cool 45 minutes.

YIELD: MAKES 8 SERVINGS

4 pounds chicken breasts with skin and
    bones
4 to 6 cups canned low-sodium chicken
    broth
3 large carrots, peeled and cut into
    ½-inch pieces
1 pound turnips, peeled and cut into
    ½-inch pieces
1 large bunch turnip greens (about 8 to
    10 ounces), center stem cut away,
    leaves cut into 1-inch pieces
¼ cup (½ stick) butter
3 medium leeks (white and pale green
    parts only), sliced
2 large shallots, minced
2 tablespoons minced fresh thyme leaves
½ cup all-purpose flour
½ cup dry white wine
½ cup heavy whipping cream
Herb Crust (recipe follows)

do ahead:

The **FILLING** can be made 1 day ahead. Cover and refrigerate.

The **DOUGH** can be made 2 days ahead. Keep chilled. Let dough soften slightly before rolling out.

recipe continues

5. Position a rack in the top third of the oven and place a baking sheet on the bottom rack. Preheat the oven to 400°F.

6. Roll out the dough for the crust on parchment to a 15 by 10½-inch rectangle. Using the parchment as an aid, turn the dough over onto the filling. Trim the overhang; tuck the dough edge inside the dish. Roll out any dough scraps to ¼-inch thickness. Cut out leaf shapes. Brush the bottom of the cutouts with water and place on the crust; cut slits in the crust to allow steam to escape.

7. Place the pot pie on the top rack and bake until the crust is golden and the sauce is bubbling, about 50 minutes. Let stand 10 minutes before serving.

herb crust

YIELD: MAKES CRUST FOR 1 POT PIE

2½ cups all-purpose flour
2 tablespoons chopped fresh parsley
1 tablespoon chopped fresh thyme
1 teaspoon salt
1 teaspoon sugar
½ cup (1 stick) chilled unsalted butter, cut into ½-inch pieces
½ cup chilled vegetable shortening, cut into ½-inch pieces
6½ tablespoons ice water, as more as needed

1. Blend the flour, parsley, thyme, salt, and sugar in a food processor until the herbs are very finely chopped. Add the butter and shortening. Blend until the mixture resembles coarse meal.

2. Transfer the mixture to a large bowl. Using a fork, mix enough ice water into the flour mixture to form moist clumps. Gather the dough into a ball; flatten into a rectangle. Cover and chill 30 minutes.

chicken chili

A blender and a saucepan are all you'll need to cook this peanut-thickened chili. In authentic Mexican fashion, the nuts, along with the dried chiles, garlic, cilantro, and cumin, are blended with tomatoes and chicken broth to create an earthy, spicy stew base. Pulled rotisserie chicken—a brilliant time-saver—and fiber-rich beans complete the magic. To turn this into a "meatless Monday" meal, replace the chicken with another can of beans and use a good-quality veggie broth. And always remember to wear gloves while handling chiles.

1. Purée the broth, tomatoes with their juice, chiles, onion, garlic, cilantro, peanuts, cumin, and salt in a blender until smooth, about 2 minutes.

2. Heat the oil in a wide 3- to 4-quart heavy saucepan over moderately high heat until hot but not smoking, then pour in the sauce and boil, uncovered, stirring occasionally, 5 minutes.

3. Meanwhile, coarsely shred the chicken, discarding skin and bones.

4. Stir the chicken and beans with their liquid into the chili, then reduce the heat to moderately low and simmer, covered, 10 minutes. Serve with cilantro and sour cream.

"I used chipotle peppers instead of guajillo chiles, cut back on the garlic by one clove, and added corn and a bit of butternut squash—loved it with a slice of corn bread, a dollop of sour cream, and avocado cubes."

Fab40, Calgary, Canada

YIELD: MAKES 4 SERVINGS

1¼ cups reduced-sodium chicken broth
1 (14-ounce) can stewed tomatoes
4 dried New Mexican or guajillo chiles, stems and seeds discarded and chiles torn into pieces
1 (¾-inch-thick) crosswise slice of medium white onion
2 garlic cloves, peeled
½ cup coarsely chopped fresh cilantro
¼ cup dry-roasted peanuts
1 teaspoon ground cumin
¼ teaspoon salt, or to taste
2 tablespoons olive oil
1 (2-pound) rotisserie-cooked chicken
1 (15-ounce) can pink beans in liquid
Chopped fresh cilantro and sour cream, for garnish

beef stew *with potatoes and carrots*

This recipe is flexible enough that you can add whatever vegetables you have on hand; root vegetables and winter squash are ideal candidates. And as with many one-pot dishes, the stew will taste better the next day, so plan accordingly.

YIELD: MAKES 12 SERVINGS

FOR BRAISED BEEF

5 pounds boneless beef chuck (not lean), cut into 2-inch pieces
2½ teaspoons salt
1 teaspoon black pepper
3 tablespoons olive oil
3 medium carrots, quartered
3 celery ribs, quartered
2 medium onions, quartered
1 head garlic, halved crosswise
3 tablespoons tomato paste
⅓ cup balsamic vinegar
1 (750-ml) bottle dry red wine (about 3¾ cups)
2 Turkish bay leaves or 1 California
2 sprigs fresh thyme
3 cups low-sodium beef broth
3 cups water

FOR POTATOES AND CARROTS

2½ pounds small white boiling potatoes
1½ pounds carrots
Crusty bread, for serving

Special equipment: Wide 6- to 8-quart heavy pot with a tight-fitting lid

do ahead:

The **STEW** improves in flavor if made at least 1 day ahead. Chill up to 5 days. Reheat, covered, over medium heat or in a 350°F oven.

BRAISE BEEF

1. Preheat the oven to 350°F, with the rack in the middle.

2. Pat the beef dry and season with salt and pepper.

3. Heat the oil in a heavy 8-quart pot over medium-high heat until it shimmers, then brown the meat, without crowding, in 3 batches, turning, about 8 minutes per batch. Transfer to a platter.

4. Reduce the heat to medium, then add the carrots, celery, onions, and garlic and cook, stirring occasionally, until well browned, about 12 minutes.

5. Push the vegetables to one side of the pot. Add the tomato paste to the cleared area and cook the paste, stirring, 2 minutes, then stir it into the vegetables. Add the vinegar and cook, stirring, 2 minutes. Stir in the wine, bay leaves, and thyme and boil until the wine is reduced by about two-thirds, 10 to 12 minutes.

6. Add the broth to the pot along with the water, beef, and any juices from the platter and bring to a simmer. Cover and braise in the oven until the meat is very tender, about 2½ hours.

7. Set a large colander in a large bowl. Pour the stew into the colander. Return the meat to the pot, then discard the remaining solids. Let cooking liquid stand 10 minutes.

MAKE POTATOES AND CARROTS

1. While beef braises, peel the potatoes and cut into ½-inch-wide wedges. Slice the carrots diagonally (1-inch).

2. Add the potatoes and carrots to the stew (make sure they are submerged) and simmer, uncovered, stirring occasionally, until the potatoes and carrots are tender, about 40 minutes.

beef empanadas

Long the star of South American street snacks, the empanada gets a dinner close-up with this hearty version that puts an entire meal in the palm of your hand. This recipe adapts easily to the stuffing of your choice. Substitute lean ground turkey and bake for a lighter alternative.

1. Cut each egg crosswise into 10 thin slices.

2. Cook the onion in the olive oil in a heavy medium skillet over medium heat, stirring frequently, until softened. Add the garlic, cumin, and oregano and cook, stirring, 1 minute. Stir in the beef and cook, breaking up lumps with a fork, until no longer pink, about 4 minutes.

3. Add the raisins, olives, salt, pepper, and tomatoes with reserved juice, then cook, stirring occasionally, until the liquid is reduced but the mixture is still moist, about 5 minutes. Spread on a plate to cool.

4. Preheat the oven to 200°F, with the rack in the middle.

5. Lay a large sheet of plastic wrap on a dampened work surface (to help keep plastic in place), then roll out an empanada disk on the wrap to measure about 6 inches. Place 3 tablespoons of meat mixture on the disk and top with 2 slices of egg. Moisten the edges of the disk with water and fold over to form a semicircle, then crimp with a fork. Make 9 more empanadas in the same manner.

6. Heat ¾ inch of vegetable oil in a deep 12-inch skillet over medium heat until it registers 360°F on a deep-fry thermometer. Fry the empanadas, 2 or 3 at a time, turning once, until crisp and golden, 4 to 6 minutes per batch.

7. Transfer the empanadas to a shallow baking pan and keep warm in the oven. Return oil to 360°F between frying batches.

YIELD: MAKES 10 EMPANADAS

2 hard-boiled large eggs
½ medium onion, finely chopped
1 tablespoon olive oil
1 garlic clove, finely chopped
½ teaspoon ground cumin
½ teaspoon dried oregano
¾ pound ground beef chuck
2 tablespoons raisins
1½ tablespoons chopped pimiento-stuffed olives
½ teaspoon salt
¼ teaspoon pepper
1 (14-ounce) can whole tomatoes in juice, drained, reserving 2 tablespoons juice, and chopped
1 package (10) frozen empanada pastry disks, thawed
About 4 cups vegetable oil, for frying

Special equipment: Deep-fry thermometer

cook's note:

The **EMPANADAS** can be brushed with oil and baked on an oiled baking sheet in a 425°F oven until golden, about 10 minutes. (They will not be as crisp as fried empanadas.)

blackened steak salad

A signature item on the lunch menu of Chicago's famed Chop House, this salad is perfect for a hearty meal, day or night. The classic pairing of blue cheese and steak gets extra oomph from a zesty spice mixture. If you are expecting guests, throw the butter-drenched beef tenderloins on a hot grill for a minute or two before serving for a hint of smoky flavor, and pair the dish with a full-bodied red wine.

YIELD: MAKES 2 SERVINGS

FOR SPICE MIXTURE
1 tablespoon paprika
2 teaspoons ground black pepper
1½ teaspoons salt
1 teaspoon garlic powder
1 teaspoon cayenne
½ teaspoon dried oregano
½ teaspoon dried thyme

FOR SALAD
¼ cup olive oil
2 tablespoons balsamic vinegar
1 teaspoon Dijon mustard
6 cups (packed) mixed baby greens
½ green bell pepper, thinly sliced
½ cup thinly sliced red onion
2 (5- to 6-ounce) beef tenderloin steaks, each about ½ inch thick
3 tablespoons unsalted butter, melted
6 tablespoons crumbled blue cheese (about 3 ounces)
1 medium tomato, quartered

---

do ahead:

The **SPICE MIXTURE** can be made 1 week ahead. Store airtight at room temperature.

---

1. Mix all the ingredients for the spice mixture in a small bowl.

2. Whisk the oil, vinegar, and mustard in a large bowl to blend. Season with salt and pepper. Add the greens, bell pepper, and onion and toss to coat. Divide the salad between 2 plates.

3. Spread the spice mixture on a plate. Coat both sides of the steaks with the mixture. Dip both sides of the steaks into melted butter. Heat a heavy large skillet over high heat until very hot. Add the steaks and cook to desired doneness, about 2 minutes per side for medium-rare.

4. Transfer steaks to a cutting board; let stand 2 minutes. Thinly slice the steaks crosswise. Arrange the slices atop the salads. Sprinkle with cheese. Garnish with tomato and serve.

"I brushed a bit of the dressing on some portobello mushrooms and sprinkled with some of the rub. Grilled them along with the steak and sliced onto the salad. Added cucumber and extra blue cheese."

A cook, Kirkland, Washington

skillet steak and onion *on sourdough toast*

These open-faced steak sandwiches are equal parts hearty and elegant. Onions cooked in beer (ales are best) partner well with meaty rib eye, and thick toasted slices of sourdough soak up the yummy juices of both. We love this speedy skillet supper with a cup of tomato soup and a light green salad served alongside. And don't be afraid to add a sprinkle of freshly grated aged Parmesan; a hit of salty cheese will only improve what's already a knockout dish.

1. Toast the bread; arrange on plates. Pat ¼ teaspoon pepper onto each side of each steak; sprinkle the steaks lightly with salt. Melt 1 tablespoon butter in a heavy medium skillet over medium-high heat. Add the steaks and sauté to desired doneness, about 4 minutes per side for medium-rare. Place one steak on each toast; pour any pan juices over.

2. Melt the remaining 1 tablespoon butter in another medium skillet over medium-high heat. Add the onion and sauté until soft and golden, about 8 minutes. Add the beer and half of the thyme. Boil until the liquid thickens, about 2 minutes. Season with salt and pepper.

3. Spoon the onion mixture over the steaks. Sprinkle with the remaining thyme.

YIELD: MAKES 2 SERVINGS

2 (4 by 6-inch) slices sourdough bread, each about ½ inch thick
1 teaspoon coarsely cracked pepper
2 (¾-inch-thick) rib-eye steaks
2 tablespoons (¼ stick) butter
1 large onion, thinly sliced
½ cup beer
2 tablespoons chopped fresh thyme, or 2 teaspoons dried

"I substituted sourdough with rye bread the second time I made it, and it was received with rave reviews at a lunch party."
A cook, Rancho Cucamonga, California

sausage and broccoli rabe torta

Equal parts comfort and sophistication, this torta toes the line between hearty main and delicate appetizer. Flaky crespelle pastry with a rich besciamella sauce and sweet Italian sausage produce a dish worthy of every minute of effort.

YIELD: MAKES 4 SERVINGS

FOR CRESPELLE
2 large eggs
⅔ cup whole milk
½ cup all-purpose flour
¼ teaspoon salt
3 tablespoons unsalted butter, melted

FOR FILLING
¾ pound broccoli rabe
4 garlic cloves, finely chopped
½ teaspoon dried red pepper flakes
3 tablespoons olive oil
¾ pound sweet Italian sausage, casings removed

FOR BESCIAMELLA SAUCE
½ stick (¼ cup) unsalted butter
¼ cup all-purpose flour
1 ¾ cups whole milk
¼ teaspoon salt
¼ teaspoon black pepper
1 ounce finely grated Parmigiano-Reggiano cheese (½ cup)

FOR ASSEMBLY
1 tablespoon unsalted butter, melted
¼ cup dry bread crumbs
¼ pound chilled Italian fontina, coarsely grated (1 cup)
1 ounce finely grated Parmigiano-Reggiano cheese (½ cup)

Special equipment: 8-inch round springform pan

MAKE CRESPELLE

1. Blend together the eggs, milk, flour, and salt in a blender until smooth. Transfer to a bowl.

2. Lightly brush a 10-inch nonstick skillet with melted butter and heat over moderate heat until hot but not smoking. Ladle about ¼ cup batter into the skillet, tilting and rotating the skillet to coat the bottom, then pour any excess batter back into the bowl. (If batter sets before skillet is coated, reduce heat slightly for next crespella.) Cook until just set and underside is lightly browned, about 30 seconds, then invert the crespella onto a clean kitchen towel to cool completely. (It will be cooked on one side only.)

3. Make 5 more crespelle with remaining batter in same manner, brushing skillet with melted butter as needed.

MAKE FILLING

1. Cut off and discard 1 inch from stem ends of broccoli rabe, then coarsely chop remainder.

2. Cook the broccoli rabe in an 8-quart pot of boiling salted water, uncovered, until just tender, about 5 minutes. Transfer with a slotted spoon to a large bowl of ice and cold water to stop the cooking. Drain well in a colander and pat dry.

3. Cook the garlic with the red pepper flakes in the oil in a 12-inch nonstick skillet over moderate heat, stirring occasionally, until golden, about 8 minutes. Add the sausage and cook, breaking up sausage with the back of a wooden spoon, until no longer pink inside, about 5 minutes. Stir in the broccoli rabe and cook, tossing to coat with sausage, until heated through, about 3 minutes. Remove from heat.

MAKE BESCIAMELLA SAUCE

Heat the butter in a 3-quart heavy saucepan over moderately low heat until the foam subsides, then add the flour and cook, whisking, 3 minutes. Add the milk in a slow stream, whisking, and bring to a boil, whisking. Reduce the heat and simmer, whisking occasionally, 5 minutes. Stir in the salt, pepper, and cheese, then remove from the heat.

ASSEMBLE TORTA

1. Put the oven rack in the middle position and preheat the oven to 425°F. Invert the bottom of an 8-inch springform pan (torta will be easier to slide off bottom when serving), then lock. Wrap the outside of the entire bottom of the pan with a double layer of foil. Generously brush the inside bottom and side of the pan with butter, then sprinkle the bottom with bread crumbs.

2. Stir together the cheese in a bowl. Put one crespella in the bottom of the pan, then sprinkle with one-sixth of the filling and drizzle with ⅓ cup sauce. Make 5 more layers each of crespella, filling, and sauce (end with a layer of sauce). Sprinkle cheese mixture evenly over the top.

3. Bake, uncovered, until the top is bubbling and golden, about 25 minutes. Cool in the pan on a rack 15 minutes. Remove the side of the pan and carefully slide the torta off the bottom of the pan onto a plate. Cut torta into wedges.

"Mellow, delicate, even subtle. I did not have Asiago, so used Reggiano and grated Cheddar for the top. And what a lovely presentation, to boot!"
A cook, Scranton, Pennsylvania

do ahead:

The **BROCCOLI RABE** can be cooked and drained 1 day ahead and chilled in an airtight container. Bring to room temperature before using.

The **SAUCE** can be made 1 day ahead and cooled completely, uncovered, then chilled, covered.

The **CRESPELLE** can be made 3 days ahead and chilled, wrapped tightly in plastic wrap.

We think this might well be the ultimate Thanksgiving menu, one that stars Tom Colicchio's Herb-Butter Turkey, Brussels Sprout Hash with Caramelized Shallots, and New England Sausage, Apple, and Dried Cranberry Stuffing.

Brussels Sprout Hash with Caramelized Shallots (page 263)

New England Sausage, Apple, and Dried Cranberry Stuffing (page 262)

tom colicchio's herb-butter turkey

Basic but brilliant is an apt description for this never-fail Thanksgiving turkey from acclaimed restaurant-owner and *Top Chef* judge Tom Colicchio. His secret is to use a moisture-ensuring butter that is rubbed under the turkey skin; Tom's is speckled with rosemary, sage, tarragon, and thyme, but use herbs of your choosing to put a personal stamp on this dynamite bird. With its simple and traditional flavor notes, this turkey can be paired with a variety of stuffings, though we're partial to our New England Sausage, Apple, and Dried Cranberry Stuffing (page 262).

YIELD: MAKES 8 SERVINGS

FOR GRAVY BASE
2 tablespoons unsalted butter
2 pounds turkey necks and/or wings
2 cups diced onions
1 cup diced peeled carrots
1 cup diced celery
6 cups low-sodium chicken broth, or more as needed

FOR TURKEY
1 cup (2 sticks) butter, at room temperature
2 teaspoons minced fresh thyme, plus 15 fresh thyme sprigs
2 teaspoons minced fresh tarragon, plus 5 large fresh tarragon sprigs
2 teaspoons minced fresh rosemary, plus 5 fresh rosemary sprigs
2 teaspoons minced fresh sage, plus 5 fresh sage sprigs
1 (14- to 16-pound) turkey
4 cups low-sodium chicken broth
¼ cup all purpose flour

do ahead:

The **GRAVY BASE** can be prepared 2 days ahead. Cool slightly. Refrigerate uncovered until cold, then cover and keep chilled. Rewarm before using.

MAKE GRAVY BASE

1. Melt the butter in a heavy large deep skillet over high heat. Add the turkey necks and/or wings and sauté until deep brown, about 15 minutes. Add the onions, carrots, and celery and sauté until vegetables are deep brown, about 15 minutes. Add the 6 cups chicken broth and bring to boil. Reduce the heat to medium-low and simmer uncovered 45 minutes, stirring occasionally.

2. Pour the gravy base through a strainer set over a 4-cup measuring cup, pressing on the solids to extract liquid. If necessary, add enough more chicken broth to gravy base to measure 4 cups.

MAKE TURKEY

1. Mix ½ cup butter and all the minced herbs in a small bowl; season the herb butter with salt and pepper. Transfer 2 generous tablespoons to another small bowl and reserve for gravy; let stand at room temperature.

2. Set a rack at lowest position in the oven and preheat the oven to 425°F. Rinse the turkey inside and out; pat dry. Starting at the neck end, slide your hand between the skin and the breast meat to loosen the skin. Rub 4 tablespoons of herb butter over the breast meat under the skin. Place the turkey on a rack set into a large roasting pan. Sprinkle the main cavity generously with salt and pepper. Place 4 tablespoons of plain butter and all the herb sprigs in the main cavity. Tuck the wing tips under. Tie the legs together loosely. Rub the 2 tablespoons remaining herb butter over the outside of the turkey. Sprinkle the turkey generously with salt and pepper.

3. Place the turkey in the oven and roast 20 minutes. Reduce the oven temperature to 350°F. Roast 30 minutes more, then pour 1 cup broth over and add 1 tablespoon plain butter to the roasting pan. Roast 30 minutes more; baste with pan juices, then pour another 1 cup broth over and add another 1 tablespoon butter to pan. Cover the turkey loosely with foil. Roast until a thermometer inserted into thickest part of the thigh registers 175°F, basting with pan juices and adding 1 cup broth and 1 tablespoon butter to pan every 45 minutes, about 1 hour 45 minutes longer. Transfer the turkey to a platter; let stand 30 minutes (internal temperature will rise 5 to 10 degrees).

4. Strain the pan juices into a bowl; whisk in the gravy base. Melt the reserved 2 tablespoons herb butter in a heavy large saucepan over medium heat; add the flour and whisk constantly until the roux is golden brown, about 6 minutes. Gradually add the pan juice–gravy base mixture; increase the heat and whisk constantly until gravy thickens, boils, and is smooth. Reduce the heat to medium; boil gently until gravy is reduced to 4½ cups, whisking often, about 10 minutes. Season the gravy with salt and pepper and serve with the turkey.

"I did add a lemon to the cavity and some lemon zest to the herb butter. The result was a beautifully browned, moist bird with the most delicious gravy we have ever had."
A cook, Fairport, New York

new england sausage, apple, and dried cranberry stuffing

There's a lot to like about this classic American stuffing. Sweet Italian sausage has salty appeal, while the combination of tart green apples and dried cranberries delivers a one-two punch of tangy sweetness.

YIELD: MAKES 14 SERVINGS (ABOUT 18 CUPS)

14 ounces white bread, cut into ¾-inch cubes (about 12 cups)
1 pound sweet Italian sausages, casings removed
¼ cup (½ stick) butter
6 cups sliced leeks (white and pale green parts only; about 3 large leeks)
1 pound tart green apples, peeled, cored, and chopped
2 cups chopped celery with leaves
4 teaspoons poultry seasoning
1 cup dried cranberries (about 4 ounces)
4 teaspoons chopped fresh rosemary
⅔ cup chopped fresh parsley
3 large eggs, beaten to blend
1⅓ cups low-sodium chicken broth, or as needed

cook's note:

To bake the **STUFFING** in pan, butter a 15 by 10-inch baking dish. Mix 1⅓ cups broth into stuffing and transfer to the prepared dish. Cover with buttered foil and bake at 350°F until heated through, about 45 minutes. Uncover and bake until top is golden brown, about 15 minutes.

1. Preheat the oven to 350°F. Divide the bread cubes between 2 large baking sheets. Bake until slightly dry, about 15 minutes. Cool completely.

2. Sauté the sausages in a heavy large skillet over medium-high heat until cooked through, crumbling coarsely with the back of a spoon, about 10 minutes. Using a slotted spoon, transfer the sausage to a large bowl.

3. Pour off any drippings from the skillet. Melt the butter in the same skillet over medium-high heat. Add the leeks, apples, celery, and poultry seasoning; sauté until leeks soften, about 8 minutes. Mix in the cranberries and rosemary. Add the mixture to the sausage, then mix in the bread and parsley. Season the stuffing to taste with salt and pepper.

4. When ready to stuff the bird, mix the eggs into the stuffing. Fill the main turkey cavity with the stuffing. Mix enough chicken broth into the remaining stuffing to moisten (about ¾ to 1 cup chicken broth, depending on amount of remaining stuffing). Spoon into a buttered baking dish. Cover with buttered aluminum foil and bake alongside the turkey until heated through, about 45 minutes. Uncover stuffing and bake until top is golden brown, about 15 minutes.

"Challah bread is a wonderful substitute, but more often I use potato bread. Raisins and dried apricots are a good substitute for dried cranberries."

A cook, New Jersey

brussels sprout hash
with caramelized shallots

Thanks to caramelized shallots and a brown sugar–cider vinegar glaze, this surprisingly elegant hash wins over even the most adamant of Brussels sprout naysayers. Plus, it requires almost no preparation; everything is quickly sautéed, making this an ideal addition to the holiday table. This hearty hash is also perfect for the morning. Pair it with a sunny-side egg, and you have a well-rounded breakfast or an impressive, guest-worthy brunch.

1. Melt 3 tablespoons butter in a medium skillet over medium heat. Add the shallots; sprinkle with kosher salt and pepper. Sauté until soft and golden, about 10 minutes. Add the vinegar and sugar. Stir until brown and glazed, about 3 minutes.

2. Halve the sprouts lengthwise. Cut lengthwise into thin (⅛-inch) slices. Heat the oil in a large skillet over medium-high heat. Add the sprouts; sprinkle with salt and pepper. Sauté until brown at the edges, 6 minutes. Add the water and remaining 3 tablespoons butter. Sauté until most of the water evaporates and the sprouts are tender but still bright green, 3 minutes. Add the shallots; season with salt and pepper.

YIELD: MAKES 8 TO 10 SERVINGS

6 tablespoons (¾ stick) butter
½ pound shallots, thinly sliced
Kosher or other coarse salt
2 tablespoons apple cider vinegar
4 teaspoons sugar
1½ pounds Brussels sprouts, trimmed
3 tablespoons extra-virgin olive oil
1 cup water

"I found that by prepping all of the ingredients and storing them in tight plastic, I can throw the sauté together a few minutes before dinner and not lose the greenness and crispness of the sprouts. It's a Thanksgiving staple."
Oh_wow, Frenchtown, New Jersey

turkey pot pie *with cheddar biscuit crust*

This simple-to-prepare pot pie is a perfect excuse for all that leftover Thanksgiving turkey. The cheesy crust is so good that you'll want to bake it as a stand-alone biscuit—use just a cup of buttermilk for a stiffer consistency.

YIELD: MAKES 8 SERVINGS

FOR STOCK

Carcass and skin from 12- to 14-pound roast turkey
10 cups water

FOR FILLING

1 medium onion, coarsely chopped
2 large carrots, cut into ½-inch pieces
2 celery ribs, cut into ½-inch pieces
1 large parsnip, peeled, cored, and cut into ½-inch pieces
1 teaspoon chopped fresh thyme
½ teaspoon salt
¼ teaspoon pepper
3 tablespoons unsalted butter
½ pound mushrooms, trimmed and quartered
¼ cup all-purpose flour
4 cups roast turkey meat, cut into ½-inch pieces
1 (10-ounce) package frozen baby peas, thawed

FOR BISCUIT CRUST

2 cups all-purpose flour
2 teaspoons baking powder
1 teaspoon baking soda
½ teaspoon salt
½ teaspoon black pepper
1 cup coarsely grated extra-sharp Cheddar cheese
¼ cup grated Parmigiano-Reggiano cheese
¾ stick (6 tablespoons) cold unsalted butter, cut into ½-inch pieces
1¼ cups well-shaken buttermilk

MAKE STOCK

Separate parts of the carcass and put, along with skin, in an 8-quart pot. Cover the bones with the water and simmer until liquid is reduced by one-third, about 1½ hours. Strain through a fine-mesh sieve into a large bowl. Set aside 3½ cups stock (reserve remainder for another use).

MAKE FILLING

1. Cook the onion, carrots, celery, parsnip, thyme, salt, and pepper in the butter in a 12-inch-wide shallow pot (3- to 4-quart), covered, over medium heat, stirring occasionally, until the vegetables are almost tender, 10 to 12 minutes. Add the mushrooms and cook, uncovered, stirring, until tender, 5 to 7 minutes.

2. Sprinkle with the flour and cook, stirring constantly, 2 minutes. Stir in the reserved stock, scraping up any brown bits, and bring to a boil, stirring, then simmer until slightly thickened, about 3 minutes. Stir in the turkey, peas, and salt and pepper to taste. Reheat over low heat just before topping with biscuit crust.

MAKE BISCUIT CRUST AND BAKE PIE

1. Preheat the oven to 400°F, with the rack in the middle.

2. Sift together the flour, baking powder, baking soda, salt, and pepper into a medium bowl. Add the cheeses and toss to coat. Blend in the butter with a pastry blender or your fingertips until the mixture resembles coarse meal. Add the buttermilk and stir just until a dough forms.

3. Drop the biscuit dough onto the filling in 8 large mounds, leaving spaces between the biscuits. Bake until the biscuits are puffed and golden brown and the filling is bubbling, 35 to 40 minutes. Let stand 10 minutes before serving.

cornbread stuffing *with fresh and dried fruit*

Buttermilk-enriched cornbread combines with onions, apples, dried apricots, and prunes in this simple and versatile Thanksgiving stuffing. While prep is fairly minimal, take note: You'll need to dry the bread overnight, so be sure to start this recipe the day before. And if you'd like to offer a vegetarian-friendly option, swap a high-quality vegetable stock for the chicken broth.

1. Cut the bread lengthwise into 1-inch-wide slices. Place on a baking sheet; cover with a kitchen towel and let dry overnight. Cut the bread slices into 1-inch cubes.

2. Preheat the oven to 375°F. Butter a 13 by 9-inch glass baking dish. Melt the butter in a heavy large skillet over medium heat. Add the onions and sauté until translucent, about 10 minutes. Add the apples and celery; sauté until celery begins to soften, about 10 minutes. Scrape the contents of the skillet into a very large bowl. Add the prunes, apricots, fennel seeds, salt, pepper, and thyme; toss. Add the dried bread cubes and toss until evenly combined. Transfer the stuffing to the prepared dish. Pour the broth evenly over.

3. Bake the stuffing uncovered until heated through and the top begins to form a crust, about 40 minutes.

YIELD: MAKES 6 SERVINGS

Buttery Cornbread (recipe follows)
½ cup (1 stick) unsalted butter
4 cups chopped onions
4 cups chopped unpeeled McIntosh or Golden Delicious apples (about 2 large)
2 cups chopped celery with leaves
24 pitted prunes, diced (about 10 ounces)
12 dried apricot halves, diced (about 2 ounces)
1 tablespoon fennel seeds
2 teaspoons kosher or other coarse salt
1 teaspoon freshly ground black pepper
1 teaspoon dried thyme
1 cup low-sodium chicken broth

buttery cornbread

1. Butter a 9 by 5 by 3-inch metal loaf pan. Mix the cornmeal, flour, sugar, baking powder, and salt in a large bowl. Add the buttermilk, melted butter, and beaten eggs. Stir with a wooden spoon until well blended. Let the mixture stand 30 minutes to absorb the liquid. Meanwhile, preheat the oven to 375°F.

2. Pour the batter into the prepared pan. Bake the bread until browned around the edges and a tester inserted into the center comes out clean, about 40 minutes. Let the bread rest in the pan 5 minutes. Turn bread out onto a rack and cool completely.

YIELD: MAKES 1 LOAF

1⅓ cups coarse stone-ground yellow cornmeal
1 cup unbleached all-purpose flour
¼ cup sugar
2 teaspoons baking powder
¾ teaspoon kosher or other coarse salt
1 cup plus 2 tablespoons buttermilk
9 tablespoons (1 stick plus 1 tablespoon) unsalted butter, melted
1 large egg plus 1 large egg yolk, lightly beaten

fresh herb spaetzle

Is it a dumpling or a noodle? Spaetzle, the beloved dish of Austrians, Germans, Hungarians, and the Swiss, is infinitely easier to make than it is to classify. While some spaetzle dishes are cheesy and rich, this version is lightened with fresh herbs—a lot of them.

YIELD: MAKES 4 SERVINGS

2¼ cups all-purpose flour
1 teaspoon salt
¼ teaspoon ground white pepper
⅛ teaspoon ground nutmeg
3 large eggs
¾ cup whole milk
8 teaspoons minced assorted fresh herbs
  (parsley, thyme, rosemary, and chives)
4 tablespoons (½ stick) butter
2 tablespoons extra-virgin olive oil
8 ounces button mushrooms, thinly sliced
1 medium onion, chopped
¾ cup low-sodium chicken broth, or as
  needed

do ahead:

The **SPAETZLE** can be prepared
3 hours ahead (through step 2). Let
stand at room temperature.

1. Blend the flour, salt, pepper, and nutmeg in a large bowl. Whisk in the eggs and milk, forming a soft batter. Mix in half of the herbs.

2. Bring a large pot of salted water to a boil. Butter a large bowl. Working with ⅓ cup batter at a time and using a rubber spatula, press the batter directly into the boiling water through ¼-inch holes on a coarse grater, strainer, or wide ladle. Stir the spaetzle to separate and boil 2 minutes. Using a fine sieve, scoop the spaetzle from the pot, drain well, and transfer to the buttered bowl.

3. Melt 2 tablespoons butter with 1 tablespoon oil in a heavy large skillet over medium heat. Add the mushrooms; sauté until beginning to soften, about 4 minutes. Add the onion; sauté until beginning to soften, about 5 minutes. Add the remaining 2 tablespoons butter, remaining 1 tablespoon oil, and the spaetzle. Sauté until the spaetzle begin to brown, stirring often, about 10 minutes. Add the broth. Simmer until absorbed, adding more broth if dry. Mix in the remaining herbs; season with salt and pepper.

"This was ridiculously easy, yet delicious. Our family made the spaetzle together and had so much fun. The cheese grater was easier than the colander. We only used thyme, but will try the other herbs next time."

Timozero2, New York, New York

wild rice stuffing *with pearl onions*

Whoever believes that bread-based stuffing is the only one worth eating hasn't tried this wild rice version. Alongside perfectly cooked poultry, its blend of sweet and savory stands out as a great-tasting, healthier alternative to plain old stuffing. Pearl onions are sweeter than their larger cousins and they add a nice visual touch, so seek them out in the market's frozen section. And to fortify nutrients, substitute with brown rice, which requires a little more cooking time than white.

1. Melt 2 tablespoons butter in a large skillet over medium heat. Add the onions and sauté until brown, about 15 minutes. Set aside.

2. Bring the broth and 1 tablespoon thyme to a boil in a large saucepan. Add the wild rice. Bring to a boil, reduce the heat, cover, and simmer 30 minutes. Add the white rice, cover, and simmer until all the rice is tender and the liquid is almost absorbed, about 15 minutes longer.

3. Stir the apricots, cherries, raisins, and remaining 2 tablespoons thyme into the rice mixture; cover and simmer 3 minutes. Stir the pearl onions and remaining 4 tablespoons butter into the rice, then mix in the pecans. Season generously with salt and pepper.

4. Loosely fill the main cavity of a turkey with cool stuffing. Butter a glass baking dish. Spoon the remaining stuffing into the prepared dish and cover with buttered foil, buttered side down. Bake the stuffing alongside the turkey until heated through, about 20 minutes.

"My husband and daughter were diagnosed with celiac disease, so we have been searching for a gluten-free dressing that all of us like! Even our non-celiac son loved this, as did everyone else at our Thanksgiving supper! We could not find dried tart cherries, so we substituted a mix of fresh and dried cranberries, and it was superb."
A cook, Ottawa, Canada

YIELD: MAKES 8 TO 10 SERVINGS

6 tablespoons (¾ stick) butter
18 ounces pearl onions, blanched in boiling water 1 minute and peeled
4½ cups low-sodium chicken broth
3 tablespoons chopped fresh thyme
1¼ cups wild rice (about 6½ ounces)
1¼ cups long-grain white rice
1 (6-ounce) package dried apricots, coarsely chopped
1 cup dried tart cherries
1 cup raisins
1 cup pecans, toasted and chopped

cook's note:

To bake the **STUFFING** in a baking dish, preheat oven to 350°F. Butter a 13 by 9-inch glass baking dish. Transfer the stuffing to a prepared dish. Cover with buttered foil, buttered side down, and bake until heated through, about 30 minutes.

cranberry sauce *with dried cherries and cloves*

The cherry-cranberry combination achieves the perfect balance of flavors alongside a roasted turkey or ham—or drizzled on vanilla ice cream. If cherry cider is hard to find, substitute a sweet-tart fruit juice such as cranberry or pomegranate.

YIELD: MAKES 4½ CUPS

2½ cups cherry cider or black cherry cider or cranberry juice cocktail
1 (8-ounce) package dried tart cherries (2 cups)
1 cup sugar
1 (12-ounce) package cranberries
¼ (generous) teaspoon ground cloves

Bring the cider to a simmer in a heavy, large saucepan. Remove from the heat. Add the cherries and let stand 8 minutes. Mix in the sugar, then the cranberries and cloves. Cook over medium-high heat until cranberries burst, stirring occasionally, about 9 minutes. Refrigerate until cold, about 4 hours (sauce will thicken as it cools).

butternut squash *with pumpkin-seed pesto*

This zinger of a pesto sauce breathes new life into a nutritious winter staple, and works well with acorn and kabocha squash, too.

YIELD: MAKES 6 SERVINGS

1 (3-pound) butternut squash, peeled and cubed (½ inch; about 6 cups)
¼ cup olive oil
¾ teaspoon salt
½ cup green (hulled) pumpkin seeds (pepitas; not toasted)
½ cup (packed) cilantro sprigs
1½ teaspoons fresh lemon juice
¼ teaspoon black pepper

"I couldn't find pumpkin seeds at the grocery store, so I substituted sunflower seeds, which worked just fine."
A cook, Pleasant Hill, California

1. Preheat the oven to 500°F with the rack in the middle.

2. Toss the butternut squash with 2 tablespoons oil and ½ teaspoon salt, then arrange in a single layer in a 17 by 12-inch baking pan and roast, turning occasionally, until golden brown on edges, 20 to 25 minutes.

3. Toast the pumpkin seeds in 1 tablespoon oil in a large heavy skillet over medium-high heat, stirring frequently, until the seeds are puffed and beginning to brown, 2 to 4 minutes. Transfer to a large plate and cool.

4. Pulse the cooled seeds in a food processor with the cilantro, lemon juice, ¼ teaspoon each of salt and the pepper and 1 remaining tablespoon oil to a coarse paste. Toss the squash with the pesto and salt and pepper to taste. Serve immediately.

sweet potato purée *with smoked paprika*

Transform a traditional holiday side into something bold and beautiful using smoked paprika (hot or sweet) and cayenne. This dish couldn't be simpler to prepare, requiring just a handful of ingredients and yielding a result that's sweet, savory, and delicious.

1. Put the oven rack in the middle position and preheat the oven to 400°F.

2. Prick each potato once with a fork, then bake potatoes in a foil-lined shallow baking pan until tender, about 1 hour. When cool enough to handle, peel, then cut away any dark spots. Purée the potatoes with the butter, cream, paprika, salt, and cayenne in a food processor until smooth.

YIELD: MAKES 8 SERVINGS

3 pounds sweet potatoes
½ stick (¼ cup) unsalted butter, cut into
    ½-inch cubes and softened
⅓ cup heavy cream
¼ teaspoon sweet or hot smoked paprika
¼ teaspoon salt, or to taste
⅛ teaspoon cayenne, or to taste

do ahead:

The **PURÉE** can be made 1 day ahead and chilled in an airtight container. Reheat in a double boiler or a metal bowl set over a saucepan of simmering water, stirring occasionally.

"I had an urge to try out a new kitchen torch, so I did serve this in individual ramekins and sprinkled about 2 teaspoons of sugar on the top and hit it with the flame. . . . Sort of a sweet/savory sweet potato brûlée."

A cook, Washington, D.C.

polenta fries *with roasted red pepper ketchup*

If you've ever made polenta, you know about the "polenta dilemma." Freshly made polenta is so filling and luscious that there are almost always leftovers, but reheated polenta is disappointing: it's never quite as creamy. Happily, this satisfying side dish, courtesy of the much-loved Roy's restaurant on Hawaii's Big Island, offers a great solution. Dredging firmed-up polenta in a little bit of flour and then frying it ever so lightly results in a divine finger food—and the accompanying roasted red pepper ketchup is a recipe you'll want to use for turkey burgers and beyond.

YIELD: MAKES 10 TO 12 SERVINGS

4 cups whole milk
1 cup water
2 tablespoons butter
2¼ cups yellow cornmeal
1 cup grated smoked Gouda cheese
  (about 4 ounces)
2 tablespoons chopped fresh basil
2 tablespoons chopped fresh thyme
½ cup olive oil, or more as needed
All-purpose flour, for dusting
Roasted Red Pepper Ketchup (recipe
  follows)

*"I served this at an all-out veggie
party. They all loved it! I plan to
use the red pepper ketchup in my
pasta sauces."*
A cook, Caracas, Venezuela

1. Lightly oil a 13 x 9-inch metal baking pan. Bring the milk, water, and butter to a boil in a heavy large saucepan. Gradually whisk in the cornmeal. Reduce the heat to low and cook until the polenta is very thick and starts to pull away from the sides of the pan, stirring often, about 8 minutes. Remove polenta from the heat. Stir in the cheese, basil, and thyme. Season to taste with salt and pepper. Immediately transfer the polenta to the prepared baking pan, spreading evenly to cover. Refrigerate until cool and firm, about 1 hour.

2. Cut the polenta lengthwise in the pan into 3 (3-inch-wide) rectangles. Cut each rectangle crosswise into ¾-inch-wide strips. Set the polenta strips aside.

3. Preheat the oven to 300°F. Heat ½ cup oil in a heavy large skillet over medium-high heat. Place some flour in a pie plate. Lightly coat the polenta strips with flour; shake off excess. Working in batches, fry the polenta strips until golden brown on all sides, adding more oil if necessary, about 5 minutes. Using a slotted spoon, transfer the fries to paper towels and drain. Place fries on a baking sheet and keep warm in the oven while cooking the remaining batches. Transfer the fries to a large platter and serve with Roasted Red Pepper Ketchup.

roasted red pepper ketchup

Combine the tomatoes with their juices and all remaining ingredients in a heavy large saucepan over high heat. Bring to a boil. Reduce the heat to medium and simmer until reduced to about 3 cups, about 30 minutes. Discard the bay leaf. Working in batches, purée the mixture in a blender until smooth. Season with salt and pepper. Cool slightly, then chill until cold.

YIELD: MAKES ABOUT 3 CUPS

1 (14½-ounce) can diced tomatoes in juice
1 (7.25-ounce) jar roasted red peppers, drained
1 cup chopped red onion
½ cup dry red wine
6 tablespoons light brown sugar
2 large dried ancho chiles, seeded and coarsely chopped
2 tablespoons tomato paste
2 tablespoons red-wine vinegar
1 tablespoon fennel seeds
2 teaspoons chopped garlic
1½ teaspoons ground cumin
1 bay leaf

bourbon sweet potatoes

member recipe

Epicurious member **Eileen La Mendola** tells us that her husband's family preferred their sweet potatoes roasted and topped with melted marshmallows. But it was her husband who inspired this revamped version of the family classic featuring bourbon and pecans. It's been a hit ever since.

1. Position a rack in the middle of the oven and preheat the oven to 350°F. Butter a 2-quart baking dish.

2. In a medium pot over moderately high heat, combine the potatoes with enough cold water to cover by 1 inch. Bring to a boil, then reduce the heat to moderately low and simmer, uncovered, until the potatoes are tender, about 15 minutes. Drain the potatoes and transfer to the bowl of a stand mixer fitted with a paddle attachment. Add the butter, bourbon, orange juice, brown sugar, salt, cinnamon, nutmeg, and cloves and beat on medium speed until smooth, about 1 minute.

3. Transfer the mixture to the prepared baking dish and sprinkle the pecans on top. Bake until golden brown, about 45 minutes. Serve immediately.

YIELD: MAKES 6 TO 8 SERVINGS

4 pounds sweet potatoes, peeled and cut into 1-inch chunks
½ cup (1 stick) unsalted butter, softened
½ cup bourbon
⅓ cup orange juice
¼ cup (packed) light brown sugar
1 teaspoon kosher salt
1 teaspoon ground cinnamon
½ teaspoon ground nutmeg
¼ teaspoon ground cloves
⅓ cup chopped pecans

Special equipment: 2-quart baking dish

wild mushroom–potato gratin

Layers of potatoes smothered in cheese and mushrooms provide cozy comfort at any winter or holiday meal. This side—rich and creamy on the inside, toasted and crunchy on the top—will definitely warm you on a cold night. Gruyère cheese, sweet and salty, affords this dish its smooth texture, while the mushrooms add a distinctive flavor that will keep the family asking for seconds.

YIELD: MAKES 8 SERVINGS

½ pound fresh wild or exotic mushrooms, such as chanterelles or shiitakes (discard shiitake stems), trimmed and coarsely chopped

2½ tablespoons unsalted butter

¾ pound fresh cremini mushrooms, trimmed and sliced ¼ inch thick

1½ teaspoons minced garlic

3 pounds russet (baking) potatoes

1½ cups heavy cream

1½ cups whole milk

1½ teaspoons salt

½ teaspoon white pepper

¼ teaspoon freshly grated nutmeg

1 cup finely grated Gruyère cheese (2 ounces)

Special equipment: a 15 by 10 by 2-inch oval gratin dish or other 3-quart shallow baking dish

"I mix smoked and nonsmoked Gruyère and add an extra layer of cheese over the mushrooms. Yum!"

A cook, Kansas City, Missouri

1. Put the oven rack in the middle position and preheat the oven to 400°F.

2. Cook the chanterelles or shiitakes with salt and pepper to taste in 1 tablespoon butter in a large nonstick skillet over moderate heat, stirring, until liquid mushrooms give off is evaporated and the mushrooms are tender, about 8 minutes; transfer to a bowl. Cook the cremini in the remaining 1½ tablespoons butter in the skillet, stirring, until the liquid is evaporated and the mushrooms are tender, about 8 minutes; transfer to the bowl with the wild mushrooms. Toss the mushrooms with 1 teaspoon garlic.

3. Peel the potatoes and cut crosswise into ⅛-inch-thick slices (preferably with an adjustable-blade slicer). Bring the potatoes, cream, milk, salt, white pepper, nutmeg, and remaining ½ teaspoon garlic to a boil in a 4- to 6-quart heavy pot, stirring once or twice, then remove from the heat. Transfer half of the potatoes to a buttered gratin dish with a slotted spoon, spreading evenly. Spread the mushrooms evenly over the potatoes, then top with the remaining potatoes. Pour the cooking liquid over the potatoes and sprinkle with the cheese.

4. Bake the gratin until the top is golden brown and the potatoes are tender, 45 to 55 minutes. Let stand 10 minutes before serving.

thai fried eggplant *with basil*

Think of this dish from Epicurious member **WCASS,** from Toronto, as an Asian-style ratatouille. The key to this recipe is speed: the vegetables need little more than a quick toss in a wok or large sauté pan to cook. Look for Chinese eggplants and Thai basil, but small Italian eggplants and regular basil will do. If you like spicier food, you can leave in the chile ribs and some or all of the seeds, and complement the Asian flavors with some sriracha and a mung bean garnish.

1. In a small bowl, whisk together the fish sauce, soy sauce, brown sugar, and warm water; set aside.

2. In a wok over moderately high heat, warm 2 tablespoons oil until hot but not smoking. Add the eggplant and stir-fry, tossing occasionally, until softened and light golden brown, about 2 minutes. Transfer the eggplant to a paper-towel–lined plate to drain.

3. Return the wok to moderately high heat and warm 1 tablespoon of oil until hot but not smoking. Add the onion and stir-fry until soft and translucent, 3 to 4 minutes. Transfer the onion to a bowl and reserve.

4. Return the wok to moderately high heat and warm the remaining 1 tablespoon oil until hot but not smoking. Add the garlic, ginger, and chiles and stir-fry until fragrant, about 30 seconds. Add the sliced peppers and reserved onion and stir-fry until the peppers just begin to soften, about 30 seconds. Add the reserved eggplant and toss to combine. Stir in the fish sauce mixture and the basil, and simmer for 1 minute.

5. While the sauce is simmering, whisk the cornstarch with the cold water until dissolved. Add the cornstarch mixture to the wok and continue simmering, stirring occasionally, until the sauce thickens and coats the vegetables, about 1 minute. Serve immediately.

YIELD: MAKES 6 SERVINGS

2 tablespoons Asian fish sauce, such as nam pla or nuoc mam
1 tablespoon light soy sauce
1 tablespoon light brown sugar or palm sugar
¾ cup warm water
4 tablespoons canola or sunflower oil
3 medium Chinese eggplants, halved and cut into 1-inch pieces
1 medium onion, roughly chopped
4 to 5 garlic cloves, minced
1 (3-inch) piece peeled fresh ginger, minced
3 fresh Thai or serrano chiles, seeds and ribs removed and minced
1 large red bell pepper, thinly sliced
1 large green bell pepper, thinly sliced
Generous handful of fresh Thai basil leaves, roughly chopped (about ½ cup)
2 teaspoons cornstarch
4 tablespoons cold water

beets and caramelized onions *with feta*

Enjoy this rustic salad as a palate-opening starter or as a hearty side—the combination of robust beets, salty feta, sweet onions, and toasted pine nuts pairs particularly well with the lamb and beef recipes in this book. If you prefer fresh beets, roast them ahead of time and toss them in the dressing once they've cooled. Use a combination of red and yellow beets for a more colorful presentation, and to trim some fat and calories, seek out light feta; you'll never notice the difference.

YIELD: MAKES 4 SERVINGS

2 tablespoons cider vinegar
1 teaspoon Dijon mustard, preferably whole-grain or coarse-grain
¼ teaspoon black pepper
¾ teaspoon salt
5 tablespoons olive oil
1 pound onions (2 medium), quartered lengthwise, then cut crosswise into 1-inch pieces
2 (15-ounce) cans small whole beets, drained and quartered (or halved if very small)
½ cup crumbled feta cheese (3 ounces)
¼ cup pine nuts, toasted and coarsely chopped (1 ounce)

1. Whisk together the vinegar, mustard, pepper, and ½ teaspoon salt in a large bowl, then add 3 tablespoons oil in a slow stream, whisking until combined well.

2. Cook the onions with the remaining ¼ teaspoon salt in the remaining 2 tablespoons oil in a 12-inch heavy skillet over moderate heat, stirring occasionally, until golden brown, 18 to 20 minutes. Add the onions to the dressing, then add the beets and cheese, stirring gently to combine. Serve sprinkled with pine nuts.

"I added a diced chicken breast, and served it as a light summer dinner."

A cook, Vancouver, Canada

multi-grain bread
with sesame, flax, and poppy seeds

With a recipe that is simple enough for beginners yet customizable for experienced bakers, this bread will end the days of buying overpriced loaves. Choose your favorite 7- or 10-grain cereal and then experiment with your own mixture of seeds and nuts to determine the taste and texture that suit you. This loaf is special enough to be a gift but requires less than an hour of active prep time. Use it for sandwiches or eat it toasted with a smear of butter or jam.

1. Place the cereal in a large heatproof bowl. Pour the boiling water over. Let stand until the mixture cools to between 105° and 115°F, about 20 minutes.

2. Sprinkle the yeast over the cereal. Add 1 cup bread flour, the oil, sugar, and salt, and stir until smooth. Gradually mix in enough remaining bread flour to form a dough. Cover the dough; let rest 15 minutes.

3. Turn out dough onto a floured surface. Knead until smooth and elastic, adding more flour if sticky, about 10 minutes. Oil a large bowl. Add the dough to the bowl and turn to coat. Cover the bowl with a clean kitchen towel. Let the dough rise in a warm area until doubled, about 1 hour.

4. Mix all the seeds in a bowl. Punch down dough. Turn out onto a lightly oiled surface. Knead briefly. Shape into a 12 by 4-inch loaf. Sprinkle a baking sheet with 2 teaspoons seeds. Place the loaf atop the seeds. Cover with a towel. Let rise in a warm area until almost doubled, about 30 minutes.

5. Position the oven rack in the center and another just below center in the oven. Place a baking pan on the lower rack and preheat the oven to 425°F. Brush the loaf with water. Sprinkle with the remaining seed mixture. Using a sharp knife, cut 3 diagonal slashes in the surface of the loaf. Place the baking sheet with the loaf in the oven. Immediately pour 2 cups of water into the hot pan on the lower rack (water will steam).

6. Bake the loaf until golden and crusty and a tester inserted into the center comes out clean, about 35 minutes. Transfer to a rack and cool.

YIELD: MAKES 1 LOAF

½ cup unsweetened multi-grain cereal
  (such as 7-grain)
2 cups boiling water
1 envelope active dry yeast
4⅓ cups bread flour, or as needed
1 tablespoon olive oil
1 tablespoon dark brown sugar
1½ teaspoons salt
2 teaspoons sesame seeds
2 teaspoons flax seeds
2 teaspoons poppy seeds
2 cups water

do ahead:

The **BREAD** can be made 1 day ahead. Wrap in plastic; store at room temperature.

"Soft, tasty crumb, and an excellent, crunchy crust. I made one loaf in a loaf pan and one hand-shaped loaf, and both were perfect (although the loaf pan took a little longer to bake)."
Stefanie_1973, the United Kingdom

cheddar jalapeño bread

While several hours are required for the dough to rise twice, this top-rated bread recipe demands little more than 20 minutes of active time. If you prefer milder heat, omit the chile seeds and ribs, as that's where the majority of their fire resides. A shopping note: Always purchase extra yeast. If it doesn't foam when combined with water, it's past its prime and you'll need to start over with new. Active dry yeast will keep for about a year, but with this recipe in your repertoire, you're likely to use it much sooner than that.

YIELD: MAKES 1 LOAF

1 teaspoon active dry yeast (less than a ¼-ounce package)

1¾ cups plus 1 tablespoon warm water (105°-115°F)

4 cups all-purpose flour, plus additional for dusting

1½ teaspoons salt

¼ cup olive oil

3 tablespoons chopped fresh jalapeño chile, including seeds and ribs, plus 2 tablespoons chopped fresh jalapeño without seeds and ribs (from 3 medium total)

1½ cups plus 2 tablespoons coarsely grated extra-sharp Cheddar cheese (5 ounces)

¾ cup finely grated Parmigiano-Reggiano cheese (1½ ounces)

1 large egg, beaten with a pinch of salt

1. Stir together the yeast and 1 tablespoon warm water in a small bowl; let mixture stand until foamy, about 5 minutes. (If it doesn't foam, discard and start over with new yeast.)

2. Mix the flour, salt, oil, yeast mixture, and remaining 1¾ cups warm water in the bowl of a mixer with paddle attachment at low speed until a soft dough forms. Increase the speed to medium-high and beat 3 minutes more. Add the jalapeño, 1½ cups Cheddar, and ½ cup Parmigiano-Reggiano and mix until combined.

3. Scrape the dough down the side of the bowl (all around) into the center, then sprinkle lightly with flour. Cover the bowl with a clean kitchen towel (not terry cloth) to keep a crust from forming and let the dough rise in a draft-free place at warm room temperature until doubled in bulk, 2 to 2½ hours. (Alternatively, let the dough rise in the bowl in the refrigerator 8 to 12 hours.)

4. Turn the dough out onto a well-floured surface and gently form into a roughly 11 by 8-inch rectangle. Fold dough in thirds (like a letter) with floured hands (dough will be sticky), pressing along seam of each fold to seal. Put the dough seam side down in an oiled 9 by 5-inch loaf pan. Cover the pan with the same clean kitchen towel and let rise in a draft-free place at warm room temperature until dough completely fills pan and rises above it slightly, 1 to 1¼ hours.

5. Put the oven rack in the middle position and preheat the oven to 400°F.

6. Brush the loaf with beaten egg, then sprinkle the remaining 2 tablespoons Cheddar and remaining ¼ cup Parmigiano-Reggiano down the center of the loaf. Bake until the bread is golden and sounds hollow when tapped on bottom, 50 minutes to 1 hour. Run a knife around the edge of the pan to loosen the loaf, then remove from the pan to test for doneness. Return the bread to the oven and turn on its side, then bake 10 minutes more to crisp the crust. Cool completely on a rack, about 1½ hours.

"Amazingly good bread that goes with almost any main course— especially if there is a sauce so you can soak up every bit with the bread! We've cut it into slices to make sandwiches. I buy the finest (sharpest) Cheddar cheese and grate it at home—really makes a difference."

Carolineau, Chicago, Illinois

mini provolone popovers

"Popover" may be one of the most inherently cheerful words in the language; it evokes something baked, warm, and fragrantly delicious. Infused with two savory cheeses, these foolproof, airy popovers, made in a mini-muffin pan, more than live up to their enticing name. They take little time to prepare and are best served hot, but if your oven is juggling multiple priorities, you can mix the batter a day ahead and chill, covered, until you're ready to bake.

1. Whisk together the milk, eggs, flour, 1 tablespoon butter, the salt, and pepper until smooth, then stir in the cheeses and chives. Chill 1 hour to allow batter to rest.

2. Preheat the oven to 425°F with the rack in the upper third. Butter a mini-muffin pan with the remaining tablespoon butter, then heat in the oven until the butter sizzles, about 2 minutes.

3. Gently stir the batter, then divide among the muffin cups (they will be about two-thirds full). Bake until puffed and golden brown, 18 to 20 minutes. Serve immediately.

YIELD: MAKES 24 POPOVERS

1 cup whole milk
2 large eggs
1 cup all-purpose flour
2 tablespoons unsalted butter, melted
½ teaspoon salt
⅛ teaspoon black pepper
⅓ cup finely chopped provolone cheese
2 tablespoons grated Parmesan cheese
1½ tablespoons chopped chives

Special equipment: 24-cup mini-muffin pan

"I used a sharp aged provolone and served for brunch with peach mimosas."

Lamclaughlin, Greenville, South Carolina

pretzel rolls

While these German-style pretzel rolls are perfect for an Oktoberfest celebration, we like to think they complete just about any meal. Boiling the rolls before baking might seem overly fussy, but it's the secret to creating their delightful chewiness. Speaking of secrets, the egg wash gives the bread its sheen, and it helps all that addictive salt adhere to the dough. Pair the rolls with a tangy, hearty whole-grain mustard for an afternoon snack.

YIELD: MAKES 8 ROLLS

2¾ cups bread flour
1 envelope quick-rising yeast
1 teaspoon salt
2 tablespoons plus 1 teaspoon sugar
1 teaspoon celery seeds
1 cup plus 2 tablespoons hot water
  (125°–130°F)
Cornmeal
8 cups water
¼ cup baking soda
1 egg white, lightly beaten
Coarse salt

"These are adorable, very chewy, and fun. These rolls were perfect for my sliders topped with stone-ground mustard and homemade pickles!"

Cafenator, Manteca, California

do ahead:

The **ROLLS** can be prepared 6 hours ahead. Let stand at room temperature. Rewarm in 375°F oven 10 minutes.

1. Combine the bread flour, yeast, 1 teaspoon salt, 1 teaspoon sugar, and celery seeds in a food processor and blend. With the machine running, gradually pour the hot water through the feed tube, adding enough water to form a smooth, elastic dough. Process 1 minute to knead.

2. Grease a medium bowl. Add the dough to the bowl, turning to coat. Cover the bowl with plastic wrap, then a towel; let the dough rise in a warm draft-free area until doubled in volume, about 35 minutes.

3. Flour a baking sheet. Punch the dough down and knead on a lightly floured surface until smooth. Divide into 8 pieces. Form each dough piece into a ball. Place the dough balls on the prepared sheet, flattening each slightly. Using a serrated knife, cut an *X* in the top center of each dough ball. Cover with a towel and let the dough balls rise until almost doubled in volume, about 20 minutes.

4. Preheat the oven to 375°F. Grease another baking sheet and sprinkle with cornmeal. Bring 8 cups of water to a boil in a large saucepan. Add the baking soda and remaining 2 tablespoons sugar (water will foam up). Add 4 rolls and cook 30 seconds per side. Using a slotted spoon, transfer the rolls to the prepared sheet, arranging *X* side up. Repeat with the remaining rolls.

5. Brush the rolls with the egg-white glaze. Sprinkle the rolls generously with coarse salt. Bake the rolls until brown, about 25 minutes. Transfer to racks and cool 10 minutes. Serve rolls warm or at room temperature.

valrhona chocolate pudding

Bittersweet chocolate gives this creamy pudding a decidedly grown-up taste. It's a favorite at the City Limits Diner in Stamford, Connecticut, where it originated. The ingredient list calls for Valrhona, but any good-quality bittersweet chocolate will do. With only six ingredients, the hardest thing you'll have to do is wait for dessert to be ready.

1. Put the oven rack in the middle position and preheat the oven to 275°F.

2. Scrape the seeds from the vanilla bean into a 3-quart heavy saucepan with the tip of a paring knife, then add the pod, milk, cream, and sugar and bring just to a boil, stirring until sugar is dissolved. Add the chocolate and cook over moderately high heat, stirring gently with a whisk, until the chocolate is melted and the mixture just boils. Remove from the heat.

3. Pour the mixture into a metal bowl. Set the bowl in a larger bowl of ice and cold water and cool to room temperature, stirring occasionally, about 5 minutes. Whisk in the yolks, then pour through a fine-mesh sieve into a 1-quart measure, discarding the pod and any other solids.

4. Divide the mixture among 6 (¼-cup) ramekins. Bake in a water bath until the puddings are just set around edge but the centers wobble when the ramekins are gently shaken, about 1 hour.

5. Cool the puddings in the water bath 1 hour, then remove from the water and chill, uncovered, until cold, at least 1 hour.

YIELD: MAKES 6 SERVINGS

½ vanilla bean, halved lengthwise
1½ cups whole milk
½ cup heavy cream
⅓ cup sugar
4½ ounces Valrhona or other bittersweet chocolate (61%), finely chopped
5 large egg yolks

Special equipment: 6 (¼-cup) ramekins

do ahead:

The **PUDDINGS** can be chilled, covered with a sheet of plastic wrap after 4 hours, up to 2 days. Blot very gently with paper towels before serving to remove the "stain" that formed.

"This is simple to make, silky smooth, with lush chocolate flavor, and just the right amount of sweetness. I might [add] a dash of cinnamon in the future."
Leisadeffenbaugh, Quinton, Virginia

vanilla hot chocolate mix

Homemade hot cocoa is in a category all by itself, and once you try this rich, vanilla-infused version developed by cookbook author Tracey Seaman, you'll find just how much is missing from the store-bought variety. Use the highest-quality chocolate and vanilla you can find—Valrhona, Lindt, and Ghirardelli are all great options. And if you really love the delicate warm notes of vanilla, go ahead and use the full bean. Turn this decadent treat into an edible gift with decorative canisters, crocks, jars, or even cellophane bags, then trim your presents in festive ribbon and attach gift tags with the serving directions.

**YIELD: MAKES 10 CUPS MIX,
SERVING 24 TO 32**

4 cups sugar
½ vanilla bean, split crosswise (see Note)
1½ pounds high-quality semisweet
  chocolate, coarsely chopped
8 ounces milk chocolate, coarsely
  chopped
2 cups unsweetened cocoa powder,
  preferably Dutch process (see Note)

cook's note:

Save the other half of the **VANILLA BEAN** for another use, such as a second batch of vanilla sugar, which keeps indefinitely and can be used in baking, coffee, or simply to sprinkle on fruit or waffles.

The **DUTCH-PROCESSED COCOA** has been treated with an alkaline solution, which gives it a darker color and less bitter flavor and makes it dissolve more easily. Dröste is a good brand.

MAKE MIX

1. Place the sugar in a large bowl. Split the vanilla bean in half lengthwise, scrape the seeds into the sugar, and add the pod. Work the seeds in with your fingers. Cover snugly with plastic wrap and let stand overnight at room temperature.

2. In food processor fitted with the metal blade, process the chocolates until finely ground, using 4-second pulses. (Process in 2 batches if necessary.)

3. Remove the pod from the sugar. Add the ground chocolate and cocoa powder to the sugar and whisk to blend. Store mix airtight at room temperature for up to 6 months.

TO SERVE

For each serving, heat 8 ounces milk in a small saucepan over medium heat until scalded (or microwave 2½ minutes at full power). Whisk in ¼ to ⅓ cup of the mix. Serve with unsweetened softly whipped cream or marshmallows.

"I'll use a whole vanilla bean next time for more vanilla flavor. The hot chocolate needed a little extra stirring to make sure it was all dissolved. But the texture was very smooth; not at all grainy like hot chocolate can sometimes be."
Jamimess, Los Angeles, California

double-nut maple bars

These deliciously sticky nut bars are like miniature maple pecan pies and are perfect as a dessert, snack, or indulgent breakfast. Swap out the walnuts and pecans with other varieties, or try mixing some dried fruit into the filling to add another layer of sweetness. Make a batch to share with friends—or store them in a container as a gift to yourself.

MAKE CRUST

1. Preheat the oven to 350°F. Butter an 8 by 8-inch metal baking pan.

2. Combine the flour, sugar, and a pinch of salt in a food processor and blend. Add the butter and process until the mixture resembles coarse meal. Combine the egg yolk and milk in a small bowl. Drizzle the egg mixture into the processor bowl; process using on/off pulses just until the dough clumps together but is still dry. Transfer the dough crumbs to the prepared pan. Press the crumbs onto the bottom and halfway up the sides of the pan. Bake until the crust is set and pale golden, about 25 minutes. Transfer the crust to a rack and cool.

MAKE FILLING

1. Combine the maple syrup, sugar, cream, and butter in a heavy medium saucepan. Bring the mixture to a boil and boil 2 minutes. Remove from the heat and stir in the nuts and vanilla.

2. Pour the filling over the crust, spreading the nuts evenly, and bake until the filling bubbles all over, about 8 minutes. Transfer to a rack and cool completely. Cut into bars and serve at room temperature.

"This recipe really satisfied on all levels: It was easy, looked great (I added chopped dried cranberries to the filling for color/flavor), was a bit different, and tasted delicious!"

A cook, Canada

YIELD: MAKES 16 BARS

FOR CRUST
1¼ cups unbleached all-purpose flour
⅓ cup granulated sugar
6 tablespoons (¾ stick) chilled unsalted butter, cut into pieces
1 large egg yolk
1 tablespoon whole milk

FOR FILLING
⅓ cup pure maple syrup
⅓ cup (packed) light brown sugar
¼ cup heavy whipping cream
2 tablespoons (¼ stick) unsalted butter
¾ cup pecans, toasted, coarsely chopped
¾ cup walnuts, toasted, coarsely chopped
½ teaspoon pure vanilla extract

Special equipment: 8-inch square metal baking pan with 2-inch sides

do ahead:

The **BARS** can be prepared 1 day ahead. Store between sheets of wax paper in airtight container at room temperature.

amazing chocolate chip– peanut butter cookies

Crisp on the outside and gooey on the inside, these irresistible cookies get extra crunch from dry-roasted peanuts. The recipe, from Epicurious member **Ashlee L. Galletta** of Winnipeg, Canada, was inspired by Reese's Peanut Butter Cups, so get ready for a heady dose of peanuts balanced by creamy milk chocolate. If you prefer your cookies a little less sweet, skim a couple of tablespoons of sugar from the recipe and swap in semisweet chocolate chips for the milk chocolate ones.

1. Position a rack in the middle of the oven and preheat the oven to 375°F. Line 2 large baking sheets with parchment paper.

2. In the bowl of a stand mixer fitted with the paddle attachment, combine the butter and sugars, and beat on high speed until pale and fluffy, about 5 minutes. Add the eggs 1 at a time, beating well after each addition and scraping down the bowl as necessary. Reduce the mixer speed to low and add the vanilla, baking soda, baking powder, and salt, and beat until just incorporated. Add the flour in 2 additions, mixing at a very low speed, until just incorporated. Stir in the milk chocolate chips, peanut butter chips, and peanuts.

3. Drop 1½-inch balls of dough about 2 inches apart on the prepared baking sheets. Bake until the cookies are light golden brown on top and beginning to brown around the edges, about 12 minutes. Let cookies stand 1 minute, then transfer to a rack to cool and continue making cookies using cooled baking sheets.

Keep your eye on the oven! If you wait too long, they won't be soft inside.

–Ashlee L. Galletta

YIELD: MAKES ABOUT 30 COOKIES

1 cup (2 sticks) unsalted butter, at room temperature
¾ cup granulated sugar
¾ cup (packed) light brown sugar
2 large eggs
2 teaspoons pure vanilla extract
1 teaspoon baking soda
1 teaspoon baking powder
1 teaspoon salt
2¼ cups all-purpose flour
1½ cups milk chocolate chips
1½ cups peanut butter chips
½ cup dry-roasted unsalted peanuts, chopped

Special equipment: 2 large baking sheets; parchment paper

cook's note:

The **COOLED COOKIES** can be stored, in an airtight container, at room temperature, up to 1 week.

banana nut oatmeal cookies

Sometimes the simplest things are the most delicious. Epicurious member **JynnJynn** of Louisville, Kentucky, ensured these moist cookies are easy to make and easier to enjoy. Follow JynnJynn's advice and add coconut, or use white chocolate and other fruit or nuts. Save a few cookies for the next day, as the banana flavor truly comes out the day after baking.

YIELD: MAKES ABOUT 30 COOKIES

1 cup all-purpose flour
1 teaspoon ground cinnamon
½ teaspoon baking soda
¼ teaspoon kosher salt
½ cup (1 stick) unsalted butter, at room temperature
½ cup granulated sugar
½ cup (packed) light brown sugar
1 large egg
1 teaspoon pure vanilla extract
1 very ripe banana, peeled and cut into 1-inch chunks
1½ cups old-fashioned rolled oats
½ cup chopped walnuts
For the garnish: 3 ounces dark chocolate or white chocolate, coarsely chopped, or caramel candies, coarsely chopped (optional)

Special equipment: 2 large baking sheets, parchment paper

cook's note:

The **COOKIES** can be baked and stored in an airtight container up to 4 days. If drizzling with chocolate or caramel, place sheets of parchment between the layers to keep the cookies from sticking together.

1. Position a rack in the middle of the oven and preheat the oven to 350°F. Line 2 large baking sheets with parchment.

2. In a medium bowl, whisk together the flour, cinnamon, baking soda, and salt. In the bowl of a stand mixer fitted with a paddle attachment, combine the butter and sugars, and beat on high until pale and fluffy, about 3 minutes. Add the egg, vanilla, and banana and continue beating, scraping down the bowl as necessary, until fully incorporated, about 1 minute. Add the flour mixture, along with the oats and walnuts, to the bowl and gently stir to combine.

3. Drop rounded tablespoons of dough about 2 inches apart on the prepared baking sheets. Bake the cookies, rotating the pans halfway through the baking time, until the edges are light brown, about 15 minutes total. Let the cookies stand 5 minutes, then transfer to a rack to cool completely. Continue making cookies on cooled baking sheets.

4. If making the garnish, in a double boiler, or in a heat-proof bowl set over a saucepan of barely simmering water (the bottom of the bowl should not touch the water), melt the chopped chocolate or caramel candies, stirring occasionally, until smooth. Using a small spoon, drizzle the melted chocolate or caramel over the cookies in a zigzag pattern. Let stand until the topping sets, about 30 minutes, or refrigerate the cookies for about 10 minutes to set the topping faster.

cherry double-chocolate cookies

With toasted pecans, dried sour cherries, and creamy milk chocolate chunks, these cocoa-based cookies feature a mix of flavors guaranteed to appeal to every palate. Seek out a high-quality milk chocolate for the richest, smoothest experience, or experiment by replacing some or all of the chunks with premium white chocolate.

1. Preheat the oven to 375°F, with racks in the upper and lower thirds.

2. Whisk together the flour, cocoa powder, baking soda, and salt in a small bowl. Beat together the butter and brown sugar with an electric mixer at medium-high speed until pale and fluffy, then add the eggs 1 at a time, beating until combined well. Reduce the speed to low and add the flour mixture, mixing until just combined. Add the chocolate chunks, pecans, and cherries and mix until just incorporated.

3. Drop 2 level tablespoons of dough per cookie about 2 inches apart onto 2 ungreased large baking sheets. With dampened fingers, flatten cookies slightly.

4. Bake, switching position of sheets halfway through baking, until puffed and set, 12 to 14 minutes. Transfer the cookies to a rack to cool.

"I used walnuts instead of pecans, a mix of semisweet and milk chocolate, and kosher salt. I don't even like chocolate all that much, and I had to use all my willpower to keep from eating a second."

Ehbergman, Atlanta, Georgia

YIELD: MAKES ABOUT 2 DOZEN COOKIES

1¼ cups all-purpose flour
¾ cup unsweetened Dutch-process cocoa powder
¾ teaspoon baking soda
Scant ½ teaspoon salt
¾ cup (1½ sticks) unsalted butter, softened
1½ cups (packed) light brown sugar
2 large eggs
3½ ounces fine-quality milk chocolate, cut into ½-inch chunks
1 cup pecans, toasted and coarsely chopped
1 cup dried sour cherries

cook's note:

The **COOKIES** keep in an airtight container at room temperature up to 5 days.

cinnamon crumble apple pie

The classic apple pie elements are flawless as is, but we think this version topped with a thick layer of cinnamon crumble is pure genius. The buttery, brown sugar–infused topping crowns a generous mound of tart Granny Smith apples, while a traditional American-style pastry features equal parts butter and shortening, with a touch of cider vinegar to ensure tenderness.

MAKE CRUST

1. Mix the flour, salt, and sugar in a large bowl. Add the butter and shortening; rub in with your fingertips until coarse meal forms. Mix 3 tablespoons ice water and the vinegar in a small bowl. Drizzle over the flour mixture; stir with fork until moist clumps form, adding more water by teaspoonfuls if dough is dry. Gather the dough into a ball; flatten into a disk. Wrap in plastic; refrigerate 30 minutes.

2. Position a rack in the center of the oven and preheat the oven to 400°F. Roll out the dough on a lightly floured surface to a 12-inch round. Transfer to a 9-inch-diameter glass pie dish. Trim the overhang to ½ inch; turn the edge under and crimp decoratively. Refrigerate while preparing the filling and topping.

MAKE FILLING AND TOPPING

1. Mix the filling ingredients in large bowl to coat apples.

2. Blend the flour, sugars, cinnamon, and salt in a processor. Add the chilled butter cubes; using on/off pulses, cut in until the mixture resembles wet sand.

ASSEMBLE AND BAKE PIE

1. Toss the filling to redistribute juices; transfer to the crust, mounding in the center. Pack the topping over and around the apples. Bake the pie on a baking sheet until the topping is golden, about 40 minutes (cover top with foil if browning too quickly).

2. Reduce the oven temperature to 350°F. Bake until the apples in the center are tender when pierced and the filling is bubbling thickly at the edges, about 45 minutes longer. Cool until warm, about 1 hour. Serve with ice cream.

YIELD: MAKES 8 SERVINGS

FOR CRUST

1⅓ cups all-purpose flour
½ teaspoon salt
½ teaspoon granulated sugar
¼ cup (½ stick) chilled unsalted butter, cut into ½-inch cubes
¼ cup frozen vegetable shortening, cut into ½-inch cubes
3 tablespoons ice water, or more as needed
½ teaspoon apple cider vinegar

FOR FILLING

3¼ pounds Granny Smith apples, peeled, cored, and sliced ¼ inch thick
⅔ cup granulated sugar
2 tablespoons all-purpose flour
2 teaspoons ground cinnamon
2 tablespoons unsalted butter, melted

FOR TOPPING

1 cup all-purpose flour
½ cup granulated sugar
¼ cup (packed) light brown sugar
1½ teaspoons ground cinnamon
½ teaspoon salt
6 tablespoons chilled unsalted butter, cut into ½-inch cubes

Vanilla ice cream, for serving

spiced pumpkin layer cake

Foolproof and moist, this cake is suitable for birthdays or other celebrations. Tip: It's better to underbeat the frosting than overbeat it for a frosting that's easier to spread.

YIELD: MAKES 12 SERVINGS

FOR CAKE

3 cups all-purpose flour
2 teaspoons baking powder
1 teaspoon baking soda
1 tablespoon ground cinnamon
2 teaspoons ground ginger
1¾ teaspoons ground allspice
½ teaspoon ground nutmeg
1 teaspoon salt
1½ cups granulated sugar
1 cup (packed) light brown sugar
1 cup canola oil
4 large eggs
1 (15-ounce) can pure pumpkin
1 tablespoon vanilla extract
1 tablespoon grated orange peel
¾ cup raisins
¾ cup sweetened flaked coconut, plus
  additional for garnish

FOR FROSTING

1 (8-ounce) package cream cheese, at
  room temperature
10 tablespoons (1¼ sticks) unsalted
  butter, at room temperature
1 tablespoon dark rum
1 teaspoon pure vanilla extract
4½ cups confectioners' sugar (measured,
  then sifted)

Special equipment: 2 (9-inch) round cake
  pans

MAKE CAKE

1. Position the rack in the center of the oven and preheat the oven to 350°F. Butter two 9-inch-diameter cake pans with 1½-inch-high sides. Line the bottoms of the pans with parchment; dust with flour.

2. Sift 3 cups flour, the baking powder, baking soda, spices, and salt into a medium bowl. Using an electric mixer, beat both sugars and the oil in a large bowl until combined (mixture will look grainy). Add the eggs 1 at a time, beating until well blended after each addition. Add the pumpkin, vanilla, and orange peel; beat until well blended. Add the flour mixture; beat just until incorporated. Stir in the raisins and ¾ cup coconut. Divide the batter between the pans and smooth the tops.

3. Bake the cakes until a tester inserted into the center comes out clean, about 1 hour. Cool the cakes completely in pans on a rack. Run a knife around the cakes to loosen. Invert the cakes onto racks; remove parchment. Turn the cakes over, rounded side up. Using a serrated knife, trim the rounded tops of the cakes to level them.

MAKE FROSTING AND ICE CAKE

1. Using an electric mixer, beat the cream cheese and butter in a large bowl until smooth. Beat in the rum and vanilla. Add the sugar in 3 additions, beating just until the frosting is smooth after each addition (do not overbeat or frosting may become too soft to spread).

2. Place one cake layer, flat side down, on a platter. Spread half of the cream-cheese frosting over the top to the edges. Top with the second cake layer, trimmed side down. Spread the remaining frosting over the top (not sides) of cake. Sprinkle additional coconut over.

"Made it as cupcakes and gave them out as party favors at the end of the night. Make sure you use good-quality rum. The cake was moist and stayed that way for several days."

A cook, New York, New York

apple tart *with caramel sauce*

This elegant dessert evokes all the fun of a caramel apple but is a whole lot cleaner and easier to eat—and to share. McIntosh and Golden Delicious apples tend to break down when cooked, so use firmer cooking apples such as Cameo, Cortland, or Braeburn. Save leftover sauce for another use, such as an ice cream topping, a sweet fondue, or dip.

YIELD: MAKES 8 SERVINGS

FOR CARAMEL SAUCE
1½ cups (packed) dark brown sugar
1½ cups heavy whipping cream
6 tablespoons (¾ stick) unsalted butter

FOR CRUST
1¼ cups unbleached all-purpose flour
¾ cup confectioners' sugar
¼ teaspoon kosher or other coarse salt
½ cup (1 stick) chilled unsalted butter, diced
2 large egg yolks

FOR FILLING
2 tablespoons granulated sugar
1 tablespoon unbleached all-purpose flour
½ teaspoon ground cinnamon
½ teaspoon ground cardamom
6 large McIntosh or Golden Delicious apples (about 2¾ pounds), peeled, quartered, and cored

Special equipment: 9-inch tart pan with removable bottom

do ahead:

The **CARAMEL SAUCE** can be made 5 days ahead. Cover; chill. Whisk over low heat until warm before using.

The **DOUGH** for the tart crust can be made 1 day ahead. Keep chilled.

MAKE CARAMEL SAUCE
Bring sugar, cream, and butter to a boil in a heavy medium saucepan over medium-high heat, whisking constantly until the sugar dissolves. Boil until the caramel thickens enough to coat spoon thickly, whisking often, about 10 minutes.

MAKE CRUST
Blend the flour, sugar, and salt in a food processor. Add the butter and blend until coarse meal forms. Add the egg yolks; pulse until moist clumps form. Gather the dough into a ball, then flatten into a disk. Wrap and chill at least 1 hour.

MAKE FILLING AND BAKE TART
1. Whisk the sugar, flour, cinnamon, and cardamom in a large bowl to blend. Add the apples and toss until evenly coated.

2. Preheat the oven to 375°F. Roll out the dough on a lightly floured surface to a 13-inch round. Transfer to a 9-inch-diameter tart pan with removable bottom. Cut the overhang even with the top of the pan sides. Press the sides of the dough to bring ¼ inch above sides of pan. Arrange the apple quarters cut side down in a circle around the outer edge of the pan, fitting snugly. Cut the remaining apple quarters lengthwise in half; stand in the center of tart, fitting snugly.

3. Bake the tart until the apples are tender, about 1 hour 15 minutes. Remove the tart from the oven; brush with some of the caramel sauce. Cool the tart to room temperature. Rewarm the remaining caramel sauce and drizzle tart lightly with the sauce. Serve, passing remaining sauce separately.

chocolate pumpkin brownies

member recipe

Rich chocolate brownies get jazzed up with fresh or canned pumpkin. Epicurious member **Sharon Perry Murphy** of Fort Knox, Kentucky, often bakes hers with fresh pumpkin, which is runnier. (To achieve the desired consistency with fresh pumpkin, Murphy recommends adding a little extra flour, 1 tablespoon at a time, or substituting 1 egg for ¼ cup pumpkin.)

1. Position a rack in the middle of the oven and preheat the pan to 350°F. Using coconut oil, grease a 9-inch square baking pan.

2. In a medium bowl, whisk together the remaining coconut oil, the pumpkin, sugar, and salt. In a second medium bowl, whisk together the flour, cocoa powder, and baking soda. Add the dry ingredients to the wet in 3 batches, folding the mixture to thoroughly incorporate the ingredients in each addition. (The batter will be thicker than traditional brownie batter.)

3. Transfer the batter to the prepared pan and bake until the top is dry and a toothpick inserted into the center comes out mostly clean, 45 to 50 minutes. Cool the brownies completely in the pan before cutting and serving.

My husband and I were stationed in Germany, and there was a local farm selling pumpkins and squash of all kinds. I went by to pick up a few to use for baby food and decided to save some for baking. Add in my love for chocolate and desire to make foods that are healthy and (almost) vegan, and you have this lovely recipe!

–Sharon Perry Murphy

YIELD: MAKE 16 BROWNIES

6 tablespoons coconut oil, melted
1 (15-ounce) can solid-pack pumpkin (not pie filling)
2½ cups sugar
½ teaspoon kosher salt
1½ cups all-purpose flour
1½ cups unsweetened cocoa powder
¼ teaspoon baking soda

Special equipment: 9-inch square baking pan

cook's note:

The **BROWNIES** can be baked in advance and stored, in an airtight container, at room temperature, and will keep for about 3 days.

gianduia mousse cake

Chocolate and hazelnut: Consider this combination the "Meg Ryan and Tom Hanks" of flavor profiles—sweet, nutty, and guaranteed to produce a blockbuster. Baking expert Carole Bloom's indulgent cake recipe calls for an easy homemade hazelnut butter, but store-bought will do just as well. Top it off with some crushed hazelnuts for added texture, and then serve it with a glass of Sauternes or port, or a shot of espresso.

YIELD: MAKES 12 TO 14 SERVINGS

9 ounces fine-quality bittersweet
    chocolate (not unsweetened)
7 ounces fine-quality milk chocolate
1 cup Nutella (chocolate-hazelnut spread;
    from a 13-ounce jar)
¾ cup Unsweetened Hazelnut Butter
    (recipe follows)
6 large eggs
½ cup superfine granulated sugar
1 cup well-chilled heavy cream
Whipped cream

Special equipment: 10-inch springform
    pan

do ahead:

The **CAKE** keeps, covered and chilled, 3 days.

"Serve with fresh fruit (I recommend light fruits like mangos, plums, nectarines, etc.), and you can't get a better, more sophisticated dessert."
A cook, Salt Lake City, Utah

1. Preheat the oven to 350°F and butter a 10-inch springform pan. Wrap the bottom and side of the pan with a large piece of heavy-duty foil to waterproof.

2. Chop the chocolates into small pieces and melt in a double boiler or a metal bowl set over a saucepan of barely simmering water, stirring until smooth. Remove the top of the double boiler or bowl from the heat and stir in the Nutella and hazelnut butter until combined well.

3. In a large bowl of a standing electric mixer or in a large bowl with a handheld mixer, beat the eggs until frothy, about 1 minute. Gradually add the sugar, beating the mixture at high speed until thick and pale and until it holds a slowly dissolving ribbon when the beaters are lifted, about 4 minutes if using a standing mixer and about 8 minutes if using a handheld mixer. Pour the chocolate mixture into the egg mixture and stir until combined well. In a chilled bowl, beat the cream until it holds soft peaks and fold into the batter gently but thoroughly.

4. Pour the batter into the springform pan and put springform pan in a larger roasting pan. Add enough hot water to the roasting pan to reach halfway up the side of the springform pan. Bake the cake in the middle of the oven 1 hour and 10 minutes. Turn off the oven and let the cake stand in the oven 40 minutes. Remove the springform pan from the water and cool cake in pan on a rack 30 minutes. Remove the side of the pan from cake. Let cake cool completely before serving. Serve with whipped cream.

unsweetened hazelnut butter

Toast and skin the hazelnuts, but do not cool. In a food processor, grind the hazelnuts into a fine paste. Add the oil and pulse until combined well.

YIELD: MAKES ABOUT 1 CUP

1½ cups hazelnuts (about 7 ounces)
3 tablespoons vegetable oil

prune, cherry, and apricot frangipane tart

This classic almond-flavored dessert gets a boost from a dried-fruit compote steeped overnight in grappa syrup. Once drained, this compote is coupled with the frangipane filling—an almond paste, not marzipan—to give the beautiful tart its luscious, unforgettable taste. The reserved syrup is brushed over the golden brown tart for a sparkling finish.

MAKE DRIED FRUIT COMPOTE

Heat the grappa with the sugar in a medium saucepan over low heat, stirring, until the sugar has dissolved. Add the fruit and gently simmer 1 minute. Remove from the heat and let macerate, stirring occasionally, 24 hours.

MAKE TART SHELL

1. Blend together the flour, butter, and salt in a bowl with your fingertips or a pastry blender (or pulse in a food processor) just until the mixture resembles coarse meal with some small (roughly pea-size) butter lumps.

2. Drizzle 2 to 3 tablespoons ice water evenly over mixture. Gently stir with a fork (or pulse) until incorporated. Squeeze a small handful of dough: if it doesn't hold together, add more water, ½ tablespoon at a time, stirring (or pulsing) until incorporated. Do not overwork dough, or pastry will be tough.

YIELD: MAKES 8 SERVINGS

FOR DRIED FRUIT COMPOTE
⅔ cup grappa, preferably Julia brand
3½ tablespoons sugar
½ cup pitted prunes, halved
⅓ cup dried cherries
⅓ cup dried California apricots

FOR PASTRY DOUGH
1¼ cups all-purpose flour
½ cup (1 stick) cold unsalted butter, cut into ½-inch cubes
½ teaspoon salt
2 to 3 tablespoons ice water, or as needed

recipe continues

FOR FRANGIPANE FILLING

7 ounces almond paste (not marzipan; about 1 cup)

½ stick unsalted butter, softened

3 tablespoons sugar

⅛ teaspoon pure almond extract

½ teaspoon salt

2 large eggs

3 tablespoons all-purpose flour

Special equipment: 11-inch flan ring or round tart pan with removable bottom; pie weights or dried beans

do ahead:

The **DRIED FRUIT** can be macerated up to 3 days.

The **TART SHELL** can be baked 1 day ahead and kept (once cool), wrapped in plastic wrap, at room temperature.

The **TART** is best eaten the day it is baked but can be made 1 day ahead, covered with foil, kept at room temperature.

The **DOUGH** can be chilled 2 days or frozen, wrapped well, 3 months.

"I didn't think it was a particularly difficult or time-consuming dessert if you spread the work over a few days. Started the fruit three days ahead—that only takes five minutes. Made the tart dough and baked the shell the day before, and made the filling and finished the tart the day of serving."

A cook, Moscow, Idaho

3. Turn out dough onto a work surface and divide into 4 portions. With the heel of your hand, smear each portion once or twice in a forward motion to help distribute fat. Gather the dough together with a pastry scraper, if you have one. Press into a ball, then flatten into a 5-inch disk and wrap in plastic wrap. Chill until firm, at least 1 hour.

4. Set an 11-inch flan ring on a parchment-lined baking sheet. (If using a tart pan, parchment is not necessary.) Roll out the dough on a lightly floured surface with a lightly floured rolling pin into a 13-inch round, then fit into the flan ring and trim excess dough. Chill until firm, at least 30 minutes.

5. Preheat the oven to 375°F, with the rack in the middle.

6. Lightly prick the bottom of the shell all over with a fork, then line with foil and fill with pie weights or dried beans. Bake until the side is set and the edge is pale golden, 18 to 20 minutes. Remove the foil and weights and bake until the bottom is golden, about 10 minutes more. Cool completely in the pan, about 30 minutes. Leave oven on.

MAKE FRANGIPANE FILLING

Beat the almond paste, butter, sugar, extract, and salt in a bowl with an electric mixer at medium speed 3 minutes. Add the eggs 1 at a time, beating well after each addition, then beat in the flour.

FILL TART AND BAKE

Spread the frangipane filling in the cooled shell. Drain the fruit in a sieve set over a bowl, reserving the syrup, and scatter the fruit over the filling, pressing in slightly. Bake until puffed and golden, 30 to 40 minutes. Transfer the tart on parchment to a rack. Brush the reserved syrup over the tart and cool to warm or room temperature.

W

inter

extreme granola *with dried fruit*

Dried blueberries and plump dates partner with old-fashioned rolled oats and toasty nuts in this hearty granola created by Epicurious editor-in-chief Tanya Steel and her *Real Foods for Healthy Kids* coauthor Tracey Seaman. Sesame seeds lend extra crunch while pure maple syrup (cane syrup or honey are excellent substitutes) kisses the mix with sweetness. With milk or yogurt, this granola is an easy breakfast, but don't limit yourself: it's delightful sprinkled on pancakes or as a topping for ice cream.

YIELD: MAKES ABOUT 7 CUPS

¾ cup pecans
½ cup natural almonds
4 cups old-fashioned rolled oats
¼ cup sesame seeds (optional)
1 stick (8 tablespoons) unsalted butter
⅓ cup pure maple syrup, cane syrup, or honey, at room temperature
¼ teaspoon fine salt
¾ cup chopped pitted dates
½ cup dried blueberries, raisins, and/or cranberries

"A tasty and exceptionally versatile recipe. I've made this with various combinations: no fixins (pure oats), pepitas, unsalted pistachios, smidgens of ground ginger or cardamom, apricot, whatever is on hand or of interest."
A cook, Boston, Massachusetts

1. Preheat the oven to 375°F. Line a large shallow baking sheet with foil. Spread the pecans and almonds on the sheet and roast for 8 to 10 minutes, until lightly toasted. Transfer the nuts to a board, let cool, and chop the nuts. Set aside.

2. Reduce the oven temperature to 300°F. Pour the oats and sesame seeds, if using, in a mound on the same baking sheet. Melt the butter in a small bowl in the microwave; stir in the maple syrup and salt, and drizzle on top of the oats. Stir well with a rubber spatula and then spread out the oats in an even layer. Bake the oats for 30 minutes, stirring once with the spatula halfway through, until the oats are lightly colored. Let cool; the mixture will crisp as it cools.

3. Add the dates, dried fruit, and reserved nuts to the oats and toss. Store the granola in covered glass jars at room temperature for up to 1 month.

cinnamon rolls *with cream cheese glaze*

Whether you are baking for Christmas morning, a brunch with family, or a plain old lazy Sunday, these cinnamon rolls from Molly Wizenberg of Orangette.com make it an occasion. If you're crunched for time, try popping the prepared dough into a warm oven to help it rise.

YIELD: MAKES 18 ROLLS

FOR DOUGH

1 cup whole milk
3 tablespoons unsalted butter
3½ cups unbleached all-purpose flour, or
  more as needed
½ cup granulated sugar
1 large egg
2¼ teaspoons rapid-rise yeast (from
  2 envelopes yeast)
1 teaspoon salt
Nonstick vegetable-oil spray

FOR FILLING

¾ cup (packed) light brown sugar
2 tablespoons ground cinnamon
¼ cup (½ stick) unsalted butter, at room
  temperature

FOR GLAZE

4 ounces cream cheese, at room
  temperature
1 cup confectioners' sugar
¼ cup (½ stick) unsalted butter, at room
  temperature
½ teaspoon pure vanilla extract

MAKE DOUGH

1. Combine the milk and butter in a glass measuring cup. Microwave on high until the butter melts and the mixture is just warmed to 120° to 130°F, 30 to 45 seconds. Pour into the bowl of a stand mixer fitted with the paddle attachment. Add 1 cup flour, the sugar, egg, yeast, and salt. Beat on low speed 3 minutes, stopping occasionally to scrape down sides of bowl. Add 2½ cups flour and beat on low until the flour is absorbed and the dough is sticky, scraping down the sides of the bowl. If the dough is very sticky, add more flour by tablespoonfuls until it begins to form a ball and pulls away from the bowl. Turn the dough out onto a lightly floured work surface and knead until smooth and elastic, adding more flour if sticky, about 8 minutes. Form into a ball.

2. Lightly coat a large bowl with nonstick spray. Transfer the dough to the bowl, turning to coat. Cover the bowl with plastic wrap, then a kitchen towel. Let the dough rise in a warm draft-free area until doubled in volume, about 2 hours.

MAKE FILLING AND FILL ROLLS

1. Mix the brown sugar and cinnamon in a medium bowl.

2. Punch down the dough. Transfer it to a floured work surface and roll out to a 15 by 11-inch rectangle. Spread the butter over the dough, leaving a ½-inch border. Sprinkle the cinnamon sugar evenly over the butter. Starting at the long side, roll the dough into a log, pinching gently to keep it rolled up. With the seam side down, cut the dough crosswise with a thin sharp knife into 18 equal slices (each about ½ to ¾ inch wide).

3. Spray 2 (9-inch) square glass baking dishes with non-stick spray. Divide the rolls between the baking dishes, arranging cut side up (there will be almost no space between rolls). Cover the baking dishes with plastic wrap, then a kitchen towel. Let the dough rise in a warm draft-free area until almost doubled in volume, 40 to 45 minutes.

BAKE AND GLAZE ROLLS

1. Position the rack in the center of the oven and preheat the oven to 375°F. Bake the rolls until the tops are golden, about 20 minutes. Remove from oven and invert immediately onto a rack. Cool 10 minutes. Turn rolls right side up.

2. Combine the cream cheese, sugar, butter, and vanilla in a medium bowl. Using an electric mixer, beat until smooth. Spread the glaze on the rolls. Serve warm or at room temperature.

"I don't have a stand mixer, so I did all the mixing by hand, which helped me to preemptively burn off some calories. I found the glaze to be a little thick, so I thinned it out with a bit of milk and maple syrup. Probably the best cinnamon rolls I've ever had!"
Alliedoesstuff, Seattle, Washington

almond-banana smoothies

A sweet blend of ripe bananas, brown sugar, and nutmeg that only tastes decadent, this dairy-free, low-calorie smoothie uses almond milk to pump up the protein. Add a touch of almond extract to increase the flavor, or use chocolate almond milk and a tablespoon of peanut butter.

Combine the bananas, milk, ice, sugar, and vanilla in a blender until smooth. Divide among 4 small glasses. Sprinkle lightly with nutmeg.

"If you freeze your bananas (out of the skin, in plastic wrap) you eliminate the need for ice cubes. I let a bunch of bananas go black and then freeze them; this makes them sweet enough for me to also forgo the sugar."
UrbanGypsy, New York, New York

YIELD: MAKES 4 SERVINGS

2 large ripe bananas, peeled and sliced
2 cups almond milk or whole milk
2 cups ice cubes
2 tablespoons light brown sugar
1 teaspoon pure vanilla extract
Ground nutmeg

crispy waffles *with salted caramel coulis*

These sophisticated waffles were originally conceived as the dessert course in a modern Parisian bistro menu, but make this the sweet dish for your next brunch—every good brunch includes at least one dish that could pass for dessert! If salted caramel is just too much before noon, skip it and serve these ethereal waffles with real maple syrup, or fruit and a dusting of confectioners' sugar. And take note—the caramel is a dream drizzled over ice cream.

MAKE SALTED CARAMEL COULIS

1. Combine the sugar and water in a heavy medium saucepan. Stir over medium-low heat until the sugar dissolves. Increase the heat and boil without stirring until the syrup is a deep amber color, occasionally brushing down the sides with a wet pastry brush and swirling the pan, about 10 minutes.

2. Add the cream (mixture will bubble vigorously) and stir over low heat until any caramel bits dissolve. Remove from the heat. Stir in the butter and salt. Transfer the caramel to a small pitcher or bowl. Cool.

MAKE WAFFLES

1. Whisk the flour, sugar, baking powder, and salt in a large bowl to blend. Whisk the milk, eggs, and melted butter in a medium bowl to blend. Add the milk mixture to the dry ingredients in the large bowl and whisk until batter is smooth.

2. Heat a waffle iron according to the manufacturer's instructions (medium-high heat). Brush the grids lightly with peanut oil. Pour enough batter onto each waffle grid to cover generously (heaping ½ cup batter for an 4½ by 3½-inch grid); spread evenly with an offset spatula. Close the waffle iron and cook until the waffles are golden brown and crisp on both sides, 5 to 6 minutes.

3. Cut each waffle in half, forming either rectangles or triangles. Divide the waffles among 4 plates. Dust with confectioners' sugar and drizzle with the coulis. Serve waffles, passing remaining salted caramel coulis separately.

YIELD: MAKES 4 SERVINGS

FOR SALTED CARAMEL COULIS
½ cup granulated sugar
¼ cup water
½ cup heavy whipping cream
3½ tablespoons unsalted butter
½ teaspoon fleur de sel or kosher salt

FOR WAFFLES
1¾ cups all-purpose flour
2 tablespoons granulated sugar
1½ teaspoons baking powder
½ teaspoon salt
1¾ cups whole milk
2 large eggs
6 tablespoons (¾ stick) unsalted butter, melted, slightly cooled
Peanut oil, for coating iron
Confectioners' sugar, for serving

Special equipment: Waffle iron

"A drop of vanilla in the batter, maybe even a few chopped pecans, and some sliced strawberries makes it heaven."
A cook, Pawling, New York

sweet and spicy bacon

Can't believe that bacon could get any better? Brown sugar and a pinch of cayenne add both sweet and hot components to the meat's smoky flavor. As the bacon sizzles in the oven, the spicy mixture forms a glaze over each strip, packing even more flavor and crunch. Serve this traditionally, with scrambled eggs and an English muffin, or go rogue and pile this crispy treat onto a club sandwich with turkey and avocado for an extra-special lunch break.

YIELD: MAKES 6 SERVINGS

1½ tablespoons light brown sugar
Rounded ¼ teaspoon cayenne
Rounded ¼ teaspoon black pepper
1 pound thick-cut bacon (about 12 slices;
    see Cook's Note)

cook's note:

If thick-cut **BACON** is not available, regular packaged bacon can be used but will need to be cooked in batches with slightly shorter cooking times.

"When draining on paper towels, lift the bacon edges often, because the caramelized sugar will cause the bacon to stick, and the paper is difficult to peel off later when the bacon has cooled completely."
A cook, Mississippi

1. Put the oven rack in the middle position and preheat the oven to 350°F.

2. Stir together the brown sugar, cayenne, and black pepper in a small bowl.

3. Arrange the bacon slices in a single layer (not overlapping) on the rack of a large broiler pan or baking sheet. Bake 20 minutes. Turn the slices over and sprinkle evenly with the spiced sugar. Continue baking until the bacon is crisp and deep golden, 20 to 35 minutes more (check bacon every 5 minutes). Transfer to paper towels to drain.

egg burritos

Epicurious member and Maine resident **Jesse Wakeman** first made this ultimate breakfast burrito when he was in fifth grade. It's fast (under 20 minutes), tasty, and simple to make. To warm the tortillas, arrange them in a single layer on a baking sheet and bake in a 350°F oven until just heated through, about 30 seconds. Alternatively, wrap the tortillas loosely in a damp towel and place in the microwave on high for about 20 seconds.

1. In a medium nonstick skillet over moderate heat, heat ½ tablespoon oil until hot but not smoking. Add the sausage and sauté, stirring occasionally and breaking into small crumbles, until cooked through, 4 to 5 minutes. Transfer the sausage to a paper-towel–lined plate to drain.

2. In a medium bowl, whisk together the eggs, salsa, ½ cup of cheese, garlic, and cayenne, if using, and season with freshly ground black pepper.

3. Return the nonstick skillet to moderate heat and warm the remaining ½ tablespoon oil. Add the egg mixture and sprinkle with the cooked sausage. Using a heatproof spatula, gently scramble the mixture until the eggs are cooked through, 2 to 3 minutes.

4. Divide the eggs evenly between the warmed tortillas and top each with the remaining cheese. Roll up the tortillas to form burritos, then cut them in half and serve immediately.

YIELD: MAKES 2 SERVINGS

1 tablespoon olive or canola oil
½ pound favorite loose or ground
  sausage
4 large eggs
2 tablespoons favorite salsa
1 cup coarsely grated sharp Cheddar
  cheese (about 4 ounces)
2 garlic cloves, minced
1 teaspoon cayenne (optional)
2 large flour tortillas, warmed

I like to serve the egg-sausage mixture in a big bowl in the middle of the table, with warmed tortillas and cheese on the side, so that everyone can make his own. The art of burrito folding is a sort of rite of passage for my group of friends. You have to learn how to do it properly before you can eat this.

—Jesse Wakeman

eggs benedict *with hollandaise sauce*

Eggs Benedict with a dash of Worcestershire sauce? Trust us—and Epicurious member **Gromney**—on this one: it lends a compelling touch to this brunch classic. To make this dish a touch healthier, substitute turkey bacon or smoked salmon and reach for whole-wheat English muffins instead of the plain old white.

YIELD: MAKES 4 SERVINGS

FOR HOLLANDAISE SAUCE
4 large egg yolks
3 tablespoons lemon juice
¼ teaspoon salt
Dash of Worcestershire sauce
1 cup (2 sticks) unsalted butter, melted

FOR EGGS BENEDICT
8 slices Canadian bacon
2 teaspoons distilled white vinegar
8 large eggs
4 English muffins, split and toasted

MAKE HOLLANDAISE SAUCE
In a double boiler or a heatproof bowl set over a saucepan of barely simmering water (the bottom of the bowl should not touch the water), whisk together the egg yolks, lemon juice, salt, and Worcestershire sauce for 1 minute. Gradually add the melted butter, whisking vigorously. Remove the pan from the heat and cover to keep warm.

MAKE EGGS BENEDICT
1. Line 2 large plates with paper towels. In a medium skillet over moderate heat, cook the bacon until golden brown and beginning to crisp, 1 to 2 minutes per side. Transfer to a paper-towel–lined plate.

2. Add enough water to a large skillet to reach a depth of 1¼ inches. Add the vinegar and bring to a simmer over moderate heat. Crack the eggs 1 at a time and gently slip into the water. Cover and cook until the whites are just set and the yolks are still runny, about 3 minutes. Using a slotted spoon, carefully remove the eggs and transfer to the other paper-towel–lined plate.

3. Place 2 English muffin halves on each of 4 plates. Top each half with a slice of bacon and a poached egg. Drizzle with hollandaise sauce and serve immediately.

dates *with goat cheese wrapped in prosciutto*

Plump Medjool dates stuffed with creamy herbed goat cheese and wrapped in fresh basil and crispy prosciutto make for seriously addictive eating. Plus, these salty-sweet bundles are quite possibly the easiest hors d'oeuvre you'll ever make. Stuff and wrap the dates a couple of hours ahead, then arrange on a baking sheet, cover with plastic, and refrigerate until party time. When your guests arrive, pop the dates under the broiler and serve immediately.

Heat the broiler to low. Spoon 1 teaspoon cheese into each date. Wrap dates with a basil leaf, then a prosciutto strip, and secure with a toothpick. Broil until the cheese bubbles, about 3 minutes. Serve warm.

YIELD: MAKES 8 APPETIZER SERVINGS

⅓ cup soft herbed goat cheese
16 Medjool dates, pitted
16 large basil leaves
4 wide, thin slices prosciutto di Parma,
    each cut into 4 long strips
16 toothpicks, soaked in water 10 minutes

meatballs *with parsley and parmesan*

Meatballs are usually the spicy sidekick to spaghetti, but with a crusty roll, zesty tomato sauce, and some fresh mozzarella, they are transformed into hero material. Proving their versatility, these beefy bites from home cook Gayle Gardener of New Mexico also work as hors d'oeuvres. Just add a dipping sauce, and they'll be the hit of the party. If you're counting calories, substitute ground turkey or chicken for the beef and bake them.

1. Stir the eggs, bread crumbs, cheese, 3 tablespoons olive oil, the parsley, garlic, salt, and pepper in a large bowl to blend. Add the beef and mix thoroughly. Form the mixture into 1½-inch meatballs.

2. Pour enough oil into a heavy large skillet to coat the bottom; heat over medium-low heat. Working in batches, add meatballs and fry until brown and cooked through, turning frequently and adding more oil as needed, about 15 minutes per batch. Transfer to plate.

YIELD: MAKES ABOUT 44 MEATBALLS

4 large eggs
½ cup fresh bread crumbs
6 tablespoons grated Parmesan cheese
3 tablespoons olive oil
¼ cup chopped fresh parsley leaves
3 large garlic cloves, minced
2 teaspoons salt
1 teaspoon ground black pepper
2 pounds lean ground beef
Olive oil, for frying

quick cucumber pickles
with rye bread and cheese

The ultimate beer-hall food is also quite possibly one of our most versatile recipes. Arrange the pickles on a board with Gouda and a soft, dark loaf of rye from the bakery for a satisfying ploughman's lunch. Whip up a batch to present in an attractive jar for a delectable edible gift that comes together in minutes. Or just serve alongside sandwiches in a buffet—the tart, lightly spicy crunch of the cucumber is a refreshing complement to most cheeses, from Cheddar to goat.

1. Cut the cucumbers crosswise into ⅛-inch-thick slices, then toss with the salt in a bowl and let stand 15 minutes. Rinse and drain the cucumbers and pat dry with paper towels.

2. Whisk together the vinegar, sugar, mustard, horseradish, and dill until the sugar is dissolved. Stir in the cucumbers and let stand at least 5 minutes.

3. Slice the bread and serve with the pickles and the cheese.

"This crisp and lively pickle is a favorite of my frequent dinner guests. The pickles are good with many types of cheeses and go well with barbecue, fried chicken dinners, and for potlucks. I make the pickles at least once a month."
Dbolton, Kansas

YIELD: MAKES 6 HORS D'OEUVRE SERVINGS

2 English cucumbers
2 teaspoons kosher salt
½ cup cider vinegar
¼ cup sugar
1 tablespoon dry mustard
2 teaspoons drained bottled horseradish
1 tablespoon chopped fresh dill
1 loaf rye bread (1 pound)
2 (6- to 8-ounce) pieces semisoft cheese (preferably German, such as Cambozola or Mirabo)

do ahead:

The **PICKLES** can be made 2 to 4 hours ahead and chilled, covered.

duck pizza *with hoisin and scallions*

This fusion pizza was inspired by one that Wolfgang Puck created years ago. Traditional Asian ingredients—Chinese five-spice powder, hoisin sauce, scallions, and black sesame seeds—are an excellent change of pace from your usual pizza seasonings. Bonus: At fewer than 150 calories per serving, these mini pizzas, or pizzettes, are a low-fat alternative to traditional tomato and cheese pies. Just 3 inches across, they are designed to be canapés or hors d'oeuvres, but you can, of course, easily bake one large pizza for a family-style meal.

1. Preheat the oven to 400°F. Sprinkle the duck with five-spice powder, salt, and pepper. Heat the oil in an oven-proof medium skillet over high heat. Cook the duck until browned, 4 to 5 minutes per side, then transfer the skillet to the oven. Bake the duck until the outside is cooked but inside is rare, 8 to 10 minutes. Cool 4 to 5 minutes. Thinly slice the duck on the diagonal into 8 pieces, then cut each in half. Set aside.

2. Form the pizza dough into 8 even balls, then flatten to form 3-inch disks and place on an ungreased baking sheet. Spread hoisin sauce on the crusts with a pastry brush. Top with the spinach, cheese, bell pepper, and duck. Bake until the cheese is melted and bubbly, 20 to 25 minutes. Remove and garnish with onions and sesame seeds.

YIELD: MAKES 8 SERVINGS

1 duck (or chicken) breast, fat trimmed
½ teaspoon Chinese five-spice powder
¼ teaspoon salt
⅛ teaspoon freshly ground black pepper
1 teaspoon olive oil
½ pound whole-wheat pizza dough
3 tablespoons hoisin sauce
1 cup baby spinach, chopped
½ cup shredded part-skim mozzarella
½ red bell pepper, cored, seeded, and diced
4 green onions, thinly sliced
2 tablespoons black sesame seeds

"Made this for a cocktail party with the small pizzas cut into quarters . . . I prepared all the ingredients the night before, and assembled the pizzas immediately before the party. I coated the bell peppers with high-quality olive oil and roasted them ahead of time. These were easy, unusual, and a huge hit with guests."
A cook, San Francisco, California

caramelized-onion dip
with cilantro-garlic pita chips

Too often chips and dip are left out as a makeshift hors d'oeuvre at cocktail parties. Here's a deliciously unconventional version of an entertaining favorite. The dip highlights the rich flavors of sweet caramelized Vidalia or Maui onions with cinnamon-like garam masala and tangy crème fraîche or sour cream. Homemade pita chips are cooked in extra-virgin olive oil infused with garlic and cilantro.

YIELD: MAKES 8 SERVINGS

FOR DIP
2 tablespoons vegetable oil
3 cups chopped sweet onions, such as Vidalia or Maui (about 2 medium)
1½ teaspoons garam masala
1 (8-ounce) container crème fraîche or sour cream (1 cup)
Chopped fresh chives, for serving

FOR PITA CRISPS
½ bunch fresh cilantro
¼ cup extra-virgin olive oil
2 garlic cloves, crushed
6 pita breads

do ahead:

The **DIP** can be made 2 days ahead. Keep refrigerated.

The **PITA CHIPS** can be made 1 day ahead. Store airtight at room temperature.

"I loved the recipe and used Vidalia onions but added a bit of cayenne for kick. I also stirred some of the mixture in my eggs and scrambled them, and I really enjoyed it."
Bhixon, California

MAKE DIP
1. Heat the oil in heavy large skillet over medium heat. Add the onions and sauté until slightly softened, about 5 minutes. Reduce the heat to medium low and cook until the onions are deep brown and begin to crisp slightly, stirring often, about 40 minutes.

2. Add the garam masala; stir 1 minute. Transfer to a small bowl and cool completely. Mix in crème fraîche and season to taste with salt and pepper. Cover and refrigerate at least 2 hours.

MAKE PITA CRISPS AND SERVE
1. Finely chop enough cilantro leaves to measure 2 tablespoons. Chop enough cilantro stems to measure 3 tablespoons. Combine the oil and garlic in a heavy small saucepan; cook over medium heat until the oil begins to bubble around the garlic, about 5 minutes. Add the chopped cilantro stems. Remove from heat and let steep 10 minutes. Strain the oil into a small bowl; discard the solids in the strainer.

2. Preheat the oven to 350°F. Cut each pita bread horizontally in half. Cut each round into 6 wedges. Place the pita wedges on 2 rimmed baking sheets; drizzle with the cilantro-garlic oil, and toss gently to coat. Arrange the pita wedges in a single layer; bake 5 minutes. Sprinkle with the chopped cilantro leaves and bake until the pita wedges are crisp and golden, about 5 minutes longer. Cool.

3. Sprinkle the dip with chives; place on a platter and surround with the pita crisps.

classic spinach and artichoke dip

Creamy, tangy, cheesy, and easy, this time-tested recipe for a party dip from Epicurious member **Kristen Warner** of Stamford, Connecticut, might just be the reason pita chips were invented. But it's just as delicious with salty tortilla chips, which stand up well to the chunky bits of artichoke and deliciously gooey spinach.

1. Position a rack in the middle of the oven and preheat the oven to 350°F.

2. Using paper towels, squeeze the spinach to remove as much liquid as possible, then finely chop and place in a large bowl. Add the artichokes, mozzarella, ¾ cup Parmesan, the mayonnaise, sour cream, garlic, pepper, and salt and stir to combine. Transfer to a 1½-quart baking dish. Sprinkle with the remaining ¼ cup Parmesan, and cover snugly with foil. Bake until the top is golden brown, about 30 minutes.

I love this dish. I've been making it since college. It's super easy; the ingredients are ones you commonly have in your kitchen, it's quick to make, and it's always delicious! It also tastes great the next day as leftovers (sometimes I even eat it cold!).

–Kristen Warner

YIELD: MAKES 8 TO 10 SERVINGS

10 ounces frozen spinach, thawed and drained
1 (14-ounce) can artichoke hearts, drained and cut into quarters
2 cups shredded mozzarella cheese
1 cup freshly grated Parmesan cheese
1 cup mayonnaise
1 cup sour cream
3 garlic cloves, minced
1 teaspoon freshly ground black pepper
¼ teaspoon salt

Special equipment: 1- to 1½-quart baking dish

warm tofu *with spicy garlic sauce*

Chances are if you've ever eaten at a Korean restaurant, you've already had a variation of this specialty served to you as one of the *banchan,* or small dishes that accompany your meal. Traditionally, the tofu is lightly fried, but gentle simmering preserves the soft tofu's smooth delicacy. Using firm tofu won't yield the same texture, but the slices will maintain their shape a bit better. Considering how easy this dish is to prepare, it's amazing that such complex tastes abound. Serve with a hot bowl of rice for a simple meal.

1. Carefully rinse the tofu, then cover with cold water in a medium saucepan. Bring to a simmer over medium-high heat, then keep warm, covered, over very low heat.

2. Meanwhile, mince and mash the garlic to a paste with a pinch of salt. Stir together with the remaining ingredients.

3. Just before serving, carefully lift the tofu from the saucepan with a large spatula and drain on paper towels. Gently pat dry, then transfer to a small plate. Spoon some sauce over the tofu and serve warm. Serve remaining sauce on the side.

"I served the tofu over lightly sautéed bok choy seasoned with a bit of mirin. Instead of rice, I made quinoa in a miso broth; once it had cooked up, I tossed in some soaked hijiki seaweed (which had been tossed with a bit of sesame oil and soy sauce). Looked good on the plate and made for a lovely light dinner."

A cook, Oakland, California

YIELD: MAKES 8 SERVINGS

1 (14- to 18-ounce) package soft tofu (not silken)
1 teaspoon chopped garlic
¼ cup chopped green onions
2 teaspoons sesame seeds, toasted and crushed with side of a heavy knife
3 tablespoons soy sauce
1 tablespoon Asian sesame oil
1 teaspoon coarse Korean hot red pepper flakes
½ teaspoon sugar

do ahead:

The **SAUCE** can be made 1 day ahead and chilled. Bring to room temperature before using.

The **TOFU** can be kept warm up to 4 hours.

winter squash soup *with gruyère croutons*

While this recipe calls for the common butternut and acorn squash, you can also use other varieties, such as kabocha, delicata, and pumpkin—just avoid stringy spaghetti squash. If you aren't comfortable peeling uncooked squash with a paring knife, just cut the squash into quarters, drizzle with some olive oil, toss with a few garlic cloves, and roast until soft enough to scoop out the flesh. Lastly, don't forget the croutons, which make the soup a standout.

YIELD: MAKES 8 SERVINGS

FOR SOUP

¼ cup (½ stick) butter
1 large onion, finely chopped
4 large garlic cloves, chopped
3 (14½-ounce) cans low-sodium chicken broth
4 cups (1-inch) cubed peeled butternut squash (about 1½ pounds)
4 cups (1-inch) cubed peeled acorn squash (about 1½ pounds)
1¼ teaspoons minced fresh thyme
1¼ teaspoons minced fresh sage
¼ cup heavy whipping cream
2 teaspoons sugar

FOR CROUTONS

2 tablespoons butter
24 (¼-inch-thick) baguette bread slices
1 cup grated Gruyère cheese
1 teaspoon minced fresh thyme
1 teaspoon minced fresh sage

do ahead:

The **SOUP** can be made 1 day ahead. Chill. Rewarm over medium heat before serving.

MAKE SOUP

1. Melt the butter in a large pot over medium heat. Add the onion and garlic and sauté until tender, about 10 minutes. Add the broth, squash, and herbs. Bring to a boil, reduce the heat, cover, and simmer until the squash is very tender, about 20 minutes.

2. Working in batches, purée the soup in a blender. Return the soup to the pot. Stir in the cream and sugar. Bring to a simmer and season with salt and pepper.

MAKE CROUTONS AND SERVE SOUP

1. Preheat the broiler. Butter one side of each bread slice. Arrange the slices, buttered side up on a baking sheet. Broil until golden, about 1 minute. Turn over; sprinkle with cheese, then thyme and sage. Sprinkle with salt and pepper. Broil until the cheese melts, about 1 minute.

2. Ladle the soup into bowls. Top each with croutons and serve.

"I've been known to accidentally slip a tablespoon of bourbon into the recipe; it adds just a little more personality. Wonderful soup for parties or cold rainy days."

Akdale, Soldotna, Alaska

sweet potato and basil cream soup

A homemade chicken stock spiced with a Scotch bonnet or habanero chile lays the foundation for this tropical dish. Coconut powder and sweet potatoes add to the island feel. "It's a sweet soup and is more appropriate as an appetizer than an entrée, though I have to admit I've indulged in several bowls for dinner," Epicurious member **JTucci** says. Although Tucci calls it a soup, the coconut chicken broth will be scant—just enough to cover the chicken and cabbage at the bottom of the bowl.

1. In a heavy large pot over moderate heat, heat the oil until hot but not smoking. Add the chicken breast and wings and brown on all sides, about 4 minutes total. Transfer the chicken breast to a plate and set aside.

2. Add enough water to the pot to cover the chicken wings by 1 inch. Add the thyme, bay leaf, cinnamon stick, and the chile, if using. Season with salt and pepper and bring to a simmer. Continue simmering, scraping up any browned bits sticking to the bottom of the pot and skimming the fat as necessary, until reduced by half, about 15 minutes.

3. Pour the stock through a fine-mesh strainer, discarding the solids. Return the stock to the large pot and bring to a simmer. Add the sweet potato and simmer until barely tender, about 10 minutes. Coarsely chop the reserved chicken breast and add it to the soup, along with the shredded cabbage and the coconut milk. Simmer gently until the chicken is heated through, about 5 minutes.

4. Divide the banana slices among 4 bowls, then pour some soup into each bowl, making sure to evenly distribute the chicken and the cabbage. Garnish with basil and serve immediately.

YIELD: MAKES 4 SERVINGS

1 tablespoon vegetable oil
1 boneless skinless chicken breast
2 to 4 skin-on chicken wings
1 teaspoon dried thyme
1 bay leaf
1 (2-inch) cinnamon stick
1 habanero chile (optional)
1 large sweet potato, peeled, quartered, and cut into ¼-inch dice
½ large head green cabbage, very thinly sliced
¼ cup unsweetened coconut milk
1 banana, peeled, halved lengthwise, and cut into ¼-inch-thick slices
4 large basil leaves, thinly sliced

salmon chowder

Forty-five minutes is all the time you'll need to make this hearty, creamy chowder with bacon, salmon, and corn. A family-pleasing favorite for a winter night, the recipe also holds up to health-conscious variations. Sub in turkey bacon and low-fat milk, or swap in yams for the red potatoes for an extra dose of beta-carotene.

1. Cut the potatoes into ½-inch cubes, then cook in a 1½-quart heavy saucepan of boiling salted water until just tender, 8 to 10 minutes. Drain in a colander and set aside.

2. Cook the bacon in a 5-quart heavy pot over moderate heat, stirring occasionally, until crisp, about 8 minutes. Transfer with a slotted spoon to paper towels to drain.

3. Pour off all but 2 tablespoons of fat from the pot, then cook the onions, corn, garlic, thyme, bay leaf, and red pepper flakes over moderately low heat, stirring occasionally, until onions are tender, about 5 minutes.

4. Add the milk and cream and bring just to a boil. Reduce the heat to moderately low, then add the potatoes, the salmon, bacon, salt, and pepper and cook, gently stirring occasionally, until salmon is just cooked through and begins to break up as you stir, 5 to 8 minutes. Stir in the lemon juice and salt and pepper to taste. Discard the bay leaf and sprinkle with chives before serving.

YIELD: MAKES 6 SERVINGS

½ pound red potatoes
½ pound sliced bacon, cut crosswise into ¼-inch-wide strips
2 cups chopped green onions (from 2 bunches)
1 cup fresh or frozen corn kernels
1 tablespoon finely chopped garlic (3 cloves)
1 teaspoon finely chopped fresh thyme
1 Turkish or ½ California bay leaf
⅛ teaspoon dried red pepper flakes
3 cups whole milk
⅔ cup heavy cream
1 (1½-pound) piece salmon fillet (preferably wild), skin discarded and fish cut into 1-inch pieces
½ teaspoon salt
¼ teaspoon black pepper
2 teaspoons fresh lemon juice
Chopped fresh chives, for garnish

"This would also be great if you quartered a habanero pepper to steep in the soup and pulled it out before serving. Nice heat without the burn."
Ragde, Seattle, Washington

roasted squash, chestnut, and chicory salad *with cranberry vinaigrette*

With tender acorn squash, salty pancetta, a pungent and tart vinaigrette, and bitter chicory, this hearty salad is layered in flavor and texture. It will take you through all of winter, and would fit perfectly on most holiday buffets. You can use other winter squashes, including butternut, and bacon or prosciutto can easily stand in for the pancetta.

YIELD: MAKES 6 SERVINGS

1 (2-pound) acorn squash
2 tablespoons extra-virgin olive oil, plus additional for greasing pan
1 teaspoon salt
½ teaspoon black pepper
1 cup peeled whole chestnuts, cut into thirds (from a 7- to 8-ounce jar)
4 (¼-inch-thick) slices pancetta, cut into ¼-inch dice (6 ounces total)
¼ cup fresh cranberries, finely chopped
1 tablespoon dark brown sugar
¼ cup water
2 tablespoons whole-grain mustard
¾ pound chicory (curly endive), trimmed and torn into 2-inch pieces (10 cups)

"I made the components and then transported it piecemeal to my mother-in-law's and it was a big success—elegant and not heavy."
Zfmt, Brooklyn, New York

1. Put the oven rack in the middle position and preheat the oven to 450°F. Line a large shallow baking pan with foil and coat generously with olive oil.

2. Cut off the stem end of the squash, then put cut side down and halve lengthwise. Discard the seeds, then cut the squash into ½-inch-thick slices. Peel if desired with a paring knife and transfer the slices to a bowl. Add 1 tablespoon olive oil, ½ teaspoon salt, and ¼ teaspoon pepper and gently toss to coat. Arrange in a single layer in the lined baking pan and roast until golden, about 15 minutes. Remove from the oven and turn the squash over with a spatula. Add the chestnuts to the pan in an even layer, and continue to roast until squash is golden and tender, 10 to 15 minutes. Keep warm, covered with foil.

3. Cook the pancetta in a dry 10-inch heavy skillet over high heat until browned, about 4 minutes total. Transfer the pancetta with a slotted spoon to paper towels to drain, reserving the fat in the skillet.

4. Reheat the pancetta fat over moderately high heat until hot but not smoking, then add cranberries and brown sugar and stir once to combine. Remove from the heat and add the water, stirring and scraping up browned bits from bottom of skillet.

5. Transfer the cranberry mixture to a medium bowl and whisk in the mustard, remaining tablespoon olive oil, remaining ½ teaspoon salt, and remaining ¼ teaspoon pepper.

6. Toss together the chicory, roasted acorn squash, and chestnuts. Just before serving, toss with dressing and sprinkle with pancetta.

iceberg wedge salad
with warm bacon and blue cheese dressing

Iceberg-wedge salads have been a restaurant staple, but this simple starter begs to be made at home. Hot pepper sauce adds zing to the blue cheese dressing, which is easy and delicious enough that you'll want to save any extra and use as a dip for veggies or toss with cold cooked pasta for lunch. Serve with a grilled fillet of fish or steak, and you've got yourself an at-home meal that trumps anything you'd find on a menu.

YIELD: MAKES 6 SERVINGS

1½ cups mayonnaise
2 tablespoons fresh lemon juice
1 tablespoon coarsely ground black
   pepper
1 teaspoon hot pepper sauce
1 cup coarsely crumbled blue cheese
Buttermilk (optional)
½ pound thick-cut bacon, cut crosswise
   into 1-inch pieces
1 large head iceberg lettuce, cut into
   6 wedges, each with some core
   attached
½ red onion, very thinly sliced

do ahead:

The **DRESSING** can be made 1 day ahead. Cover and chill.

1. Mix the mayonnaise, lemon juice, pepper, and hot sauce in a medium bowl. Add the cheese and stir until well blended. If too thick, thin with buttermilk by tablespoon-fuls to desired consistency.

2. Cook the bacon in a large skillet over medium heat until golden brown and beginning to crisp.

3. Arrange the lettuce wedges on plates. Spoon the dressing over. Using a slotted spoon, transfer the warm bacon from the skillet onto the salads, dividing equally. Garnish with red onion.

"I took a cue from the low-cal world and replaced most (but not all) of the mayo with Greek yogurt, and the dressing still tastes rich and tangy."
SauteLA

shaved brussels sprout salad
with fresh walnuts and pecorino

Adapted from a recipe by Chez Panisse alum and *Top Chef Masters* veteran Jonathan Waxman, this delicate, fuss-free dish proves that Brussels sprouts can be just as tasty raw as they are roasted. Use a food processor or mandoline to shave the sprouts, unless you're really confident with your knife skills. The slaw also makes an incredible pizza topping; just wait to add the walnuts until the dough is out of the oven and the pecorino has melted.

1. Holding each Brussels sprout by its stem end, cut into very thin slices; discard the stem ends. Toss in a bowl to separate the layers.

2. Lightly crush the walnuts with your hands and add to the sprouts along with the cheese, oil, and lemon juice, then toss to combine. Season with pepper.

YIELD: MAKES 6 SERVINGS

1½ pounds Brussels sprouts (preferably on the stalk), any discolored leaves discarded and stem ends left intact
1 cup walnuts, lightly toasted (3½ ounces)
2 tablespoons finely grated pecorino romano, or to taste
¼ cup olive oil
3 tablespoons fresh lemon juice

Special equipment: Adjustable-blade slicer (mandoline)

do ahead:

The **WALNUTS** can be toasted 1 day ahead and kept in an airtight container at room temperature.

The **BRUSSELS SPROUTS** can be sliced 3 hours ahead and chilled, covered. Toss with remaining ingredients just before serving.

"Using a food processor is definitely the way to go—fast, safe, and creates very thin slices. I added more lemon juice, a touch more oil (I used half olive, half walnut oil)."
KateCinOH

pear, arugula, and pancetta salad

Let's be clear: If you're hosting the dinner party to end all dinner parties—Grandma's good china is out of storage, the napkins have been *ironed,* and you're polishing the silver—this is the ultimate first course. At first glance it may resemble a basic pear-and-arugula salad, but look closer and you'll find that everything about it is just a little bit special, from the Champagne vinaigrette, to the creamy, salty ricotta salata, to the rich and savory pancetta. The ingredients do cost a little more, but it's worth it.

YIELD: MAKES 4 SERVINGS

FOR VINAIGRETTE
1 tablespoon Champagne vinegar
1 tablespoon mild honey
½ tablespoon fresh lemon juice
⅛ teaspoon salt
⅛ teaspoon coarsely ground black pepper
3 tablespoons olive oil

FOR SALAD
2 ounce thinly sliced pancetta (4 to 5 slices)
1 tablespoon olive oil
2 firm-ripe pears
4 cups baby arugula or torn larger arugula (1¼ pounds)
3 ounces ricotta salata, thinly shaved with a vegetable peeler

MAKE VINAIGRETTE
Whisk together the vinegar, honey, lemon juice, salt, and pepper in a salad bowl. Add the oil in a slow stream, whisking until combined well.

MAKE SALAD
1. Cook the pancetta in the oil in a 10-inch heavy skillet over moderate heat, turning frequently, until just crisp, about 5 minutes. Transfer to paper towels to drain (pancetta will crisp as it cools). Tear into bite-size pieces.

2. Halve the pears lengthwise, core, and cut lengthwise into ¼-inch-thick slices.

3. Add the pears to the dressing along with arugula, cheese, and pancetta, tossing to coat.

"Instead of mixing everything together with the dressing, I arranged the components on top of the greens and drizzled the dressing on top, on individual plates. It was a nice presentation, and I could make sure that each person got all the components. The dressing is yummy—can definitely be used on any salad."

A cook, Dresher, Pennsylvania

avocado, asparagus, and hearts of palm salad

Crisp, tender asparagus spears get friendly with hearts of palm, cherry tomatoes, scallions, and avocado in this lovely starter salad from Epicurious member **Theonike**. A simple mustard-and-garlic-infused vinaigrette serves as dressing, while a sprinkle of toasted pine nuts gives this dish some crunch. Use soft, ripe avocados but wait to peel and dice them until just before serving so they retain their beautiful pale green hue.

YIELD: MAKES 6 TO 8 SERVINGS

1 pound asparagus, trimmed and cut into 1-inch pieces

1 (14-ounce) can hearts of palm, drained, rinsed, and cut into ½-inch pieces

About 12 cherry tomatoes, halved

2 green onions (white and light green parts only), thinly sliced

3 tablespoons red-wine vinegar

2 tablespoons lemon juice

1½ tablespoons Dijon mustard

1 garlic clove, minced

½ teaspoon freshly ground black pepper

¼ teaspoon sugar

½ cup extra-virgin olive oil

2 avocados, halved, peeled, pitted, and diced

¼ cup pine nuts, toasted

1. In a medium skillet over high heat, bring 1 inch of salted water to a boil. Add the asparagus and cook, uncovered, until crisp-tender, about 3 minutes. Drain and rinse with cold water to stop the cooking. Pat dry and transfer to a large salad bowl.

2. Add the hearts of palm, cherry tomatoes, and onions to the salad bowl.

3. In a small bowl, whisk together the vinegar, lemon juice, mustard, garlic, pepper, and sugar. Gradually whisk in the oil, then pour over the salad and toss to coat the vegetables. Add the diced avocado, season with salt and pepper, and toss gently. Sprinkle the salad with toasted pine nuts and serve immediately.

spiced lentil tacos

"Vegetarian taco" is typically code for a taco with a black or pinto bean filling. But you can use heart-healthy lentils instead. Standard brown lentils are easy to find, but if you opt for French green lentils, they will take a bit more time to cook. If you're craving lentil burritos—just add rice and tortillas.

1. Heat the oil in a large skillet over medium-high heat. Cook the onion, garlic, and salt until the onion begins to soften, 3 to 4 minutes. Add the lentils and taco seasoning. Cook until the spices are fragrant and lentils are dry, about 1 minute. Add the broth. Bring to a boil, reduce the heat, cover, and simmer until the lentils are tender, 25 to 30 minutes.

2. Mix the sour cream, chile, and adobo sauce in a bowl. Uncover the lentils and cook until mixture thickens, 6 to 8 minutes, then mash with a rubber spatula.

3. Spoon ¼ cup lentil mixture into each taco shell. Top with 2 heaping teaspoons sour cream mixture, the lettuce, tomato, and cheese.

YIELD: MAKES 4 SERVINGS

1 tablespoon olive oil
1 cup finely chopped onion
1 garlic clove, chopped
½ teaspoon salt
1 cup brown lentils, rinsed
1 (2.25-ounce) package taco seasoning
2½ cups vegetable broth
½ cup fat-free sour cream
1 chipotle chile in adobo sauce, finely chopped (use half for less heat), and 2 teaspoons adobo sauce
8 taco shells
1¼ cups shredded lettuce
1 cup chopped ripe tomato
½ cup shredded reduced-fat (2 percent) Cheddar cheese

"I used Middle Eastern labaneh yogurt instead of sour cream, chipotle Tabasco instead of the chile in adobo, and shredded red cabbage instead of lettuce, to increase the nutritional value."
Kaikaikido, California

three-bean veggie chili

Epicurious member **Benjamin Tevelow** of Woodside, New York, offers this easy and delicious vegetarian chili, which will satisfy even those who live for bacon. To simplify the recipe, throw this hearty chili in a slow-cooker. Simply sauté the onion, garlic, and spices in a pot, transfer that plus the other ingredients to the cooker, and cook for four hours on medium heat. Green onions, cilantro, sour cream, and grated Cheddar cheese combine for a tasty garnish.

YIELD: MAKES 8 SERVINGS

¼ cup olive oil
1 large onion, chopped
8 ounces button mushrooms, thinly sliced
4 garlic cloves, minced
1 tablespoon plus 1 teaspoon chili powder
1½ teaspoons ground cumin
⅛ teaspoon ground cinnamon
1 bottle dark beer, such as brown ale
1 (28-ounce) can diced tomatoes with their liquid
1 (15-ounce) can black beans, drained and rinsed
1 (15-ounce) can kidney beans, drained and rinsed
1 (15-ounce) can white beans, such as cannellini, navy, or great northern, drained and rinsed
1 red bell pepper, seeded and finely diced
1 jalapeño chile, seeded and minced
2 cups frozen corn kernels, thawed
Thinly sliced green onions (white and light green parts only), chopped fresh cilantro, sour cream, coarsely grated Cheddar cheese, lime wedges, and tortilla chips, for garnish

1. In a 6-quart heavy pot over moderate heat, warm the olive oil. Add the onion and mushrooms and sauté, stirring occasionally, until the onion is translucent, 6 to 7 minutes. Add the garlic, chili powder, cumin, and cinnamon, and sauté, stirring occasionally, for an additional 2 minutes.

2. Stir in the beer, tomatoes and their liquid, beans, bell pepper, and jalapeño and bring to a boil, stirring occasionally. Reduce the heat to low, cover, and simmer until the tomatoes are broken down and the chili is thick, about 1 hour.

3. Just before serving, stir in the corn, and simmer until heated through, 1 to 2 minutes. Season with salt and pepper and serve in bowls, along with the garnish.

vegetarian cassoulet

In this protein-packed vegetarian version of the French bistro classic, tangy leeks and a garlic-herb bread-crumb topping mean that you won't miss the sausage and duck that you'd find in a traditional cassoulet. Best of all, this one-pot wonder takes considerably less time to assemble and cook than a meat-lover's cassoulet. For an easy flavor boost, substitute vegetable broth for the water, and add a can of fire-roasted tomatoes.

MAKE CASSOULET

1. Halve the leeks lengthwise and cut crosswise into ½-inch pieces, then wash well and pat dry.

2. Cook the leeks, carrots, celery, and garlic in the oil with the herb sprigs, bay leaf, cloves, and salt and pepper in a large heavy pot over medium heat, stirring occasionally, until softened and golden, about 15 minutes. Stir in the beans, then the water, and simmer, partially covered, stirring occasionally, until carrots are tender but not falling apart, about 30 minutes.

MAKE GARLIC CRUMBS

1. Preheat the oven to 350°F, with the rack in the middle.

2. Toss the bread crumbs with the oil, garlic, and salt and pepper in a bowl until well coated. Spread in a baking pan and toast in the oven, stirring once halfway through, until crisp and golden, 12 to 15 minutes.

3. Cool the crumbs in the pan, then transfer to a bowl and stir in the parsley.

SERVE CASSOULET

Discard the herb sprigs and bay leaf, and mash some of the beans in the pot with a potato masher or back of a spoon to thicken the broth. Season with salt and pepper. Sprinkle with garlic crumbs and serve.

"Even better as leftovers for lunch. I made big chunky croutons rather than bread crumbs. They were like big cassoulet sponges, which, frankly, were delicious."
A cook, New England

YIELD: MAKES 4 TO 6 SERVINGS

FOR CASSOULET

3 medium leeks (white and pale green parts only)
4 medium carrots, halved lengthwise and cut into 1-inch pieces
3 celery ribs, cut into 1-inch pieces
4 garlic cloves, chopped
¼ cup olive oil
4 sprigs fresh thyme
2 sprigs fresh parsley
1 Turkish or ½ California bay leaf
⅛ teaspoon ground cloves
½ teaspoon salt
½ teaspoon pepper
3 (19-ounce) cans cannellini or great northern beans, rinsed and drained
1 quart water

FOR GARLIC CRUMBS

4 cups coarse fresh bread crumbs from a baguette
⅓ cup olive oil
1 tablespoon chopped garlic
¼ teaspoon salt
¼ teaspoon pepper
¼ cup chopped fresh parsley

quinoa *with moroccan winter squash and carrot stew*

Remember the scene in *The Wizard of Oz* where Dorothy steps out of her house and everything turns Technicolor? This gorgeous, colorful vegetarian supper from chefs Bruce Aidells and Nancy Oakes has the same effect on a winter day. Butternut squash absorbs the laundry list of zingy spices, but if you're sensitive to spices, feel free to cut the cayenne by half. Add chickpeas for a hearty, nutty dose of protein, and top with a cooling dollop of Greek yogurt.

YIELD: 4 TO 6 SERVINGS

FOR STEW

2 tablespoons olive oil
1 cup chopped onion
3 garlic cloves, chopped
2 teaspoons Hungarian sweet paprika
1 teaspoon salt
½ teaspoon ground black pepper
½ teaspoon ground coriander
½ teaspoon ground cumin
½ teaspoon turmeric
½ teaspoon ground ginger
½ teaspoon cayenne pepper
Pinch of saffron
1 cup water
1 (14½-ounce) can diced tomatoes, drained
2 tablespoons fresh lemon juice
3 cups 1-inch cubes peeled butternut squash (from 1½-pound squash)
2 cups ¾-inch cubes peeled carrots

FOR QUINOA

1 cup quinoa
1 tablespoon butter
1 tablespoon olive oil
½ cup finely chopped onion
¼ cup finely chopped peeled carrot
2 garlic cloves, minced
½ teaspoon salt
½ teaspoon turmeric
2 cups water
½ cup chopped fresh cilantro, divided
2 teaspoons chopped fresh mint, divided

FOR STEW

Heat the oil in a large saucepan over medium heat. Add the onion; sauté until soft, stirring often, about 5 minutes. Add the garlic; stir 1 minute. Mix in the paprika and the next 8 ingredients. Add 1 cup water, tomatoes, and lemon juice. Bring to boil. Add the squash and carrots. Cover and simmer over medium-low heat until the vegetables are tender, stirring occasionally, about 20 minutes. Season with salt and pepper.

FOR QUINOA

1. Rinse quinoa; drain. Melt the butter with oil in a large saucepan over medium heat. Add onion and carrot. Cover; cook until vegetables begin to brown, stirring often, about 10 minutes. Add the garlic, salt, and turmeric; sauté 1 minute. Add the quinoa; stir 1 minute. Add 2 cups water. Bring to a boil; reduce heat to medium-low. Cover; simmer until the liquid is absorbed and the quinoa is tender, about 15 minutes.

2. Rewarm the stew. Stir in half of the cilantro and half of the mint. Spoon the quinoa onto a platter, forming a well in center. Spoon the stew into the well. Sprinkle with the remaining herbs.

"I didn't think this could get any better until I subbed one preserved lemon, diced, for the lemon juice. It was exquisite. The prep can be a little time-consuming, what with all the chopping, but it is impossible to screw this up, and the actual cooking is practically a one-pot, one-shot deal."
Veruka2

spaghetti *with turkey-pesto meatballs*

In addition to being packed with meaty flavor, turkey is a healthy alternative to beef, rendering this a great dinner option for the whole family; to really save on fat and calories, stick to lean ground turkey. Pair this dish with a green salad and red wine, then finish off the meal with bowls of your favorite ice cream.

YIELD: MAKES 2 SERVINGS (CAN BE DOUBLED)

2 cups favorite chunky tomato pasta sauce
½ pound ground turkey
¾ cup fresh bread crumbs made from crustless Italian bread
2¾ tablespoons favorite pesto
1 large egg white
¼ teaspoon salt
8 ounces spaghetti

"Leftover meatballs make great snacks by themselves and are awesome in a meatball sub with roasted red peppers, Provolone, and pesto mayo."

Lhourin, Gulf Coast, Mississippi

1. Spread 1 cup of pasta sauce over the bottom of a heavy medium skillet. Mix the turkey, bread crumbs, pesto, egg white, and salt in a medium bowl. Using moistened hands, form mixture into 8 meatballs. Place the meatballs in a single layer in the sauce. Spoon the remaining sauce over and bring to a simmer. Cover, reduce the heat to medium-low, and simmer until the meatballs are cooked through, stirring occasionally, about 20 minutes.

2. Cook the pasta in a large pot of boiling salted water until just tender but still firm to the bite. Drain pasta; divide between bowls. Top with meatballs and sauce.

turkey jambalaya

A satisfying budget-friendly Southern supper with leftovers that pack up easily for lunch the next day—what else could you ask for? This one-pot feast is packed with turkey, rice, and peppers, plus a little cayenne for spice. If you don't like turkey, use chicken instead and add a dash of smoked paprika or lean bacon for a warm, earthy effect.

1. Cut the turkey meat off the bone with a paring knife, then cut (or pull off) and discard the tendons and skin. Cut the turkey into 1-inch pieces.

2. Heat the oil in a 6-quart wide heavy pot over moderately high heat until hot but not smoking. Cook the onion, bell pepper, and celery, stirring frequently, until the onion begins to brown, about 5 minutes.

3. Add the garlic and cook, stirring, 30 seconds. Add the turkey, the tomatoes, broth, water, salt, and cayenne and bring to a boil, covered, over high heat. Stir in the rice and bring to a full rolling boil. Cover the pot, then cook over low heat until the rice is tender and the liquid is absorbed, about 20 minutes. Let stand off the heat, covered, 5 minutes. Stir in the onion greens.

YIELD: MAKES 6 SERVINGS

2¾ pounds smoked turkey drumsticks
2 tablespoons vegetable oil
1 medium onion, chopped
1 small green bell pepper, chopped
1 large celery rib, chopped
1 large garlic clove, finely chopped
1 (14- to 16-ounce) can diced tomatoes in juice, drained
1¾ cups reduced-sodium chicken broth
1¼ cups water
½ teaspoon salt
½ teaspoon cayenne
2 cups long-grain white rice
½ cup chopped tops of green onions

"I used smoked chipotle chicken sausage for a super-easy turkey substitute. Also, I added a can of black beans, drained. It makes a really easy and healthy comfort meal."

A cook, San Diego, California

halibut in hazelnut romesco
with potatoes

A traditional Spanish romesco sauce calls for almonds, but in this recipe hazelnuts spruce up simple halibut fillets. The sauce freezes well and also partners with chicken, steak, or pasta. For a more budget-friendly dish, substitute tilapia. You can also swap roasted red peppers for the piquillos and use whatever nuts you happen to have in the pantry.

YIELD: MAKES 4 SERVINGS

1 large tomato
½ cup husked toasted hazelnuts (about 2½ ounces)
½ cup coarsely chopped drained piquillo chiles from jar or can
4 tablespoons extra-virgin olive oil
2 garlic cloves, chopped
1½ teaspoons smoked paprika (see Note)
1 teaspoon Sherry vinegar or red-wine vinegar
½ teaspoon salt
¼ teaspoon cayenne
1 tablespoon unsalted butter
4 (6-ounce) halibut fillets
½ cup low-sodium chicken broth
12 small Yukon Gold potatoes, halved, steamed until tender
Chopped fresh parsley, for serving

cook's note:

The **SMOKED PAPRIKA** is sometimes labeled pimentón dulce or pimentón de la vera dulce. It is available at some supermarkets and at specialty food stores.

do ahead:

The **ROMESCO SAUCE** can be made 1 day ahead. Cover and refrigerate.

1. Preheat the broiler. Place the tomato on a rimmed baking sheet and broil until the skin is blistered and slipping off, turning once with tongs, about 3 minutes. When cool enough to handle, peel the tomato, then cut in half and squeeze out the seeds.

2. Chop the nuts in a food processor; add the tomato, chiles, 2 tablespoons olive oil, the garlic, paprika, vinegar, salt, and cayenne, then purée. Transfer the romesco sauce to a bowl.

3. Melt the butter with the remaining 2 tablespoons oil in a heavy large skillet over medium-high heat. Add the halibut and cook until golden brown, about 2 minutes per side (fish will not be cooked through). Transfer the halibut to a plate.

4. Add the broth to the same skillet and bring to a boil; stir in the romesco sauce. Add the halibut. Reduce the heat to medium-low, cover, and simmer until the halibut is opaque in center, about 2 minutes. Transfer the halibut to plates. Place the steamed potatoes alongside and spoon romesco sauce over. Sprinkle with parsley, if desired, and serve.

"I substituted cod, since halibut was not available. Canned fire-roasted tomatoes, drained, are a time-saver for roasting your own tomatoes."
A cook, USA

crispy skate *with cauliflower, bacon, capers, and croutons*

This lightly fried, fleshy white fish paired with crisp bacon and cauliflower is surprisingly hearty. Cream of Wheat gives the rice-flour crust an airy texture that won't drown the fish, and the bacon drippings infuse the cauliflower with a smoky flavor. To cut the fat, drain the drippings and sauté the vegetables in olive oil instead. Dover sole is a suitable flat-fish substitute.

MAKE CAULIFLOWER

1. Sauté the bacon in a heavy large skillet over medium heat until browned and crisp. Using a slotted spoon, transfer the bacon to paper towels to drain. Add the cauliflower to the drippings and sauté until crisp-tender and beginning to brown, about 5 minutes.

2. Add the tomatoes, lemon juice, capers, and thyme; simmer 1 minute to blend flavors. Remove from heat.

MAKE SKATE AND SERVE

1. Whisk the rice flour, Cream of Wheat, and herbs in a large shallow bowl to blend. Sprinkle the fish with salt and pepper, then coat fish on both sides with the flour mixture. Heat the oil in a heavy large skillet over medium-high heat. Add the fish and sauté until browned and just opaque in the center, about 3 minutes per side.

2. Rewarm the cauliflower mixture over medium heat. Mix in the reserved bacon and the croutons. Season to taste with salt and pepper. Spoon the cauliflower mixture into the center of 2 plates; top with the fish.

"Wondra flour is a good substitute for the rice flour. Wondra fries up lighter and crispier than all-purpose flour. Fast, easy, delicious."
Springhop, USA

YIELD: MAKES 2 SERVINGS

FOR CAULIFLOWER

4 slices thick-cut bacon, cut into 1-inch pieces
2 cups small (¾-inch) cauliflower florets
10 cherry tomatoes, halved
1½ tablespoons fresh lemon juice
1 tablespoon drained capers
¼ teaspoon chopped fresh thyme

FOR SKATE

¼ cup rice flour (see Note)
¼ cup Cream of Wheat
¼ teaspoon chopped fresh tarragon
¼ teaspoon chopped fresh thyme
2 (7-ounce) pieces boned skate wing (or Dover sole fillets)
¼ cup canola oil
2 tablespoons coarsely chopped purchased plain croutons

cook's note:

The **RICE FLOUR** is available at some supermarkets, specialty food stores, and natural food stores.

fish and chips

We owe the Brits big time for this classic pub dish. The beer batter highlights the freshness of the fish while also creating a light and crispy coating. Serve these with the accompanying homemade "chips" and watch as adults and children alike flock for seconds, thirds, and fourths.

4 large boiling potatoes (2¼ pounds)
3 quarts vegetable oil, for frying
2 cups all-purpose flour
1 (12-ounce) bottle cold beer,
    preferably ale
1 teaspoon salt
1½ pounds haddock or cod fillets,
    skinned, pin bones removed, and fish
    cut diagonally into 1-inch-wide strips
¼ teaspoon pepper
Malt vinegar, for serving

Special equipment: Deep-fry
    thermometer

do ahead:

The **CHIPS** can be fried for the first time 3 hours ahead and kept, uncovered, at room temperature until refrying.

1. Peel the potatoes and halve lengthwise, then cut lengthwise into ½-inch-thick wedges, transferring as cut to a large bowl of ice and cold water. Chill 30 minutes.

2. Heat the oil in a deep 6-quart heavy pot or deep-fat fryer over moderately high heat until it registers 325°F on a deep-fry thermometer. Meanwhile, drain the potatoes and dry thoroughly with paper towels. Fry one-third of the potatoes, stirring gently, until the edges are just golden, about 4 minutes. Transfer with a slotted spoon to fresh paper towels to drain. Fry the remaining potatoes in 2 batches, returning the oil to 325°F between batches. Remove the oil from the heat and reserve. Cool the potatoes, about 25 minutes.

3. Reheat the oil over moderately high heat until it registers 350°F. Put the oven racks in the upper and lower thirds of the oven and preheat the oven to 250°F.

4. Fry the potatoes again, in 3 batches, until deep golden brown and crisp, about 5 minutes per batch. Return the oil to 350°F between batches. Transfer the potatoes with a slotted spoon to fresh paper towels as fried and drain briefly. Arrange in a shallow baking pan and keep warm in the oven. Increase the oil temperature to 375°F. Sift 1½ cups of flour into a bowl, then whisk in the beer gently until just combined. Stir in ¼ teaspoon salt.

5. Pat the fish dry, then sprinkle on both sides with the remaining ¾ teaspoon salt and the pepper. Dredge in the remaining ½ cup flour, shaking off any excess. Coat 4 pieces of fish in the batter, 1 at a time, and slide into the oil as coated. Fry, turning over frequently, until deep golden and cooked through, 4 to 5 minutes. Transfer to a paper-towel–lined baking sheet and keep warm in the oven. Fry remaining fish in batches of 4, returning the oil to 375°F between batches. Season with salt and malt vinegar and serve.

spicy orange tilapia

Looking for a fast, inexpensive, and tempting weeknight meal? Epicurious member **Leah Hook** of Reading, Massachusetts, has a fish dish that's just the ticket. The breaded tilapia fillets are quickly seared in a hot pan, and then drenched in a sauce made from orange juice and sriracha sauce and served over brown rice. "Don't stress about whether the flour sticks evenly to the tilapia," Hook says. "The idea is that some flour will stick on some parts of the fillet, and those parts will soak up the tasty sauce."

YIELD: MAKES 4 SERVINGS

⅓ cup all-purpose flour
½ teaspoon salt
½ teaspoon freshly ground black pepper
4 (6-ounce) tilapia fillets
¼ cup olive oil
1 medium onion, thinly sliced
½ cup orange or orange-pineapple juice
2 tablespoons lemon juice
2 tablespoons finely grated fresh ginger
1 tablespoon sriracha sauce
2 tablespoons unsalted butter

1. In a shallow bowl, whisk together the flour, salt, and pepper. Coat the tilapia fillets in the flour mixture, shaking off any excess.

2. In a large skillet over moderately high heat, heat 2 tablespoon of the oil until hot but not smoking. Carefully add the fillets and cook for 3 minutes. Flip the fillets and continue cooking until firm to the touch, about 2 minutes. Transfer to a platter and cover to keep warm.

3. Wipe the pan clean, add the remaining 2 tablespoons oil, and place over moderate heat. Add the onion and sauté, stirring frequently, until tender, 6 to 7 minutes. Add the orange juice, lemon juice, ginger, and sriracha and bring to a simmer. Whisk in the butter, then remove the sauce from the heat, spoon over the tilapia, and serve immediately.

I was a new lawyer with lots of school debt so I set out to create some low-cost, easy dinners that didn't skimp on flavor, and this was my favorite. I love sweetening curried and peppery dishes with honey or maple syrup, but both can be expensive condiments. I scoured my kitchen for something sweet and cheap—juice! I found the spice in the equally inexpensive sriracha sauce and my canvas was cheap and delicious tilapia fillets.

—Leah Hook

southwestern-style chicken soup *with barley*

Get a full serving of the Southwest with this bowl of beans, barley, and chicken from Epicurious member **Mike Kubin.** This hearty soup is perfect for midweek eating. If you prefer a meatless version, simply omit the chicken and substitute vegetable broth for the chicken stock. You can even bump up the bean count for additional protein—and extra fiber. Store any leftovers in the fridge, and take this soup to work for lunch.

1. In a small bowl, whisk together the lemon juice, 1 tablespoon vegetable oil, 1 tablespoon chili powder, ½ teaspoon cumin, and the garlic powder. Place the chicken breasts in a large bowl. Add the lemon juice mixture and toss to thoroughly coat the chicken.

2. In an 8-quart Dutch oven over moderate heat, warm 1 tablespoon vegetable oil. Add the chicken and cook, turning once or twice, until browned and cooked through, about 12 minutes total. Transfer the chicken to a plate.

3. Add the remaining 1 tablespoon vegetable oil along with the onions and garlic to the Dutch oven and sauté, stirring occasionally, until the onions are translucent, about 6 minutes. Add the black pepper along with the remaining 1 tablespoon chili powder and the remaining 1 teaspoon cumin and cook, stirring frequently, for 2 minutes. Add the tomatoes and their liquid, chicken stock, black beans, barley, chiles, and tomato paste and bring to a boil, stirring occasionally. Reduce the heat to moderately low, cover, and simmer until the barley is tender, about 45 minutes.

4. Cut or tear the chicken into bite-size pieces. Once the barley is tender, stir the chicken into the soup along with the corn, and cook until heated through, about 3 minutes. Season with salt and pepper and serve.

YIELD: MAKES 8 SERVINGS

3 tablespoons lemon juice
3 tablespoons vegetable oil
2 tablespoons chili powder
1½ teaspoons ground cumin
½ teaspoon garlic powder
4 boneless skinless chicken breast halves
2 medium onions, chopped
4 garlic cloves, minced
½ teaspoon freshly ground black pepper
1 (28-ounce) can diced tomatoes with their liquid
5½ cups chicken stock or low-sodium chicken broth
1 (15-ounce) can black beans, drained and rinsed
½ cup medium pearl barley
1 (4-ounce) can diced mild or hot green chiles
1 tablespoon tomato paste
2 cups frozen corn kernels, thawed

mahogany chicken

This sweet, sour, and salty chicken gets its name from the rich, dark soy sauce. It's quick to prepare, and the one-pan prep makes it easy to clean up. "Using a splatter screen (or a large, inverted strainer/colander) is helpful for reducing the mess when browning the chicken," says Epicurious member **Joy Vaughns.** Serve the chicken with steamed rice and a crunchy green vegetable.

YIELD: MAKES 4 SERVINGS

⅓ cup soy sauce

2 tablespoons sugar

2 tablespoons mirin, sweet sherry, or white wine

2 teaspoons grated fresh ginger

1 garlic clove, minced

½ teaspoon cornstarch

8 bone-in skin-on (5-ounce) chicken thighs, trimmed of excess fat

2 teaspoons vegetable oil

2 green onions (white and light green parts only), thinly sliced on the diagonal

1. In a small bowl, whisk together the soy sauce, sugar, mirin, ginger, garlic, and cornstarch.

2. Pat the chicken dry and season with freshly ground black pepper.

3. In a large nonstick skillet over moderate heat, heat the oil until hot but not smoking. Add the chicken skin side down, and cook until the skin is crisp and deep golden brown, 15 to 20 minutes. Flip and continue cooking until the other side is browned and the meat is thoroughly cooked, about 10 minutes. Transfer the chicken to a plate and drain the fat from the pan.

4. Add the soy sauce mixture to the skillet and bring to a simmer. Return the chicken to the skillet and turn to coat in the sauce. Simmer the chicken, skin side up, until the sauce is thick and glossy, 4 to 5 minutes. Transfer the chicken to a platter, spoon the sauce over the top, sprinkle with the sliced onions, and serve.

smoked chicken chowder

In this comforting chowder, heavy cream, flour, and potatoes provide rich, velvety texture, while the smoky flavor of chipotle chile in adobo sauce adds heat. The recipe calls for about a pound of smoked chicken, which is available at some butcher shops and specialty food stores, but you can also use (unsmoked) chicken breasts.

1. In a 6-quart heavy pot, cook the onions in the oil over moderate heat, stirring, until softened. Add the potato, garlic, and jalapeño and cook, stirring, 1 minute. Stir in the flour, and cook over moderately low heat, stirring, for 2 minutes.

2. Whisk in 2 cups broth and the heavy cream, and bring to a boil, stirring. Add the tomatoes, corn, cheese, parsley, chipotle, and chicken, and simmer, stirring occasionally and adding enough of the remaining cup of broth to thin soup to desired consistency, 20 minutes, or until the vegetables are tender. Season the soup with salt and pepper.

"We did alter the recipe slightly by increasing the quantity of potatoes and omitting flour (using the potato to thicken the recipe instead). This would be a good option for those on a wheat-free diet."

A cook, Wellington, New Zealand

YIELD: MAKES 4 SERVINGS

3 medium onions, chopped (about 2½ cups)

½ cup vegetable oil

1 large russet (baking) potato, peeled and diced (¼ inch)

3 garlic cloves, minced

1 fresh jalapeño chile, seeded and minced fine (wear rubber gloves)

¼ cup all-purpose flour

3 cups low-sodium chicken broth

2 cups heavy cream

3 plum tomatoes, seeded and cut into ¼-inch dice (about 1 cup)

2 cups fresh or frozen corn kernels

1 cup shredded Monterey Jack cheese (about 4 ounces)

1 tablespoon chopped fresh flat-leaf parsley

½ canned chipotle chile in adobo sauce, finely minced (about 1 teaspoon)

1½ whole boneless smoked chicken breasts (about 1 pound), skin and fat removed and meat cut into ½-inch dice

pork roast *with winter fruits and port sauce*

Inside this beautiful pork roast is a sweet and savory fruit surprise: apricots, prunes, and apples. A coat of bacon keeps the meat moist as it cooks. Stuff and wrap the pork a day ahead to let the flavors marinate. The port sauce not only provides a lovely glaze for the meat but is also a great topper for side dishes like mashed potatoes and green beans.

MAKE STUFFING

1. Simmer the apricots, prunes, and wine in a small heavy saucepan, covered, 5 minutes. Remove from the heat and let stand 10 minutes.

2. Cook the onion and shallot in the butter in a 12-inch heavy skillet over medium heat, stirring occasionally, until softened, 4 to 5 minutes. Add the apple and salt and pepper and cook, stirring occasionally, until apple is just tender, about 5 minutes. Stir in the apricot mixture and cool.

STUFF AND ROAST PORK

1. Preheat the oven to 500°F, with the rack in the middle.

2. Make a pocket in the center of the roast by cutting a horizontal 1½-inch-wide slit into one end with a long thin knife and repeating from the opposite end so a pocket runs all the way through. Make a vertical cut through the center (forming a cross) to widen the pocket. Push about 1 cup stuffing into the pocket using a long-handled wooden spoon (you may need to stuff from both sides if roast is long). Reserve the remaining stuffing for the sauce.

3. Season the roast with salt and pepper and put in a large flameproof roasting pan. Wrap with the bacon between rib bones, tucking the ends under the roast. Roast the pork 20 minutes, then reduce the oven to 325°F and roast until an instant-read thermometer inserted 2 inches into the center (do not touch bone or stuffing) registers 155°F, 1¼ to 1½ hours total.

4. Transfer the roast to a cutting board and let stand, loosely covered with foil, 15 to 20 minutes. (Temperature

recipe continues

YIELD: MAKES 8 SERVINGS

FOR STUFFING

¼ pound California dried apricots, cut into ½-inch pieces
¼ pound pitted prunes, cut into ½-inch pieces
⅔ cup ruby port wine
1 medium onion, finely chopped
1 small shallot, finely chopped
6 tablespoons unsalted butter
1 tart apple such as Granny Smith, peeled and cut into ½-inch pieces
½ teaspoon salt
½ teaspoon pepper

FOR ROAST AND SAUCE

1 (6-pound) bone-in pork loin roast (about 10 ribs), frenched, at room temperature 1 hour
1½ teaspoons salt
½ teaspoon pepper
9 or 10 bacon slices
½ cup ruby port wine
1 small shallot, finely chopped
1½ cups water
2 teaspoons arrowroot

"I used a ribless roast, so the cook time was very fast. I also used cranberries because I did not have apricots on hand. Even with the substitution, this recipe is delicious!"

Marybee88, Chicago, Illinois

of the meat will rise to about 160°F; meat will be slightly pink.)

MAKE SAUCE

1. Skim the fat from the pan drippings and reserve 1½ tablespoons fat. Straddle the pan across 2 burners and add port to drippings, then deglaze by boiling over high heat, stirring and scraping up browned bits, 1 minute. Strain the pan juices through a fine-mesh sieve into a bowl, discarding the solids.

2. Cook the shallot in the reserved fat in a heavy medium saucepan over medium heat, stirring occasionally, until softened, about 3 minutes. Stir in the pan juices, 1¼ cups water, and any reserved fruit stuffing and bring to a simmer. Whisk together the arrowroot and remaining ¼ cup water until smooth, then whisk into the sauce along with any juices from the cutting board. Simmer the sauce, whisking occasionally, until slightly thickened, about 5 minutes. Season with salt and pepper.

3. Carve the roast into chops by cutting between ribs, then serve with the sauce.

red wine–braised duck legs

These slow-cooked duck legs take several hours to braise, but the hardest thing about this recipe is waiting for the tender meat to finish cooking. Make this inexpensive yet elegant dish for a dinner party and watch as guests break into a smile after the first bite. Dried fruits and a hearty dry red give the sauce its rich appeal. Serve with buttered noodles, mashed potatoes, or fluffy quinoa.

1. Preheat the oven to 350°F. and season the duck legs with salt and pepper.

2. In a heavy pot just large enough to hold legs in one layer, cook the legs over moderately high heat 10 to 15 minutes, or until the skin is crisp and mahogany colored, removing fat from the pot as it is rendered with a metal bulb baster (or very carefully tilting the pot and spooning off). Turn the legs over and cook until browned all over, about 2 minutes, transferring to a plate.

3. Pour off the fat and deglaze with the wine, scraping up browned bits. Boil the wine until reduced to a syrup and add the garlic, thyme, and ½ cup dried fruit. Return the duck legs and add the broth. Bring the mixture to a simmer and braise, uncovered, in the oven 2 hours, or until legs are very tender. Transfer the legs to a platter and keep warm.

4. Pour the braising mixture into a 1-quart measuring cup and let stand until the fat rises to the top. Skim off the fat and pour the liquid through a sieve into a saucepan, pressing hard on the solids. Boil until reduced by about one-third and slightly thickened, then add the remaining ½ cup dried fruit. Simmer the sauce until the fruit is softened, about 5 minutes, and season with salt and pepper.

5. Serve duck legs with sauce and noodles or roasted and mashed potatoes.

YIELD: MAKES 6 SERVINGS

6 large whole duck legs (about 4½ pounds total), trimmed of excess fat
½ cup dry red wine
2 heads garlic, cloves separated and peeled
8 sprigs fresh thyme
1 cup mixed dried fruit, such as sour cherries, chopped apricots, chopped pitted prunes, and raisins
5 cups low-sodium chicken broth
Accompaniment: buttered noodles or roasted and mashed potatoes

"I made this recipe using chicken legs and thighs, which are such a bargain. A great recipe for a low-cost meat!"
A cook, Gatlinburg, Tennessee

moroccan slow-cooked lamb

Get a taste of North Africa with this lamb slow-cooked with stewed apricots, tomatoes, cinnamon, ginger, and lemon. To complete the Moroccan theme, serve the winter stew atop couscous. Alternatively, pair it with crusty bread for a heartier meal. Just be sure to save some leftovers, as the meat will be even tastier the following day.

YIELD: MAKES 6 SERVINGS

1 tablespoon ground cumin
2 teaspoons ground coriander
1½ teaspoons salt
1 teaspoon fennel seeds
½ teaspoon cayenne
½ teaspoon ground black pepper
2½ pounds trimmed boned lamb
    shoulder, cut into 1½- to 2-inch pieces
4 tablespoons olive oil
1 large onion, finely chopped
1 tablespoon tomato paste
2 cups low-sodium chicken broth
1 (15½-ounce) can garbanzo beans
    (chickpeas), drained
1 cup dried apricots (about 5 ounces)
2 large plum tomatoes, chopped
2 cinnamon sticks
1 tablespoon minced peeled fresh ginger
2 teaspoons (packed) grated lemon peel
2 tablespoons chopped fresh cilantro

do ahead:

The **STEW** can be prepared 1 day ahead through step 2. Cool slightly. Refrigerate uncovered until cold, then cover and keep chilled. Rewarm over medium-low heat, stirring occasionally.

1. Mix the cumin, coriander, salt, fennel seeds, cayenne, and pepper in a large bowl. Add the lamb and toss to coat. Heat 2 tablespoons oil in a heavy large skillet over medium-high heat. Working in batches, add the lamb to the skillet and cook until browned on all sides, turning occasionally and adding 2 more tablespoons oil to skillet between batches, about 8 minutes per batch. Transfer the lamb to another large bowl after each batch.

2. Add the onion and tomato paste to the drippings in the skillet. Reduce the heat to medium; sauté until onion is soft, about 5 minutes. Add the broth, beans, apricots, tomatoes, cinnamon sticks, ginger, and lemon peel and bring to boil, scraping up browned bits. Return the lamb to the skillet and bring to a boil. Reduce the heat to low, cover, and simmer until the lamb is just tender, about 1 hour. Uncover and simmer until the sauce thickens enough to coat a spoon, about 20 minutes. Season with salt and pepper.

3. Transfer the lamb and sauce to a bowl. Sprinkle with cilantro and serve.

"I have often made this with ground lamb—lamb stew meat is very hard for me to find. I made it with ground chicken for our 'no red meat' daughter, and it was wonderful."

Fancycooks, Bayside, Wisconsin

rosemary lamb chops
with swiss chard and balsamic syrup

Rosemary and garlic are often used to season lamb, but rarely are they part of such a complex taste arrangement as this recipe produces. The powerful duo is sprinkled on lamb chops that are quickly broiled. Garlic also flavors a hearty side of sautéed chard, while additional rosemary is simmered in balsamic vinegar, creating a beautiful, aromatic syrup to drizzle over the chops and greens. With only 35 minutes of prep time, this recipe is perfect any night of the week.

MAKE SYRUP

Simmer the syrup ingredients in a 1½-quart nonreactive saucepan over moderate heat until just syrupy and reduced to about ¼ cup, about 8 minutes. Pour through a sieve into a small bowl, discarding rosemary and peppercorns.

MAKE CHARD

1. Cut the stems and center ribs from the chard, discarding any tough portions, then cut the stems and ribs crosswise into ¼-inch-thick slices. Stack the chard leaves and roll into cylinders; cut the cylinders crosswise to make 1-inch-wide strips.

2. Cook the onion and garlic in oil in a 12-inch nonstick skillet over moderate heat, stirring occasionally, until the onion begins to soften, about 4 minutes. Add the chard stems and ribs, the salt, and pepper and cook, stirring occasionally, until stems are just tender, about 6 minutes. Stir in the chard leaves and water and cook, stirring occasionally, until tender, about 8 minutes.

MAKE CHOPS

Preheat the broiler. Sprinkle the chops with the garlic, salt, rosemary, and pepper, then broil on a lightly oiled broiler pan, 4 to 5 inches from heat, turning over once, until medium-rare, 6 to 7 minutes total. Serve the chops and chard drizzled with the balsamic syrup.

YIELD: MAKES 4 SERVINGS

FOR BALSAMIC SYRUP
¾ cup balsamic vinegar
¼ teaspoon minced fresh rosemary
⅛ teaspoon black peppercorns

FOR CHARD
1 bunch Swiss chard (1 pound)
¼ cup chopped red onion
1 teaspoon finely chopped garlic
1 tablespoon olive oil
½ teaspoon salt
¼ teaspoon black pepper
1 tablespoon water

FOR LAMB CHOPS
8 rib lamb chops (1¼ pounds total), trimmed of all fat
1 teaspoon finely chopped garlic
½ teaspoon salt
½ teaspoon finely chopped fresh rosemary leaves
¼ teaspoon black pepper

"The balsamic reduction was wonderful, and I now make it with many other meats (duck, steak)."
A cook, France

beef short ribs tagine
with honey-glazed butternut squash

This thick Moroccan stew gets its name from the conical earthenware pot traditionally used by North African cooks and known for producing moist, tender meats and vegetables. Here you can accomplish the same effect by slow-roasting beef short ribs in a pot at 325°F. The best part is that the short ribs can be prepped up to two days ahead of time.

YIELD: MAKES 8 SERVINGS

5 tablespoons olive oil
1 pound onions, chopped
16 (3- to 4-inch) pieces meaty beef short ribs, any tough membranes trimmed
3 tablespoons all-purpose flour
4 cups low-sodium chicken broth
1½ cups dry red wine
1 cup prune juice
1 tablespoon tomato paste
½ teaspoon ground cumin
½ teaspoon ground allspice
½ teaspoon ground ginger
½ teaspoon ground cinnamon
2 ounces pitted dates, diced
2 ounces dried pears, diced
1 tablespoon honey
Honey-Glazed Butternut Squash (recipe follows)
Fresh parsley, for garnish

do ahead:

The **SHORT RIBS** can be made 2 days ahead. Refrigerate until cold; then cover and keep chilled.

"Ran out of allspice, so I used garam masala instead. Added red pepper flakes and about 1 tablespoon chipotle with the honey for some kick."

A cook, Boston, Massachusetts

1. Preheat the oven to 325°F. Heat 3 tablespoons oil in a heavy large Dutch oven or flameproof casserole over medium-high heat. Add the onions and sauté until browned, about 20 minutes. Using a slotted spoon, transfer the onions to a large bowl. Season the short ribs with salt and pepper. Add 1 tablespoon oil to the pot and add half the short ribs. Brown on all sides, about 10 minutes, then transfer ribs to the bowl with the onions. Add the remaining 1 tablespoon oil to the pot, then the remaining ribs and brown on all sides, about 10 minutes. Transfer to same bowl.

2. Whisk the flour into the drippings in the pot. Whisk in 2 cups broth, and bring to a boil, scraping up browned bits. Mix in the remaining 2 cups broth, the wine, prune juice, tomato paste, and spices. Return the ribs to the pot, arranging close together on their sides in a single layer if possible. Add the dates and pears; add the onions and any juices. Bring the liquid to a boil. Cover the pot and place in oven. Bake until the ribs are tender, about 1 hour 45 minutes.

3. Using tongs, transfer the ribs to a large bowl. Strain the cooking liquid into a medium bowl, pressing on the contents of the strainer. Freeze the liquid until the fat rises to the top, about 30 minutes. Spoon off the fat and return liquid to the pot. Add the honey and boil until the sauce is thick enough to coat a spoon and is reduced to 3 cups, about 12 minutes. Season with salt and pepper. Return the ribs to the pot, spooning the sauce over to coat.

4. Rewarm the ribs over medium-low heat, stirring occasionally. Mound the ribs on a platter. Top with the squash; garnish with parsley.

honey-glazed butternut squash

Heat the oil in a heavy large nonstick skillet over medium heat. Add the squash, cover, and cook until just tender and beginning to color, stirring occasionally, about 12 minutes. Add the honey and toss until squash is glazed. Season with salt and pepper.

YIELD: MAKES 8 SERVINGS

¼ cup olive oil
2 medium butternut squash, peeled and
    cut into ¾-inch cubes (about 6 cups)
¼ cup honey

filet mignon *with gorgonzola sauce*

Filet mignon gets a Southwestern twist from Cucina Rustica restaurant in Sedona, Arizona, with smoky chipotle chiles amping up the creamy Gorgonzola and shiitake mushroom sauce. Any leftover steak and sauce makes a delicious sandwich on crusty bread with peppery arugula.

YIELD: MAKES 8 SERVINGS

 3 tablespoons olive oil
½ pound fresh shiitake mushrooms, stemmed and sliced
3 garlic cloves, minced
1½ cups heavy whipping cream
1 cup crumbled Gorgonzola cheese (about 4 ounces)
2 teaspoons minced canned chipotle chiles (from canned chipotles in adobo)
8 (6-ounce) filet mignon steaks

do ahead:

The **SAUCE** can be made 2 hours ahead. Let stand at room temperature.

1. Heat 2 tablespoons olive oil in a heavy large skillet over medium heat. Add the shiitake mushrooms and sauté until soft, about 4 minutes. Add the garlic and stir 1 minute. Add the cream and bring to a boil. Reduce the heat to medium and simmer the sauce until thickened, about 4 minutes. Stir in the cheese and chipotles. Season the sauce to taste with salt and pepper.

2. Sprinkle the steaks with salt and freshly ground black pepper. Heat the remaining 1 tablespoon olive oil in another heavy large skillet. Cook the steaks in the skillet until browned on both sides and cooked to desired doneness, about 5 minutes per side for medium-rare.

3. Rewarm the sauce. Transfer a steak to each of 8 plates. Pour the sauce over the steaks and serve.

"I love the creamy Gorgonzola sauce, and I used the leftover sauce to toss with some penne pasta. I use different mushrooms, depending on what I have. Portobellos always work great."
Jessicafolliett, Fort Lauderdale, Florida

beef brisket *with merlot and prunes*

Need a festive centerpiece for a holiday dinner? Choose this recipe, which calls for a tender cut of inexpensive meat. Although the instructions seem complex, preparation time and effort can be considerably reduced with some advance planning so that the day of serving, all you need to do is reheat.

YIELD: MAKES 8 SERVINGS

1 (4- to 4½-pound) flat-cut (also called first-cut) beef brisket, trimmed of most fat
2 tablespoons olive oil
1 (14½-ounce) can diced tomatoes in juice, preferably fire-roasted
1 cup merlot or other dry red wine
2 pounds onions, sliced
4 medium carrots, peeled and thinly sliced
16 garlic cloves, peeled
1½ cups pitted large prunes (about 8 ounces)
1 tablespoon finely chopped fresh thyme
½ cup plus 1 tablespoon prune juice
3 tablespoons plus 1 teaspoon balsamic vinegar
2 tablespoons chopped fresh flat-leaf parsley

1. Position a rack in the bottom third of the oven and preheat the oven to 325°F. Pat the brisket dry; sprinkle all over with salt and pepper. Heat the oil in a heavy extra-large skillet over high heat. Add the brisket and cook until deep brown, about 7 minutes per side.

2. Transfer the brisket, fat side up, to a large flameproof roasting pan. Add the tomatoes with their juice and the wine to the skillet. Remove from heat, scrape up any browned bits from the skillet, and pour mixture over the brisket. Distribute the onions, carrots, and garlic around the brisket. Add the prunes and thyme; drizzle with ½ cup prune juice and 3 tablespoons vinegar. Sprinkle lightly with salt and pepper. Place the pan over 2 burners and bring to a boil. Cover with heavy-duty foil; place in the oven.

3. Braise the brisket until tender, about 3 hours 15 minutes. Uncover and cool 1 hour at room temperature.

4. Remove the brisket from the roasting pan, scraping off juices, and let rest. Place on a work surface; cut across the grain into ¼-inch-thick slices. Spoon off the fat from the top of the pan juices. Place 1 cup vegetables (no prunes) and 1 cup braising liquid from the pan into a food processor and purée. Return purée to pan and add remaining 1 tablespoon prune juice and 1 teaspoon vinegar. Heat the sauce; season with salt and pepper.

5. Overlap the brisket slices in a 13 by 9-inch glass baking dish. Pour the sauce over the brisket, separating the slices to allow some sauce to flow between.

6. Rewarm the brisket, covered, in a 350°F oven for 30 minutes. Sprinkle the brisket with parsley; serve.

do ahead:

The **BRISKET** can be braised 2 days ahead. Cover with foil and chill. Bring just to a simmer over 2 burners before continuing.

The **BRISKET** can be made 1 day ahead (through step 5). Cover; chill.

sweet 'n' smoky meatloaf

"This recipe will prove all meatloaf doubters wrong!" says Epicurious member **Jamie Monahan**, of Martinez, California. She has perfected it over the years and it combines sweet and smoky flavors harmoniously. Serve with mashed potatoes and roasted carrots—and if you have leftovers, slice onto crusty bread for a stick-to-your-ribs sandwich.

YIELD: MAKES 6 SERVINGS

2 pounds ground beef chuck
1 cup finely grated Parmesan cheese
¾ cup plain dry bread crumbs
½ cup ketchup, plus more for serving
½ medium onion, coarsely grated using the large holes on a box grater
1 garlic clove, minced
2 large eggs, beaten
2 tablespoons light brown sugar
½ teaspoon salt
½ teaspoon freshly ground black pepper
5 to 7 thin slices bacon (optional)

Special equipment: 1 (9 by 13-inch) baking dish

cook's note:

The **COOKED MEATLOAF** can be covered and refrigerated, up to 3 days.

1. Position a rack in the middle of the oven and preheat the oven to 400°F.

2. In a large bowl, crumble the ground beef. Add the cheese, bread crumbs, ketchup, onions, garlic, eggs, brown sugar, salt, and pepper. Using your hands, gently mix to combine.

3. Transfer the meat mixture to a 9 by 13-inch baking dish and form it into a roughly 5 by 12-inch loaf. Drape the bacon slices diagonally over the top and sides of the meatloaf and bake until the bacon is browned and the meatloaf gives slightly when pressed in the center, about 45 minutes. Let the meatloaf stand about 10 minutes before slicing and serving.

When I'm mixing in all of the ingredients, I always stop and smell the meat mixture. I try to pick up the scent of every ingredient. If I don't smell something, I toss a little bit more of it in! This method may be pretty unconventional, but it has always worked for me.

—Jamie Monahan

persian rice salad

This unassuming rice salad from Mustard Seed Market & Café in Akron, Ohio, is so unusual it's likely to shift everyone's attention from the main course. Dates and cinnamon, two Middle Eastern staples, are paired with cashews, green onions, and cilantro and are punched up with freshly squeezed lemon juice. Use a cast-iron pot to get what Persian-style rice is best known for—the crispy toasted bits. Topped with a fried egg, it's a casual supper; paired with simple roasted fish, it's a proper formal meal.

1. Bring the broth to a boil in a large saucepan over medium-high heat. Mix in the rice. Return to a boil, reduce the heat to low, cover, and cook without stirring until the rice is tender, about 40 minutes. Spread out the rice in a large baking pan and cool.

2. Transfer the rice to a large bowl. Add the cashews, dates, and green onions; toss to blend.

3. Whisk the olive oil, lemon juice, cilantro, and cinnamon in a small bowl. Add to the rice and toss to coat. Season the salad to taste with salt and pepper.

YIELD: MAKES 8 TO 10 SERVINGS

2 (14-ounce) cans vegetable broth
2 cups long-grain brown rice
1½ cups roasted salted cashews, coarsely chopped
1½ cups pitted dates, sliced (about 7 ounces)
4 green onions, thinly sliced
½ cup olive oil
¼ cup fresh lemon juice
¼ cup chopped fresh cilantro
¼ teaspoon ground cinnamon

do ahead:

The **SALAD** can be made 2 hours ahead. Let stand at room temperature.

"I substituted golden raisins for dates and used chicken broth instead of veggie broth for the rice."

Dpatrice, Bay Area, California

wild rice *with pecans, raisins, and orange essence*

Bright orange, cooling mint, sweet raisins, and earthy pecans—yep, this wild rice salad by Epicurious member **Jruz** has pretty much nothing in common with the salty kitchen-sink rice salad from the school cafeteria. Try this alongside pork tenderloin or roasted poultry for a welcome change from starchy mashed potatoes.

YIELD: MAKES 4 TO 6 SERVINGS

3 cups water
½ cup long-grain wild rice
½ cup long-grain white rice
1 cup pecans, toasted and coarsely
    chopped
1 cup golden raisins
4 green onions (white and light green
    parts only), thinly sliced on a diagonal
¼ cup (loosely packed) fresh mint leaves,
    finely chopped
3 tablespoons extra-virgin olive oil
2 tablespoons balsamic vinegar
Zest and juice of 1 large orange

do ahead:

The **RICE SALAD** can be prepared ahead and refrigerated, covered, overnight. Bring to room temperature before serving.

1. In a medium pot over high heat, bring 2 cups of water to a boil. Add the wild rice, cover, and reduce the heat to low. Simmer until the rice grains are tender, about 1 hour. Drain the cooked rice and transfer to a bowl to cool.

2. Meanwhile, in a second medium pot over high heat, bring remaining 1 cup of water and the white rice to a boil. Cover, reduce the heat to low, and simmer until the rice is tender and all the water is absorbed, about 15 minutes. Remove from the heat and let the rice rest in the pot for 5 minutes. Transfer to a bowl to cool.

3. Combine the wild and white rice, then add the pecans, raisins, onions, and mint and toss to combine.

4. In a small bowl, whisk together the olive oil, vinegar, orange zest, and juice, then pour it over the rice salad and toss to coat. Cover the salad and let it sit at room temperate for 2 hours. Season with salt and pepper and serve at room temperature.

bacon smashed potatoes

Perfect with roast chicken on a casual Monday night with family, this seven-ingredient dish is great to throw together at the last minute. Steam the potatoes instead of boiling—this will keep them fluffy and light. Then, taking inspiration from German-style potato salad, smash them with a hot and smoky bacon dressing and toss with fresh dill, cider vinegar, and sugar. Planning an elegant winter spread? Serve this hearty side with pork chops.

1. Steam the potatoes in a large steamer rack set over boiling water, covered, until very tender, 20 to 25 minutes.

2. Meanwhile, cook the bacon in a 12-inch heavy skillet over medium heat until crisp. Transfer the bacon with a slotted spoon to paper towels to drain, reserving the fat in the skillet. Add 2 tablespoons vinegar, the sugar, and the salt and pepper to the hot bacon fat, scraping up the browned bits.

3. Transfer the potatoes to a large bowl, reserving ½ cup steaming water. Add the vinegar mixture to the potatoes and smash with a potato masher to desired texture, adding the reserved water if desired. Stir in the dill and bacon.

"I used small chunks of pancetta instead of bacon, and fresh thyme instead of dill."

Gmcinto, Toronto, Canada

YIELD: MAKES 8 SERVINGS

3 pounds Yukon Gold potatoes, peeled and cut into 2-inch chunks
½ pound bacon, cut into ½-inch pieces
2 to 3 tablespoons cider vinegar
1 teaspoon sugar
¾ teaspoon salt
¾ teaspoon pepper
2 tablespoons chopped fresh dill

do ahead:

The **POTATOES** can be made 3 hours ahead and kept at room temperature. Reheat, covered, in a microwave or in a 300°F oven.

wilted kale and roasted-potato winter salad

For those who've not already jumped on board, it's time to embrace kale! It stars in this hearty potato salad, versatile enough for a stand-alone meal or an accompaniment to pork tenderloin. Strip the kale quickly by turning the leaf upside down, grasping the top of the stem with one hand, and wrapping the other hand around the stem just below. Pull the leaf down with your lower hand; it will easily peel away. Then, save time by preparing the tahini dressing as the seasoned potatoes roast in the oven.

YIELD: MAKES 6 SERVINGS

2 pounds Yukon Gold potatoes, cut into
    1-inch pieces
⅓ cup olive oil
1 teaspoon salt
½ teaspoon pepper
4 garlic cloves, 3 thinly sliced and
    1 minced
⅓ cup grated Parmigiano-Reggiano
    cheese
¼ cup well-stirred tahini
2 tablespoons water
3 tablespoons fresh lemon juice
¾ pound kale, stems and center ribs
    discarded and leaves very thinly sliced
    crosswise
Lemon wedges, for serving

"I find it's easier to make the potatoes and the kale separately. I cook the potatoes ahead of time and reheat them in the oven just before serving. I wilt the kale in the microwave for about 15 or 20 seconds. Then I mix them together with the sauce."
CountryFoodie

1. Preheat the oven to 450°F, with the rack in the upper third.

2. Toss the potatoes with the oil and ½ teaspoon of the salt and the pepper in a large 4-sided sheet pan, then spread evenly. Roast, stirring once, 10 minutes. Stir in the sliced garlic and roast 10 minutes more. Sprinkle with the cheese and roast until the cheese is melted and golden in spots, about 5 minutes more.

3. Purée the tahini, water, lemon juice, minced garlic, and remaining ½ teaspoon salt in a blender until smooth, about 1 minute. (Add a bit more water if sauce is too thick.)

4. Toss the kale with the hot potatoes (to wilt the leaves) and any garlic and oil remaining in pan, then toss with tahini sauce and salt and pepper to taste.

kale and potato purée

With just three ingredients, this sophisticated take on creamed spinach is extremely easy to make. In a pinch, use an immersion blender to mix the sauce, or try ricing the potatoes to make this winter side a tad thicker.

1. Cook the kale in a pot of boiling salted water (1½ tablespoons salt for 4 quarts water), uncovered, until tender, about 7 minutes. Drain, then immediately transfer the kale to an ice bath to stop the cooking. When kale is cool, drain but do not squeeze.

2. While kale cooks, peel the potatoes and cut into ½-inch pieces. Simmer in the cream, salt, and pepper in a heavy medium saucepan, covered, stirring occasionally, until tender, 15 to 20 minutes.

3. Purée the potato mixture with the kale in 2 batches in a food processor until just smooth (use caution when blending hot liquids). Transfer to a 4- to 5-quart heavy saucepan and cook over low heat, stirring frequently, until heated through. Season with salt and pepper.

YIELD: MAKES 8 SERVINGS

2 pounds kale, stems and center ribs discarded and leaves chopped
1½ pounds large boiling potatoes
2 cups heavy cream
½ teaspoon salt
¼ teaspoon pepper

do ahead:

The **PURÉE** can be made 1 day ahead and chilled. Reheat over low heat, stirring frequently.

"I puréed the greens separately and added them to the coarsely mashed potatoes. Finally, I added some butter and cheese to add a bit more flavor. It tastes like mashed potatoes, but with the added nutrients from the greens."
Megp47, Scottsdale, Arizona

roasted sweet-potato rounds
with garlic oil and fried sage

Had your fill of sweet potatoes made even sweeter with brown sugar? These quick-baked sweet potato "chips" flip the script with garlic and melt-in-the-mouth fried sage. Serve as colorful hors d'oeuvres at a cocktail party; as a crisp side course for barbecued pork, roasted turkey, or a holiday ham or tenderloin; or as a stand-in for movie popcorn on the couch with a beer on a chilly Friday night. Not bad for a recipe that only takes 25 minutes and four ingredients.

YIELD: MAKES 8 SERVINGS

FOR SWEET POTATOES
3 large garlic cloves
¼ cup olive oil
¾ teaspoon salt
2½ pounds sweet potatoes, peeled and
    sliced into ½-inch-thick rounds

FOR FRIED SAGE
⅓ cup olive oil
24 fresh sage leaves

do ahead:

The **SWEET POTATOES** can be cut and tossed with garlic oil 4 hours ahead and chilled in a sealable bag. Sage leaves can be fried 4 hours ahead and kept at room temperature.

ROAST SWEET POTATOES

1. Preheat the oven to 450°F, with the rack in the upper third.

2. Purée the garlic with the oil and salt in a blender until smooth. Toss the sweet potatoes with the garlic oil in a large bowl, then spread in a single layer in a 15 by 10-inch shallow baking pan. Bake until golden in patches and cooked through, 20 to 30 minutes.

FRY SAGE LEAVES AND SERVE

1. Heat the oil in a small heavy skillet over medium-high heat until it shimmers, then fry the sage leaves in 2 batches, stirring, until crisp, 30 seconds to 1 minute per batch. Transfer with a slotted spoon to paper towels to drain.

2. Serve the sweet potatoes with sage leaves scattered on top.

"I couldn't find sage leaves anywhere, so I just chopped up a combination of fresh basil, parsley, dill, and cilantro that I had at home and sprinkled over just before serving. It was so lovely. I can say that of all the herbs, the parsley complemented the best."

Kathrynlynn, USA

sweet potato soufflé

Here's a sweet Southern dish from the heart of Texas; the recipe originated from the Dallas-based mother of a friend of Epicurious member **Tina Jones.** The spuds are baked with a blend of milk, vanilla, sugar, and butter, and topped with a crunchy walnut topping. This goes with almost any roasted meat.

1. Position a rack in the middle of the oven and preheat the oven to 375°F. Arrange the sweet potatoes on a baking sheet and bake until very tender, 60 to 90 minutes, depending on the thickness of the potato.

2. Once the potatoes are cool enough to handle, scoop out the flesh and transfer to the bowl of a stand mixer fitted with a paddle attachment. Beat the potatoes until smooth, about 1 minute. Add the milk, eggs, half the melted butter, the vanilla, sugar, and salt and stir to combine; the mixture will be somewhat thin. Transfer to a 2-quart baking dish and set aside.

3. In a small bowl, stir together the walnuts, flour, and brown sugar, then drizzle with the remaining melted butter and stir to combine. Sprinkle the mixture evenly over the sweet potato mash. Bake until the topping is golden brown and the sweet potato mixture is slightly puffed, about 30 minutes. Serve immediately.

YIELD: MAKES 6 TO 8 SERVINGS

3½ pounds sweet potatoes (about 5 medium)
½ cup whole milk
2 large eggs
11 tablespoons unsalted butter, melted
1 tablespoon pure vanilla extract
¾ cup sugar
1 teaspoon kosher salt
1 cup chopped walnuts
⅓ cup all-purpose flour
¾ cup (packed) light brown sugar

roasted acorn squash *with chile vinaigrette*

The chile vinaigrette here will perk up an otherwise ho-hum dish with some heat and tang. For a tasty variation, use sweet potatoes instead of acorn squash.

1. Put the oven racks in the upper and lower thirds of the oven and preheat the oven to 450°F.

2. Halve the squash lengthwise, then cut off and discard the stem ends. Scoop out the seeds and cut the squash lengthwise into ¾-inch-wide wedges. Toss with the pepper, ¾ teaspoon salt, and 2 tablespoons oil in a bowl. Arrange cut side down in 2 large shallow baking pans.

3. Roast the squash, switching position of pans halfway through roasting, until tender and undersides of wedges are golden brown, 25 to 35 minutes.

4. While squash roasts, mince the garlic and mash to a paste with the remaining ¼ teaspoon salt. Transfer the paste to a small bowl and whisk in the lime juice, chile to taste, cilantro, and remaining ¼ cup oil until combined.

5. Transfer the squash, browned sides up, to a platter and drizzle with vinaigrette.

YIELD: MAKES 4 SERVINGS

2 (1½-pound) acorn squash
½ teaspoon black pepper
1 teaspoon salt
6 tablespoons olive oil
1 garlic clove
1½ tablespoons fresh lime juice, or to taste
1 to 2 teaspoons finely chopped fresh hot red chile, including seeds
2 tablespoons chopped fresh cilantro

"I added the squash seeds to the roasting pan after tossing them in the leftover oil. It added a great crunch to the dish."
JKealey, Ottawa, Canada

stir-fried chinese broccoli

Thai cuisine is known for its flavor combinations of sweet, salty, sour, bitter, and hot, and this dish encapsulates them all. Find Thai yellow bean sauce (or paste) at your local Asian market, or substitute miso paste or black bean sauce. If Chinese broccoli isn't available, use broccoli rabe or broccolini. A heavy sauté pan or cast-iron skillet can replace a wok.

YIELD: MAKES 8 SERVINGS

3 tablespoons vegetable oil
4 garlic cloves, smashed
2 pounds Chinese broccoli (sometimes known as Chinese kale), ends of stems trimmed and broccoli cut into 1-inch pieces
½ cup Thai Chicken Stock (recipe follows) or canned chicken broth
2 tablespoons Thai yellow bean sauce
2 tablespoons oyster sauce
2 teaspoons sugar

Special equipment: Wok (optional)

Heat the oil in a wok over high heat until hot but not smoking, then stir-fry the garlic until pale golden, 10 to 15 seconds. Add the broccoli and stock, and stir-fry 2 minutes. Add the bean sauce, oyster sauce, and sugar, and stir-fry until broccoli is crisp-tender, 4 to 5 minutes.

"The trick is to not overcook the broccoli, so make sure everything else is finished (rice, whatever else you're making) and cook the broccoli just before serving for three to four minutes max."

Caniolhav4, Berlin, Germany

thai chicken stock

YIELD: MAKES ABOUT 10 CUPS

6 pounds chicken wings, halved at joint
4 quarts cold water
½ cup coarsely chopped fresh cilantro stems
3 garlic cloves, smashed
3 (¼-inch-thick) fresh ginger slices, smashed
1½ teaspoons salt

do ahead:

The **STOCK** can be chilled 3 days or frozen 1 month.

1. Crack the chicken bones in several places with the back of a cleaver or a large knife on a cutting board. Bring all the ingredients to a boil in an 8-quart pot, skimming the froth as necessary, then reduce the heat and gently simmer, partially covered, 2½ hours. Remove the pot from the heat and cool stock to room temperature, about 1 hour.

2. Pour the stock through a large fine-mesh sieve lined with a triple thickness of cheesecloth into a large bowl and discard the solids. Measure the stock: if there is more than 10 cups, boil in a cleaned pot until reduced; if there is less, add water.

3. If using stock right away, skim off and discard the fat. If not, cool stock completely, uncovered, before skimming fat (it will be easier to remove when cool), then chill, covered.

gnocchi alla romana

A departure from the more common potato gnocchi, these light, pillowy rounds feature semolina and are baked instead of boiled. Parmesan cheese and a glaze of butter make them quite rich and delicious. They go well with meat or poultry but you can also top the gnocchi with your favorite tomato sauce or pesto.

1. Whisk together the milk, semolina, and salt in a 2-quart heavy saucepan and bring to a boil over moderate heat, whisking. Simmer, stirring constantly with a wooden spoon, until very stiff, 5 to 8 minutes. Remove from the heat and stir in 2 tablespoons butter and ¾ cup cheese. Beat in the egg.

2. Spread the gnocchi mixture ½ inch thick on an oiled baking sheet and chill, uncovered, until very firm, about 1 hour.

3. Preheat the oven to 425°F. Cut out rounds from the gnocchi mixture with a 2-inch round cookie cutter (push scraps into remaining mixture as you go) and arrange, slightly overlapping, in a well-buttered 13 by 9-inch baking dish. Make a small second layer in the center of the dish with any remaining rounds. Brush the gnocchi with the remaining 4 tablespoons melted butter and sprinkle with the remaining ¾ cup cheese.

4. Bake in the middle of the oven until the gnocchi are beginning to brown, 15 to 20 minutes. Let stand 5 minutes before serving.

YIELD: MAKES 6 SERVINGS

3 cups whole milk
¾ cup semolina
1 teaspoon salt
6 tablespoons unsalted butter, melted
3 ounces finely grated Parmigiano-Reggiano cheese (1½ cups, divided)
1 large egg

"Ethereal, not only for their lightness but also their marriage of butter and Parmigiano-Reggiano."
Clementine651, St. Paul, Minnesota

roasted cauliflower *with kalamata vinaigrette*

This dish calls for just five commonly used ingredients, making it a last-minute cinch. Roasting the cauliflower in either slices or mini-florets tenderizes it, and the olive vinaigrette adds tanginess to the already nutty base, pumping up the dish with the perfect sharp flavor note. Serve this alongside any cut of lamb or beef.

YIELD: MAKES 4 SERVINGS

1 (2½- to 3-pound) head cauliflower
¼ cup extra-virgin olive oil
¾ teaspoon salt
1 teaspoon pepper
1 small garlic clove
1 to 2 tablespoons fresh lemon juice
¼ cup pitted kalamata olives, finely
　　chopped

1. Preheat the oven to 450°F, with the rack in the lower third.

2. Cut the cauliflower lengthwise into ¾-inch-thick slices. Put in a large baking pan and toss with 2 tablespoons oil and ½ teaspoon each of salt and pepper. Roast, turning once or twice, until golden and just tender, about 25 minutes.

3. While cauliflower roasts, mince and mash the garlic to a paste with a pinch of salt, then whisk together with the lemon juice, remaining 2 tablespoons oil, the olives, remaining ⅛ teaspoon salt, and remaining ½ teaspoon pepper. Serve the cauliflower drizzled with kalamata vinaigrette.

roasted broccoli *with asiago*

Consider roasting broccoli over steaming it—doing so allows it to caramelize under the high heat. Add some slightly nutty and mildly tangy Asiago, and your taste buds will tell you this cruciferous vegetable deserves its place in the pantheon of vegetables. Be sure not to cut the broccoli into tiny pieces, as those will burn.

YIELD: MAKES 4 SERVINGS

1½ pounds (about 1 large bunch)
　　broccoli, stalks trimmed to 2 inches
　　below crowns
3 tablespoons olive oil
1 cup grated Asiago cheese

Preheat the oven to 450°F. Cut each crown of broccoli lengthwise into 4 spears. Place the broccoli in a large bowl; toss with the olive oil and sprinkle with salt and pepper. Transfer the broccoli to a large rimmed baking sheet. Add the grated cheese to the large bowl. Roast the broccoli until crisp-tender and the stalks begin to brown, about 25 minutes. Return the broccoli to the bowl with the cheese. Using tongs, toss to coat.

roasted brussels sprouts

New York's Momofuku Ssäm Bar is certainly worth a visit at least once, but you're sure to make these Brussels sprouts from chef David Chang at least twice—in the same week. While this signature dish is deep-fried at Ssäm Bar, the secret to Chang's home preparation is roasting the mini cabbages at 450°F, maximizing their sweet, nutty flavor and crisping their beautiful green leaves. The recipe is written for slightly charred results; if you prefer your vegetables more green than golden brown, check them after 20 minutes or so.

MAKE BRUSSELS SPROUTS

1. Preheat the oven to 450°F, with a rack in the upper third.

2. Toss the Brussels sprouts with the oil, then arrange cut side down in a 17 by 12-inch shallow baking pan. Roast, without turning, until the outer leaves are tender and very dark brown, 40 to 45 minutes. Add butter and toss to coat.

MAKE DRESSING AND PUFFED RICE

1. Stir together all dressing ingredients until sugar has dissolved.

2. Cook the cereal, oil, and seasoning in a small skillet over medium heat, shaking the skillet and stirring, until rice is coated and begins to turn golden, about 3 minutes. Transfer to a bowl and cool, stirring occasionally.

FINISH AND SERVE

Put the Brussels sprouts in a serving bowl, then toss with just enough dressing to coat. Sprinkle with the puffed rice and serve the remaining dressing on the side.

"I confess that I didn't make the dressing or the puffed rice—I just used this method to roast the Brussels sprouts. To those looking for a terrific veggie dish—roast the sprouts as directed, salt well, add pine nuts and a squeeze of lemon. Terrific."

Tew11, Sydney, Australia

YIELD: MAKES 8 SERVINGS

FOR BRUSSELS SPROUTS

2 pounds Brussels sprouts, trimmed and
   halved lengthwise
3 tablespoons canola oil
2 tablespoons unsalted butter

FOR DRESSING

¼ cup Asian fish sauce, preferably Tiparos
   brand
¼ cup water
¼ cup sugar
3 tablespoons finely chopped fresh mint
2 tablespoons finely chopped cilantro
   stems
1 garlic clove, minced
1 (1½-inch) fresh red Thai chile, thinly
   sliced crosswise, including seeds

FOR PUFFED RICE

½ cup crisp rice cereal, such as Rice
   Krispies
¼ teaspoon canola oil
¼ teaspoon shichimi togarashi (Japanese
   seven-spice blend)
Cilantro sprigs, torn mint leaves, chopped
   scallions, for garnish

brown-butter creamed winter greens

From Southern food aficionado John T. Edge, this recipe calls for bitters such as collards, mustard greens, and kale and then amps up the flavor with red pepper flakes, garlic, and crunchy bacon. Homemade béchamel sauce sends it over the top. Serve this as a savory addition to any winter feast in place of the usual creamed spinach; it's a spectacular pledge-of-undying-love-to-the-chef kind of dish.

YIELD: MAKES 6 SERVINGS

¾ stick (6 tablespoons) unsalted butter
2 tablespoons all-purpose flour
2 cups whole milk
2 tablespoons minced shallot
1 Turkish or ½ California bay leaf
6 black peppercorns
3½ pounds mixed winter greens, such as
    collards, mustard greens, and kale
6 ounces slab bacon, rind discarded,
    bacon cut into ¼-inch-thick slices, then
    cut crosswise into ¼-inch sticks
1 cup finely chopped onion
½ cup heavy cream
2 garlic cloves, minced
1 teaspoon dried red pepper flakes
¾ teaspoon salt
½ teaspoon pepper
1 tablespoon cider vinegar, or to taste

do ahead:

The **BÉCHAMEL SAUCE** can be made 1 day ahead and chilled, its surface covered with parchment; stir before using. The greens can be chopped 1 day ahead and chilled in a large sealed bag.

1. Melt 2 tablespoons butter in a heavy medium saucepan over medium heat, then add the flour and cook, stirring, 1 minute.

2. Add the milk in a stream, whisking, then add the shallot, bay leaf, and peppercorns. Bring to a boil, whisking, then simmer, whisking occasionally, 5 minutes. Strain the béchamel sauce through a fine-mesh sieve into a bowl, discarding solids, and cover the surface with parchment.

3. Discard the stems and center ribs from the greens, then coarsely chop the leaves.

4. Cook the bacon in a wide 8-quart heavy pot over medium heat, stirring occasionally, until golden brown but not crisp, about 8 minutes. Transfer to paper towels to drain, then pour off the fat from the pot and wipe clean.

5. Heat the remaining 4 tablespoons butter in the pot over medium-low heat until browned and fragrant, about 2 minutes, then cook the onion, stirring, until softened, about 3 minutes.

6. Increase the heat to medium-high, then stir in the greens, 1 handful at a time, letting each handful wilt before adding the next. Add the béchamel, cream, garlic, red pepper flakes, salt, and pepper and boil, uncovered, stirring, until the sauce coats the greens and the greens are tender, about 10 minutes.

7. Stir in the bacon, vinegar, and salt and pepper to taste.

sesame noodles

A modern version of a Cantonese classic, this noodle dish got a reworking in Epicurious member **Roni Jordan**'s Massachusetts kitchen and has been a family staple for more than twenty-five years. These sesame- and soy-sauced noodles will easily become a favorite whether you enjoy them warm, at room temperature, or straight out of the fridge three days later. Toss in your favorite veggies for a multifaceted vegetarian meal or serve it alongside grilled chicken or flank steak.

In a large bowl, whisk together the soy sauce, sesame oil, peanut oil, honey, chili garlic sauce, sesame seeds, onions, garlic, and ginger along with any garnishes you may want to use. Add the noodles and toss to coat evenly.

We were fortunate to have a large Asian population in Boston and a huge Asian market. I enjoy lo mein, and when I first saw refrigerated packages of thin Chinese egg noodles at the market, I was inspired to develop my own take on this dish.

—Roni Jordan

YIELD: MAKES 4 SERVINGS

¼ cup light soy sauce
¼ cup Asian sesame oil
1 tablespoon peanut or vegetable oil
1 tablespoon honey
½ tablespoon chili garlic sauce
¼ cup white sesame seeds, lightly toasted, or black sesame seeds, untoasted
⅓ cup green onions (white and light green parts only), thinly sliced on a diagonal
1 garlic clove, minced
1 (1-inch) piece fresh ginger, peeled and minced
Optional extras: thinly sliced mushrooms such as black, shiitake, or cremini; blanched and slivered pea pods; thinly sliced red bell peppers; julienned carrots
1 pound fresh Chinese egg noodles, cooked and drained

do ahead:

The **NOODLES** may be prepared ahead and refrigerated, covered, up to 24 hours. Toss well before serving.

sage and honey skillet cornbread

Down-home cornbread gets a beautiful, fragrant makeover with the addition of warming honey and flowery sage. But don't worry, it's still the same cornbread from the block. The ingredient list is short, the prep is straightforward, and the whole dish takes so little time to prepare that you could bake it while your roasted turkey rests or chili simmers.

YIELD: MAKES 10 TO 12 SERVINGS

1 cup cornmeal, preferably whole-grain, medium grind
1 cup unbleached all-purpose flour
1 tablespoon baking powder
1 teaspoon salt
2 teaspoons chopped fresh sage, plus 12 whole fresh sage leaves
1 cup whole milk
½ cup honey
1 large egg
½ cup (1 stick) unsalted butter

"I recommend a fine-grind cornmeal. Very moist, and the whole sage leaves on top made this a very festive-looking dish."
Lovelyreeda, Saint Paul, Minnesota

1. Preheat the oven to 400°F. Heat a heavy 10-inch ovenproof skillet (preferably cast-iron) in the oven for 10 minutes.

2. Whisk the cornmeal, flour, baking powder, salt, and 2 teaspoons chopped sage in a large bowl to blend. Whisk the milk, honey, and egg in a medium bowl to blend.

3. With a pot holder, remove the skillet from the oven and add the butter. Swirl until the butter is melted, then pour all except 2 tablespoons butter into the egg mixture. Add the whole sage leaves to the butter in the skillet; toss to coat. Arrange the leaves over the bottom of the skillet, spacing apart.

4. Add the egg mixture to the cornmeal mixture; stir until just combined (do not overmix; batter will be wet and runny). Pour the batter over the sage leaves in the skillet.

5. Bake until browned around edges and a tester inserted into center comes out clean, about 22 minutes. Cool in the skillet 10 minutes, then invert onto a platter. If necessary, reposition the sage leaves atop the cornbread.

thyme focaccia and parmesan focaccia

This double-batch recipe for focaccia gives you the flexibility to make two different breads at once. Feel free to mix things up with other cheeses and your favorite herb and spice combinations. We love this bread as the base for sandwiches, served alongside soup or salad, or when it starts to go stale, toasted and turned into fabulous, flavor-packed croutons.

YIELD: MAKES 2 FOCACCIA

2 (¼-ounce) packages active dry yeast (5 teaspoons)
1 teaspoon sugar
2 cups warm water (105°–115°F)
1 tablespoon table salt
About 5½ cups all-purpose flour
⅓ cup olive oil
2 teaspoons minced fresh thyme leaves
2 tablespoons cornmeal
½ cup coarsely grated Parmesan cheese
Coarse salt, for sprinkling
Freshly ground black pepper, for sprinkling

"I made a half-recipe, preparing the Parmesan focaccia only. The great thing about this recipe is how quickly you can produce a really nice pan of focaccia. Very tender. I only sprinkled with pepper (no salt); the Parmesan is plenty salty."

A cook, Santa Fe, New Mexico

1. In a standing electric mixer fitted with the paddle attachment, beat together the yeast, sugar, and water and let stand 5 minutes, or until foamy. In a bowl, stir together the table salt and 5 cups flour. Stir the oil into the yeast mixture. With the motor on low speed, gradually add the flour mixture to the yeast mixture. With a dough hook, knead the dough 2 minutes, or until soft and slightly sticky.

2. Transfer the dough to a floured surface and knead in enough remaining flour to form a soft but not sticky dough. Form the dough into a ball and put in an oiled large bowl, turning to coat. Cover the bowl with a kitchen towel and let the dough rise in a warm place until doubled in bulk, about 45 minutes.

3. Transfer the dough to a lightly floured surface and divide in half. Knead the thyme into one half for 1 minute and knead the plain half for 1 minute. Form each half into an oval and invert bowls over them. Let dough rest 5 minutes for easier rolling.

4. Preheat oven to 450°F. Oil 2 (13 by 9-inch) baking pans and sprinkle each with 1 tablespoon cornmeal. On lightly floured surface with a floured rolling pin, roll out the dough halves into 13 by 9-inch rectangles and fit into the pans. Cover each pan with a kitchen towel and let the dough rise in a warm place until doubled in bulk, about 20 minutes.

5. Sprinkle the plain dough with Parmesan and sprinkle both doughs with coarse salt and pepper. With lightly oiled fingertips, make indentations about ½ inch deep and 1 inch apart all over the dough rectangles. Bake in the middle of the oven for 12 minutes, or until golden. Remove the focaccia from the pans and cool on racks.

grilled cheese *with onion jam, taleggio, and escarole*

Skip the side salad and serve these greens with a hot cup of tomato soup for an easy, comforting winter dinner. If meat is a must, add some fried bacon or prosciutto for a heartier bite.

1. Brush one side of the bread slices with oil and arrange, oiled side down, on a work surface. Spread jam on 2 slices of bread and divide the cheese between the remaining 2 slices. Mound the escarole on top of the cheese and season with salt and pepper, then assemble the sandwiches.

2. Heat a dry 12-inch heavy skillet (not nonstick) over medium-low heat until hot. Cook the sandwiches, turning once and pressing with a spatula to compact, until the bread is golden brown and the cheese is melted, 6 to 8 minutes total.

YIELD: MAKES 2 SANDWICHES

4 (½-inch-thick) center slices sourdough bread (from a 9- or 10-inch round)
4 teaspoons extra-virgin olive oil
1½ tablespoons onion or fig jam
12 to 14 ounces chilled Taleggio or Italian fontina, sliced
4 ounces escarole, center ribs discarded and leaves cut crosswise into 1-inch pieces (about 2 cups)

ultimate grilled cheese sandwiches

The Italian influences of Asiago, prosciutto, and basil dress up this childhood favorite. Take it further by adding thinly sliced red onion or avocado. If you want to omit the prosciutto, add a little salt to the sandwich to really bring out the flavors of the other ingredients.

1. Preheat the oven to 400°F. Lightly butter one side of each bread slice. Place 2 bread slices, buttered side down, on a work surface. Top each with 2 prosciutto slices, then 4 basil leaves, then 4 cheese slices. Sprinkle with salt and red pepper flakes. Top with the remaining 2 bread slices, buttered side up.

2. Heat the olive oil in a heavy large ovenproof skillet over medium-high heat. Add the sandwiches to the skillet and cook until golden on bottom, about 4 minutes. Turn the sandwiches over; transfer the skillet to the oven, and bake until golden and cheese melts, about 5 minutes.

3. Remove the skillet from the oven. Carefully lift off the top bread slices from the sandwiches and insert 3 tomato slices into each, then cover with bread tops and serve.

YIELD: MAKES 2 SANDWICHES

Butter
4 slices country white sourdough bread, cut on deep diagonal into ⅓-inch-thick slices (each about 7 by 3½ inches)
4 thin slices prosciutto
8 large fresh basil leaves
8 (¼-inch-thick) slices Asiago cheese or drained fresh mozzarella cheese
¼ teaspoon dried red pepper flakes
2 tablespoons olive oil
6 (⅓-inch-thick) slices heirloom tomato (about 1 large)

"I put my tomatoes on the sandwiches a few minutes before the end of their time on the press so they were warm and gooey with the cheese!"

Cmtc517, Chicago, Illinois

Ultimate Grilled Cheese Sandwiches (page 371)

Grilled Cheese with
Onion Jam, Taleggio, and
Escarole (page 371)

miniature gougères

Traditional *pâte à choux*—cream-puff pastry—gives these addictive cheese puffs their light and airy consistency. The recipe calls for Gruyère and crushed dill seeds, but experiment with different cheeses and seasonings to create your own signature appetizer. The gougères can be made ahead and frozen for up to a week. Simply reheat and serve warm, paired with a flute—or two—of Champagne.

YIELD: MAKES ABOUT 40 GOUGÈRES

1 cup water
½ cup (1 stick) unsalted butter, cut into
    small pieces
½ teaspoon salt
1 cup all-purpose flour
4 to 5 large eggs
1 tablespoon dill seeds
1½ cups coarsely grated Gruyère cheese

do ahead:

The **GOUGÈRES** keep, chilled in sealable plastic bags, 2 days, or frozen 1 week. Reheat gougères, uncovered, in a preheated 350°F oven 10 minutes if chilled or 15 minutes if unthawed frozen.

"Don't waste your time spooning these out—use a pastry bag. It is faster and makes a better presentation."
A cook, Ennui, Maryland

1. In a heavy saucepan bring the water to a boil with the butter and salt over high heat and reduce the heat to moderate. Add the flour all at once and beat with a wooden spoon until mixture pulls away from the side of the pan.

2. Transfer the mixture to a bowl, and with an electric mixer on high speed, beat in 4 eggs, 1 at a time, beating well after each addition. The batter should be stiff enough to just hold soft peaks and fall softly from a spoon. If the batter is too stiff, in a small bowl beat the remaining egg lightly and add to the batter, a little at a time, beating on high speed, until batter is desired consistency.

3. Preheat the oven to 375°F with the racks in the upper and lower thirds. Lightly grease 2 baking sheets or line with parchment.

4. In a small heavy skillet, dry-roast the seeds over moderate heat, shaking the skillet, until fragrant and slightly darker, being careful not to burn them, 3 or 4 minutes. Transfer the seeds to a small bowl and cool. With a mortar and pestle or in an electric coffee/spice grinder, grind seeds coarse.

5. Stir the cheese and 1 teaspoon ground seeds into the batter and arrange level tablespoons about 1 inch apart on the baking sheets. Sprinkle the tops with the remaining ground seeds and bake, switching positions of sheets halfway through baking, 30 minutes, or until puffed, golden, and crisp. Serve gougères warm.

chocolate and peppermint candy ice cream sandwiches

These super-simple, kid-pleasing treats are delicious any time of year, but make for an especially festive dessert at a winter wonderland–themed get-together. Best of all, the recipe calls for just four ingredients: vanilla ice cream, peppermint extract, peppermint hard candies, and chocolate wafers. Try strawberry, mint, or chocolate chip ice cream for a sweet twist.

1. Stir together the ice cream (reserve pint container), extract, and ½ cup crushed candy in a bowl until combined. Transfer the mixture to the reserved pint container and freeze until just firm enough to scoop, about 1 hour.

2. Working very quickly, scoop the ice cream onto the flat sides of 8 wafers (1 scoop per wafer), then top with the remaining 8 wafers, flat side down. Wrap each sandwich individually with plastic wrap and freeze until firm, about 1 hour.

3. Unwrap sandwiches and roll the edges in the remaining ½ cup crushed candy. Rewrap and freeze until firm, about 1 hour.

YIELD: MAKES 8 SANDWICHES

1 pint premium vanilla ice cream, softened slightly
¼ teaspoon pure peppermint extract
1 cup finely crushed peppermint hard candies (4 ounces)
16 chocolate wafers, such as Nabisco Famous

Special equipment: ¼-cup ice cream scoop

"I made a few changes to these and they were still delicious. I had some great peppermint ice cream from a local place so I used that. Also, I couldn't find the chocolate wafers the recipe called for so I used some thin sugar cookie wafers instead."

Phillihg, Cincinnati, Ohio

dried cranberry and white chocolate biscotti

This variation on the classic biscotti from home cook Andrea Daly in Plymouth, Massachusetts, which first appeared in *Bon Appétit,* integrates almond extract and dried cranberries, packing both sweet and tart flavors into each biscuit. The inclusion of fruit gives them a characteristic chewy-crisp texture. These visually appealing treats make great holiday gifts, excellent accompaniments to tea and coffee, and lovely endings for a holiday feast.

1. Preheat the oven to 350°F. Line a heavy large baking sheet with parchment. Combine the flour, baking powder, and salt in a medium bowl; whisk to blend. Using an electric mixer, beat the sugar, butter, eggs, and almond extract in a large bowl until well blended. Mix in the flour mixture, then add the cranberries.

2. Divide the dough in half. Using floured hands, shape each piece into a 2½-inch-wide, 9 ½-inch-long, 1-inch-high log. Transfer both logs to the prepared baking sheet, spacing evenly. Whisk the egg white in a small bowl until foamy, then brush egg white glaze on top and sides of each log.

3. Bake the logs until golden brown (logs will spread), about 35 minutes. Cool completely on the sheet set on a rack. Maintain oven temperature.

4. Transfer logs to a work surface. Discard the parchment. Using a serrated knife, cut the logs on the diagonal into ½-inch-wide slices. Arrange the slices cut side down on the same sheet. Bake 10 minutes; turn biscotti over and bake until just beginning to color, about 5 minutes. Transfer to a rack to cool.

5. Stir the chocolate in the top of a double boiler over simmering water until smooth. Using a fork, drizzle the melted chocolate over the biscotti. Let stand until the chocolate sets, about 30 minutes.

YIELD: MAKES ABOUT 28 BISCOTTI

2½ cups all-purpose flour
1 teaspoon baking powder
½ teaspoon salt
1½ cups sugar
½ cup (1 stick) unsalted butter, at room temperature
2 large eggs
½ teaspoon almond extract
1½ cups dried cranberries (about 6 ounces)
1 large egg white
6 ounces good-quality white chocolate (such as Lindt or Baker's), chopped, or white chocolate chips

do ahead:

The **BISCOTTI** can be made 1 week ahead. Freeze in airtight container. Thaw at room temperature.

"The almond flavoring is what, for me, makes it so special. I added ground almonds to the dough to enhance the flavor and texture."
A cook, Connecticut

triple chocolate cookies

A chocoholic's dream, these cookies from renowned Seattle chef Tom Douglas incorporate melted chocolate, cocoa powder, and chocolate chips. The soft and chewy, decadently fudgy texture makes them brownie-like, and their generous size will satisfy the strongest of chocolate cravings. For a smaller cookie, use a tablespoon to portion the dough and reduce the baking time by a few minutes. Wrap either size cookie in parchment or wax paper and tie with a pretty ribbon to create a sweet edible gift, but be warned: if you take even one bite, you'll want to keep them all for yourself.

YIELD: MAKES ABOUT 16 COOKIES

10 ounces bittersweet or semisweet chocolate, chopped
½ cup plus 2 teaspoons all-purpose flour
3 tablespoons unsweetened cocoa powder
¼ teaspoon baking powder
¼ teaspoon salt
1 cup plus 1 tablespoon sugar
5 tablespoons unsalted butter, at room temperature
3 large eggs
1½ teaspoons pure vanilla extract
6 ounces semisweet chocolate chips (1 cup)

cook's note:

The **COOKIES** can be made 3 days ahead. Keep frozen. If giving as gifts, using a metal spatula, carefully transfer 4 cookies to each of 4 large resealable plastic bags, arranging in single layer, and freeze.

1. Position a rack in the center of the oven and preheat the oven to 350°F. Line 2 large rimmed baking sheets with parchment. Stir the chopped chocolate in the top of a double boiler set over simmering water until melted and smooth; remove from heat and cool melted chocolate 10 minutes.

2. Meanwhile, sift the flour, cocoa powder, baking powder, and salt into a medium bowl. Using an electric mixer, beat the sugar and butter in another medium bowl until crumbly. Add the eggs 1 at a time, beating well after each addition. Continue to beat until the mixture is light, pale, and creamy, about 5 minutes. Add the lukewarm melted chocolate and the vanilla, and beat just until blended. Fold in the dry ingredients, then add the chocolate chips.

3. Drop the batter by ¼ cupfuls onto the prepared baking sheets, spacing 2 inches apart. Bake the cookies, one sheet at a time, until the tops are evenly cracked but cookies are not yet firm to touch, about 16 minutes. Cool the cookies completely on the baking sheets.

"I made these with a hint of cinnamon and bourbon-soaked cherries, and they were killer. The chocolate is really intense, and I thought the cherries broke up the flavor nicely. I bet these would be great with mint chips or as ice cream sandwiches."

GizelleMarie, Chicago, Illinois

double chip christmas fudge

Homey, comforting, chocolatey goodness: that's Mama Braun's Christmas fudge, as captured by her daughter and Epicurious member **Meridith Braun Schmalz** of Ontario, Canada. As one of seven children raised on a farm in Idaho, Schmalz grew up with this fudge recipe and considers it the best there is—maybe it's the mellow butterscotch, maybe it's the gooey marshmallow, or maybe it's just the dense but crumbly fudge consistency. Any way you cut it, it's a fabulous baked gift.

1. Butter the baking pan.

2. In a medium pot over moderately high heat, bring the sugars, evaporated milk, and butter to a boil. Continue boiling until the mixture turns a deep golden brown and registers 245°F on a candy thermometer, 10 to 15 minutes.

3. Remove the pot from the heat and add the marshmallow cream, butterscotch chips, chocolate chips, and vanilla. Stir until smooth, then stir in the walnuts, if using. Transfer to the prepared pan and cool at room temperature until set, at least 1 hour. Cut into squares and serve.

Make sure the butter is room temperature before starting, otherwise the sugar cooks too long while the butter melts and the 15 minutes of boil time is compromised. You end up with fudge that crumbles when cut instead of staying nice and smooth.

—Meridith Braun Schmalz

YIELD: MAKES ABOUT 36 (1½-INCH) SQUARES

2 cups (packed) light brown sugar
1 cup sugar
1 cup evaporated milk
½ cup (1 stick) salted butter
1 (7½-ounce) jar marshmallow cream
6 ounces butterscotch chips
6 ounces milk chocolate chips
1 teaspoon pure vanilla extract
½ cup walnuts, toasted and finely chopped (optional)

Special equipment: 9-inch square baking pan; candy thermometer

do ahead:

The **FUDGE** can be made ahead and stored in an airtight container at room temperature for 1 week.

peanut butter and fudge brownies
with salted peanuts

A much-loved brainchild of the legendary cookbook author Dorie Greenspan, this recipe features a dense, peanut-studded cake topped with a creamy layer of peanut butter, which is in turn topped with a thick, rich ganache. The recipe yields 30 pieces, but you can cut the brownies into even smaller squares for larger parties.

YIELD: MAKES 30 BROWNIES

FOR BROWNIES

¾ cup (1½ sticks) unsalted butter

7 ounces bittersweet or semisweet chocolate, chopped

3 ounces unsweetened chocolate, chopped

1½ cups granulated sugar

1½ teaspoons pure vanilla extract

¼ teaspoon salt

4 large eggs

1 cup all-purpose flour

1 cup roasted salted peanuts, coarsely chopped

FOR FROSTING AND GANACHE

1 cup chunky peanut butter (not natural or old-fashioned)

½ cup (1 stick) unsalted butter, at room temperature

¾ cup confectioners' sugar

⅛ teaspoon salt

⅛ teaspoon ground nutmeg

1 tablespoon whole milk

1 teaspoon pure vanilla extract

7 ounces bittersweet or semisweet chocolate, chopped

do ahead:

The **BROWNIES** can be made 1 day ahead. Cover and keep chilled until ready to cut and serve.

MAKE BROWNIES

1. Position a rack in the center of the oven and preheat the oven to 325°F. Line a 13 by 9-inch metal baking pan with foil, leaving a long overhang; butter the foil.

2. Place the butter in a heavy large saucepan. Add both chocolates, stir over low heat until smooth, and remove from heat. Whisk in the sugar, vanilla, and salt, then add the eggs 1 at a time. Fold in the flour, then the nuts. Spread the batter in the prepared pan. Bake until a tester inserted into the center comes out with moist crumbs attached, about 30 minutes. Place the pan on a rack; cool.

MAKE FROSTING AND GANACHE

1. Using an electric mixer, beat the peanut butter and ¼ cup butter in a medium bowl to blend. Beat in the sugar, salt, and nutmeg, then add the milk and vanilla. Spread the frosting over the brownies.

2. Stir the chocolate and remaining ¼ cup butter in a heavy small saucepan over low heat and stir until smooth. Drop the ganache all over the frosting, spreading to cover. Chill until set, about 1½ hours.

3. Using the foil as an aid, transfer the brownie cake to a work surface. Cut into squares. Bring to room temperature and serve.

"For the best results use the best quality chocolate possible (I used Callebaut), especially in the ganache. If you are short on time, make the brownies by themselves, and sprinkle with powdered sugar for a nice presentation."

A cook, Mexico

hazelnut chocolate mousse

member recipe

Hazelnut and chocolate have long been dessert partners, and it's easy to see why. They bring out the best in each other, as in this mousse, from Epicurious member **Derrinl.** If you don't have Frangelico, you can substitute Amaretto.

YIELD: MAKES 6 TO 8 SERVINGS

8 ounces whole hazelnuts
3 ounces cream cheese, at room
    temperature
½ cup hazelnut-flavored liqueur, such as
    Frangelico
9 ounces bittersweet chocolate, coarsely
    chopped
2 large eggs
1 cup whole milk
½ cup sugar
1 cup heavy whipping cream

do ahead:

The **MOUSSE** can be prepared and refrigerated, loosely covered, up to 1 day ahead.

1. Arrange a rack in the middle of the oven and preheat to 350°F. Arrange the hazelnuts in a single layer on a baking sheet and toast until golden, 10 to 12 minutes. Lay a tea towel out flat and transfer the hot toasted nuts onto it. Fold the edges of the towel over to cover the nuts and gently roll them to loosen the skins. Reserve about ¼ cup nuts for the garnish and transfer the rest to the bowl of a food processor. Process the nuts, scraping the sides down, until a smooth paste forms, about 2 minutes.

2. In a large bowl, mix the cream cheese with a wooden spoon or rubber spatula until smooth. Add the liqueur and chocolate and set aside.

3. In a medium bowl, whisk together the eggs. In a medium pot over moderate heat, combine the nut paste, the milk, and sugar. Warm to just below the boiling point, then slowly whisk a few splashes of the hot milk into the beaten eggs. Add the warmed egg mixture to the pot and return to moderately low heat. Stir constantly, until it thickens and holds a slight ribbon when stirred, about 2 minutes.

4. Pour the hot egg-milk mixture into the bowl with the chocolate mixture and whisk until smooth. Nest the bowl in an ice water bath and stir until cool but still easy to stir, 5 to 8 minutes. (Or, chill the mixture in the refrigerator, stirring occasionally, until cool, about 45 minutes.)

5. Using a large wire whisk or an electric mixer, whip the cream until it holds distinct peaks. Fold about one-third of the cream into the chocolate mixture to lighten it, then gently fold in the remaining two-thirds until just incorporated. Transfer the mousse to individual dishes or 1 large serving dish and chill, loosely covered, at least 1 hour. Before serving, roughly chop the reserved ¼ cup toasted hazelnuts and use them to garnish each portion.

eggnog ice cream

This ice cream can be made up to a week in advance, which helps free up precious prep time during the always-hectic holiday season. The lovely aroma of freshly grated nutmeg will put you, and everyone who enjoys this treat, in the holiday spirit.

1. Bring the milk and salt to a boil in a 3-quart heavy saucepan over moderate heat. Remove from the heat.

2. Whisk together the yolks and sugar in a bowl, then gradually add ¼ cup of the hot milk, whisking. Add the yolk mixture to the milk remaining in pan in a slow stream, whisking, and cook over low heat, stirring constantly with a wooden spoon, until the mixture is slightly thickened, coats the back of the spoon, and registers 175°F on an instant-read thermometer, 3 to 5 minutes.

3. Immediately pour the mixture through a fine-mesh sieve set into a clean bowl and stir in the cream, rum, vanilla, and ¼ teaspoon nutmeg. Chill the custard, covered, until cold, at least 2 hours.

4. Freeze the custard in an ice-cream maker according to manufacturer's directions. Transfer to an airtight container and put in freezer to harden, at least 2 hours. Soften slightly in refrigerator before serving, about 20 minutes.

YIELD: MAKES ABOUT 1½ QUARTS

1 cup whole milk
¼ teaspoon salt
7 large egg yolks
¾ cup sugar
2 cups heavy cream, chilled
3 tablespoons dark rum
1 teaspoon pure vanilla extract
¼ teaspoon freshly grated nutmeg, plus additional for garnish

Special equipment: an ice-cream maker

do ahead:

The **CUSTARD** can be chilled up to 1 day.

"This ice cream tastes just like frozen eggnog, and who doesn't like that?! To increase the eggnog flavor, I added extra ground nutmeg and ground cloves."
A cook, New York, New York

double chocolate layer cake

The most reviewed recipe on Epicurious, this is classic birthday cake material. Using premium chocolate gives this cake subtle sweetness and a refined taste. But, if you're on a budget, a more affordable option still gets the job done.

YIELD: MAKES 12 TO 14 SERVINGS

FOR CAKE LAYERS

3 ounces fine-quality semisweet chocolate, such as Callebaut
1½ cups hot brewed coffee
3 cups sugar
2½ cups all-purpose flour
1½ cups unsweetened cocoa powder (not Dutch process)
2 teaspoons baking soda
¾ teaspoon baking powder
1¼ teaspoons salt
3 large eggs
¾ cup vegetable oil
1½ cups well-shaken buttermilk
¾ teaspoon pure vanilla extract

FOR GANACHE FROSTING

1 pound fine-quality semisweet chocolate, such as Callebaut
1 cup heavy cream
2 tablespoons sugar
2 tablespoons light corn syrup
½ stick (¼ cup) unsalted butter

do ahead:

The **CAKE LAYERS** may be made 1 day ahead and kept, wrapped well in plastic wrap, at room temperature.

The **CAKE** keeps, covered and chilled, 3 days. Bring cake to room temperature before serving.

MAKE CAKE LAYERS

1. Preheat the oven to 300°F and grease 2 (10 by 2-inch) round cake pans. Line the bottoms with rounds of wax paper and grease the paper.

2. Finely chop the chocolate and combine in a bowl with the hot coffee. Let the mixture stand, stirring occasionally, until the chocolate is melted and mixture is smooth.

3. Into a large bowl sift together the sugar, flour, cocoa powder, baking soda, baking powder, and salt. In another large bowl with an electric mixer, beat the eggs until thickened slightly and lemon colored (about 3 minutes with a standing mixer or 5 minutes with a handheld mixer).

4. Slowly add the oil, buttermilk, vanilla, and melted chocolate mixture to the eggs, beating until combined well. Add the sugar mixture and beat on medium speed until just combined well. Divide the batter between the pans and bake in the middle of the oven until a tester inserted in center comes out clean, 1 hour to 1 hour and 10 minutes. Cool layers completely in pans on racks.

5. Run a thin knife around the edges of the pans and invert the layers onto racks. Carefully remove the wax paper and cool the layers completely.

MAKE FROSTING

1. Finely chop the chocolate. In a 1½- to 2-quart saucepan, bring the cream, sugar, and corn syrup to a boil over moderately low heat, whisking until the sugar is dissolved. Remove the pan from the heat and add the chocolate, whisking until the chocolate is melted. Cut the butter into pieces and add to the frosting, whisking until smooth.

2. Transfer the frosting to a bowl and cool, stirring occasionally, until spreadable (depending on chocolate used, it may be necessary to chill frosting to spreadable consistency). Spread the frosting between the cake layers and over the top and sides.

"You want to know how much I LOVE this cake? After baking it, I gave a copy of the recipe to MY baker, and asked him to make this for my wedding cake!"

A cook, Madison, Wisconsin

old-fashioned pecan pie

The perfect slice of pecan pie delivers a dollop of nutty sweetness with every bite. Our version calls for orange zest, which adds a sprightliness to this holiday staple. The pecan halves will rise to the top of the rich custard filling for an attractive display. It's fine to use frozen crust when you need to save time, but make your own pastry for a truly delightful dessert.

YIELD: MAKES 8 SERVINGS

Pastry Dough (recipe follows)
¾ stick (4 tablespoons) unsalted butter
1¼ cups (packed) light brown sugar
¾ cup light corn syrup
2 teaspoons pure vanilla extract
½ teaspoon grated orange zest
¼ teaspoon salt
3 large eggs
2 cups pecan halves (½ pound)
Whipped cream or vanilla ice cream

do ahead:

The **PIE** can be baked 1 day ahead and chilled. Bring to room temperature before serving.

The **DOUGH** can be chilled up to 3 days.

1. Roll out the dough on a lightly floured surface with a lightly floured rolling pin into a 12-inch round and fit into a 9-inch pie plate. Trim the edge, leaving a ½-inch overhang. Fold the overhang under and lightly press against the rim of the pie plate, then crimp decoratively. Lightly prick the bottom all over with a fork. Chill until firm, at least 30 minutes (or freeze 10 minutes).

2. Preheat the oven to 350°F, with a baking sheet on the middle rack.

3. Melt the butter in a small heavy saucepan over medium heat. Add the brown sugar, whisking until smooth. Remove from the heat and whisk in the corn syrup, vanilla, zest, and salt. Lightly beat the eggs in a medium bowl, then whisk in the corn syrup mixture.

4. Put the pecans in the pie shell and pour the corn syrup mixture evenly over them. Bake on the hot baking sheet until the filling is set, 50 minutes to 1 hour. Cool completely.

"We loved the addition of the orange zest—it cut some of the oversweet taste that typical pecan pie can have. Make sure to make the pie the day before serving so that it has time to set. I would recommend warming the pie before serving and putting a small scoop of vanilla ice cream on the top of each slice."

Lisaincaz, Cazenovia, New York

pastry dough

1. Blend together the flour, butter, and salt in a bowl with your fingertips or a pastry blender (or pulse in a food processor) just until the mixture resembles coarse meal with some roughly pea-size butter lumps. Drizzle 3 table-spoons ice water evenly over the mixture and gently stir with a fork (or pulse in processor) until incorporated. Squeeze a small handful. If it doesn't hold together, add more ice water, ½ tablespoon at a time, stirring (or puls-ing) until incorporated, then test again. Do not overwork dough or pastry will be tough.

2. Turn out the dough onto a lightly floured surface and divide into 4 portions. With the heel of your hand, smear each portion once or twice in a forward motion to help distribute the fat. Gather the dough together, with a pastry scraper if you have one, and press into a 5-inch disk. Chill, wrapped in plastic wrap, until firm, at least 1 hour.

YIELD: MAKES SINGLE CRUST FOR 9-INCH PIE

1¼ cups all-purpose flour
½ cup (1 stick) cold unsalted butter, cut into ½-inch pieces
¼ teaspoon salt
3 to 5 tablespoons ice water

vermont maple bread pudding
with walnut praline

There are few things better than rich and custardy bread pudding topped with sweet and sticky praline, but pair this dessert with vanilla ice cream and you've reached nirvana. Another option: skip the ice cream and serve this dish for brunch. If you need to accommodate a nut allergy, just leave the walnuts out; the caramelized sugar topping will provide plenty of crunch.

MAKE PRALINE

Coat a rimmed baking sheet with nonstick spray. Stir the sugar and water in a heavy small saucepan over medium heat until the sugar dissolves. Increase the heat to high and boil without stirring until the mixture turns deep amber color, occasionally swirling the pan and brushing down the sides with a wet pastry brush, about 7 minutes. Stir in the nuts. Quickly spread the mixture on the prepared sheet. Cool, then chop the praline into small pieces.

MAKE BREAD PUDDING

1. Whisk the eggs, cream, sugar, 1 cup maple syrup, and the vanilla in a large bowl to blend. Add the brioche; stir to coat. Let stand at room temperature 1 hour, stirring occasionally.

2. Preheat the oven to 375°F. Butter a 13 by 9-inch baking dish. Transfer the bread mixture to the prepared dish. Bake until puffed and golden and a toothpick inserted into the center comes out clean, about 40 minutes. Cool slightly.

3. Cut pudding into 6 to 8 pieces. Place 1 piece on each plate. Place a scoop of ice cream atop the pudding, drizzle with maple syrup, sprinkle with praline, and serve.

YIELD: MAKES 6 TO 8 SERVINGS

FOR PRALINE
Nonstick vegetable-oil spray
2 cups sugar
¼ cup water
1 cup walnuts, toasted and chopped

FOR BREAD PUDDING
8 large eggs
1 quart heavy whipping cream
1 cup sugar
1 cup maple syrup, plus more for drizzling
1 tablespoon pure vanilla extract
1 (1-pound) loaf brioche or egg bread, torn into bite-size pieces
Vanilla ice cream

> **do ahead:**
>
> The **PRALINE** can be made 1 day ahead. Store in airtight container at room temperature.

"My substitutions included using week-old panettone instead of brioche, throwing in a handful of raisins, and using half-and-half instead of cream. Also, butter pecan ice cream instead of vanilla. This was easy to prepare, and results were excellent."
A cook, Brooklyn, New York

menus and recipes for any occasion

It's sometimes hard to figure out what dish goes with what, so we've taken out the guesswork for you and pulled together some seasonal menus.

Easy Weeknight Dinners
Faux Arrabbiata with Penne (page 126)
Grilled Shrimp Satay with Peaches and Bok Choy (page 138)
Grilled Asian Flank Steak with Sweet Slaw (page 161)
Shrimp and Penne Rigate Alfredo (page 230)
Salmon Chowder (page 319)
Spaghetti with Turkey-Pesto Meatballs (page 332)
Mahogany Chicken (page 340)

Weekend Suppers
Grilled Caesar Salad (page 125)
Pork Barbecue Sandwiches (page 157)
Dilled Potato and Pickled Cucumber Salad (page 164)
Classic Sour Cherry Pie with Lattice Crust (page 186)
SERVE WITH:
Basil Lime Spritzer (page 111)

Lacinato Kale and Ricotta Salata Salad (page 223)
Deviled Fried Chicken (page 146)
Bacon Smashed Potatoes (page 355)
Double-Nut Maple Bars (page 281)
SERVE WITH:
Iced tea or summer cocktail like Papaya Margarita

Beef Short Ribs Tagine with Honey-Glazed Butternut Squash (page 348)
Peanut Butter and Fudge Brownies with Salted Peanuts (page 380)
SERVE WITH:
Pinot Noir

Brunch Menus
Meyer Lemon and Dried Blueberry Scones (page 109)
Belgian Leek Tart with Aged Goat Cheese (page 32)
SERVE WITH:
Freshly squeezed fruit juices, coffee, tea

Three Cheese, Spinach, and Tomato Quiche (page 108)
Pear, Arugula, and Pancetta Salad (page 324)
Mini Provolone Popovers (page 277)
SERVE WITH:
Mimosas made from fresh orange juice and Prosecco

Kitchen Sink Frittata (page 203)
Featherlight Yeast Rolls (toasted) (page 179)
Pound Cake with Blueberries and Lavender Syrup (page 194)
SERVE WITH:
Bloody Marys, iced tea, iced coffee

VIP Dinner
Bourbon Chicken Liver Pâté (page 212)
Wild Rice with Pecans, Raisins and Orange Essence (page 354)
Oven-Roasted Sea Bass with Ginger and Lime Sauce (page 247)
SERVE WITH:
Sauvignon Blanc, coffee, Port

Courtship and Cocktails
Dates with Goat Cheese Wrapped in Prosciutto (page 307)
Oysters with Champagne-Vinegar Mignonette (page 28)
Cheese Fondue (page 221)
Gianduia Mousse Cake (page 292)
SERVE WITH:
Champagne cocktail

A Chill Picnic
Tuscan Tuna-and-Bean Sandwiches (page 76)
Orzo with Grilled Shrimp, Summer Vegetables, and Pesto Vinaigrette (page 127)
Tomato and Watermelon Salad with Feta and Toasted Almonds (page 123)
Chocolate Chip Zucchini Cake (page 197)
SERVE WITH:
Agua fresca, lemonade

Backyard BBQ
Grilled Caesar Salad (page 125)
Corn on the Cob with Cheese and Lime (page 168)
Coffee-Rubbed Cheeseburgers with Texas Barbecue Sauce (page 148)
Peruvian Grilled Chicken (page 143)
Bourbon-Glazed Baby Back Ribs (page 154)
SERVE WITH:
Craft American beer

Kid's Birthday Party

Ultimate Grilled Cheese Sandwiches (page 371)
Grilled Jerk Chicken (page 54)
Baked Zucchini Fries with Tomato Coulis Dipping Sauce (page 167)
Double Chocolate Layer Cake (page 384)
SERVE WITH:
Fruit smoothies or juice

HOLIDAY MENUS

Super Bowl Party

Three-Bean Veggie Chili (page 328)
Meatballs with Parsley and Parmesan (page 307)
Caramelized-Onion Dip with Cilantro-Garlic Pita Chips (page 312)
Triple-Layer Carrot Cake with Cream Cheese Frosting (page 95)
SERVE WITH:
Beer from your team's hometown

Valentine's Day

Avocado, Asparagus, and Hearts of Palm Salad (page 326)
Filet Mignon with Gorgonzola Sauce (page 350)
Wild Mushroom–Potato Gratin (page 272)
Hazelnut Chocolate Mousse (page 382)
SERVE WITH:
Syrah or a sparkling rose

Passover Seder

Mediterranean Couscous and Lentil Salad (omit feta) (page 71)
Beet and Carrot Pancakes (omit sour cream) (page 69)
Beef Brisket with Merlot and Prunes (page 351)
Persian Rice Salad (page 353)
SERVE WITH:
Kosher Cabernet Sauvignon

Easter Lunch

Golden and Crimson Beet Salad with Oranges, Fennel, and Feta (page 222)
Rosemary Lamb Chops with Swiss Chard and Balsamic Syrup (page 347)
Roasted Potato Salad (page 65)
Lattice-Topped Strawberry-Rhubarb Pie (page 92)
SERVE WITH:
Sangria

Kid-Friendly Halloween Party

Caprese Pizza (page 51)
Chocolate Pumpkin Brownies (page 291)
SERVE WITH:
Apple cider

Holiday Dessert Party

Chocolate and Peppermint Candy Ice Cream Sandwiches (page 375)
Triple Chocolate Cookies (page 378)
Peanut Butter and Fudge Brownies with Salted Peanuts (page 380)
Eggnog Ice Cream (page 383)
SERVE WITH:
Mulled wine or spiked apple cider

Edible Holiday Gifts

Double Chip Christmas Fudge (page 379)
Dried Cranberry and White Chocolate Biscotti (page 377)
Extreme Granola with Dried Fruit (298)
Thyme Focaccia and Parmesan Focaccia (page 370)
Vanilla Hot Chocolate Mix (page 280)

Christmas Dinner

Shaved Brussels Sprout Salad with Fresh Walnuts and Pecorino (page 323)
Pork Roast with Winter Fruits and Port Sauce (page 343)
Kale and Potato Purée (page 357)
Vermont Maple Bread Pudding with Walnut Praline (page 389)
SERVE WITH:
Cabernet Sauvignon

New Year's Eve

Miniature Gougères (page 374)
Spicy Adobo Shrimp Cocktail (page 115)
Polenta Fries with Roasted Red Pepper Ketchup (page 270)
Red Wine–Braised Duck Legs (page 345)
Double Chocolate Layer Cake (page 384)
SERVE WITH:
Champagne

index

notes

....

....

....

....

....

....

....

....

....

....

....

....

....

....

....

....

....